Human Capital and America's Future

A Johns Hopkins Institute for Policy Studies Book

An Economic Strategy for the '90s

Human Capital and America's Future

edited by David W. Hornbeck and Lester M. Salamon

The Johns Hopkins University Press   Baltimore and London

This book has been brought to publication with the generous assistance of the Institute for Policy Studies at the Johns Hopkins University.

The Johns Hopkins University Press
701 West 40th Street
Baltimore, Maryland 21211
The Johns Hopkins Press Ltd., London

⊗ The paper used in this book meets the minimum requirements of American National Standards for Information Sciences—Permanence of Paper for Printed Library Materials, ANSI Z39.48-1984.

Library of Congress Cataloging-in-Publication Data

Human capital and America's future : an economic strategy for the nineties / edited by David W. Hornbeck and Lester M. Salamon.
          p.   cm.
   Includes bibliographical references and index.
   ISBN 0-8018-4143-7.—ISBN 0-8018-4144-5 (pbk.)
   1. Manpower policy—United States.   2. Human capital—United States.   I. Hornbeck, David W., 1941–   .   II. Salamon, Lester M.
HD5724.H8425   1991
331.11'0973—dc20   90-48566

Contents

Acknowledgments

Work on this book began in the fall of 1988. The project reflected our conviction that an important moment was at hand in the social and economic history of our nation because of an unusual coincidence of the nation's social welfare and economic agendas, but that this moment had yet to be fully seized.

To remedy this, we set out to document the developments that made greater attention to the needs of the nation's disadvantaged populations a matter of economic, and not just moral, necessity; and to identify in a more comprehensive and coherent way than was yet available the human capital investments that seemed appropriate in response.

Fortunately, we were able to enlist an extraordinary group of experts to assist us in this task and to attract crucial support from the Ford Foundation, the Carnegie Corporation, and the William T. Grant Foundation. To all of these we express our deep appreciation for their contributions.

We are also grateful to Ms. Jacquelyn Perry, who ensured the project strong secretarial and administrative support; to our copyeditors, Miriam Kleiger, Marie Blanchard, and Elizabeth Champney, who helped us achieve greater clarity and textual consistency; to Pat Kramer, who provided invaluable assistance with the many graphics included in the text; and to Henry Y. K. Tom of the Johns Hopkins University Press, who guided us through all phases of the publication process with great professionalism and care.

Since the launching of this project, important advances have been made in educating key publics about the importance of human capital investment and in authorizing improvements in some of the crucial human capital systems. Thus, the president and the nation's governors joined forces in 1989 at an Education Summit to articulate a set of national education goals. Then, in a budget agreement reached in the fall of 1990, health and day care coverage for poor children were significantly expanded.

Despite these advances, however, the nation has yet to come fully to terms with the human capital crisis it faces or to articulate a coherent human capital investment strategy. The premise that inspired this book therefore remains very much alive and in need of attention. Indeed, the evidence of growing concern about our human capital problems makes this volume all the more timely since it pulls together in one convenient place much of what needs to be known about the demographic and economic realities that make attention to human capital investment so important and about the range of human capital systems that require attention. It is our hope that the result is a volume that will be useful to policymakers and the general public in dealing with this topic that is so crucial to our national future.

D.W.H.
L.M.S.

Contributors

Nancy S. Barrett is provost and vice-president for academic affairs at the University of Western Michigan. She is co-author of *The Subtle Revolution,* an analysis of the changing position of women in the American economy, and has written widely on women in the labor force.

Ernest L. Boyer is president of the Carnegie Foundation for the Advancement of Teaching and is one of the nation's leading authorities on public education. He is the author of *High School* and numerous other books and articles on public education. Prior to joining the Carnegie Foundation, Dr. Boyer was president of the State University of New York and then United States commissioner of education. He is also a senior fellow at the Woodrow Wilson School, Princeton University.

Anthony Carnevale is the vice-president of national affairs and chief economist for the American Society for Training and Development. Dr. Carnevale has served in senior positions of the federal government, the U.S. Congress, organized labor, and industry.

Sheldon Danziger is professor of social work and public policy at the University of Michigan in Ann Arbor. He formerly served as director of the Institute for Research on Poverty at the University of Wisconsin and is the author or editor of numerous books and articles on the causes and consequences of poverty, including *Fighting Poverty: What Works and What Doesn't* (Harvard, 1986).

Marian Wright Edelman is president of the Children's Defense Fund, a policy research and advocacy organization focusing on the problems of children. A lawyer by training, Ms. Edelman has become a leading authority on the problems of children and on the range of public and private responses to children's needs.

R. Scott Fosler is vice-president of the Committee for Economic Development (CED) and an expert on intergovernmental relations and public-private partnerships. He has played a key role in conceptualizing and guiding a number of CED studies on human capital issues and has written extensively on human capital and economic development issues. Mr. Fosler's most recent book is *The New Economic Role of American States* (Oxford, 1987).

Daniel S. Greenberg edits *Science and Government Report* and writes a syndicated column on U.S. science policy that appears in numerous other papers throughout the United States.

David W. Hornbeck served from 1976 to 1988 as the state superintendent of schools for the State of Maryland. During 1986 and 1987 he was president of the Council of Chief State School Officers. He is the immediate past chairman of the board of the Carnegie Foundation for the Advancement of Teaching and serves on the board of the Children's Defense Fund and as chairman of the Public Education Foundation Network, among other posts. Mr. Hornbeck is a partner in the Washington, D.C., law firm of Hogan and Hartson.

Jason Juffras is a research associate with the Urban Institute's Changing Domestic Priorities Project, where he has examined a variety of budget and human resource issues.

Ray Marshall is Rapoport Centennial Professor of Economics and Public Affairs in the Lyndon B. Johnson School of Public Affairs at the University of Texas at Austin. Between 1977 and 1981 Dr. Marshall was secretary of the U.S. Department of Labor. He has written widely on human capital issues and also serves on the board of the Carnegie Corporation of New York.

Arnold H. Packer is executive director, Secretary's Commission on Achieving Necessary Skills, U.S. Department of Labor. Prior to this he was senior research associate at the Hudson Institute in Arlington, Virginia. Dr. Packer served as co-project director on the *Workforce 2000* report that the Hudson Institute prepared for the U.S. Department of Labor. A labor economist, Dr. Packer has written widely on human capital issues and served between 1977 and 1981 as assistant secretary for policy in the U.S. Department of Labor.

Marion Pines is a senior fellow at the Johns Hopkins Institute for Policy Studies and chairs the U.S. Department of Labor's Job Training Partnership Act Advisory Committee. Ms. Pines served from 1972 to 1987 as the administrator of employment and training programs for the City of Baltimore and from 1984 to 1987 as housing commissioner. In these capacities she earned a national reputation for innovative approaches to human capital problems.

Lester M. Salamon is professor and director of the Institute for Policy Studies at the Johns Hopkins University. Between 1980 and 1986, he was director of the Center for Governance and Management Research and of the Nonprofit Sector Project at the Urban Institute in Washington, D.C. Prior to that Dr. Salamon served from 1977 to 1980 as deputy associate director of the U.S. Office of Management and Budget and from 1973 to 1977 as associate professor of policy sciences at Duke University. Dr. Salamon has written or edited numerous books and articles on social welfare and economic development issues. His most recent book is *Beyond Privatization: The Tools of Government Action,* published by the Urban Institute Press in March 1989.

Isabel V. Sawhill is a senior fellow at the Urban Institute in Washington, D.C. She is director of the institute's Changing Domestic Priorities Project, served as executive director of the National Commission for Employment Policy, and has written numerous books and articles, including *Youth Employment and Public Policy, Time of Transition: The Growth of Families Headed by Women,* and *Economic Policy in the Reagan Years.* Her most recent book is *Challenge to Leadership: Economic and Social Issues for the Next Decade.*

Donald M. Stewart is president of the College Board in New York City, and president emeritus of Spelman College in Atlanta, Georgia. He was formerly a program officer in the Ford Foundation and associate dean of Arts and Sciences at the University of Pennsylvania. He has written and lectured widely on the subject of higher education.

Human Capital and America's Future

1

Overview: Why Human Capital? Why Now?

Lester M. Salamon

The United States finds itself today at a unique, historical moment. For the first time in our history, the nation's social agenda and its economic agenda seem to have converged. Policies to deal with poverty, drug abuse, employment discrimination, and related problems, which formerly could be justified only in terms of morality or political expediency, have now come to be seen as essential for the nation's economic progress, as critical investments in its "human capital."

The reason for this fortuitous turn of events is a set of social and economic forces that have importantly reshaped American economic circumstances. On the one hand, significant technological and other changes have increased the competition that America faces throughout the world and put a special premium on "brain power" instead of "brawn power" as the engine of economic growth. On the other hand, however, significant demographic trends have altered the flow of new entrants to the labor force to the point that over 85 percent will come during the next 15 or 20 years from segments of the population that have historically had the most limited educational and economic advantages—minorities, immigrants, and women. The upshot is a potentially serious mismatch between the labor force the nation needs and the one that our population dynamics and our educational institutions are making available.

Evidence of this mismatch is already apparent. "Area Businesses Tap New Source to Solve Severe Labor Shortage: The Homeless, Welfare Mothers among Workers Being Recruited," reported the *Washington Post* in September 1989 (Brenner 1989: 1). "Impending U.S. Jobs 'Disaster': Work Force Unqualified to Work" is how the *New York Times* put it in a front page series the same month (Fiske 1989: 1). Increasingly, the conviction has been growing that the nation can no longer afford to waste the talents and potentials of millions of unemployed inner-city poor people or put up with educational institutions that fail as many as a quarter of their students. "NEEDED: HUMAN CAPITAL" was *Business Week's* succinct summary of the problem in 1988 (Nussbaum 1988), and a broad cross section of national leadership seems to be reaching a similar conclusion. In its 1985 report to the nation, for example, the President's Commission on Industrial Competitiveness identified improvements in human resources and technology as the most crucial prerequisites of national competitiveness. (President's Commission on Industrial Competitiveness 1985: 21, 30). More recently, Xerox chairman David Kearns called education and human resource development "our most serious national problem" (Kearns 1988: 6). And improved human capital investment emerged as the most often cited requirement for future U.S. economic progress in a recent Conference Board survey of 2,300 business executives.

Although important efforts have been launched to upgrade public education in many states and localities around the country in response to these concerns, and the president and the nation's governors committed themselves to a bold set of educational goals in 1990, progress in developing a coherent human capital investment strategy, particularly at the national level, has still been limited. Indeed, it is not even clear what the components of such a strategy should be, how they should be carried out, or what they can realistically be expected to accomplish. The past record in this field, moreover, is not entirely encouraging. It was, after all, twenty years ago that economist Ivar Berg reported that "few other topics enjoy the favored place accorded education on the contemporary American agenda of public concerns" (Berg 1969: 1). But when Berg assessed the actual impact of the tremendous educational investments undertaken in the 1960s in response to this concern, he concluded that the nation had been the victim of a "great training robbery."

What, then, is the case for greater investments in human capital in contemporary America? If a case truly exists, what shape should a "human capital investment strategy" take? What is "human capital investment" and what evidence is there that it contributes to personal well-being or overall economic growth? If human capital investment makes sense, how should it be structured and how can it be financed?

The purpose of this book is to answer these and related questions and thus provide a basic overview of the human capital challenges facing the United States in the years ahead and the policy options available to deal with them. The individual chapters report on different facets of human capital policy, from the basic demographic and economic trends that have stimulated increased attention to human capital policies, to the question of how such policies, if adopted, could be financed.

To lay the foundation for the discussion that follows, this chapter introduces the basic concept of human capital investment and provides an overview of the major issues that the book addresses.

The Concept of Human Capital

Human capital refers to the acquired skills, knowledge, and abilities of human beings. Underlying the concept is the notion that such skills and knowledge increase human productivity, and that they do so enough to justify the costs incurred in acquiring them. It is in this sense that expenditures on improving human capabilities can be thought of as "investments." They generate future income or output that justifies the amounts spent on them. As the authoritative *Palgrave's* puts it, "human capital refers to the productive capacities of human beings as income producing agents in the economy"(Rosen 1987: 681).[1]

The concept of human capital is by no means a new one. More than two centuries ago economist Adam Smith pointed out in his classic treatise, *The Wealth of Nations,* that a crucial part of a nation's wealth lies in its people. For much of the ensuing two hundred years, however, economic thought largely ignored Smith's insight, and focused instead on the role of land, capital stock, and hours of labor as the crucial ingredients of economic growth. To the extent that people were considered part of the production process, it was in terms of their numbers, not their skills or knowledge. The quantity, rather than the quality, of human inputs was thus the exclusive focus of concern. Instead of treating knowledge and skills as a form of capital, as an input to the production process, economists tended to treat them as a form of consumption, as an output of the production process. This was consistent with the philosophical basis of classical economics, which stressed the individual's role as a consumer, as the end to be served by economic activity, not as a means of production. As human capital theorist Theodore Schultz (1961: 4) has explained, "to treat human beings as wealth that can be augmented by investment runs counter to deeply held values. It seems to reduce man once again to a mere material component, to something akin to property."

The rise of quantitative economics in the post-World War II period dealt a decisive blow to this line of thought, however. Detailed analyses of the sources of American economic growth demonstrated that national income grew at a much faster rate than the combined traditional inputs of land, person-hours worked, and the stock of reproducible capital. This created a puzzle about how to explain the remaining growth that occurred (Rosen 1987). In a pioneering address to the American Economic Association in 1960, Theodore Schultz argued that the answer to this puzzle was the tremendous growth that had occurred in the skills and abilities of workers, in the quality of human inputs to the economy. These skills, Schultz suggested, represented a form of capital that was every bit as important to economic growth as the more traditional forms of capital long considered by economists (Schultz 1961). According to this line of thinking, education and other forms of human capital investment increase output in a variety of ways: by generating new ideas and techniques that can be embodied in production equipment and procedures; by equipping workers to utilize the new production techniques and initiate changes in production methods; by improving the links among consumers, workers, and managers; and by extending the useful life of the stock of knowledge and skills that people embody (Berg 1969: 25). Subsequent work by Edward Denison verified Schultz's argument, demonstrating that educational improvements contributed a substantial 42 percent to the growth of per capita income in the United States between 1929 and 1957 (Denison 1962). As Schultz (1981: 4, ix) summarized the argument recently: "The decisive factors of production in improving the welfare of poor people are not space, energy, and cropland; the decisive factors are the improvement in population quality and advances in knowledge ... Increases in the acquired abilities of people throughout the world and advances in useful knowledge hold the key to future economic productivity and to its contributions to human well-being."

The Rationale for Government Involvement

To say that improved human skills and abilities boost productivity and output is not yet to establish a case for *public* investment in human capital. After all, if investments in human capital boost productivity and earning power, individuals should be willing to finance these investments themselves since they will ultimately reap the rewards in the form of higher earnings. Alternatively, employers could be expected to invest in the skills and abilities of their workers since they can expect to reap the rewards in the form of higher output per worker. Either way, the private market might be expected to handle the human capital investment needs of the country quite satisfactorily. Why then should human capital investment become a subject for government involvement?

As Jason Juffras and Isabel Sawhill point out in Chapter 12, the answer to this question lies fundamentally in a number of imperfections in the human capital market that make it unlikely that reliance on market mechanisms alone will produce the level of human capital investment that is best for the economy. In the first place, the mobility of labor makes it irrational for employers to invest as much as they might think desirable in their labor force since the newly trained workers might be attracted away by other employers who can pay higher wages because they did not have to bear the cost of the training. As a result, employers have an incentive not to pay for the training themselves since they have no guarantee that they will reap the benefits.

In the second place, serious information gaps exist in the human capital market. Young people are often not in a good position to understand the value of education, and even their parents often lack the information to make choices about the kind of training that makes sense for them. Left to their own devices, therefore, people may underinvest in human capital or invest unwisely.

In the third place, significant portions of the population lack the savings to afford extensive human capital investments. This would not be as serious a problem if private capital markets were available to finance such investments on credit. But the credit markets for this kind of investment have historically been deficient. One obvious reason for this is that human capital investments are not used to acquire tangible assets that can serve as collateral for loans. In addition, there is no guarantee that the skills once acquired will be used productively. As a result, human capital investments entail significant risks. Without some kind of public involvement, therefore, investment in human capital is likely to be limited in scale. What is more, it is likely to be distributed inequitably, undermining the important social value of equal opportunity.

Beyond this, there are social and economic benefits of human capital investment that are not captured by the market because they accrue to society as a whole rather than just to the people who acquire the skills and abilities or those who employ them. More able and informed consumers, parents, voters, and citizens contribute to the overall quality of life in a society. Yet these benefits do not show up in a form that the market can reward. As a result, the market systematically underestimates the value of human capital and therefore has a further tendency to reduce the incentives to invest in it.

In short, for a wide variety of reasons, human capital investment cannot be left to the automatic operations of the market. Significant public involvement is needed.

Caveats

Although a strong case can be made that improved skills and abilities can lead to increases in productivity and output, and that the optimal level of human capital investment cannot be achieved without significant public-sector involvement, a number of complexities make the case for human capital investment more problematic than it would otherwise be. For one thing, the cost of this form of capital is difficult to assess. Unlike physical capital, the costs of which are more or less direct, human capital also involves important indirect costs in the form of forgone earnings, while the training or skills are being acquired. How to value these forgone earnings, and hence how to calculate the real costs of human capital in order to determine what the rate of return on this type of investment is, consequently becomes a serious empirical problem.

Similarly, it is difficult to assess what the quantity of human capital really is, in that some part of what is spent on improving human skills and abilities often really does represent consumption rather than investment. In other words, it is valued in and of itself rather than being valued chiefly because of what it contributes to the production of other goods and services. This is true even of some forms of education and training, which are pursued because of what they contribute to the quality of life rather than for what they contribute to worker productivity or earnings. But if this problem exists for education and training, it exists even more so for other forms of "human capital." Conceptually, anything that contributes to population quality can be considered a form of human capital, particularly if it extends the useful life of the human capital stock or otherwise enhances the ability of people to contribute to the production process. Thus improvements in nutrition, in health, in housing, and in the quality of life generally can be considered forms of human capital. But these improvements also have significant consumption components. Distinguishing the investment from the consumption aspects of these forms of human capital thus becomes a difficult philosophical as well as empirical challenge.

Human capital theorists attempt to get around this problem by defining human capital as "the abilities and know-how of men and women that have been acquired at some cost and that *can command a price in the labor market because they are useful in the productive process*" (Parnes 1984: 32). But this merely shifts the problem rather than solving it since the quantity of human capital in existence comes to be determined by the economy's demand for it. A year of schooling may or may not be a contribution to the stock of human capital, therefore, depending on whether the training acquired has a productive use in the labor market. And this can change over time.

One final complication arises from the fact that, unlike physical capital, human capital cannot be owned by someone else. This introduces a significant volitional quality to human capital. Because of tastes, or values, or preferences, individuals can choose to make little productive use of the human capital embodied in them. As a result, the productivity of a given quantity of human capital can vary greatly (Parnes 1984: 32).

The Past Record

Because of these complications, the connection between investments in human capital and improvements in output and economic performance may be far less direct in practice than it appears in theory. To be sure, empirical analyses in the 1960s and 1970s confirmed the basic point that improvements in human quality are associated with gains in income, both for individuals and for national economies. Thus Schultz (1981: 88) reports that the share of income accruing to property declined from 45 percent in 1900 to 20 percent in 1975, while the share accruing to labor, broadly defined, increased from 55 percent to 80 percent. Especially persuasive empirical results have been obtained in the field of agriculture, where researchers have been able to document a strong relationship between education and adoption of innovations that boost earnings and improve productivity (Welch 1976; Welch 1979; Wozniak 1984; Wozniak 1987). Similar relationships between education and the adoption of new technologies have also been established in the manufacturing sector (Bartel and Lichtenberg 1987).

But the early enthusiasm for increased investments in education in the 1960s gave way by the late 1960s and the early 1970s to significant doubts as evidence began to accumulate that the results were considerably less impressive than had been hoped. Thus economist Ivar Berg (1969), charging that existing studies failed to take sufficient account of the inherent complexities of the human capital concept, concluded from a direct examination of jobs and educational levels that educational achievements actually exceeded job requirements in most job categories in the United States in the late 1960s. What is more, employer beliefs about the superior capabilities of educated employees turned out not to be confirmed in practice: educated employees have higher turnover rates, lower job satisfaction, and poorer promotion records than less educated employees. On the basis of this evidence, Berg concluded that education may be more important as a credential for getting a job than as a requirement for performing the job, a situation that poses particular problems for the disadvantaged who may lack the credential but not necessarily the ability to perform (Berg 1969: 60).

Similarly, Richard Freeman (1976) found that the tremendous investments in higher education in the 1960s and early 1970s, which boosted the number of workers with at least one year of college above the number of manufacturing workers, had turned sour by the mid-1970s. Although college graduates still earned more than nongraduates and had better chances to obtain high-level managerial positions, the "college premium"—that is, the income position of college graduates relative to other workers—dropped sharply in the 1970s. For example, as of 1969 college graduates among men earned 53 percent more than high school graduates. By 1974, however, they earned only 35 percent more. By the same token, the proportion of college graduates who obtained professional jobs dropped from 71 percent in the late 1950s to 46 percent in the early 1970s. In other words, the nation was "over-educating" its work force, creating more college-educated workers than the economy could absorb and reducing the returns to education as a consequence.

One other disappointing body of evidence emerged from the record of the War on Poverty of the 1960s and 1970s. As Isabel Sawhill (1988) reports in a recent, careful assessment of the evidence, the poverty program constituted almost a natural test of the "human capital investment" approach to the alleviation of poverty. Between 1963 and 1985, the federal government alone spent roughly $282 billion on targeted education and training programs in addition to $469 billion on improved health care for the poor. Although early evaluations reporting little or no effect from these expenditures have been refuted by more recent studies, the overall result was still, at best, only "mixed." Compensatory education expenditures seem to have produced significant, long-term effects, but only in the case of investments targeted on preschool children. Employment and training programs proved moderately effective in boosting the employment levels of adult women, but have done little to improve their earnings and have had little discernible effect on adult men. For youth, only intensive interventions such as the federal Job Corps program seem to have had an effect, but these are also the most expensive kinds of activities.

Lessons

Three major conclusions emerge from this discussion of the basic concept of human capital investment and from the experience with such investments in the recent past. In the first place, the return on investments in human capital do seem to be positive, even though they may not be as high, or as automatic, as early thinking seemed to suggest. Even during the slump period of the 1970s, for example, Freeman (1976) found that college graduates earned more than high school graduates, although the disparity was lower than it had been in the 1960s. By the same token, Sawhill (1988) estimates that the poverty rate as of 1985 would have been anywhere from 0.4 to 2.2 percent above its actual rate of 14 percent had it not been for the federal spending on employment, training, and education in the 1960s and 1970s. Coupled with the longer-term, macroeconomic evidence on the contribution of population quality to overall economic growth, the case for human capital investment remains fairly strong.

In the second place, however, the discussion above also makes clear that human capital investments cannot be considered in a vacuum. Such investments focus on the supply side of the labor market. But their value depends heavily on the demand side as well. In fact, this is what distinguishes human capital as an "investment" from human capital as a "consumption good." The latter has a value in and of itself that does not depend on market demand. The former, by contrast, has only the value that the market puts on it. If more skilled workers are produced than can be productively employed at a given point in time, then the value of human capital and the return on investments in it decline. According to Freeman (1976: 64–67), this is exactly what happened in the United States in the mid-1970s as the growth of college-intensive industries slowed while the supply of college educated personnel increased. The same thing occurred, moreover, in many developing countries in the 1960s as the level of investment in human capital increased beyond the capacity of the economies to absorb.

In addition to general economic circumstances, artificial barriers such as racial or sexual discrimination can also limit the returns on human capital investment by keeping certain classes of workers from acquiring the jobs or the salaries to which they would otherwise be entitled. Critics of the human capital investment approach have argued, in fact, that the approach tends systematically to overlook this point, that it focuses so heavily on the shortcomings of potential workers that it ignores, or at least downplays, the shortcomings of the broader market in which they must function and the disadvantages they must overcome (Bowles and Gintis 1976). Any serious human capital investment strategy must take explicit account of this issue.

Finally, the discussion here also makes clear that the concept of human capital investment must be interpreted fairly broadly. While education and the acquisition of marketable skills may form the heart of the concept, they do not exhaust it. To the contrary, anything that materially affects the size, productive capabilities, or useful life of the work force can properly be considered a form of human capital. Thus Schultz (1981: 7) includes within his definition of human capital child care, home and work experience, the acquisition of information and skills through schooling, and other improvements in health and education that can improve population quality. Improved health, for example, increases the useful life of human capital and thereby enhances its value. Parnes (1984: 42) adds migration to the list of forms of human capital on grounds that it involves costs incurred to enhance earnings and employment prospects. Similarly, immigration, the provision of labor market information, anti-discrimination policies, and advances in knowledge can also be considered forms of human capital investment since their effect is to increase the size of the labor force or the effective use that can be made of human resources.

For the sake of convenience, it is possible to divide these various forms of human capital investment into three major categories, as Scott Fosler suggests in Chapter 11. The first category includes factors that affect the *size and composition of the work force.* Included here are such obvious factors as birth rates, death rates, health status, migration patterns, and labor force participation rates. Also relevant, however, are patterns of discrimination that affect access to particular jobs, cultural traditions that affect the propensity for labor force participation, and the availability of day care and other supports that affect accessibility to work. The second category includes factors that affect *worker capacity,* such as early childhood development, basic schooling, on-the-job training, and job-related skill development. The third category includes factors that affect *worker productivity,* such as the structure of employment opportunities, mobility among jobs and regions, motivation, and the mechanisms for matching skilled workers to the jobs for which they are qualified.

Any particular activity can, of course, affect more than one of these dimensions. Nevertheless, this division provides a useful framework for identifying the range of activities that can appropriately be considered as part of a human capital investment strategy. Which of these make the most sense at a particular point in time, however, is something that can only be evaluated in the light of the particular demographic and economic circumstances that exist.

The Current Case for Human Capital Investment: The Demand Side

What, then, are the demographic and economic circumstances that exist at the present time in America? What is it that now makes human capital investment particularly important? And what types of human capital investment seem most appropriate given these circumstances?

To answer these questions, Part I of this book reviews the basic economic and demographic realities that define the need for human capital over the next couple of decades. Part II then assesses the performance of some of the principal vehicles for human capital development. The overwhelming conclusion that emerges from this analysis is that market conditions seem unusually opportune for significant returns to human capital investment. In fact, the competitiveness of the nation may depend on it.

Three broad sets of factors seem to point in this direction: first, the shifting structure and character of the American economy; second, the evolving composition of the American work force; and third, the performance of existing human capital institutions, such as our schools, our research institutions, our on-the-job training, and our social welfare system. In this section, we consider the first of these. The second and third are the focus of the sections that follow.

Overview: A Basic Economic Shift

Unlike the situation in the 1960s, when the case for human capital investment was framed chiefly in terms of the needs of potential workers, today the case for human capital investment results largely from the needs of the economy. In a word, a fundamental change has occurred in the economic situation confronting the United States over the past two decades, and this change makes attention to human capital investment increasingly urgent. Four key dimensions of this change are particularly important.

Technological Advance

At the heart of the dramatic changes affecting the U.S. economy over the past several decades has been a startling acceleration in the speed of technological innovation and in the application of new technologies. Most fundamental have been the invention and widespread application of the computer and the associated improvements in communications technologies. These changes have literally revolutionized long-standing production processes and industrial structures, automating production, speeding up the processing of information, reducing the number of people required in manufacturing, and encouraging decentralized forms of organization. Technology is not only what one analyst has called "the wild card of the future" (Choate 1986: 14); it is also the wild card of the present, exposing businesses to intense competition, accelerating the pace of change, and placing increasing emphasis on the processing of information instead of the manufacture of products.

Expanded International Competition

One major consequence of the microelectronic revolution of the past several decades has been a stunning increase in international competition and in the integration of the world economy. Thanks to vastly improved communications technologies, American manufacturing workers find themselves in direct competition with their counterparts in Korea, Singapore, and Mexico, not to mention Japan and Germany. Technological advances in one country are applied in others at a speed that would earlier have been considered impossible. As a consequence, while in 1960 an estimated 20 percent of the goods produced in the United States faced active competition from foreign products, by the early 1980s an estimated 70 percent did (President's Commission 1985: 175). What is more, the competition is not only in manufacturing; it is also in services, such as insurance, finance, engineering, and data processing. Thanks to telecommunications advances, corporations in the United States can locate back-office data processing centers overseas, process records at these locations, and ship the information back to the United States at considerable savings compared to what it would cost to hire data processors in the United States. Similarly, large manufacturing firms can contract out the production of specific components to overseas suppliers who can take advantage of low-cost native labor and then import either the components or the finished product into the United States.

Reflecting this, a sixth of all U.S. manufacturing imports consist of U.S. components assembled overseas. According to one estimate, 70 percent of the total value of the components of every IBM personal computer is made in Japan and Singapore (Choate 1986: 21). Overall, the share of our gross national product represented by imports tripled between 1955 and 1985, from 4.5 percent to 13.1 percent; and the export share doubled. More generally, between 1965 and 1983 exports climbed from 12 percent to 18 percent of gross domestic product in the developed world (Johnston and Packer, 1987: 2).

This increased integration of the global economy has produced a number of positive results, allowing Americans to benefit from less-expensive imports and spreading some of the benefits of economic growth throughout the world. At the same time, however, it has also led to a significant deterioration of the U.S. competitive position in the world, at least if competitiveness is defined, as the President's Commission on Industrial Competitiveness suggests (1985: 8), as "the degree to which [a nation] can, under free and fair market conditions, produce goods and services that meet the test of international markets while simultaneously maintaining and expanding the real incomes of its citizens." In point of fact, the U.S. has neither been able to produce goods and services that meet the test of international markets nor maintain and expand the real incomes of its citizens.

As far as the former is concerned, although the value of exports has continued to grow, the American share of international trade has declined steadily since the 1960s. In 1960, for example, the United States devoted 6 percent of its gross national product (GNP) to exports but controlled 20 percent of world trade; in 1984, it devoted 10 percent of its GNP to exports but its share of world trade declined to 9 percent (Johnston and Packer 1987: 6). By the mid-1980s, one out of every four cars driven in the U.S. was foreign made, reflecting the decline in the U.S. share of world automotive production from 52 percent in 1960 to 23 percent in 1983. Similarly, the U.S. share of world crude steel production declined from 26 percent in 1960 to 12 percent in 1983. Comparable deterioration occurred in high-technology products, where the U.S. share declined from 25 percent to 20 percent; and in services, where a similar decline occurred (President's Commission 1985: 174). Reflecting these developments, the U.S. merchandise trade balance, which was positive from 1893 to 1970, turned negative in 1971, and except for 1973 and 1975, has been negative every year since.

Accompanying this loss in market share and the increased exposure of American workers to competition from lower-paid workers overseas has been a deterioration in the real value of wages of new entrants to the American labor force. As Arnold Packer shows in Chapter 2, the average annual earnings of 20- to 24-year old males in the United States declined, after adjusting for inflation, by 26 percent between 1973 and 1986. And among high school graduates, the decline was 28 percent. Moreover, real wages, after rising by 2.6 percent a year between 1963 and 1973, remained largely stagnant over the ensuing decade (President's Commission 1985: 12).

Changing Economic Structure

Taken together, these two forces, technological advance and internationalization of the economy, have in turn had profound effects on the basic structure of the American economy. In a sense, they have rendered obsolete the traditional, mass-production, assembly-line factory system as a viable base for future American economic growth. This system, with its stress on high-volume production of standardized goods using relatively static technology and relying on unskilled labor, has been undermined by the rapidity of technological change and the ability of manufacturers of standardized products to tap the much less expensive pools of unskilled labor in the developing countries. The upshot has been what Piore and Sabel (1982) term "the second industrial divide," the emergence of a new economic system that stresses quality over quantity and puts a special premium on flexibility, decentralization, rapid applications of new technology, and competitiveness (Reich 1984; Osborne 1988; Choate 1986).

Evidence of this shift is apparent everywhere. Virtually all of the growth in employment in the U.S. economy during the 1970s and 1980s, for example, took place in the service sector. By 1985, as Packer shows in Chapter 2, goods-producing industries (including manufacturing, mining, construction, and agriculture) consequently accounted for only 26 percent of the labor force compared to 74 percent in services. Not surprisingly, given the small size of most service firms, this trend has been accompanied by a decline in employment in large firms and a burst of employment in small firms. Thus, between 1980 and 1985, America's 500 largest companies lost 3 million jobs, while businesses with fewer than 100 employees gained 10 million (Reich 1984: 121).

Even more significant, perhaps, has been the change that has occurred in the nature of the jobs that remain. As Packer observes, the number of old-fashioned, narrowly defined jobs is shrinking even in large manufacturing firms. Job classifications are being broadened to encourage workers to master a wide variety of tasks. Increasing use of the team approach in the automobile industry, for example, is requiring production workers to communicate with engineers and understand make-buy decisions. What is more, similar changes are under way in the service sector. As the number of word processors increases from 500,000 in 1978 to an estimated 2.5 million in 1990 (President's Commission 1985: 147), for example, secretaries must increasingly master computer technology to function on the job. In other spheres as well, workers at all levels are having to shift from manual to mental work, to deal with quantitative and symbolic information, and to master multiple tasks.

Nor does this trend seem likely to abate. To the contrary, as Johnston and Packer report: "Overall, the skill mix of the economy will be moving rapidly upscale." Thus only 4 percent of the jobs likely to be created in the economy between 1984 and 2000 will be in the lowest skill levels, which now represent 9 percent of existing jobs. By contrast, 41 percent of the likely new jobs will require the highest skill levels, compared to the 24 percent of all jobs that require such proficiency now (Johnston and Packer, 1987: 96, 97).

Increased Pressure for Productivity Improvements

Underlying this steady upgrading of skill requirements is the growing pressure on American businesses to increase their productivity. As Packer shows in Chapter 2, the period from the end of the Second World War to the early 1970s was a "golden era" for the American economy, during which employment, productivity, and output all grew at quite healthy rates. As the spread of new technology undermined the U.S. competitive position in the world economy during the 1970s, however, the country's ability to sustain its high living standards began to be called into question. Between 1970 and 1985, economic growth slowed to 2.7 percent a year from 3.3 percent during the previous 15 years despite a healthy, 2.1 percent a year growth in the labor force.

The principal reason for this slowdown was a sharp decline in U.S. productivity, in its output per worker. Instead of growing by 1.6 percent a year as it did during 1955–70, output per worker during 1970–85 grew by a much more meager 0.7 percent per year, much lower than for our major overseas competitors. This was due in large part to the shift in employment from manufacturing, where productivity growth has traditionally been relatively high, to services, where it has traditionally been relatively low; and to the virtual disappearance of productivity growth altogether in the service sector during this period.

Although per capita consumption in the United States continued to grow during 1970–85 by about 2 percent a year despite this slowdown in productivity and overall economic growth, this was largely due to the growth that occurred in the size of the labor force, in federal deficit financing, and in borrowing from abroad. But these sources will not be available to sustain consumption growth in the years ahead. For one thing, as we will see below, changing demographic patterns are almost certain to slow the growth in the labor force. At the same time, the federal budget and trade deficits will have to be reduced, the latter either by increasing exports or by reducing imports. In order to sustain growth in living standards, or avoid reductions, productivity must consequently increase, and it must increase not only in the manufacturing sector, but in the service sector as well. In fact, productivity improvement in the service sector is more essential since so much of the country's employment and output is tied up in this sector. This means that unskilled workers already displaced from manufacturing will increasingly be displaced from service occupations as well. Even more so than the recent past, the future will belong to those with skills. As Johnston and Packer put it in their influential *Workforce 2000* report (1987: 103):

> During the 1985–2000 period, the good fortune to be born in or to immigrate to the United States will make less difference than the luck or initiative to be well-educated and well-trained. For individuals, the good jobs of the future will belong to those who have skills that enable them to be productive in a high-skill, service economy. For the nation, the success with which the workforce is prepared for high-skilled jobs will be an essential ingredient in maintaining a high-productivity, high-wage economy.

The Current Case for Human Capital Investment: The Supply Side

If economic changes constitute one side of the need for increased attention to human capital investment in the years ahead, demographic changes constitute the other. The former have established a demand for increasing numbers of skilled workers. The latter, regrettably, indicate that such workers are likely to be in short supply.

Three Demographic Challenges

As Packer shows in Chapter 2 below, three fundamental demographic developments explain why this is so: first, the baby boom of the 1940s and 1950s; second, the "birth dearth" of the 1960s and 1970s; and third, the shifting composition of new entrants to the work force.

The Baby Boom

The baby boom of 1946–62, which set the demographic framework for the past thirty years of American social and economic life, will also help define a significant part of the economic challenge that the nation faces in the years ahead. This is so because the baby boomers who overloaded our school systems in the 1950s and 1960s, and our housing markets in the 1970s and 1980s, will now overload our retirement systems in the 1990s and beyond, especially given the increase in life expectancy that has occurred over the past generation. The result will be a "squaring" of the U.S. population pyramid, as the number of elderly people comes to equal or exceed the number of people under 20 years of age.

The Birth Dearth

What makes this situation particularly troubling is that the working population will not grow anywhere near as fast as those 65 and older because the baby boom of the 1940s, 50s, and early 60s was followed by a "birth dearth" in the 1960s and 1970s, as birth rates fell from 3.2 per woman in 1964 to 1.74 in 1976. As a result, the annual growth of the labor force will fall from 3 percent in the 1970s to 1 percent in the 1990s, and will disappear almost completely in the first decade of the new century. As a consequence, the number of active workers available to support each elderly person will decline, from 3.3 in 1985 to 2.0 in 2030. Since retirees are supported mostly out of the current earnings of existing workers, this situation will add further to the need for productivity improvements so that the working population can not only continue to increase its own standard of living but also support a larger pool of retired persons.

Changing Work Force Composition

To complicate matters further, however, the birth dearth of the 1970s and 1980s has not affected all segments of the population uniformly. To the contrary, fertility rates for minorities remained high longer than they did for whites. In addition, immigration of nonwhites has also been substantial. As a consequence, the limited number of newcomers to the labor force between 1988 and 2000 will differ markedly from those already in it. In particular, minorities, women, and immigrants will comprise almost 90 percent of the net increase, compared to only 53 percent of those currently at work. But these are the populations that our educational system and our labor market have historically served least well. By contrast, native white males, who comprise 47 percent of the labor force at present, will account for only 10 percent of the increase.

In short, at a time when technological developments, international competition, and growing pressures for productivity advances are increasing the skill requirements of available jobs, demographic developments are generating a labor force whose ability to meet these requirements is very much in question as a product of past disadvantage, inexperience, or other factors. Under these circumstances, it becomes essential to understand more fully the human capital challenges confronting the three segments of the population that will comprise most of the new entrants to the labor force in the years ahead.

Three Special Target Groups

Women

The entry of women into the labor force constitutes one of the most dramatic changes in American economic life over the past thirty years. Between 1960 and 1988, the proportion of married women working outside the home increased from 31 percent to 65 percent, as the number of women working or looking for work increased by more than 30 million. As a consequence, by 1985 women constituted 44 percent of the U.S. labor force. More startling still, they are projected to constitute 64 percent of the new entrants expected between 1985 and 2000.

As Nancy Barrett shows in Chapter 3 of this volume, the movement of women out of homemaking into paid employment is every bit as fundamental in character as the massive shift of farmers out of agriculture earlier in this century, but larger and possibly more serious in its implications, especially its human capital implications. This is so in the first instance because the movement of women out of homemaking, while significantly increasing output in the market economy, deprived the economy of substantial human capital investments that women have made in their children. The change in female labor-force participation rates was most pronounced, in fact, among women with children. For those with children under six years of age, labor-force participation increased from 18.6 percent in 1960 to 57.1 percent in 1988; for those with children between 6 and 17 years of age, it rose from 39.0 percent to 72.5 percent. Correspondingly, the proportion of school age children with mothers in the work force increased from 29 percent in 1970 to 53 percent in 1988. Yet no coherent child care policy exists to help parents cope with the strains that this produces. The result is to decrease the incentives for women to work and to decrease the human capital investments in children.

A second problem facing women in the work force is the persistence of occupational segregation and a resulting pay gap. Despite some gains for an elite group of women, the occupational profile of the vast majority of women has not changed much over the past generation. To be sure, more women are in the professions, and clerical employment has replaced domestic work as a source of upward mobility for black women. But as of 1987, 70 percent of all employed women worked in occupations in which three-fourths of the employees were female. And even in the professional fields, over half of all employed women work in five predominantly female professions. Nor can this be explained in terms of differential educational levels. Almost 70 percent of the women who joined the labor force between 1975 and 1985 had at least some college education; and by 1985, the proportion of women aged 25–34 in the labor force who had attended college exceeded the proportion of men (50 percent versus 47 percent). Nevertheless, women are still restricted to certain "female occupations." Worse still, they suffer a pay gap as a consequence, since female-dominated jobs tend to pay less than male jobs requiring equivalent education and skill. As a result, the return on human capital investments in women is lower than that for men, reducing the incentives for women, their families, and even employers, to underwrite such investments.

Finally, low-income women face particularly severe problems, as we will see more fully below. Because they often lack education and training, such women have relatively low income levels even when they are in the labor force. Yet the facilities for improving their education and training are meager. For the millions with children, moreover, entry into the labor force brings with it heavy child care costs. Under the circumstances, there is little incentive, and little opportunity, for these women to improve their human capital resources. Although a welfare reform bill enacted in 1988 usefully provides encouragement for states to set up job training, education, and work programs for welfare recipients, the resources made available are sufficient to allow only an estimated 5,000 welfare recipients out of 3.8 million eligible families to find work and leave the welfare system each year.

In short, although the number of women entering the labor force is likely to continue to grow in the years ahead, significant obstacles stand in the way of optimal female labor force participation and hence optimal returns on human capital investments in women. In addition, little account has yet been taken of the implications that expanded female labor force participation has for the human capital investments women were formerly able to make in their children.

Immigrants

One potential way to cope with the labor force squeeze that seems looming on the nation's horizon is to increase the levels of immigration. In Chapter 4 of this volume, however, Ray Marshall argues against this course. As Marshall points out, the United States was the destination during the 1980s of half of the world's immigrants, and immigration accounted for 30 percent of the annual U.S. population growth. Many of the immigrants coming to this country, particularly those who have entered legally, have had high levels of education and other forms of

human capital. Thus 24 percent of those who entered between 1975 and 1980 had completed four or more years of college, compared to only 16 percent of the native population. However, the far larger numbers of illegal immigrants who have entered the country have extremely low levels of education and end up in lower-status jobs with lower incomes.

Although some have argued that continued high levels of immigration even of low-skilled people can benefit the economy (Johnston and Packer, 1987: 93–94), Marshall reads the evidence differently. Drawing on recent studies of the impact of immigration in California, Marshall argues that recent Mexican immigrants depressed wage rates, displaced legal native workers, closed off job opportunities for unemployed blacks, and absorbed twice as much in public benefits as they contributed in taxes. Beyond this, the presence of large numbers of low-wage laborers may have perpetuated a disproportionate number of low-pay, weak industries that is unhealthy for the Southern California economy over the long run.

Even if nothing is done to stem the flow of illegal immigration, however, the number of Hispanics in the United States will double between 1985 and 2020. If fact, by 2020 there will be 3 million more Hispanic Americans than blacks, and they will comprise 34 percent of the U.S. population, up from 17 percent in 1987. With limited education, there is evidence that these immigrants are losing ground socially and economically. For them to contribute effectively to the knowledge-based economy likely to be needed in the future, considerable human capital investment will be needed. The alternative of leaving them without skills will exert a sizable drag on overall economic growth and detract from efforts to eliminate the urban underclass.

Minorities and the Poor

The problems facing the immigrant poor are but a part, however, of a larger problem facing poor people, and particularly poor children, in the United States today. As we have seen, the number of 18- to 24-year-olds that will enter the labor force is projected to decline during the 1990s. At the same time, a higher proportion of them will come from minority groups that suffer from a variety of economic and educational disadvantages. Given technological and economic trends demanding a more highly skilled labor force to remain competitive in the world economy, it is important that these young workers receive adequate preparation for the economy of the future. But current trends indicate that they are falling farther behind.

As Marian Wright Edelman documents in Chapter 10, a growing number of young families have lost economic ground in the United States since the early 1970s. Between 1973 and 1986 the median income of young families with children decreased by 26 percent. One reason for

this has been a decline in average hourly wages reflecting a shift from manufacturing to service employment and the lack of adjustment of the minimum wage for inflation. Also important has been a rise in the number of families headed by single teenage mothers. By 1987, one in every five children lived in a female-headed household, compared to one in eight in 1970; and 55 percent of these children are poor. More generally, the number of children in poor families increased from just over 10 million in 1979 to almost 13 million in the late 1980s. This represents one out of every five American children, and it could rise to one in four over the next decade if current trends continue.

From the perspective of human capital investment—let alone basic morality—this is distressing. Children who start out with inadequate income and nutrition often lack the educational or emotional foundation for fully productive work lives. By the time they are adolescents, in fact, over half of the 15- to 18-year-olds from poor families have reading and math problems that place them in the bottom 20 percent of all teens.

Far from correcting the problem, moreover, recent government policies have exacerbated it, as housing, welfare, employment and training, and day care assistance have all been cut back. In the process, the experience of the 1980s seems to have refuted the view put forward during the Reagan era that targeted antipoverty policies are unnecessary so long as general economic growth is strong. As Sheldon Danziger argues in Chapter 5, the policies of the 1980s were a macroeconomic success but "a distributional failure." Despite considerable economic recovery, poverty and income inequality were higher in 1989 than they had been in 1979, the previous business cycle peak. This was true, moreover, despite the fact that educational levels rose considerably during this period. Among black males between 25 and 54 years of age, for example, the proportion who completed high school rose from 63 percent to 76 percent between 1979 and 1986; yet the proportion of these men with earnings less than the poverty level, far from declining, actually increased during this period, from 37 percent to 42 percent.

This finding points up a central paradox in current human capital investment efforts. As Danziger shows, for each of three major subgroups examined (whites, blacks, and Hispanics), for each of five points in time over the past three and a half decades, those with more education are much less likely to have low earnings than those with less education. In this sense, human capital investment seems to pay off in lower poverty rates. Thus, in 1986, the poverty rate of black males between the ages of 25 and 54 with only 0–8 years of education was 74 percent, versus 43 percent for black males who completed high school.

At the same time, however, the effectiveness of education in overcoming poverty seems to have deteriorated over time. In 1969, for example, only 9 percent of white male high school graduates between the ages of

25 and 54 were low earners. By 1986, however, this had risen to 26 percent. Among black males, 20 percent of high school graduates were below the poverty line in 1969. By 1986 this had risen to 50 percent. In fact, for all three population groups (white males, black males, and Hispanic males), the rates of low earning for college graduates in 1986 was higher than it had been for high school graduates in 1969.

A number of possible conclusions flow from these findings. In the first place, these data lend credence to the argument of Ivar Berg (1969) cited earlier: that education may be more important as a credential for getting a decent job than as a requirement for performing the job. Since the number of people with a given level of educational attainment is increasing, the worth of the credential that that level of attainment signifies is declining.

In the second place, the findings also seem to demonstrate the impact on the poor of the economic changes examined earlier, particularly the decline of low-skill jobs, the shift of employment to lower-paying service industries, and the pressure on wage levels resulting from increased international competition.

In the third place, these data seem to confirm the need to interpret human capital investment broadly, at least as a remedy for poverty. Education, it seems, may be a necessary condition for coping with poverty, but it is not sufficient. Additional aid is necessary to supplement the low earnings of the working poor. As Danziger argues, however, such aid may be viewed as "indirect" human capital investment because it is likely to raise the educational attainment of the next generation. In other words, improvements in education not accompanied by direct efforts to alleviate the poverty in which many children live may not be effective in improving academic achievement.

Finally, these data raise some questions about the *content* of education, and hence about what a given number of years of schooling really represents. One reason that the antipoverty effectiveness of schooling may be declining could be that the substance of the education may be declining, or at least may be increasingly out of sync with the needs of the job market. To explore this latter point, however, it is necessary to turn from the characteristics of the work force to the characteristics of the major instruments or institutions of human capital investment.

The Current Case for Human Capital Investment: Mechanisms and Institutions

A great many institutions and instruments are involved in the task of improving the capacity and quality of the American population and work force. At the core of the effort are our formal educational institutions, from elementary school through college and university. Equally important, however, are a variety of less formal training institutions, such as on-the-job training, specialized skills upgrading, continuing education, and remedial education and training. Finally, there are a number of activities outside of training per se that are also crucial prerequisites for work force quality, such as research, the development of new technology, and the various supportive services (e.g., health care, day care) that people often need to acquire skills and put them to productive use.

How well are these various institutions performing? To what extent do we have a well-structured, smoothly operating system of human capital investment in this country capable of responding to the economic and demographic realities that exist?

Overall Level of Effort

The chapters in Part III of this book explore these questions in some detail, focusing specifically on each of the major human capital investment institutions. Unfortunately, the answer that emerges from these analyses is not encouraging. Although America's human capital investment institutions have many strengths, they also have numerous, quite serious weaknesses, and these weaknesses have come to be quite costly given the economic and demographic circumstances that prevail. What is more, our nation's investment in human capital, far from increasing in response to the new demands detailed above, has declined in recent years, at least at the federal level. Thus, as Juffras and Sawhill show in Chapter 12, federal human capital investments declined by 21 percent between 1981 and 1982 and have barely recovered any ground since then. As a share of total federal spending, human capital expenditures declined from 3.6 percent in 1981 to 2.3 percent in 1989. Relative to federal investments in physical capital (roads, buildings, equipment), federal education and training investments declined by 50 percent during this same period.

State and local governments have performed better, at least so far as public education is concerned. Between 1970 and 1986, for example, combined state and local education expenditures increased by 40 percent after adjusting for inflation. Nevertheless, in relative terms, even state and local government performance was disappointing. Thus, as a percentage of gross national product, state and local governments spent less on education in 1986 than they had in 1975. What is more, state and local involvement in other forms of human capital investment, such as job training, welfare-to-work initiatives, and preschool education, while growing, remains quite small in absolute terms. For example, the 26 states that were providing preschool education as of 1987 served only 140,000 students, compared to the 450,000 served by the federal government's Head Start program.

Beyond these overall funding problems, other issues have arisen in the basic structure and content of our human capital investment efforts. Let us review the evidence briefly.

Elementary and Secondary School

The nation's elementary and secondary schools have the chief responsibility for producing a capable work force. For much of the 1980s, moreover, significant effort was devoted to improving the nation's public schools. Academic standards were improved, teacher education upgraded, and teacher salaries raised significantly. By the end of the decade, these efforts were beginning to bear fruit. Scores on standardized college entrance exams, after declining for years, began to improve. Test scores also improved for black and Hispanic students. And partnerships have been forged between business and the schools in cities throughout the country.

As Ernest Boyer reports in Chapter 6, however, the gains to date have been spotty and we still lack a public school system capable of meeting the nation's labor force needs. While 10 to 15 percent of the nation's schools provide an education as fine as any in the world, most students attend schools where quality ranges from good to mediocre, and some 20 to 30 percent attend schools where the educational experience is a failure. Reflecting this, nearly three-quarters of a million students drop out of school each year. And of those who remain, fewer than half read at levels that allow them to carry out even moderately complex tasks. Similar problems exist with mathematics, science, and computer competence. Compared to other leading countries, American education seems to be falling woefully behind. One recent survey of student scientific knowledge revealed, for example, that American ninth grade students ranked next to last compared to 14 other countries. Nor are the schools doing a better job on the vocational side. Vocational training is increasingly ill-equipped to provide the skills or cover the fields that the job market needs.

These problems are particularly severe, moreover, in the nation's central city schools. Attrition rates in these schools exceed 50 percent. For those who do graduate, average reading and math scores are well below the already disappointing national averages. This is particularly distressing in view of the demographic evidence reviewed earlier suggesting that the nation will be relying increasingly on the minority and poor students who attend these inner city schools in the years ahead to provide the new growth that will be needed in the nation's labor force and productivity levels. Despite this, Boyer argues, we have failed to generate the sense of urgency that is needed to respond adequately to the nation's educational crisis. In addition, what has been done has been done piecemeal, with no overall strategy. Finally, there is too little accountability for results in the system and therefore too great an acceptance of failure.

Higher Education

The problems with the 3,000 colleges and universities that comprise the nation's higher education system may be less severe, but are still serious. As Donald Stewart shows in Chapter 7, the quantity and quality of the products demanded from America's higher education system are increasing but the supply of human and financial resources available to these institutions has decreased. On the demand side, the institutions have been torn between a new-found emphasis on job-specific training and their traditional attention to liberal arts and basic thinking skills. Between 1970 and 1986, a significant increase occurred in technical and professional training to the point where degrees in these fields outdistanced liberal arts by 2:1, compared to 1:1 in 1970.

On the supply side, higher education institutions are paying the price for the inadequate performance of our elementary and secondary schools. Incoming students are increasingly ill-prepared in reading, mathematics, science, and basic thinking skills, necessitating heavy remedial efforts on the part of colleges and universities. Perhaps because of this, retention rates are low. Only half of all white college students graduate within six years of entering college. Among minority students, the retention rate is barely one-fourth. Another reason for this is the rapid escalation of college costs. College tuition has risen an average of 8 percent per year since 1980 compared to a 4 percent per year rise in the consumer price index. At a time of decreasing real family income, this puts a significant strain on family budgets, particularly since scholarship aid has declined in real value and the composition of aid has shifted increasingly from grants to loans. Nevertheless, these tuition increases have still barely kept pace with the growth in costs. In fact, salary levels of professors at colleges and universities are just beginning to recover the ground they lost in the 1970s and the nation faces a serious problem in maintaining its professorate in the years ahead. Between 1985 and 2000, a third of the nation's higher education faculty will have to be replaced. Yet the number of Ph.D.'s issued each year has declined and almost half of those with Ph.D.'s now work outside of academic institutions. What is more, the supply of black Ph.D.'s is declining. The number of blacks in graduate school declined by 20 percent between 1976/77 and 1984/85.

Research and Development

Beyond these general problems of higher education, Daniel Greenberg identifies in Chapter 8 a number of more specific problems associated with the nation's scientific research effort. The discovery and application of new knowledge is a crucial part of human capital investment because it provides the base of knowledge that ultimately translates into new technologies and productivity advances. As Greenberg shows, America has historically had great strengths in this area. Thus America produces one-third of the world's scientific, technical, and biomedical literature and employs more scientists and engineers than Japan, West Germany, France, and the United Kingdom combined. But we are in danger of squandering this advantage by giving inadequate attention to the preparation of the next generation of scientific personnel, by focusing our scientific research too heavily on military objectives, and by neglecting to link our research enterprise effectively enough to the economic needs of the nation.

Because of reductions in support for graduate training in the sciences and engineering as well as a structure of economic rewards that reduces the incentives for scientific careers, for example, the number of people entering scientific fields of study has declined markedly in recent years, as has the general science literacy of the nation's student body. Although an influx of foreign students has filled part of the resulting gap, one reliable source estimates that the number of science and engineering Ph.D.'s produced annually if present trends continue will be 40 percent below the annual number needed by the year 2000 (Atkinson 1989).

Similarly, the orientation of available federal research support increasingly toward military purposes during the 1980s has also inhibited the development of the nation's scientific infrastructure and its use to promote national productivity. Between 1980 and 1989, federal support for scientific research more than doubled, from $30 billion to $63 billion. However, within this total the defense portion tripled while the amount available for other purposes increased only about 50 percent. By the end of the decade, therefore, the defense share of the total had climbed from 51 percent to 69 percent.

Defense research does produce spinoffs in other fields. But there is a widespread consensus that defense research produces far fewer advantages for the economy than other research, in part because of the increasingly exotic focus of much defense research, and in part because of the defense establishment's single-source contracting methods, which put more emphasis on performance than cost or market acceptance. Similar problems exist, moreover, with the national laboratories, which absorb about a third of the nation's research and development expenditures. The links between these laboratories and the economic marketplace have been tenuous at best. Indeed, the lack of a sufficient link between national investments in scientific research and industrial applications of the resulting knowledge has come to be considered one of the great challenges of U.S. competitiveness. According to Greenberg, the problem is not the absence of sufficient resources but an institutional structure that fails to give sufficient salience to the applied side of the investment in new knowledge.

Employment and Training

Beyond the problems of formal education and basic research, the human capital challenges facing the nation today also involve ongoing skill development and training outside of the formal educational institutions. This is so for at least two reasons. In the first place, the demographic developments discussed above have made it increasingly necessary for employers to dip into the "at-risk" segment of the labor pool, those who drop out of school or suffer from social and economic ills that reflect historical deficiencies in our human capital investments. Since these individuals are not easily reached through the formal educational system, special training and intervention strategies are needed. In the second place, however, the speed of technological change coupled with the decentralized modes of operation that the new technologies make possible have produced changes in the nature of work that require continuous skill upgrading for all workers. Since 80 percent of those who will comprise the work force in the year 2000 are already out of school and working, the notion that training can be restricted to a person's first 18 or 22 years of life, after which he or she goes "to work," never an accurate characterization of reality, has become grossly inaccurate in recent years. The typical worker now changes jobs five times in the course of his or her occupational life, and even those on the same "job" increasingly find its content changing rapidly in response to technological developments and organizational shifts. As a consequence, employers must increasingly "make" instead of "buy" skilled employees.

Unfortunately, the nation's non-school training systems have failed to keep pace with these changing needs. As Marion Pines and Anthony Carnevale show in Chapter 9, significant efforts were made to forge an employment and training system for at-risk populations in the 1960s and 1970s, but these efforts were fragmented, tended to focus almost exclusively on the supply side of the labor market, and failed to engage the attention or interest of employers. What is more, the amount of training or skill upgrading that has been available has typically lagged far behind the quantity that would be needed to make a significant difference in people's lives. Although a new structure involving greater employer participation was put in place in the early 1980s through the Job Training Partnership Act (JTPA), this was accompanied by a drastic cutback in funding so that the new system was able to reach an even smaller portion of those in need of assistance.

So far as the broader skill upgrading issue is concerned, progress has also been slow. Pines and Carnevale report that American employers have recently been devoting more attention to work force training, but that their commitments to formal training and development remain woefully insufficient, particularly compared to that of our principal overseas competitors. This is especially true of small employers, who have been the source of most of the country's employment growth. Such employers typically lack the resources to invest very heavily in skills upgrading. Yet we lack a system of public programs to assist them in their work force needs, or to link these needs to the existing training institutions, such as community colleges or vocational training in secondary school. Therefore, while America may be able to develop new ideas, it has a harder time translating them into products and getting the products to market.

Supportive Services

One final aspect of human capital investment that the discussion above suggests is necessary concerns not training and skill development per se but the more basic supportive services such as health care, nutrition, social services, and day care that are needed to enable individuals to benefit fully from training and skill development. As Marian Edelman notes in Chapter 10, past neglect of human capital investment has a multiplier effect: by keeping people in poverty, it retards the educational and social development of their children. One study showed, as already noted, that over half of all 15- to 18-year-olds from poor families develop reading and math problems that place them in the bottom 20 percent of all teens on standardized tests. Past experience has shown, moreover, that poverty's damage begins before birth in the form of poor prenatal care and nutrition, that preventive help focused on the early years is preferable to symptomatic relief provided later, that lasting change requires family change, and that vulnerable families have multiple problems and require a combination of services.

Regrettably, however, our efforts to deal with these problems have yet to come to terms with these lessons. What is more, far from getting better, they have grown worse in recent years. Thus the value of welfare payments, housing aid, and social service support has declined sharply during the 1980s. The proportion of Americans not covered by health insurance increased by 15 percent between 1982 and 1985, and Medicaid, the joint federal-state health program for the poor, has itself been squeezed by budget reductions and has consequently been unable to fill the gap. In fact, only half of all poor children have Medicaid coverage. Head Start, one of the more successful federal programs for dealing with the pre-school problems of poor children, experienced a real decline in the value of funding available between 1981 and 1986 and is therefore able to serve only 18 percent of the eligible population. And day care has become increasingly problematic, not only for the poor but for middle-income Americans also. In 1987, for example, 10 million children under 6 needed day care, yet only 2.9 million spaces were available in licensed day care centers. Although the need to integrate services better and target them on the family unit has been increasingly recognized, efforts to build this recognition into the structure of public programs has been limited at best.

Fortunately, the federal budget compromise enacted in late 1990 made important breakthroughs in several of these areas, extending Medicaid coverage in stages to children over six living in families with incomes below the federal poverty level, expanding Head Start funding authority, and creating a new federal child care program and expanded child care funding. It remains to be seen, however, whether the resources to underwrite even these extensions will be found.

Recommendations: Key Components of a Human Capital Investment Strategy for the Future

At a time when economic and demographic changes are placing increasingly urgent demands on the nation's human capital institutions, these institutions are suffering from a variety of shortcomings and ills. The result is a serious challenge to the nation's continued ability to compete successfully in world markets, to maintain and enhance its standard of living, and to meet its obligations to all its citizens.

But if these economic and demographic realities represent a challenge, they also represent an opportunity. With economic and moral necessity pulling in the same direction, the possibility exists for a significant breakthrough in American social and economic life. But what will it take to grasp this opportunity? What changes are needed to close the gap that seems to exist between the work force the country needs and the one that seems likely to be available in the absence of corrective action? What are the key components of a human capital investment strategy for the future? And how can such a strategy be implemented and financed? In this section we explore the answers that the chapters that follow offer to these questions, focusing first on the substantive features of a human capital investment strategy for the future and then looking, in turn, at the implementation and financing of such a strategy.

Key Components

As noted earlier, to be effective, human capital investment must be conceived broadly. Investments in education not supported by changes in nutrition or health or family viability can end up having little long-run effect. By the same token, however, care must be taken not to ascribe to shortcomings of individuals problems that are really rooted in the economic circumstances that confront them. The task of formulating a human capital investment strategy is thus to match the potential array of interventions with the prevailing market circumstances and conditions.

Based on the circumstances that exist at present, two broad sets of interventions seem appropriate—the first focused on work force size and composition and the other on worker capacity and productivity. Together they define a labor force investment strategy for the future.

Work Force Supply and Composition

Some of the most serious human capital problems at the present time result from projected shortages in the basic supply of workers, particularly skilled workers. Although there is little that can be done in a democratic country to affect this, some aspects of labor force supply are amenable to change. In particular, five broad types of policy intervention geared to work force supply and composition find support in the chapters of this book.

Family planning and prenatal care. The supply of labor is importantly affected by the kind of nurturing available to infants. For numerous low-income people at the present time, an alarming rise of out-of-wedlock births coupled with inadequate access to prenatal care produces infants whose prospects for effective labor force participation are limited from birth. To correct this, expansions are needed in basic health and nutrition aid to pregnant women—for example through the Special Supplemental Food Program for Women, Infants, and Children (WIC) or Medicaid. As Marian Edelman points out in Chapter 10, prenatal care is so effective in reducing low birth weight and prematurity, which in turn often lead to life-long disabilities, that the cost of expanding Medicaid to cover maternity care for all poor women would be more than offset by subsequent savings to the Medicaid program itself from forgone health expenditures on these same children.

Immigration policy. Although it might be tempting to utilize immigration as a way to solve the labor squeeze the nation confronts in the years immediately ahead, Ray Marshall argues in Chapter 4 that such an approach would create more problems than it would solve. Particularly troubling would be an expansion of illegal immigration or the use of "guest worker" programs because these would detract from efforts to eliminate the large underclass of unskilled young people operating outside our legal economy and further burden our already overburdened inner city school systems. Rather, Marshall recommends tightening our immigration policy to impose labor market tests on incoming immigrants. At the same time, he recommends trying to integrate existing immigrants into American society as quickly as possible.

Drop-out prevention. The ability to tap the available supply of young workers for effective participation in the labor force is also affected by their tendency to drop out of school and ultimately out of the regular labor force into the underground economy of drugs and crime. From all indications, the number of young people following this course is very much on the rise, depriving the nation of talent it needs and creating serious social problems in the process. To overcome this, some local governments have launched major educational, training, and mentoring programs aimed at "at-risk" youth, youth who are most likely to drop out of school and lose contact with the legal labor market. Given the scale and consequences of this problem, these efforts should be greatly expanded.

Equal opportunity. As we have seen, occupational segregation and lack of pay equity are strong disincentives for optimal levels of human capital investment among women and minorities. Such barriers also affect the incentive to enter the labor force and remain in it. Given the likely extent of reliance on women and minorities to staff the labor force of the future, the elimination of these sex and racial barriers becomes an urgent economic necessity, in addition to a moral one. Similarly, changes are needed in the host of tax, pension, and leave policies that inhibit full female labor force participation.

Day care. Accessibility to the labor force is also affected by the availability of supportive services, the most crucial of which is child care. The United States is the only major industrial nation in the world with a large proportion of women working outside the home that lacks a national child care policy. As a result, fewer women work than would otherwise, and much time is lost by those who do work because of failed day care arrangements. The problems are particularly severe for low-income women, for whom day care is a major financial barrier to employment. Indeed, for such women the costs of child care often make employment at the wages likely to be available irrational. It also leads teen parents to leave school, further reducing their long-term employment prospects and ensuring that they will raise their children in poverty. Both to aid the employment prospects of the mothers, and to help upgrade the preschool education of the children, a major expansion of subsidized day care is therefore urgently needed. Fortunately, Congress recognized this problem in the 1990 budget agreement, but it is far from clear whether the funding to implement the newly enacted child care legislation will be made available.

Worker Capacity and Productivity

Beyond the measures needed to ensure an adequate supply of labor given the prevailing demographic realities, other steps are needed to make sure that this labor force has the capabilities that are needed for the jobs likely to be available. Broadly speaking, this will require action on five major fronts.

Early childhood education. One of the major lessons of recent efforts to cope with poverty and improve life chances is the importance of early intervention. Research on the Head Start program, for example, shows fairly convincingly that Head Start children score higher on I.Q. and achievement tests and are more likely to meet elementary school requirements than are comparable nonparticipants, and these findings have been confirmed for other preschool programs. Yet the number of children able to participate in this program remains well below the number eligible. To correct this, both Boyer and Edelman recommend an expansion of the Head Start program so that it can cover all eligible children whose parents want them to participate.

Elementary and secondary education. Significant changes are also needed in elementary and secondary education. According to Boyer, the changes needed here do not involve finances as much as direction and organization. In particular, he endorses a sixfold strategy calling for: first, a national commitment to the proposition that every child must have a quality education and can respond to it; second, the development of a coherent curriculum stressing language proficiency, basic facility with numbers, cultural knowledge, science, and familiarity with the world of work; third, attention to the pre-school years; fourth, a restructuring of public schools to stress school-based management and accountability for educational performance; fifth, greater efforts to recruit better teachers through higher salaries, improved working conditions, expanded teacher renewal programs, and efforts to upgrade the status of teaching as a profession; and sixth, expanded partnerships between the schools, on the one hand, and parents and business, on the other.

Higher education and research. In the higher education field, the most urgent changes involve finances instead of programs. Increases are needed in student financial aid, both to keep the doors of opportunity open to minority and disadvantaged students and to maintain a flow of graduate students into the professorate. Particularly critical is the need for support of science education. Greenberg, for example, calls for a significant increase in the National Science Foundation's educational budget and the establishment of a program to provide support for 3,000 science graduate students a year. Increases are also needed in federal support of research and for the upgrading of scientific research facilities at universities. This will likely require a significant shift of federal research priorities from defense to non-defense purposes as the threat of Soviet power wanes. Finally, more attention needs to be paid to the application of scientific knowledge. Given the complexity of many technological processes, expecting that industry alone will perform this function may be overly hopeful. Greenberg therefore recommends a clearer fixing of organizational responsibilities for this function in the national government, perhaps through the creation of a Department of Science or the beefing up of the system of presidential science advice.

Work force development. To fill in where the formal educational institutions leave off, a variety of important changes are needed in the broader systems of work force training and development, as Pines and Carnevale argue in Chapter 9. For one thing, a more integrated system of training and supportive services is needed for the at-risk populations and those with minimal attachment to the work force. The Private Industry Councils (PICs) created by the Job Training Partnership Act of 1982 provide a useful foundation for this system, combining as they do state and local governments and the private sector in a partnership to improve the job readiness and employment of at-risk persons. But the resources available for such training must be increased and targeted more effectively on the most disadvantaged youth and adults. In addition, efforts should be made to integrate other forms of remedial education and training, as well as needed supportive services such as day care, into the same PIC system. Similarly, the PIC system should be used to handle the new jobs emphasis in the 1988 welfare reform legislation, which provides for training services to young single mothers of young children. This should be accompanied, moreover, by efforts to restructure school-based vocational education so that it is integrated into the regular school curriculum and oriented toward mastery of certain basic thinking, problem-solving, communication, data manipulation, and decision-making skills.

Beyond this, greater efforts should be made to facilitate training and skill development for those already at work. For those affected by economic dislocations or adjustments, Pines and Carnevale suggest tapping the Unemployment Insurance trust fund to underwrite training, counseling, and job search activities, preferably well in advance of job loss. Even for those not affected by such readjustments, however, greater encouragement should be provided to employers to maintain the skill levels of their employees. In the case of smaller employers in particular, tax incentives or matching funds should be provided. Beyond this, existing pension and benefit systems should be revised to facilitate worker movement among jobs and therefore encourage the kind of flexibility that current economic circumstances require.

Supportive services. Finally, as a prerequisite to the education and training efforts described above, more serious attention must be paid to the basic supportive services required to foster physical and mental fitness and hence the ability to absorb education and training. As Danziger shows in Chapter 5, poverty is closely related to poor school performance, early parenthood, and weak attachment to the labor force. Yet education alone is insufficient to overcome poverty. To make headway on a human capital investment strategy aimed at bringing all potential workers into the work force, therefore, supplemental measures are needed, even if only to help the next generation of potential workers. Thus Danziger proposes to expand the existing Earned Income Tax Credit, which provides income supplementation to the working poor through refundable tax credits, and to make another tax provision—the Dependent Care Credit—refundable for poor families. Both of these would provide income assistance to poor families with a working parent without expanding traditional welfare assistance and thereby provide a better foundation for the children of these families to escape the debilitating effects of poverty.

Edleman suggests additional measures to ensure the physical and mental development of poor children. These include more extensive prenatal health and nutritional care, improved health care for teens, non-school recreational programs for inner-city youths to foster self-esteem and provide constructive outlets for energy, and a basic reorientation of children's services to emphasize "family preservation" by focusing counseling, nutrition, health, and other services on the family unit rather than individual family members. Each of these can be defended on strict cost-effectiveness grounds, as ways to avoid more costly corrective action later on. What is more, each is needed to make other human capital investments effective.

Implementation: Institutional Roles and Finance

Articulating a human capital investment strategy and carrying it out, however, are two different things. Where should responsibility for human capital investment be vested? And how should expanded human capital investments be financed?

Federal versus State and Local Government Roles

On theoretical grounds, a strong case can be made for vesting principal responsibility for public involvement in human capital investments in the federal government. Unlike physical capital, which is generally fixed and cannot be moved from place to place, human capital by its very nature is mobile. As a consequence, citizens in one jurisdiction may be reluctant to invest heavily in the education of their own citizens for fear that many of these citizens may decide to move elsewhere, thus robbing the jurisdiction of the return on its "investment." A human capital investment strategy that leaves everything to local discretion thus seems

likely to underinvest in human capital, at least so far as the disadvantaged are concerned. Active federal involvement thus seems imperative
to ensure the level of human capital investment that the nation as a whole
needs.

As Scott Fosler shows in Chapter 11, however, the evolution of American federalism has taken a slightly different course. By the late nineteenth and early twentieth centuries, a significant division emerged between human resource policy and economic policy, with the states and
local governments assuming principal responsibility for the former and
the federal government for the latter. Although extensive human service
programs were enacted at the federal level in the 1960s, these were
largely secondary and ad hoc, with little integration or association with
economic policy. Not until the late 1970s and early 1980s were efforts
made to integrate economic policy and human resource policy as part of
the growing concern about U.S. competitiveness, but the most promising
advances were made at the state level, not the federal level. For nearly
two decades now, states have been actively innovating in the human capital field, promoting educational reform, encouraging early childhood education, and fostering program integration between welfare and
training.

What this suggests, Fosler argues, is the need for a partnership approach to human capital investment, an approach that recognizes the
U.S. federal system as an asset and an opportunity in pursuing human
capital investment objectives. While federal leadership is imperative in
this partnership—to articulate strategy, to broaden the current school
reform movement, to provide support for the disadvantaged, and to encourage better integration of human resource policies—such leadership
should not displace active state and local government involvement. For
one thing, some of the key human capital institutions—such as the family, schools, colleges, and training institutions—are local in character or
run by state and local governments. As of 1988, for example, states and
local governments accounted for 88 percent of all governmental purchases of goods and services in the United States, and education comprised 40 percent of this. Nine out of every ten dollars state and local
governments spend on education, moreover, comes from their own-
source revenues. In the second place, regions are too diverse to permit a
single approach. To be effective, policies must be adapted to local circumstances. What is more, competition among states and regions is a source
of energy and new ideas.

What is needed, therefore, is an approach that utilizes the federal
system to promote economic growth. Fosler calls this "economic or investment federalism." It would involve both cooperation and competition—cooperation between the federal government and state and local
governments to achieve greater integration of key human capital invest-

ment programs, such as education, training, welfare, health, and social services at the point of delivery; and competition among the states and localities to "bring out the best in each." As one model of how such an approach might work, Fosler points to the PIC system endorsed also by Marion Pines. This system combines federal funding with state and local government and private-sector involvement to promote work force readiness at the local level. Guided by a more coherent concept of human capital investment and equipped with other forms of aid other than the ones now available to it, the PIC system could provide an effective vehicle for achieving some of the targeted work force assistance that is needed, especially if it can be made to work with the formal educational establishment.

Financing Increased Government Human Capital Investments

Closely related to the question of how human capital investments should be administered is the more fundamental question of how they should be financed. As we have seen, despite the increased urgency of human capital issues, government spending on human capital investment has actually been declining in recent years at both the federal and state and local government levels. Indeed, Sawhill and Juffras estimate that if human capital investments were at their historic highs as a percentage of gross national product—as economic and demographic conditions suggest is appropriate—we would have spent $33 billion more on human capital investment programs in 1988 than we did.

At a time of historically high federal deficits and intensive popular pressures to avoid increased taxation, however, where can the funds be found to carry out the human capital investment strategy outlined here? Juffras and Sawhill outline five alternative funding sources that could potentially be tapped: (1) regular budget appropriations; (2) specially earmarked taxes, such as a portion of Unemployment Insurance taxes set aside to create "individual training accounts"; (3) mandated employer investments in training and employment adjustment; (4) increased state and local spending; and (5) the Social Security trust fund.

Each of these alternatives has its advantages, but Juffras and Sawhill in the end recommend the fifth alternative—dedicating a portion of the projected increase in the Social Security trust fund over the next twenty years to a major expansion of human capital investments. The federal deficit makes the regular appropriations route essentially unavailable, particularly for "discretionary" programs like those in the human resource area, which are not mandated by law as a matter of right. Earmarked taxes are easier to raise but can create a sense of entitlement that prevents money being allocated to more productive uses as circumstances change. Mandated employer-financed benefit plans shift the cost burden to employers, but these costs can then be passed on to consumers in the form of higher prices, or to workers in the form of lower wages. Finally, reliance on state and local financing makes the country's human capital investment strategy dependent on the varied capacities and inclinations of thousands of state and local governments.

By contrast, the use of the surplus in the Social Security trust fund avoids many of these problems. This surplus is projected to grow from $40 billion in 1988 to $172 billion in 2010. At present, this surplus is being used to finance the federal deficit. But under the Gramm-Rudman-Hollings Deficit Reduction law and recent revisions, the budget deficit should be eliminated by the mid-1990s. Rather than allowing the Social Security surplus to accumulate further, Juffras and Sawhill propose to devote half of the growth in the Social Security surplus after 1993 to investments in human capital. This would generate about $22 billion in additional human capital investment funds each year between 1994 and 2005. Not only would this stimulate productivity and economic growth, but in the process it would generate the increased worker contributions to the Social Security trust fund that will ultimately be needed to finance the Social Security system after 2010, when the baby boom generation begins to retire. In other words, this arrangement would use the Social Security program to invest in the future of the Social Security program. The balance of the surplus could then be used to stimulate private investment by retiring government debt.

The Private-Sector Role

Important as government involvement is to the success of a human capital investment strategy, it is only part of the story. Also crucial will be the active involvement of the private sector. As Boyer makes clear, private-sector involvement will be crucial to turn urban schools around. Pines and Carnevale also stress the importance of private-sector action to remedy the serious workplace training deficiencies that confront the nation. They propose an interim goal of 2 percent of payroll, and an ultimate goal of 4 percent, to be devoted to workplace training efforts. Finally, private-sector investment will continue to be crucial in the research and development field. Recent findings suggesting a fall-off of corporate investments in research underline the challenge that exists and the need for active partnerships between government and the private sector to enhance America's competitive edge (Markoff 1990). Behind these specific actions, moreover, lies a more basic need for corporate understanding of the human capital challenge the nation faces, and a willingness to muster the political muscle to produce the action that is needed.

Conclusion

The United Stated stands today at a historic moment. Because of a variety of economic and demographic shifts, the nation's economic agenda and its social agenda coincide. With economic and moral necessity pulling in the same direction, there is some hope that the widespread waste of human talents that has characterized our national life for so long can be relieved. To seize this moment will require bold vision and concerted action, however. Ad hoc half-measures and disconnected experimentation will not achieve the breakthrough that both social justice and economic competitiveness require.

Fortunately, extensive experimentation at the state and local government level and a substantial body of research have created a widespread consensus about what needs to be done. A broad-gauged approach that combines changes in public education with improvements in prenatal care, early childhood intervention, specialized skill development for at-risk youth, income supplementation for the working poor, day care assistance, investments in science and engineering, the elimination of job discrimination, and ongoing skill development for those already at work is what the times require. Successful models for each of these components are already in operation. What is more, the resources are available to apply them more broadly. The task now is to develop the will to act on what we know.

How this will be done is far from clear. A recent rise of business interest in human capital issues, as reflected in the pages of *Business Week* and learned studies by the Committee for Economic Development and other groups, suggests that the message is getting through—at least to the business leadership if not to the public and their elected representatives. In Chapter 13, David Hornbeck suggests a more radical approach in the form of legislation that would give state and local governments the duty, enforceable in courts, to assure the health and well-being of each child until age 18 or graduation from high school. Whether this approach is feasible or not, it underlines the need to develop a mechanism to bring public attention squarely face to face with the realities outlined in this book.

The wealth of a nation lies in its people, Adam Smith reminded us 200 years ago. At no time in our history has this truth been more apropos. At a time of increasing international competitiveness, declining population growth, and shifting work force composition, investment in human capital has become a prerequisite to the nation's economic survival and growth. We can no longer afford to treat human resource policies as a secondary concern focused only on the symptoms of economic distress. Human capital investment must become the centerpiece of our economic strategy for the years ahead. As *Business Week* magazine put it in a statement quoted by Marion Wright Edelman in her chapter: "It is time to put our money where our future is."

Note

1. For an early theoretical development of the concept of human capital investment, see Becker 1964. For a very good collection of theoretical and empirical research on the topic, see Kiker 1971.

References

Atkinson, Richard C. (1989). "Supply and Demand for Science and Engineering Ph.D.'s: A National Crisis in the Making." Unpublished remarks to the Regents of the University of California, February 16, 1989. Cited in Daniel Greenberg, chapter 8, infra.

Bartel, Ann P., and Frank R. Lichtenberg (1987). "The Comparative Advantage of Educated Workers in Implementing New Technology." *Review of Economics and Statistics* 1 (February): 1–11.

Becker, Gary S. (1964). *Human Capital: A Theoretical and Empirical Analysis with Special Attention to Education.* New York: National Bureau of Economic Research.

Berg, Ivar (1969). *Education and Jobs: The Great Training Robbery.* New York: Praeger Publishers.

Bowles, Samuel, and Herbert Gintis (1976). *Schooling in Capitalist America.* New York: Basic Books.

Brenner, Joel Glenn (1989). "Area Businesses Tap New Source to Solve Severe Labor Shortage: The Homeless, Welfare Mothers among Workers Being Recruited." *Washington Post,* September 2, 1989, p. A1.

Choate, Pat, with J. K. Linger (1986). *The High-Flex Society: Shaping America's Economic Future.* New York: Alfred A. Knopf.

Denison, Edward F. (1962). *The Sources of Economic Growth in the United States and the Alternatives before Us.* New York: Committee for Economic Development.

Fiske, Edward B. (1989). "Impending Job 'Disaster': Work Force Unqualified to Work; Schools Lagging Far behind Needs of Employers." *New York Times,* September 25, 1989, p. 1.

Freeman, Richard B. (1976). *The Over-educated American.* New York: Academic Press.

Johnston, William B., and Arnold E. Packer (1987). *Workforce 2000: Work and Workers for the Twenty-First Century.* Indianapolis: Hudson Institute.

Kearns, David (1988). "Why Business Leaders Care about Education," in Kearns and Doyle, 1988.

Kearns, David T., and Denis P. Doyle (1988). *Winning the Brain Race: A Bold Plan to Make Our Schools Competitive.* San Francisco: Institute for Contemporary Studies.

Kiker, B. F., ed. (1971). *Investment in Human Capital.* Columbia: University of South Carolina Press.

Litan, Robert (1988). *American Living Standards: Threats and Challenges.* Washington, D.C.: Brookings Institution.

Markoff, John (1990). "A Corporate Lag in Research Funds Is Causing Worry." *New York Times,* January 23, 1990, p. A1.

Murnane, Richard (1988). "Education and the Productivity of the Work Force: Looking Ahead," in Litan, 1988.

Nussbaum, Bruce (1988). "Needed: Human Capital." *Business Week,* September 19, 1988, pp. 100–3.

Osborne, David (1988). *Laboratories of Democracy: A New Breed of Governor Creates Models for National Growth.* Boston: Harvard Business School Press.

Parnes, Herbert S. (1984). *People Power: Elements of Human Resource Policy.* Beverly Hills: Sage Publications.

Piore, Michael, and Charles Sabel (1982). *The Second Industrial Divide.* New York: Basic Books.

President's Commission on Industrial Competitiveness (1985). *Global Competition: The New Reality.* Vol. 2. Washington, D.C.: U.S. Government Printing Office.

Reich, Robert B. (1984). *The Next American Frontier.* New York: Penguin.

Rosen, Sherwin (1987). "Human Capital." In John Eatwell, Murray Milgate, and Peter Newman, eds., *The New Palgrave: A Dictionary of Economics.* Vol. 2. London: Macmillan, pp. 652–90.

Sawhill, Isabel (1988). "Poverty in the U.S.: Why Is It So Persistent?" *Journal of Economic Literature* 26 (September): 1073–1119.

Schultz, Theodore W. (1961). "Investment in Human Capital." *American Economic Review* 51 (March): 1–17; reprinted in Kiker 1971: 3–21.

———. (1981). *Investing in People: The Economics of Population Quality.* Berkeley: University of California Press.

Welch, F. (1976). *Ability Tests and Measures of Differences between Black and White Americans.* Santa Monica: The Rand Corporation.

———. (1979). "Effects of Cohort Size on Earnings: The Baby Boom Babies' Financial Bust." *Journal of Political Economy* 87(5), Pt. II (October): S65–97.

Wozniak, Gregory D. (1984). "The Adoption of Interrelated Innovations: A Human Capital Approach." *Review of Economics and Statistics* 66: 70–79.

———. (1987). "Human Capital, Information, and the Early Adoption of New Technology." *Journal of Human Resources* 22: 101–12.

PART ONE

The Need

2

The Demographic and Economic Imperatives

Arnold H. Packer

Twin Challenges: Demographic and Economic Change

The Golden Age

Picture an economy growing smoothly because, each year, there are more workers and each worker is more productive.

- The labor force is growing because the average woman is having more than the 2.1 children needed to replace those who are dying. Each generation of workers is larger than the previous generation and the ratio of retirees to workers remains constant.
- The nation's stock of factories and equipment—its capital stock—and the capabilities of its work force—its human capital—are growing smoothly. The output per worker is growing because smarter workers are using better equipment, and lower-wage, lower-productivity jobs are being replaced by better-paying, more productive work.

Picture, then, the labor force growing at 2 percent annually and the output per worker growing at an equal rate. Economic output will expand at a rate of 4 percent annually. Each new generation of workers will be better able to support their children and their retired parents as well as themselves. The population and per capita income will also grow by 2 percent annually, and both real take-home pay and retirement benefits can grow.

To some extent, this picture represented the United States during the period 1948–73, when the labor force grew by 1.6 percent annually, output grew by 3.7 percent annually, and per capita disposable income grew by 2.4 percent annually. The years after World War II were golden years for American workers and especially for union members. In the economy as a whole, the output per worker increased by 2.4 percent annually between 1950 and 1973. Although the benefits were widely shared, market power allowed unionized firms to pay unskilled and semiskilled workers relatively well. A janitor at a General Motors plant might receive five times the pay of a janitor in a nonunionized factory or service establishment. Unfortunately, the picture reflects neither the United States situation since 1973 nor the situation likely to prevail over the next 40 years. The reason is a series of demographic and economic surprises that pose serious threats to the nation's future prosperity. To overcome these threats, major policy changes will be needed to improve our human capital investment.

Demographic and Economic Surprises

Demography was the first surprise. The U.S. population has not grown smoothly since World War II. Much to the surprise of the demographers of the time, a baby boom began in 1946. Fertility rose from the Great Depression plateau of 2.1 births per female (during her full childbearing life) to a peak of 3.7 in 1957. The demographers were surprised again when the boom ended in 1964 (fertility was 3.2 in that year) and was followed by a "birth dearth" as fertility fell to 1.7 in 1976.

As a result of the baby boom and bust, the labor force, which grew by 24 million workers during the 1970s, will increase by less than 16 million during the 1990s; the ratio of retirees to workers will grow rapidly after 2010, when the baby boomers start to retire. Twenty years from now, the baby boomers who overloaded our school systems in the 1950s and 1960s, and our housing markets in the 1970s and 1980s, will overload our retirement system.

The result will be slower economic growth and a greater burden on each active worker to support the nation's retirees. Meeting this challenge requires increased productivity. Unfortunately, however, output per worker—productivity—has grown slowly over the last 18 years. If this condition persists, per capita income will also grow slowly over the next 20 years and will cease growing entirely after 2010. That is, stagnation is less than 20 years away.

The international challenge to this golden age surprised economists and everyone else in 1973, when OPEC flexed its muscles and sent oil prices through the ceiling. Previously, American institutions had set oil prices. During the following years, the United States became a "price taker" instead of a "price maker" for many goods and services. By the

1980s, our major industrial companies had lost market power to foreign competitors and our unions had lost the power to set wages.

This international shock was administered to an economy that was already moving away from manufacturing to services. The shift became a virtual earthquake in the early 1980s, when the value of the dollar rose by over 50 percent, actually 83 percent from the trough in the third quarter of 1980 to the peak in the first quarter of 1985. Over the longer term, the loss of manufacturing jobs to foreign competition is not the only reason for the growth of the service sector. Manufacturing employment naturally follows agricultural employment in its relative decline in all mature economies, and this includes Japan and Germany. International competition did, however, accelerate the long-term trend in the United States toward increasing the percentage of the work force employed by service firms or institutions (including government).

Foreign competition was also a spur to the ongoing technological revolution as United States corporations sought to increase the productivity of factory workers and, thereby, their own competitiveness. Between 1979 and 1986, output per hour in manufacturing increased by an average of 3.1 percent annually, faster than during the 1950–73 period. The adoption of new technology accelerated the shift of employment from manufacturing to services and changed the nature of work in both sectors. Strassman (1985: 93) estimates that two-thirds of United States labor costs are associated with information handling. As will be argued later, these changes in the economy outpaced the change in our education and training institutions and methods.

The Human Face of Demographic and Economic Change

Demographics, productivity, international competition, and the very idea of a national economy are abstractions that reflect the concrete reality of individual workers and their families. For the typical child of the baby boom born, say, in 1955, the past 20 or 30 years have posed real challenges. This is particularly true for those with little education. As unskilled manufacturing jobs disappeared, these baby boomers had to accept lower-paying service jobs—for example, in fast food restaurants such as McDonald's. The results are clearly evident in Table 2.1, which shows the change in real (inflation-adjusted) earnings of males aged 20 to 24 between 1973 and 1986. As Table 2.1 indicates, those who graduated from high school in the early 1980s earned 28 percent less than their older brothers who graduated 13 years earlier. For high school dropouts, the reduction was 42 percent. College graduates have suffered less decline, but even they lost some ground between 1973 and 1986.

Good jobs require good workers; high wages require high productiv-

Table 2.1 Mean Annual Earnings of 20- to 24-Year-Old Civilian Males,
1973 and 1986 (in 1986 Dollars)

	1973	1986	Change (%)
All males	12,176	9,027	−26
College graduates[a]	14,630	13,759	− 6
College dropouts and associate-degree holders[a]	13,108	10,960	−16
High school graduates[a]	15,221	10,924	−28
High school and lower-school dropouts[a]	11,815	6,853	−42

Source: William T. Grant Foundation 1988: 27.

[a]Males not citing school as major activity at time of survey.

ity. Both employers and employees have a stake in increasing productivity. In the short term, higher wages without higher productivity means inflation, high interest rates, and, inevitably, a recession and layoffs. In the long term, low productivity growth means lower wages if wages are counted in constant, inflation-adjusted dollars.

The baby boomers also have a stake in the productivity of those who come after them. The labor force of 2010 will have to carry a triple burden:

- Supporting themselves and their own children
- Supporting the elderly who depend on Social Security and private health and pension plans
- Carrying the banner of the United States in foreign competition.

Productivity must be increased. That much is clear. *How* to increase productivity is less clear. Economists are far from certain about the causes of the slowdown that began in 1973. The argument here, however, is that a significant portion of the explanation lies in our inadequate and ill-directed investment in human capital. Our hopes for a resumption of productivity growth, therefore, hinge on improving the quality of the work force.

Our argument will be that the human resource challenge has changed, while the way we educate and train children and adults has not. The changes are two:

1. The demographic profile of young Americans has shifted. New entrants to the labor force are about equally divided among white males, white females, and minorities. Whites will account for 83 percent of labor force leavers. Thus, 53 percent of the *net* new workers in the United States economy over the rest of the century (1988–

2000) will be members of these minority groups: blacks, Hispanic Americans, and Asian Americans (Fullerton 1989: 11). Thus, the students have changed.

2. The economy has also changed and requires more and different knowledge and skills. School curricula need to equip American students to cope increasingly with technological change, the service jobs, and international competition.

Why Productivity Growth Must Quicken During the 1990s

The United States cannot keep ahead of our European and Asian competitors with inadequately educated and trained workers. Moreover, the problem will not disappear during the decade of the 1990s. Why will poorly prepared workers cause such dire problems? Because:

1. Our labor shortage makes increases in wages inevitable. Unless the output per worker (i.e., productivity) also increases, prices and interest rates will rise, reducing business activity.

2. Our medium-run economic, social, and budgetary goals are incompatible unless productivity increases accelerate.

The Economic Challenge

Improving real wages and retirement benefits as the population ages is challenge enough. However, the United States must meet that goal in the face of growing international competition and rapid technological change.

The contest requires successfully competing with the nations of the Pacific Rim and, especially after 1992, the economically integrated European community. At stake are relative living standards and the leadership position of the United States. According to some forecasts, the U.S. living standard advantage will disappear by the year 2000 (*Economist* 1988: 49). The United States had a 40 percent larger gross domestic product (GDP) per person than Japan in 1987, but Japan is catching up at the rate of 3 percent annually and Japanese assets, per capita, are already much higher than ours. Korea's per capita gross national product (GNP) rose from around $500 in 1964 to around $4,000 today (both measured in 1988 dollars) (*Economist* 1989: 33, and 23).

The Short-Run Problem: Slow Economic Growth

Signs of the demographic time bomb facing the nation appeared in 1989. The nation's economy—straining to increase consumption, sup-

port its elderly population, meet newly recognized social needs, balance
the budget, and reduce the trade deficit—ran into capacity constraints.
Businesses that for years depended on waves of young people eager to
work at low wages ran out of help. Entry-level wages climbed, even before the legal minimum wage increased. Because productivity did not
grow, business costs increased. Overall in 1989, hourly compensation
increased by 3.3 percent, output per hour fell by 0.3 percent, and therefore, unit labor costs increased by 3.3 percent.

The shortage of young workers was forcing fast-food restaurants in
many parts of the country to pay close to $7.00 per hour for workers.
Nursing homes, which not long before had paid an average wage of
$4.00 per hour to the nurses' assistants who made up nearly half of their
staffs, saw these workers' wages rise also.

An increase in wages, when matched by an increase in productivity
(i.e., youngsters selling more hamburgers and nurses' assistants serving
more patients), reduces poverty and yields higher tax revenues and a
balanced budget. But, because productivity was not increasing sufficiently, food prices, health care costs, and the prices of other goods and
services were on their way up.

The Federal Reserve Board, responding to this wage-cost inflation,
raised interest rates to slow the economy, thereby risking a recession.
Sales of autos and homes slumped. Alan Greenspan, chairman of the Fed,
deemed that the economy could not grow more than 2 percent annually
in the 1990s without causing inflation. By the end of 1989, he had
reached his target and the new decade began with a recession. Greenspan's successors will be aiming for still lower rates of growth *unless*
productivity can be made to grow faster.

The Medium-Term Problem: Stagnating Take-Home Pay

President Bush's budget anticipates annual productivity increases of
1.9 percent over the 1989–94 period, considerably more than has been
seen over most of the last 18 years. This anticipation directly underlies
his hope for a balanced budget and, indirectly, for a gentler, kinder nation. Without faster productivity growth, incomes stagnate and trade
and budget deficits remain high. How likely are President Bush's anticipated productivity growth rates? Between spring 1989 and spring 1990,
productivity fell by 0.8 percent.[1] Indeed, our productivity performance
over the last 18 years has been abysmal.

The amounts of goods and services produced by the average worker
have not increased rapidly enough. That judgment holds whether the
comparison is made to earlier periods, to our international competitors,
or to our current or future needs. In the 25 years from 1948 to 1973, the
"golden age," multifactor productivity (a measure that reflects both

Table 2.2   U.S. Economic Growth: Actual (1955–1985) and Projected (1985–2000) Annual Growth (%)

	History		Forecasts for 1985–2000	
	1955–70 Balanced	1970–85 Unbalanced	Base Case	Low Growth
GNP	3.2	2.7	2.9	1.6
Employment	1.6	2.1	1.3	0.9
Manufacturing	0.92	0.0	−0.8	−0.4
Commercial and service[a]	2.3	3.3	2.1	1.4
Output per worker[b]	1.5	0.7	1.5	0.7
Manufacturing	2.0	2.9	3.9	2.5
Commercial and service	1.4	−0.2	0.9	0.1
Consumption per capita	2.1	1.9	1.8	0.7

Source: Johnston and Packer 1987: 54.

[a]The trade, finance, and service sectors.
[b]GNP/(total no. of workers).

physical and human capital) in the private sector increased by 2.0 percent annually. During the next six years growth disappeared, and from 1979 to 1987, multifactor productivity increased by only 0.6 percent annually (Bureau of Labor Statistics).

The challenge of the 1990s can be seen by analyzing the 1955–2000 period divided into three 15-year periods. The years between 1955 and 1970 were a period of balanced economic growth. As shown in Table 2.2, economic growth was balanced in the sense that

1. Employment and productivity growth (the two components of overall economic growth) contributed almost equally to economic growth. Employment grew by 1.6 percent per year, and output per worker[2] in the overall economy grew by 1.5 percent per year. As a direct result, the economy grew by 3.2 percent annually (1.6 + 1.5 + 0.1 = 3.2, the 0.1 remainder representing the compounding effect of the two basic forces).

2. Both manufacturing and the rest of the economy benefited from growing employment and productivity.

As a result, per capita consumption increased by 2.1 percent annually. Moreover, the increased personal spending did not depend on major borrowing by the federal government or on importing more than we exported (as was the story of the 1980s).

Economic growth became unbalanced in 1973. In the 1970–85 period, employment growth accelerated to 2.1 percent annually as the baby

expected to disappear completely early in the next century if current demographic trends continue. Not only will more Americans be drawing
from Social Security and pension funds but also the growth in contributors to these funds will slow and finally cease.

Today, there are 30 Social Security recipients for every 100 workers;
by 2030 there will be 50 recipients for every 100 workers. We are already
seeing the effects of the demographic trends on paychecks; Social Security tax rates increased from 11.4 percent in 1988 to 12.4 percent in
1990, further diminishing take-home pay.

Most of the goods and services consumed by the elderly are produced
by younger workers. Today, the aged earn, from current efforts, only
about 16 percent of their income. The remaining 84 percent are interge-
nerational transfers of one sort or another—38 percent from Social Security and 14 percent from pensions. Social Security is not charity but,
instead, is an agreement among the generations. Each generation of
workers pays to support the older generation of retirees and expects to
be supported by the younger generation when they reach working age.

The point is worthy of emphasis, especially in light of the confusion
regarding Social Security and private pension trust funds. The entire population consumes what the current work force produces (with the important exceptions of trade and the using up of long-lived physical assets). The Social Security trust fund is "supposed to" work by increasing
the nation's savings and thus investment, and thus increasing the productivity of tomorrow's work force. But investment funds may flow across
international boundaries, and, more important, not all investments yield
a positive return. Therefore, the nation's retirees cannot put all their trust
in the Social Security trust funds; in the end, their pensions depend upon
the growing capacity of tomorrow's workers to produce.

Not only will workers in the early part of the next century have to
support more aged people but they will also have to pay increasing
amounts for health expenditures for the aged, and especially for the very
old, who are expected to make up an increasingly large fraction of the
elderly population (Fig. 2.2). In 1985, the federal government spent a
reported $50 billion for the 6 million persons who were 80 years of age
or older (Torrey 1985: 377). Medicare expenditures are expected to
grow from 2.1 percent of the GNP in 1990 to 4.5 percent in 2030. Under
pessimistic assumptions, the share could amount to 8.5 percent of the
GNP in 2030 (Palmer 1988). Meanwhile increases of 20 percent and 30
percent for private health insurance premiums are common.

Unless productivity growth accelerates, average workers will be unable to increase their take-home pay while carrying the growing burden
of supporting the retirees. Deductions will increase faster than gross pay
as every worker will have to pay more for Social Security, pensions, and

Figure 2.2   Number and age composition of the elderly population, 1960–2050.

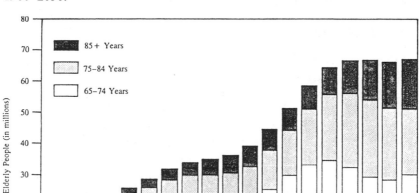

(Reprinted from Palmer 1988: 6.1.)

health insurance to support the retirees. Unless the active workers become more productive than they are now (so that their gross pay can be increased in a noninflationary manner), either their take-home pay or the retirees' retirement benefits (or both) will decline.

Why We Need to Change the Way We Invest in People

The causes of the productivity slowdown that has occurred since 1973 are controversial. The figures published by the Bureau of Labor Statistics (BLS) show no deterioration in the capital-to-labor ratio. Recent studies also indicate that, in terms of years of experience and years of schooling, the United States work force is improving as rapidly now as it did during the "golden years." So the productivity slowdown must be the result of less effective investment in the three sources of productivity improvements: knowledge, physical capital, or human capital.

In other words, what worked before 1973 is not working now, because technological or organizational innovation has slowed and/or because the nation now has a less effective education and training system. It is quite possible that schooling is less valuable today because the stu-

dent body and the economy have changed much more quickly than the
education and training system have adapted to these new realities.

The Importance of the Minority Work Force

One clue to the changes we are facing lies in a closer look at the
demographics discussed above. As it turns out, the rise and fall of birthrates did not occur simultaneously for all groups: fertility for "minorities" has remained high longer than it did for non-Hispanic whites.[4] In
addition, immigration of "minorities" has remained high. As a result,
*population growth among minorities has been almost three times that of
whites* (21 percent versus 8 percent in the 1980s). Thus, the share of
minorities among entry-level workers has increased while whites have
retired. As a result, the majority of *net* new workers being added to the
United States labor force are "minorities."

Between 1987 and 2000, a projected 42.8 million workers will enter
the work force. About one-third of these will be non-Hispanic white
men, one-third non-Hispanic white women, and one-third minorities.
During the same period, 23.4 million workers are projected to leave the
labor force, about half of whom will be non-Hispanic white males.

The net change (i.e., subtracting the leavers from the entrants), as
shown in Figure 2.3, is that 2 percent of the 19.5 million *net* additions
to the United States work force will be members of minority groups. The
major uncertainties are labor force participation rates and the level of
immigration. The latter is a function of United States policies, the vigor
of the United States economy, and political and economic conditions in
the source nations.

Current human capital systems serve minorities less well than they
do the white population. The retiring baby boom generation will be pre-
dominately white, while the replacement work force—upon whom the
retirees' retirement income ultimately depends—will be increasingly men
and women of color. Irrespective of race, will poorly paid young workers
support a retirement system that benefits *relatively* well-off retirees?

Although the gaps are narrowing, the academic and labor market
performance of black and Hispanic youth still lags considerably behind
that of whites. While solutions are far from obvious, it is clear that the
current Hispanic dropout rates and the falling college attendance of
black males are inconsistent with a healthy United States economy (see
Johnston and Packer 1987: 114–15). Part of the answer lies in school
environments that recognize differences in learning styles among individuals. Research should be able to identify—and correct—male-female differences in mathematics. Schools concerned with self-esteem of their students might pay more attention to minority and female contributions to
our society or might provide learning contexts that compensate for dif-

Figure 2.3   Minorities as a percentage of net additions to the total labor force.

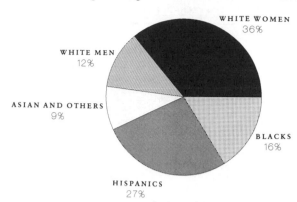

(Reprinted from the *Monthly Labor Review*, November 1989.)

ferent home environments. New technology makes it possible to tailor instruction to individual strengths, rather than force all students to read the same books and listen to the same lectures. Education must change to serve a changing student body and a changing workplace.

The Changing Economy

If our educational system is attuned to a different student body than the one it must now serve, it also focuses too heavily on skills for an economy that no longer exists. The types of jobs that are available are changing, the content of each job is changing, and both sets of changes lead to greater intellectual requirements. The new economy requires more than a strong back and willing hands.

A Growing Service Sector and Shrinking Firm Size

Human capital strategy in the United States will suffer as long as we use outdated models to think about our economy. In much of our economic system, a white male working for 20 years on an assembly line for a large manufacturing firm is no longer the typical worker (just as the "Ozzie and Harriet" family is no longer characteristic of our social system). Production workers' wages are a small and shrinking part of the GNP, currently comprising about 6 percent (Johnston and Packer 1987: 27). Nor is the fast-food industry the appropriate model for the United States economy in the 1990s.

Firms in the goods-producing sector—which includes farming, mining, and construction as well as manufacturing—now account for about

Table 2.3 Employment in the Goods-Producing and Service Sectors, 1985 and 2000 (in millions of workers, excluding self-employed workers)

	1985 (Actual)	2000 (Projected)
Goods-producing sector	28	26
Manufacturing	(19)	(17)
Other[a]	(9)	(9)
Service sector	79	105
Nongovernment[b]	(63)	(85)
Government	(16)	(20)
Other		
TOTAL	107	131

Source: Johnston and Packer, 1987: 58.

[a]Farming, forestry, fishing, mining, and construction.
[b]Wholesale and retail trade, transportation, public utilities, and financial, insurance, real estate, and other services.

one job in four (Table 2.3), and this proportion is expected to slip to one in five by the year 2000. Employment in the remainder of the economy now accounts for three in four jobs and is expected to expand by one-third, from 79 million jobs in 1985 to 97 million in 2000.

These two sectors are intimately related. Manufacturing costs—and, thus, international competitiveness—are directly or indirectly dependent on the efficiency of the service sector. Manufacturing firms buy legal, advertising, custodial, and consulting services, just as service firms purchase manufactured materials or components.

The manufacturing sector's customers are often in the service sector. The service sector buys X-ray machines for hospitals and computers for education (and for financial and technical services, legal services, restaurants, etc.). It is difficult, however, to sell high-tech products to a low-tech customer. Thus, manufacturing firms have an interest in a skilled work force for the service sector.

One factor that distinguishes service firms from manufacturing firms is that their products are typically consumed instantaneously. Traditionally, services are neither transported nor traded, and therefore the service industry is dominated by small local firms. In general, service firms and establishments (branches of large firms) are smaller than those in manufacturing (11 versus 60 employees). Small businesses generated two-thirds of the new jobs created between 1980 and 1986 and now account for 56 percent of private employment (SBA 1988b: xvi).

Investing in human capital is difficult in small firms, however. Smaller firms have more entry-level employees and—for financial reasons—are less likely to have human resources or training departments. Unions, and their training arms, are less frequently found. Moreover, employees at small firms have to solve problems that are more diverse and varied than those faced on an unchanging assembly line.

The number of old-fashioned, narrowly defined jobs is shrinking even in large, unionized manufacturing firms, however. In some of the newer steel mills, literally dozens of narrow job classifications are being replaced by a single broad job classification requiring production workers to learn a wide variety of tasks. The team approach is catching on in the auto industry, requiring that assembly line workers communicate with engineers and understand the mathematics of make/buy decisions. The need to understand statistical process control is replacing the need to operate a lathe. Foreign competition and deregulation are undermining the market power of big firms and their unions. As mini-mills and manufacturing-to-order become more widespread, distinguishing between manufacturing and services becomes a useless distraction. Both sectors require more brain power.[5]

Private, for-profit firms are not the only employers in our economy. Government agencies and nonprofit entities such as colleges and hospitals are also important. Productivity—useful output per dollar spent—is often not the foremost consideration in these activities. Although some analysts worry about cost effectiveness, the political debate is usually concerned with *how much* is spent, not with *how well. Investing* to increase the productivity of education, health, and other public services is often neglected.

Government and nonprofit institutions are especially important because they are the means by which the nation invests in human capital. Thus, the human resource needs of health care and education require special attention. Health care is crucial because it is such a large part of the economy. Health care expenditures were 11.1 percent of the GNP in 1987 and growing rapidly, up from 9.1 percent in 1980. Health care is also a large part of private sector costs. The competitiveness of U.S. manufacturing cannot improve unless the productivity of the U.S. health system improves.

Education poses a different set of problems for its own human resources: teachers and administrators. Education has, until now, been remarkably resistant to technological advance. Teachers and administrators will have to become more comfortable with change if computers and other technology are to be used effectively. Education prepares students for a new technological age that it refuses to embrace itself. Schools must use—and teach students how to use—new tools.

Two conclusions flow from this. First, improving the productivity of nurses and teachers, and hospital and school administrators, is as important as increasing the output of factory workers. Our international competitiveness will be undermined if health care costs continue to escalate and schools continue to fail one-fourth of their students, just as surely as if factories fail to modernize. Second, government has an unassailable and crucial responsibility in developing the productivity of these human resource sectors since it will likely continue to pay most of the bills for health care and education.

The Effect of International Change

Foreign competition is a spur to change in manufacturing directly and to the rest of the economy at least indirectly (e.g., by hastening the shift of the work force to the service sector). Between 1979 and 1986, manufacturing productivity increased faster than the 1950–73 average, and more than twice as fast as during 1973–79. Unfortunately, the sales of American manufactured goods did not grow as rapidly as productivity because the rise in the dollar overwhelmed the fall in production costs. Manufacturing employment fell by 2 million between 1979 and 1986. Workers were dislocated from the traditionally high-wage industries (e.g., the automobile and steel industries) as well as from the low-wage industries (e.g., the textile and shoe industries). In general, the dislocation meant that wages and family incomes were reduced (25 percent initially and 16 percent after several years).

Unions began to emphasize job security and training rather than wage increases. Manufacturing firms created new retraining programs, which were often not-for-profit training organizations created in cooperation with their unions. The best known are those negotiated by the United Automobile Workers and the major auto companies, beginning in 1982. More recently, American Telephone and Telegraph and its unions (the Communication Workers of America and International Brotherhood of Electrical Workers) formed the Alliance along similar lines. Donald Petersen, chairman of Ford, has championed this new approach, saying "people are the real resource of any enterprise" (Peterson 1988).

Government budgets also responded to the dislocations. In 1982, Congress added title III to the Job Training Partnership Act (JTPA) for retraining; it took further steps in the Economic Dislocation and Worker Adjustment Assistance Act, which was part of the trade bill of 1988.

Although the fall of the dollar from its peak in 1985 led to increased manufacturing employment in 1987, 1988, and 1989, the long-term trend is down; a fall of 10 percent is expected between 1985 and 2000 (Johnston and Packer 1987: 54). Firms that automate will increase output without adding employees and, perhaps, will be able to reduce their personnel. Firms that do not modernize will most likely be unable to compete.

Changing Employment Patterns and Job Redefinition

As we have seen, there will be a continuing shift of employment out of the manufacturing sector into the service sector. The shift will be accomplished in part because employed workers will move or be moved from one job to another and in part because entry-level workers will find employment, for example, at McDonald's rather than at Ford. Both experiences have implications for human resource policies.

The service-sector job may require more skill development although it may pay lower wages. Indeed, the evidence suggests that there will be a shift to lower-wage *industries* accompanied by a shift to more intellectually demanding *occupations* (McMahon and Tschetter, pp. 23–25). How could this happen? A General Motors assembly-line worker who, after being retrained, becomes a supervisor in a fast food restaurant is an example of a shift from a high-wage industry, lower-skill occupation to the reverse. He or she may now have more skill and less income.

Because of this change in our economic structure, the relationship between skill and wages is likely to be closer in the new economy than in the older one. The pay that a worker receives in a unionized manufacturing firm depends on union-management negotiations; in a small service firm the wage is more likely to depend on his or her human capital. Thus, the motivation to complete high school for males in Detroit and Pittsburgh is higher now than it was in the 1950s when dropouts could look forward to high-paying jobs on auto assembly lines and in steel mills.

The shift from manufacturing to services, or among industries, is one part of the changing job mix. The shift among job categories within a given industry is another, for example, from production worker to designer or accountant at Ford. The estimates of human capital needs in the 1990s that are described in the final section of this chapter are based only on these two components. They are surely underestimates, because there is a third reason why workplace requirements are changing: job redefinitions.

Changes in a worker's job can occur even if he or she does not change jobs. The work of secretaries, accountants, and inventory control specialists, whether they be in manufacturing plants or retail stores, is changing as technology advances. For example, a large supplier of temporary office workers reports that proofreading has become much more important than spelling as word processing with spell-check features becomes widespread. How will such technological change affect education and training requirements?

Technology: Dummying Down or Computer Literacy?

The proliferation of microchip-based technologies is the most important change in economic activity since the introduction of the automobile and telephone. Closely held mainframe computers, run by computer professionals, are being replaced with personal computers and work stations that are widely available in the workplace. While computer programming will remain the province of a small class of professionals, the personal computer has greatly increased the need to know how to use word processing programs, spreadsheets, and communications packages.

Microchips also are used to "dummy down" work, for example, to replace numbers with images (e.g., hamburgers) on McDonald's cash registers. In many other areas also, technology is downgrading the need for skills. On balance, will technology increase or diminish the need for education and training?

Like other epoch-making technologies, computers replace some human capacities (e.g., spelling and arithmetic) while establishing a need for other cognitive skills (learning to use a word processor or calculator). Technology is *changing* skills requirements (Spenner 1988). The new skills are not necessarily "better," but they are different. The diminishing few workers on the factory floor will be monitoring symbolic representations of physical processes on a computer screen, instead of the process itself. The steelworker will depend more on a spectrograph than on his own ability to correlate flame color with temperature; the farmer, learning to use computer-based feed-mix programs, will lose some of his "feel" for what works.

Workers need more training and education to prepare them to adapt to accelerating change. The ability to sign one's name defined workplace literacy at the beginning of this century. Today, higher level cognitive skills are necessary. As recently as 1973, the average 20- to 24-year-old male with only a high school degree earned $600 more per year than did a college graduate of the same age; extra experience counted for more than additional schooling. By 1986, the 20- to 24-year-old college graduate earned more than the high school graduate of the same age by almost $3,000 annually (Table 2.1).

Information-handling skills are a rapidly growing part of American business. From keeping medical records to filing insurance claims, from farming scientifically to doing construction work and maintaining buildings, from examining make/buy decisions on the factory floor to tracing missing luggage in baggage handling, from providing customer service in a Domino's Pizza distribution outlet to providing quality control in the manufacture of pizza dough within Domino's production facilities, job content is changing and requiring higher-order thinking skills.

Workers in the 1990s and beyond will increasingly need to understand and use information presented in written, tabular, graphic, and quantitative form, on computer screens and by word of mouth, to solve workplace problems. They will increasingly use computers and related information and communication technologies for these purposes.

John Seely Brown, one of the giants of artificial intelligence and a racing-car buff, worries about mechanics whose internal cognitive model of an auto engine no longer serves a purpose. The mechanic listening to cylinders fire with the aid of a broom handle needs to learn a new schema in which binary signals replace combustion gases and electronic gates replace cylinder valves. This change is characteristic of the new economy. Workers will have to learn to interpret abstract representations of once-visible processes.

An Estimate of the Challenge

The Challenge for the 1990s

The National Assessment of Educational Progress (NAEP) recently interviewed 3,600 persons between the ages of 21 and 25 (Educational Testing Service 1987). NAEP analyzed these young adults' ability to decipher documents (document literacy), numbers (quantitative literacy), and the spoken word, as well as their ability to read prose (prose literacy). This survey, *Literacy: Profiles of America's Young Adults,* was the first of its kind for those beyond high school age. NAEP found that

- Forty percent of whites, 60 percent of Hispanics, and 75 percent of blacks could not locate information in a news article or almanac (prose literacy);
- Sixty-six percent of whites, 80 percent of Hispanics, and 92 percent of blacks could not figure the change for a two-item restaurant meal (quantitative literacy); and
- Seventy-five percent of whites, 93 percent of Hispanics, and 97 percent of blacks could not interpret a bus schedule (document literacy).

Is this good enough? Obviously not, but what are the standards we should be aiming for, and how much upgrading is necessary to reach them? The question can only be answered by comparing the skills of the nation's work force to the demands of the jobs that the economy of the future is likely to generate.

Tomorrow's skill requirements were projected in the Hudson Institute's report *Workforce 2000* (Johnston and Packer 1987). Using the input/output tables of the Wharton econometric model, projections were made of the output and the employment required during 1985–2000 in the various industries (and government) that comprise the U.S. economy. The pattern of employment is consistent with the 2.9 percent annual growth target reflected in the "base case" scenario of Table 2.2. Thus, estimates were made of the jobs that would be filled in the year 2000.

Table 2.4   Definition of GED Language Scale

Level	Language Development
1	*Reading:* Recognize meaning of 2,500 (two- or three-syllable) words. Read at a rate of 95 to 120 words per minute.
	Writing: Print simple sentences containing subject, verb, and object and series of numbers, names, and addresses.
2	*Reading:* Passive vocabulary of 5,000 to 6,000 words. Read at a rate of 190 to 215 words per minute. Read adventure stories and comic books, looking up unfamiliar words in dictionary for meaning, spelling, and pronunciation. Read instructions for assembling model cars and airplanes.
	Writing: Write compound and complex sentences, using cursive style, proper end punctuation, and employing adjectives and adverbs.
3	*Reading:* Read a variety of novels, magazines, atlases, and encyclopedias. Read safety rules, instructions in the use and maintenance of shop tools and equipment, and methods and procedures in mechanical drawing and layout work.
	Writing: Write reports and essays with proper format, punctuation, spelling, and grammar, using all parts of speech.
4	*Reading:* Read novels, poems, newspapers, periodicals, journals, manuals, dictionaries, thesauruses, and encyclopedias.
	Writing: Prepare business letters, expositions, summaries, and reports, using prescribed format, and conforming to all rules of punctuation, grammar, diction, and style.
5	Same as level 6.
6	*Reading:* Read literature, book and play reviews, scientific and technical journals, abstracts, financial reports, and legal documents.
	Writing: Write novels, plays, editorials, journals, speeches, manuals, critiques, poetry, and songs.

Source: Dictionary of Occupational Titles, U.S. Department of Labor.

Using an estimate developed by the U.S. Department of Labor (DoL) of the language and math skills needed in each of the 12,000 jobs in the *Dictionary of Occupational Titles* (see Table 2.4), we calculated the projected skills required in the year 2000 if the "base case" productivity and economic projections shown in Table 2.2 are to be realized (Matt Jaffe, Appendix to Johnston and Packer 1987). Comparing the NAEP survey to the *Workforce 2000* projections yields the conservative estimate that 25 million workers need to upgrade their basic workplace skills in the decade of the 1990s, if the *Workforce 2000* productivity goals are to be met.[6] Twenty-five million may well be a low estimate. Hudson's projections are based only on the changing mix of jobs, not the changing requirements of any particular job. Also, the NAEP survey was one of households, missing the institutionalized and street populations.

In addition to knowing how many students need training, we need to determine how much training is needed by the average student (e.g., does he or she need a week's brushup in math or a four-year basic education?). Using the common scale, we found that the average skill level found by the NAEP survey was 2.6 on a scale of 1 to 6, substantially less than the skill level of 3.6 required by the 26 million net new jobs that *Workforce 2000* projects will be added between 1985 and 2000. Thus, 25 million workers require an average upgrading of 38 percent (Fig. 2.4). The greatest number of upgrades are not the lowest-level workers, but, rather, the 17 million who are between the second and third steps of the DoL's six-step skill level.

The Long-Term Challenge

The changing economic and demographic situation requires that during the next 20 years the nation build an education and training system capable of meeting both the problems of today and the additional demographic burden of the aging population that we will face during the years from 2010 to 2030. Over 80 percent of the work force of the year 2000 is already in the labor force. The improvement in the basic skills of 25 million adults needs to start immediately as the cost-effectiveness of the education and training system itself is increased. Emphasis must be placed on the total *system* of adult education and training, which already "serves" enough persons, but serves them not very well.

Research and development, computer-supported technology, meaningful measures of effectiveness, workplace-oriented instruction, public-private ventures, training at the work site, and others means of increasing the output per dollar spent are needed. This prescription would transform a system that now operates on a year-to-year basis and hardly understands the concept of investing. A system capable of training 3.5 million annually must be in place early in the 1990s if 25 million are to be trained by 2000 and the *Workforce 2000* goals are to be met (Packer 1988).

The nation's primary and secondary schools also must be transformed in the next 10 years. Current approaches to adult functional illiteracy have been likened to bailing a boat with a big hole in its bottom. There is enough time to affect the high school graduating class of 2001, if change begins soon. By 2010 we will need a labor force that is much more productive than today's, and one that continues to improve during the 2010–30 period when the baby boomers retire. But we must act soon and rethink who, what, how, where, and when we educate.

The nation must rethink who should receive the most assistance. The nation's human resource strategy has been to invest public dollars in the college-bound youth and to invest corporate training dollars in college graduates. The neglect of those who do not go to college has been well documented in *The Forgotten Half,* an important report of the William

Figure 2.4 The job skill gap, 1985–2000.

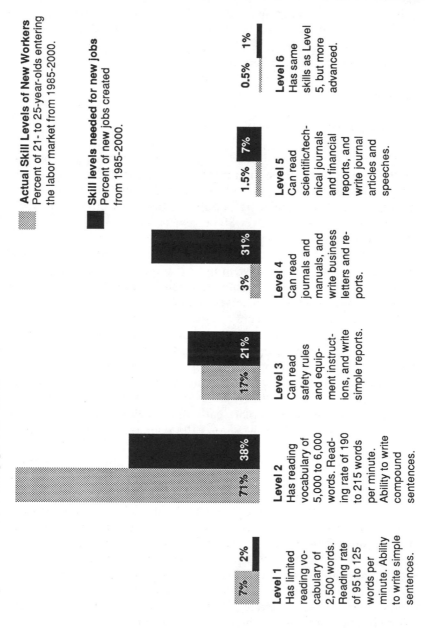

(Data are from the Hudson Institute and the U.S. Department of Labor, various years.)

T. Grant Foundation (1988). Examination of incentives in the public school systems, relative expenditures for adult basic education, community colleges, and four-year colleges, and corporate-funded training programs support the idea that equal opportunity is a distant goal. "Creaming," even within programs for the poor, seems to give the most help to those who need it least. Both the needs of the economy and concerns over poverty, teen-age pregnancy, drugs, and welfare suggest that emphasis should now be placed on the "forgotten half," the non-college bound.

The nation must rethink what it teaches. Instead of preparing students for yesterday's industrial-era economy, we must prepare them for the information and/or service jobs of tomorrow. Businesses must be involved as true partners in designing curricula and pioneering new educational approaches. Educators must listen, and have a good answer, when youngsters or adult students ask "Why do I have to learn that junk?" Table 2.5 is an initial attempt at defining job-related skills (Packer 1990).[7]

The nation must rethink how it is going to teach. No sector of our economy has been so untouched by technology as education. The current state of the art has been reviewed in *Power On,* a report of the Office of Technology Assessment (1988), and it is not good enough for the next century.

The nation must rethink when and where it teaches. Classrooms that operate with 30 students from 9:00 A.M. to 3:00 P.M., schools that close for the summer, and education that stops at graduation are not adequate. The technology now exists to facilitate education at home or at the workplace, and lifelong learning. Why not use it?

During the 1970s and 1980s the economy generated jobs that were generally appropriate to young persons who were going to school and/or were not fully serious about their careers. Employers like McDonald's were able to build a business based on near-minimum wage workers because there were many youngsters, there was relatively high unemployment, and the minimum wage was relatively low (especially in the 1980s). They invested little in increasing the productivity of their high-turnover staff.

That model no longer works for the economy, for the youngster, or for McDonald's. As the baby-boom youngsters mature they want and need better jobs. As an expanding economy coincides with the baby bust generation, McDonald's finds itself paying twice the minimum wage in low-unemployment areas. The no-longer-so-young baby boomer, the economy, and McDonald's now need a more productive, higher-paid, work force.

There are reasons to be optimistic. Business seems to recognize its need for a better-educated work force. Unions have expanded their role

Table 2.5 Ten Typical Job Clusters and Upgrading Skills

Clusters and Jobs[a]	Upgrading Skills
1. *Health and dependent care:* health care, child care, nursing homes, home care, elder care	Patient/client registration, administer medicine, keep records, respond to inquiries, fill out insurance forms
2. *Construction/maintenance:* small and large contract construction, building and facility maintenance	Read blueprints and maintenance manuals, understand cost estimates, follow directions
3. *Office skills:* financial, commercial, and manufacturing offices	Understand business forms (payroll, insurance, memos, etc.); computer literacy; oral communication skills
4. *Financial services:* insurance, banks, real estate	Read instructions, handle forms, understand business math
5. *Retailing:* sales, customer service, inventory control	Read and communicate directions, understand forms (sales slips, invoices)
6. *Distribution:* warehousing, truck driver, delivery, dispatcher	Read maps, follow directions, use forms (invoices, logs, police reports)
7. *Manufacturing:* machine operator, quality control, inventory control	Read instructions, quality control, math, production schedules, computer-controlled equipment
8. *Food service:* serving, preparing, cashier	Read menus, make out a bill, make change, follow a recipe
9. *Hotels/hospitality:* housekeeping, guest services	Understanding English, answering requests, guest registration
10. *Equipment repair and maintenance*	Maintenance manuals, filling out logs, answering complaints

Source: Packer 1990: 101.

[a]In most cases there will be entry-level and career ladder positions and, often, entrepreneurial possibilities as well.

in education. New instructional technologies that combine video with computers are maturing. The education system is more responsive. The U.S. Department of Labor is transforming its programs to provide basic skills that equip workers for better jobs. If these changes can be sustained, the goals of *Workforce 2000* can be achieved.

Notes

1. Output per hour in the business sector based on preliminary data for the second quarter of 1990. GNP per total number of workers is the productivity measure used in this chapter unless otherwise specified. The more commonly used alternative is an index of output per hour. Generally, the two measures give similar results over the extended periods discussed here.

2. GNP per worker is the productivity measurement used in this section and in *Workforce 2000*.

3. SSA makes a number of projections based on varying assumptions con-

cerning longevity and birthrates. The middle series corresponds to SSA's best judgment.

4. Minorities are defined by the Census Bureau as those who report themselves as black, Asian, Hispanic, or anything other than non-Hispanic white.

5. For example, the cry that service-sector productivity is harder to measure than manufacturing-sector productivity is not altogether valid. It is no easier to measure productivity increases in a computer manufacturing firm than in a retail store. The labor productivity involved in increasing the number of computations per second is difficult to evaluate, while it is simple to tally the sales completed (or customers served) per hour in a retail store. There may, however, be special problems in measuring productivity in the financial, insurance, and real estate sector.

6. Comparing today's capacity (from NAEP) to the year 2000 projections (from *Workforce 2000*) required a common scale. The Labor Department's surveyors were asked to evaluate the NAEP questionnaire. The DoL language scale of 1 to 6 was consistently related to the NAEP scale (of 100 to 500). Therefore, a crosswalk was possible and the comparison could proceed.

7. In February of 1990, Secretary of Labor Elizabeth Dole established SCANS, the Secretary's Commission on Achieving Necessary Skills. SCANS's purpose is to define the skills needed by high school graduates and determine means of assessing them. We expect to present this report in the spring of 1991.

References

Economist (1988). December 24.

———— (1989). April 15.

Educational Testing Services (ETS), National Assessment of Educational Progress (NAEP) (1987). *Literacy: Profiles of America's Young Adults.* Princeton, N.J.: Princeton University.

Fullerton, Howard N., Jr. (1989). "New Labor Force Projections, Spanning 1988 to 2000." *Monthly Labor Review.* Bureau of Labor Statistics, Washington, D.C.

Jaffee, Matthew P. (1987). *Forecast of Occupational Change,* Technical Appendix to *Workforce 2000.* Indianapolis, Ind.: Hudson Institute.

Johnston, William B., and Arnold H. Packer (1987). *Workforce 2000: Work and Workers for the Twenty-first Century.* Indianapolis, Ind.: Hudson Institute.

McMahon, Patrick, and John Tschetter (1986). "The Declining Middle Class: A Further Analysis." *Monthly Labor Review.* Bureau of Labor Statistics, Washington, D.C.

Office of Technology Assessment (1988). *Power On.* U.S. Congress, OTA-SET-380, September.

Packer, Arnold H. (1988). *Retooling the American Workforce: The Role of Technology in Improving Adult Literacy during the 1990's.* Washington, D.C.: Southport Foundation.

———— (1990). *Preparing For Work in the Next Century: A Workforce 2000 Report.* Indianapolis, Ind.: Hudson Institute.

Palmer, John (1988). "Financing Health Care and Retirement for the Aged." *Challenge to Leadership.* Washington, D.C.: Urban Institute.

Peterson, Donald (1988). *Interview,* American Society of Training and Development (Magazine), Alexandria, Va.

Small Business Administration (1988a). *Job Training in Small and Large Firms.* Washington, D.C.: Small Business Administration, August. Mimeo.

———— (1988b). *The State of Small Business.* Washington, D.C.: U.S. Government Printing Office.

Strassman, Paul (1985). *Information Payoff: The Transformation of Work in the Electronic Age.* New York: Free Press.

Torrey, Barbara B. (1985). "Sharing Increasing Costs on Declining Income: The Invisible Dilemma of the Invisible Aged." *Milbank Memorial Fund Quarterly* 63, no. 2.

3

Women

Nancy S. Barrett

A vast reservoir of human resources opened its floodgates into the United States labor force during the 1960s, and although the rate of increase has slowed somewhat, the influx has continued. These newcomers are the millions of women who have entered paid employment instead of opting for the traditional work role of full-time homemaker. The number of women working or looking for work outside the home increased by over 30 million between 1960 and 1988, involving an infusion of more than a million new women workers per year into the job market. By 1988, 65 percent of married women with children worked outside the home; in 1960, the comparable figure was only about 31 percent.

This development has had an extraordinary impact on our work and family lives. It represents the largest and most significant peacetime redirection of human resources our economy has ever experienced within a relatively short period of time. Although the work of a homemaker is an important human resource, it is unpaid work, and therefore the output produced by homemakers is not counted in the gross national product (GNP) or other official measures of economic activity. The movement of women from full-time homemaking into paid employment not only increases the output of the market economy but also means that fewer resources are available to meet the needs formerly taken care of by the homemaker, including the human capital investments women have traditionally made in their children and other family members. Thus, this redirection of human resources has implications not only for the paid labor market but also for the unpaid household economy.

Until recently, full-time homemaking was the major occupation of women, especially married women with children. In 1960, there were about 40 million adult women in this occupation.[1] Compared with 17 million employees in manufacturing in that year, and 11 million in wholesale and retail trade, the household economy absorbed an enormous amount of our nation's human resources. Even today, although the household labor force has lost roughly half its members—there were about 20 million full-time homemakers in 1988—the number of women in the household economy remains larger than the entire manufacturing work force (U.S. Council of Economic Advisers 1987: 282, 284, 290, 291).

In many respects, this movement of resources from homemaking into paid employment is similar to what occurred much earlier in the farm sector of our economy. In the home, as on the farm, improvements in productivity reduced the amount of time required to perform necessary tasks. In the home economy, the longer life expectancy of women and lower birthrates combined with higher levels of education for women to reduce the advantages of a lifelong career as homemaker compared with employment outside the home. Rising real wages made opportunities in paid employment more attractive to homemakers, just as was the case for work outside the farm some decades ago. As the lure of the city drew second and third generation farm workers from the land, so, too, improved labor market opportunities have drawn women from the home.

This shift of workers out of homemaking has been far larger and more rapid than that out of agriculture. Over the past generation, roughly 20 percent of the entire U.S. labor force has moved out of full-time homemaking into the manufacturing and service sectors of the economy. By comparison, the shift out of agriculture encompassed several generations and involved only about 3 million workers, or about 6 percent of the labor force.

But the analogy should not be overdrawn. There are many unmet needs in the household economy, and some—such as child care—have long-run implications for future work force productivity. How these needs will be met—whether women who work outside the home will also do the work of the traditional full-time homemaker, whether husbands will undertake more egalitarian sharing of household tasks, or whether new or existing businesses will provide the necessary services outside the family unit—is a matter of serious concern.

The rate at which the female labor force is growing may slow down even further. But the economic forces that have shaped the transition in women's work roles are unlikely to be reversed, and the erosion of mobility barriers due to changing social attitudes is unlikely to be undone.

This chapter addresses three major questions: (1) How has this phenomenon affected the economy, and what are the prospects for women's employment in the future? (2) What special human-capital issues arise with respect to women workers? and (3) What can be done to overcome

Table 3.1   Labor Force Participation Rates (%) of Women by Marital Status
and Age of Children, March 1950–88

| Year | All Women | Married, Spouse Present | | |
| | | Total | Ages of Child(ren) | |
			6–17 Only	Under 6
1950	33.9	23.8	28.3	11.9
1960	37.7	30.5	39.0	18.6
1970	43.3	40.8	49.2	30.3
1980	51.5	50.1	61.7	45.1
1983	52.3	51.8	63.8	49.9
1988	55.9	56.5	72.5	57.1

Sources: Data for 1950–83 are from U.S. Bureau of Labor Statistics (1985a: 9, 123). Data for 1988 are from U.S. Bureau of Labor Statistics (1988d: table 1).

Note: The labor force participation rate is the percentage of the civilian noninstitutional population in each category in the civilian labor force. *Child(ren)* refers to own children of the husband or wife. Included are sons, daughters, and adopted children. Excluded are other related children such as grandchildren, nieces, nephews, and cousins, and unrelated children.

existing barriers to human capital development among women and their dependents?

Women's Employment—An Overview

Recent Trends

Although female labor force participation rates have increased for all demographic categories, they have been most pronounced for married women with children, as shown in Table 3.1. In 1960, only 18.6 percent of married women with preschool children worked outside the home, compared with 57.1 percent in 1988. In 1960, 39.0 percent of married women with school-aged children (only) were in the labor force, compared with 72.5 percent in 1988. And this movement of married women out of homemaking shows no signs of letting up. Whereas in the past five years the overall labor force participation rate for women has increased by 3.6 percentage points, for married mothers of preschool children it is up by 7.2 percentage points. This represents an enormous and rapid diversion of human resources from child care and other household services to the production of market goods and services.

This change in women's work roles has not entailed an army of homemakers suddenly entering paid employment. Rather, it largely comprises women who are remaining in the work force rather than dropping out upon marriage or a first pregnancy. Because many are delaying childbearing, these married mothers on average are older and have considerably more work experience and labor-market-related human capital than did the average married woman with children a generation ago.

It is also important to recognize that women in paid employment have reduced the time they devote to the home economy by fewer hours than they have added in paid work. Although women with paid jobs, on average, spend less time in the home economy than do full-time homemakers, women still bear most of the responsibilities for housework. This means that they now contribute more hours to the economy (both paid and unpaid). Unlike the farm worker who moved to the city, women who take paid jobs have not left their former tasks behind. Few families can afford to purchase all their household services from professionals, and such services—reliable child care, for example—are often not available. The incompleteness of the household transformation is a critical factor for women in paid employment, and, as we shall discuss later, is a potential barrier to efficient levels of human capital investment for them.

Just as the female work force has gained in work experience, so has its average level of educational attainment increased. As seen in Table 3.2, between 1975 and 1985 the proportion of adult female workers with four or more years of college grew from 15 to 22 percent, while the proportion with some college increased from 29 to 42 percent. Of the 12.6 million women *added* to the labor force during this period, 8.7 million—69 percent—were in these two categories. By 1984, the median years of school completed, 12.7, was almost identical to that of male workers (U.S. Bureau of Labor Statistics 1985b: 164–65). By 1985, the proportion of young women in the labor force aged 25 to 34 who had attended college actually surpassed that of men.

For black women, the proportion in the work force with eight or fewer years of education dropped from 22.3 percent in 1970 to 7.9 percent in 1984, while the proportion with some college rose from 18.4 percent to 33.3 percent (U.S. Bureau of Labor Statistics 1985b: 164–65). As we shall see, this gain in educational attainment coincided with a sharp decline in the employment of black women as household domestic workers and a concomitant increase in their employment as clerical and sales workers.

These increased investments in schooling have undoubtedly been related to expectations of longer periods of labor market participation for most young women. But the increase in the number of years of schooling

Table 3.2 Labor Force and Labor Force Participation Rates by Age, Education, and Sex, 1975 and 1985

	Women		Men	
	1975	1985	1975	1985
Civilian Labor Force				
Workers aged 25–64 yr				
Total number (thousands)	26,161	38,779	41,842	49,647
Percentage with (max.):				
Less than 4 yr of high school	25.4	13.7	29.0	17.7
4 yr of high school	45.6	44.4	36.2	36.9
1–3 yr of college	13.8	19.9	14.7	18.3
4 yr or more of college	15.2	22.0	20.1	27.1
Workers aged 25–34 yr				
Total number (thousands)	8,511	14,708	14,005	18,553
Percentage with (max.):				
Less than 4 yr of high school	15.2	8.6	17.3	12.7
4 yr of high school	45.2	41.8	37.6	39.8
1–3 yr of college	17.3	23.3	19.3	22.0
4 yr or more of college	22.4	26.2	25.8	25.4
Labor Force Participation Rates (%)				
Workers aged 25–64 yr				
Overall rate	52.3	64.7	90.5	88.6
Rate for those with (max.):				
Less than 4 yr of high school	42.3	44.3	82.9	76.2
4 yr of high school	53.9	65.0	93.4	90.0
1–3 yr of college	57.3	72.5	93.5	91.2
4 yr or more of college	67.8	78.6	95.9	94.6
Workers aged 25–34 yr				
Overall rate	54.2	71.1	95.3	93.8
Rate for those with (max.):				
Less than 4 yr of high school	40.8	47.5	92.3	87.2
4 yr of high school	53.3	69.9	97.2	95.1
1–3 yr of college	57.5	75.5	93.8	94.4
4 yr or more of college	68.9	82.8	95.9	94.9

Source: U.S. Bureau of Labor Statistics (1985a: table 1).

does not tell the entire story. In addition, the quality of education is becoming more career oriented, with women flocking to professional schools where once they were a tiny minority. Between 1972 and 1987, the percentage of degree recipients who were female jumped from 4 to 33 percent for the M.B.A. degree, from 3.3 to 36.8 percent for the J.D.

Table 3.3 Women in the Labor Force, Aged 20 and Over by Full-time versus Part-time Status

Year	Full-time (thousands)	Part-time (thousands)	Part-time (%)
1963	18,142	4,331	19.3
1973	24,285	6,707	21.6
1983	35,854	8,782	19.7
1988	39,868	10,768	21.3

Sources: Data for 1963–83 are from the U.S. Bureau of Labor Statistics (1985b: 24–25). Data for 1988 are from U.S. Bureau of Labor Statistics (1988a: 17).

Note: The data are annual averages except for 1988, which is for August 1988. Full-time refers to 35 hours or more per week; part-time refers to 1 to 34 hours per week. Persons on part-time schedules for economic reasons are included in the full-time labor force.

degree, from 6.5 to 28 percent for the M.D., and from 0.7 percent to 19.6 percent for the D.D.S. (U.S. Social Security Administration 1987).

Most of the increase in female labor force participation has been in full-time work. Only about one-fifth of women who work outside the home do so on a part-time basis. As Table 3.3 shows, there has not been a significant increase in the proportion of adult women working part time, even though the demographic composition of the female work force has shifted in favor of married women with children. Even those women in the work force who have very young children are predominantly full-time workers, as Table 3.4 demonstrates. In 1988, two-thirds of the married women with children under age three who worked outside the home did so on a full-time basis.

This phenomenon contrasts sharply with the situation in some other industrial countries, where the growth of the female work force has been largely among part-timers. In Sweden, for instance, in 1986, 67.7 percent of mothers of preschool children who worked outside the home did so on a part-time basis. A full 48.8 percent of all Swedish women between the ages of 25 and 54 who worked outside the home were part-timers. True, the overall labor force participation rate of Swedish women is higher than that of U.S. women. (In Sweden in 1986 it was 89.8 percent for the 25–54 age group compared with 71.9 percent in the U.S.)[2] Sweden has enacted much stronger economic incentives to women's labor market participation than has the United States, including individual taxation, parental leave, the provision of child care, and the like.

The fact that American women, once they have moved into paid employment, are likely to work on a full-time basis means that the payoff for investing in their job-related human capital development is likely to be considerable. To the extent that women workers are stereotyped as

Table 3.4 Full-time versus Part-time Status of Women Aged 16 and Over, by Marital Status and Ages of Children, March 1988

	Full-time (thousands)	Part-time (thousands)	Part-time (%)
All women with children aged less than:			
18 years	14,682	5,450	27.1
6 years	5,628	2,476	30.4
3 years	3,067	1,425	31.7
Married women with spouse present and with children aged less than			
18 years	10,746	4,707	30.5
6 years	4,344	2,191	33.5
3 years	2,504	1,270	33.7

Source: U.S. Bureau of Labor Statistics (1988e: 32).

only casually attached to the labor market—a stereotype at odds with prevailing realities—the payoff to human capital investments for this group will be underestimated.

Impact on Productivity Growth

One of the major goals of human capital investment is to increase the overall rate of productivity growth, which is the key to raising real incomes and to improving our international competitiveness. Unfortunately, some experts have tied the nation's lackluster performance in this regard to the growth of the female work force, suggesting that this relatively new source of human capital has actually been a drag on the economy. The fallacy in this view is the failure to recognize the growth of the female work force as a structural transformation of the economy—a shift of resources out of household production into the marketplace. The earlier (and analogous) shift of resources out of the low-productivity agricultural sector into the rest of the economy created a substantial and widely acknowledged increase in productivity (Nordhaus 1972; Norsworthy and Fulco 1974). Similarly, workers will leave unpaid homemaking for paid employment only where the real value of market incomes exceeds that of homemaking. Thus, the shift out of housework and into paid employment has meant an increase in the value of output per hour for the female workers involved.

The resultant efficiency gain does not show up as an increase in measured productivity because of the exclusion of household output from the gross national product (GNP) and hence from the measure of aggregate national output that serves as the numerator of the productivity index. Nor does household labor show up in hours worked, which is the denominator of this index. Since the average woman worker earns less in paid employment than the average man, an increase in female participation in paid employment (and hence in the part of the economy covered by the official statistics) pulls down average worker productivity. An inclusive measure of economic activity that encompassed household production would show a productivity gain as women moved from less productive work (homemaking) to more productive work (paid employment).

Recognition that the household transformation has been accompanied by a productivity gain (if measured correctly) has important implications for human capital development strategies. For one thing, a job-market-oriented human capital strategy may lose sight of the continuing need to make home-related human capital investments as well. If household production and, in particular, child care, are to be more equally undertaken by both men and women, and/or more of these tasks are to be done outside the home, some provision for human capital investments in these activities must be made. Investments in child care are particularly important, as they not only have immediate payoffs but also lay the basis for the productivity of the next generation and enhance the potential payoff of future human capital investments.

Occupational Segregation and the Pay Gap

The movement of women workers from full-time homemaking into paid employment outside the home has occasioned a revolutionary change in women's work roles. However, because of occupational segregation in the workplace, there remains a substantial sex-based division of labor. And because jobs that are stereotypically and historically female pay less, on average, than traditionally male jobs, there is a substantial pay gap between men and women. In 1987, women who worked full time earned a median weekly wage that was just 70 percent of the median male wage. Improving women's access to higher-paying, higher-productivity jobs, as well as restructuring female-dominated jobs to enhance workers' productivity and earnings, will increase incentives to human capital investment and reduce the pay gap between men and women.

In 1987, 70 percent of all women employed full time were working in occupations in which over three-quarters of the employees were female (U.S. Bureau of Labor Statistics, unpublished tabulations). Part-time female workers are even more heavily concentrated in predominantly female occupations. Although there has been a slight reduction in the occupational segregation of women since 1970 (Blau and Beller 1988), the dynamic for change in the occupational profile of women who work for pay has been much weaker than the forces that propelled women out of the home and into paid employment, and also less robust than the conventional wisdom regarding women's economic roles would have us believe.

As seen in Table 3.5, over 40 percent of all employed women work in clerical and sales occupations, and this share has not changed substantially since 1972. Clerical employment as a proportion of the total has fallen only slightly,[3] but the employment of women in private household service has declined dramatically. The employment share in managerial and professional jobs increased for both men and women over this period. However, with the exception of the small category of managers and professionals, there are no broad occupational categories in which female representation increased substantially relative to the overall proportion of women in the work force.

Although there is considerable inertia in the overall occupational distribution, there have been some important gains. First, despite the fact that a large proportion of women work in relatively low-paying clerical jobs, clerical employment has been an important source of economic and social upward mobility for black women. In 1960, 35 percent of employed black women worked as private household domestic workers (U.S. Department of Labor 1979: 258 and 262), compared with only 3.3 percent in 1988 (U.S. Bureau of Labor Statistics 1988a: 29). Today, black women are about as likely as white women to be employed as clerical workers.

Another important gain has been the dramatic increase in the numbers of women entering the prestigious, traditionally male-dominated professions. As noted above, the percentage of women graduating from professional schools has risen substantially over the past decade. In 1987, 19.4 percent of physicians and 19.6 percent of lawyers who were employed, including self-employed, were women (U.S. Bureau of Labor Statistics, unpublished tabulations). While this development suggests a major breakthrough in the erosion of conventional stereotypes regarding women's work and represents an important potential for improved earnings opportunities for women, it is not necessarily indicative of upward mobility for women out of the low-paying female-dominated occupations. Rather, this group of college-educated women are those who, a generation ago, were most likely to have dropped out of the labor force during their childbearing years.

Since the mid-1970s, there has been a substantial increase in labor force participation among college-educated women. As seen in Table 3.2, between 1975 and 1985 the labor force participation rate increased from 69 to 83 percent for young women who were college graduates and from 58 to 76 percent for those who had attended college but not graduated.

Table 3.5 Occupational Profiles of Women and Men, 1972 and 1988

| Occupation[a] | Percentage Distribution | | | | Percentage of Women in Occupation | | Female-Male Earnings Ratio[b] |
| | Women | | Men | | | | |
	1972	1988	1972	1988	1972	1988	1987
Managerial and professional	17.0	24.9	21.2	24.8	33.0	44.6	.693
Technicians	2.4	3.3	2.3	2.9	38.4	47.9	.736
Sales	11.1	13.2	10.0	11.1	40.5	48.7	.514
Administrative support, including clerical	31.5	28.3	6.4	5.5	75.0	80.5	.731
Private household services	4.5	1.7	0.1	0.1	97.6	95.8	na
Other services	16.6	16.1	8.2	9.7	55.5	57.1	.672
Precision production, craft, and repair	1.6	2.3	19.4	19.6	4.8	8.6	.701
Operators, fabricators, and laborers	13.4	8.8	25.9	21.3	24.1	24.8	.672
Farm, forestry, and fishing	1.9	1.2	6.4	5.1	15.4	14.5	.872
TOTAL	100.0	100.0	100.0	100.0	38.0	44.4	.700

Sources: Data on 1972 employment distributions are from Klein (1984: 13–16); data on 1988 employment distributions are from U.S. Bureau of Labor Statistics (1988a: 29); data on 1987 earnings are from U.S. Bureau of Labor Statistics, unpublished tabulations.

[a]Beginning in 1983, the occupational classifications in the Current Population Survey were changed, creating a break in the historical series on occupational employers. The estimates for 1972, based on the new classifications were prepared by Deborah Klein of the Bureau of Labor Statistics. See the article cited above for a description of the conversion technique and data limitations. Totals may not sum exactly due to rounding.

[b]The female-male earnings ratio is the ratio of the median weekly earnings of wage and salary workers who usually work full time; 1987 annual averages.

The choice of professionally oriented majors among college women is clearly related to their expectation of spending many more years in paid employment than was the case for college-educated women a generation ago.

Whether these inroads into the professions will reduce the male-female pay gap remains to be seen. Over half of all women professionals work in five predominantly female (at least 75 percent female) professions: dietetics, library science, nursing, prekindergarten and kindergarten teaching, and elementary school teaching (Blau and Ferber 1986: 159–60). Moreover, within the prestigious occupations there is considerable segregation of women into the lower-paying specialities or at the bottom of the status hierarchy. In medicine, for instance, women predominate in pediatrics and nutrition, while surgeons are predominantly male. On college faculties, women account for only 10 percent of full professors and 50 percent of all instructors and lecturers (National Center for Educational Statistics 1984). In 1987, the median earnings for women physicians were 78.8 percent of those for male physicians, while women lawyers earned 74.4 percent of the male rate (U.S. Bureau of Labor Statistics, unpublished tabulations).

Despite some gains for a relatively elite group of women, it is nevertheless the case that the occupational profile of the vast majority of women has not changed much over the past generation. Blue-collar women have failed to make inroads into the skilled trades. During the first half of 1988, women accounted for only 2 percent of skilled construction and extractive workers, and 4 percent of mechanics and repairers (U.S. Bureau of Labor Statistics 1988c). Blau and Ferber (1986: 166–68) have estimated that in 1981 over 60 percent of workers would have had to change jobs in order for the detailed occupational distributions of men and women to be the same.

The occupational segregation of women is largely responsible for the substantial pay gap between men and women. Pay rates in female-dominated jobs are lower than in male-dominated jobs requiring equivalent education and skill, as seen in the examples in Table 3.6. Forty percent of all adult women employees hold jobs in the categories listed. (Men are not similarly concentrated in a handful of job categories.) For instance, a licensed practical nurse averaged $316 per week in 1987, compared with $387 for a truck driver and $403 for a furnace operator. A child care worker averaged $191, and a bank teller $234, compared with $313 for an unskilled construction laborer.

Table 3.5 shows that the female-male earnings ratio for full-time workers ranges between 51 and 87 percent within each of the occupational groups. A major source of the discrepancy is the sex-typing of jobs within broad occupational groups, and assigning them "female" and "male" pay rates. Within the sales category, for instance, women account

Table 3.6 Median Weekly Earnings in Selected Occupations, 1987

	Percent Female	Median Weekly Wage[a] ($)
Predominantly Female Occupations		
Secretary/typist	98.8	299
Receptionist	98.4	250
Licensed practical nurse	95.9	316
Teacher's aide	95.8	212
Private household worker	95.0	133
Registered nurse	93.2	483
Bookkeeper	91.0	299
Textile sewing machine operator	90.4	186
Bank teller	90.2	234
Child care worker	88.7	191
Health service worker	88.5	226
Data entry keyer	87.1	290
Elementary school teacher	85.4	462
Cashier	79.3	189
Predominantly Male Occupations		
Construction trades	1.1	415
Fire fighting/prevention	1.4	493
Truck driver	1.8	387
Construction laborer	2.5	313
Material-moving equipment operator	3.4	384
Airplane pilot/navigator	3.6	713
Extractive occupations	3.8	495
Welder	5.4	378
Engineer	6.5	720
Furnace operator	7.8	403
Architect	10.8	637
Police officer/detective	11.3	482
Lathe operator	14.0	419

Source: U.S. Bureau of Labor Statistics, unpublished tabulations.

[a]Median weekly earnings of wage and salary workers who usually work full time.

for 75.5 percent of apparel salesworkers, with median weekly earnings in 1987 of $203, but only 8.4 percent of vehicle and boat salesworkers, who averaged $424 per week.

Similarly, in the computer field, a field that is rapidly growing and so new that theoretically sex stereotyping would not have taken hold, there is substantial occupational segregation and a female-male pay gap. In 1987, only about a third of the 474,000 computer programmers averaging $543 per week were women, compared with two-thirds of the 809,000 computer operators, averaging $324 per week.[4]

Women's relatively inferior earnings opportunities reduce the incentives for human capital investments since the perceived lifetime payoff is lower than for men with similar investments. Given the labor force participation trends described earlier, it is no longer possible to dismiss the earnings discrepancy on the basis of women's lack of work experience, schooling, or future commitment to the work force. In fact, the increasing educational attainment of the female work force should form the foundation for further job-related human capital investments in women workers.

To the extent that women's jobs have been structured under the assumptions that their work force participation will be intermittent at best, with little human capital investment undertaken by employers, these governing assumptions must be changed—if we are to make full use of the potential human resources represented by women workers—to take into account the new realities of women's working lives (Viscusi 1980; Haber, Lamas, and Green 1983). And outdated attitudes about appropriate occupations for women must also be reassessed in order to create a labor market environment that will enable workers of both sexes to achieve their full productive potential.

Impact on Families

The movement of women from full-time homemaking into paid employment has had a profound impact on family life. The stereotypical family with a male breadwinner and a mother at home caring for the children and providing other family services now represents the lifestyle of a minority of the population. As shown in Table 3.7, only about one-quarter of two-parent families with children under 18 and about one-third of those with preschool children fall into this pattern. About half of all families with children are two-parent families with working mothers; nearly a quarter are single-parent families.

Although women earn less than men, their contributions to family income are substantial. As seen in Table 3.7, the median family income for married couples with children in 1988 was $30,500 when the mother was a full-time homemaker compared with $40,021 when she was in the labor force. Families maintained by a woman fared far worse than other families in terms of family income, reflecting women's relatively poor earnings opportunities. However, these families had median incomes of $15,077 when the mother was in the labor force, compared with $5,211 when she was not.

Two problematic effects of women's participation in paid employ-

Table 3.7 Number and Median Income of Families with Children by Employment Status of the Mother, 1988

	Number of Families (millions)			Percentage Distribution			Median Income ($)
		Age of Youngest Child			Age of Youngest Child		
	Total	6–17	under 6	Total	6–17	under 6	
Total families	32.3	17.5	14.9	100.0	100.0	100.0	30,721
Married couples	24.6	12.7	11.9	76.1	72.6	80.2	36,815
Mother in labor force	16.0	9.2	6.8	49.6	52.6	46.0	40,021
Mother not in labor force	8.6	3.5	5.1	26.5	20.0	34.2	30,500
Female-headed	6.7	4.1	2.6	20.6	23.4	17.4	10,279
Mother in labor force	4.5	3.1	1.4	13.9	17.7	9.4	15,077
Mother not in labor force	2.2	1.0	1.2	6.8	5.7	8.0	5,211
Male-headed	1.1	0.7	0.4	3.3	4.1	2.4	20,717

Source: U.S. Bureau of Labor Statistics (1988e).

Note: Median income is for all families with children in the category. *Child* refers to own children younger than 18 of the husband or wife. Included are sons, daughters, and adopted children. Excluded are other related children such as grandchildren, nieces, nephews, and cousins, and unrelated children. Totals may not sum exactly due to rounding.

Table 3.8 Number of Children by Labor Force Status of Mother,
1970 and 1988

	Children under Age 18 (millions)		Children under Age 6 (millions)	
	1970	1988	1970	1988
Mother in labor force	25.5	35.1	5.6	10.2
Mother not in labor force	39.6	21.8	9.6	9.2

Source: Data for 1970 are from U.S. Bureau of Labor Statistics (1985b: 124); data for 1988 are from U.S. Bureau of Labor Statistics (1988e: 42, 48).

ment are the lack of a caretaker in the home for children and the elderly, and the reduction in the time available to perform other household services. Since 1970, the number of preschool children with mothers who work outside the home has nearly doubled, from 5.6 to 10.2 million, as seen in Table 3.8. In 1970, 37 percent of preschool children had mothers in the labor force, compared with 53 percent in 1988. For all children under 18, the percentage with working mothers increased from 39 percent to 62 percent over the same period.

Despite the fact that the majority of preschoolers have mothers who work, we still lack a national child care policy of any sort, and most families resort to arrangements that are makeshift at best. In a survey conducted by the U.S. Bureau of the Census (1983), 52 percent of two-parent families with children under five and an employed mother had the youngest child cared for by a family member. Fifteen percent had the youngest child cared for at a nursery school or day care center, and another 22 percent used care by a nonrelative outside the home. In 1987 the U.S. Bureau of Labor Statistics conducted a special survey that covered 10,345 establishments (including government) with 10 or more employees; the survey found that only about 11 percent offered their employees some benefits to help them with their child care arrangements. Only 2.1 percent provided day care facilities; 9 percent provided information, referral, and counseling services (U.S. Bureau of Labor Statistics 1988b).

The lack of a national child care policy may be due to the nation's ambivalence about women's new economic roles, combined with the assumption that support for working mothers will strengthen recent trends. However, lack of attention to the need for child care and other support services can have serious long-run consequences. First, to the extent that the demands on women who work outside the home and also attempt to provide an acceptable standard of household production create heavy strains, the incentives for human capital investment by women, their employers, and the family members are reduced. There is little evidence that fathers are shouldering a proportional share of the housework burden, even when their wives are employed full time outside the home. This places women workers at a severe disadvantage relative to men in terms of discretionary time available for self-improvement.

Most women (and men) face an all-or-nothing choice when it comes to working. Part-time jobs are notoriously low-paying—the median wage was $4.42 an hour in 1987—and fringe benefits are rare. Moving from full-time to part-time work to balance the demands of work and family is not a realistic option for most working parents.

With less time available for child care, parents' contributions to their children's human capital development are likely to be lower than was the case when families allocated fewer total hours to work outside the home. Although the effect of working longer hours is undoubtedly offset to some extent by the trend toward smaller families, the potential impact on future labor force productivity, not to mention the welfare of the children themselves and the stability of the family unit, should be of concern.

This need to reconcile the labor force participation of women with the maintenance of a socially desirable level of human capital investments in children is creating a renewed interest in child care and parental leave policies in the United States. European countries faced this problem a generation ago when postwar labor shortages and pronatalist concerns combined to elicit child-oriented policies for working mothers. Although the focus in this country is not on increasing the number of children born to working mothers, there is a critical interest in enhancing the future productivity of children already born.

The increasing number of families headed by women, and their relatively meager income levels, are also serious problems. In 1987 over half of all black children lived in female-headed families, and a shocking 75.2 percent of them were below the poverty level (U.S. Bureau of the Census 1988: 30–32). Because black children are far more likely than white children to live in female-headed families, and because the poverty rate among families headed by black women is about double that for families headed by white women, the situation takes on a troubling racial dimension. Many of the problems facing our nation's school systems, and the difficulties that many minority students experience in school relative to white students, are the result of this wide and growing poverty gap between black and white children. Attempting to remedy the problems of minority youth once they enter school is likely to be less beneficial than improving earnings opportunities for their mothers and providing child care arrangements conducive to early human capital development.

A final consideration is the impact of women's employment on care of the elderly. Although the numbers are less dramatic than for mothers of preschool children, the labor force participation rates of middle-aged women, who have been the traditional caretakers of elderly parents, have also been increasing. In 1960, 45.6 percent of women aged 45 to 64 were in the labor force, compared with nearly 60 percent in 1988. As younger women, accustomed to working during the childraising years, move into this age group, their participation rates will become even higher. When no one is at home to care for the elderly, the need for other care increases. The growing shortage of long-term care for the elderly is related not only to the increasing longevity of our population but also to the increased labor force participation of middle-aged women, who are no longer available to look after the elderly. The problem of caring for the elderly is likely to intensify as the baby boom generation reaches middle age and their parents live longer than earlier generations.

Future Trends

Clearly, the rate at which the female labor force is growing, and the rate of improvement in its educational attainment, must eventually slow down. But there is no reason to expect the trend to be reversed. Strong economic forces have shaped the changes in women's work roles, and these have been reinforced by changing sex-role attitudes. In fact, if the decade of the 1990s brings forth initiatives supportive of women workers, their rate of participation and educational attainment should continue to climb fairly vigorously.

The Bureau of Labor Statistics projects that the female labor force will grow by roughly 944,000 per year during the 1990s, or an average of 0.36 percent per year (Johnston and Packer 1987: 85). This projection represents about half the rate of increase seen in the recent past, but involves a steady increase in the female share of the work force. At that rate, women would comprise 47.5 percent of the work force by the year 2000, compared with 44.9 percent in 1988 and 33.4 percent in 1960.

Several important factors could throw these projections off. For instance, the welfare reform initiative enacted in 1988 (HR1720) could potentially reduce disincentives to labor force participation among poor women. Moreover, improved earnings opportunities for all women will also increase labor force participation and will also encourage full-time participation for women who now work part time. Research has shown that the labor-supply response to higher earnings is much greater for women than for men, presumably because married women have more choice about whether to enter or leave paid employment. If continued progress is made in reducing the earnings gap, and barriers for professional women continue to come down, the official projections may be understated.

Improved child care services, expanded parental leave policies, more flexible working hours, and other supportive measures could make a considerable difference in women's labor force participation and productivity. A study by the Institute for Women's Policy Research (Levitan and Conway 1988: 10) found that women who were provided maternity leave had substantially higher lifetime earnings than those who were not, controlling for age, education, race, and other factors. Finally, and working in the opposite direction, there might be a reduction in labor force participation rates for older women as pension benefits for women improve (although changes in Social Security rules could encourage delayed retirement).

Evidence from other countries with more egalitarian pay structures and better support services (such as child care and parental leave) suggests that the female labor force participation rate could increase to over 70 percent in a relatively short time. In 1986, the Swedish labor force participation rate for women in the 25- to 54-year-old age group cited earlier was 18 percentage points above the U.S. rate. The gap between the female and male participation rates for this age group in Sweden was 5.5 percentage points, compared with a gap of 22 percentage points for the same groups in the United States (Persson-Tanimura 1988; U.S. Bureau of Labor Statistics 1986: 9). To achieve a participation rate of this magnitude by the year 2000 would involve a much higher rate of female labor force growth than is now being projected by the Bureau of Labor Statistics.

Thus, we must be cautious in making projections of future trends in the size of the female work force. Much will depend on some of the policy decisions discussed in this book.

Human Capital Policy Issues

We have seen that the potential basis for further human capital investments in women workers has been growing rapidly. As the typical woman worker gains in basic education and work experience, the opportunity to benefit from job-specific training increases. Unfortunately, continued occupational segregation and the lack of pay equity are strong disincentives to optimal levels of human capital investments among women. Perceptions of women as less committed than men to the work force exacerbate this phenomenon. As women are, and will continue to be, a substantial majority of new labor force entrants, our nation can ill afford to neglect this group if we are to achieve rapid growth in our human capital. Moreover, human capital can also be augmented substantially if we turn our attention to the vast majority of women now at work whose human capital development is far below their potential.

We must also recognize that the household transformation has reduced the incentives for human capital investments supportive of unpaid household activities. Some of this change in the qualitative aspect of women's human capital investments is not especially problematic. For instance, cooking, sewing, and the like can be accomplished efficiently outside the home, and mass-produced items can be purchased far more cheaply than they can be produced in the home. Indeed, the fact that mass production in factories is more efficient than home production was a primary reason that women's paid employment outside the home became so attractive. On the other hand, the decline of human capital investment in children is a major social concern. From the perspective of economic productivity alone, any reduction in human capital investment in today's children may have long-term effects on the productivity of tomorrow's labor force.

Recognizing that women's employment outside the home probably has been accompanied by reductions in human capital investments in children, we must reevaluate the need for governmental interventions— for instance, the provision of public child care facilities and the passage of laws regulating the conditions of employment, such as parental leave—that explicitly acknowledge the fact that most children have no parent who is not in the work force. These policies would have the double benefit of increasing the current productivity of women workers as well as the future productivity of their children. In addition, school systems must stop operating as though the availability of a homemaker-mother is the norm for their students.

Workers and employers make human capital investments when they perceive that the costs of these investments will pay off in future earnings and output. As women increase their commitment to the work force, a higher level of human capital investment should be rational for all concerned. However, removing the barriers that create occupational segregation and cause the relegation of women to the low end of the pay and productivity hierarchy will create additional incentives for investments in human capital.

An anomaly in the picture of a growing, better-educated female work force is the situation of the millions of households headed by women who live below the poverty level. As we have seen, these families have relatively low income levels even when the mother is in the labor force. And because black children are far more likely than white children to live in such families, there is a large and growing racial gap in the extent of human capital investments in early childhood.

The current "remedy" for poverty in families maintained by women in a system of cash payments [Aid to Families with Dependent Children (AFDC)] and in-kind supplements such as food stamps, Medicaid, and housing assistance. Programs to enhance the human capital development of welfare mothers are rare, and in the absence of stronger incentives for such women to enter paid employment, they have little motivation to seek such investments for themselves. Little attention is paid to the human capital needs of children in these households until they enter the public school system. By then they are already disadvantaged relative to other youngsters. An important exception is the Head Start program, but it serves only a fraction of needy preschoolers. Given the need for skilled workers in the future, we can ill afford to allow millions of children to languish in poverty simply because the nation's ambivalent view of the recent changes in sex roles and family structure has impeded a political consensus around the legitimacy of women as full participants in the labor force.

The federal welfare reform initiative enacted in 1988 is a step in the direction of creating an environment conducive to human capital development for poor women. It would require states to set up job-training, education, and work programs for welfare recipients and would require welfare parents with children three years of age or older to participate in these programs if adequate child care is available. Yet relative to the magnitude of the problem, the level of outlays envisioned is truly a drop in the bucket. The Congressional Budget Office has estimated that 5,000 people per year would find work and leave the welfare system under the new program (Congressional Caucus 1987: 1, 10). In 1988, there were 3.75 million families—the large majority headed by able-bodied young women—receiving AFDC and other benefits (U.S. Congress 1989: 559). This is a vast pool of potential resources requiring special support. And the millions of children living in these families also need immediate attention if they are to become productive members of tomorrow's labor force. The sheer magnitude of this problem suggests the need for a much larger and more comprehensive program of remediation than is presently envisioned.

A Policy Agenda

We have identified a number of barriers to human capital investments in women workers and their dependents that can be overcome or at least mitigated by public policy. Some of these interventions can be classified as market-oriented solutions; others require direct governmental involvement. And although no one policy or program can meet the needs of all women workers—professionals in male-dominated occupations, workers in low-paying, female-dominated jobs, welfare mothers lacking the skills for even minimum-wage employment—women also have many needs in common. The need for affordable and reliable child care and care of the elderly, the need for more flexible work arrangements, and the burden of traditional stereotypes that devalue women's work are universal concerns.

Market-oriented Policies

Failure to enforce equal employment opportunity laws results in a self-perpetuating cycle of underinvestment in female human capital and is a serious "market failure" in our economy. If discrimination (through occupational segregation or other means) keeps women's earnings artificially below those of men in jobs requiring equal skill and responsibility, women workers, their family members, and employers will all underestimate the social payoff to investments in their human capital development. We have seen that women have roughly the same amount of general education as do men. Most women workers have the basic educational and social skills for privately undertaken investments to pay off with no special governmental involvement. Government's role in this regard is to make sure that markets are sending the right signals by enforcing antidiscrimination laws.

Antidiscrimination policy falls into two categories. First, where women lack access to the higher-paying, male-dominated occupations described earlier, or fail to rise within them, monitoring of the conditions of entry as well as of later promotion opportunities is needed. In some cases, this means removing entry barriers such as height and weight restrictions not related to job performance; in others, affirmative action may be needed to redress past discrimination that has created stereotypes unfavorable to women's employment. Along with easing women's entry into male-dominated occupations must come greater efforts to stimulate women's interest in these lines of work, including encouraging young women to study math and science and sensitizing high school and college counselors to encourage young women to pursue nontraditional work roles. Efforts to eliminate sex-stereotyping of jobs by the media and in classroom materials should also be promoted.

Where efforts to integrate occupations fail, low rates of pay in traditionally female jobs should also be scrutinized. Many women in these jobs are not in a position to change to nontraditional occupations, even if these were to open up to women through improved enforcement of equal employment opportunity laws. Although the term *comparable worth* has become a somewhat maligned slogan, the general approach seems to be a reasonable way to redress the gender imbalance that characterizes the pay structure in most firms. Employers (over a certain size) should be required to show, on the basis of a systematic job evaluation that rates jobs on a uniform basis by a variety of skill factors, that jobs predominantly held by women are not systematically underpaid relative to other jobs with equivalent ratings. The employer need not justify differences in pay rates between specific jobs, as individual differences may well be driven by market factors. Rather, they should show the absence of a *pattern* in which the sex of the incumbents is a significant factor in the setting of pay rates. Where possible, the administrative enforcement of pay equity regulations is desirable; litigation through the courts is unnecessarily expensive and time-consuming.

Pay equity for women will lead to more human capital investments by firms, who will need to find more productive ways to utilize their female employees to justify their higher pay. Where occupational segregation exists, pay equity will not cause major reductions in the work force but should instead lead to increased productivity.

A second type of intervention involves bringing the laws that regulate the conditions of employment up to date with the new realities of the household transformation: the relatively permanent commitment of the average woman to paid employment, and the decline of full-time homemaking as the modal female occupation. Reforms are needed in the areas of taxation, Social Security, pensions, leave policy, and the like. Many rules and regulations are based on the assumption of a traditional family with a single breadwinner and a full-time homemaker, as well as lifelong marriages. These sometimes produce perverse incentives, as with the so-called "marriage penalty" in the tax code, and create undesirable inequities, such as the higher tax rate for single-parent families relative to similarly situated married-couple families.

In some of these areas, government regulations are not involved, but standard industry practice needs to be reevaluated. The household transformation has affected not only the work lives of women but also those of men. And we have repeatedly emphasized the impacts on children. Consequently, these reforms should be designed to facilitate the accommodation of all family members to the household transformation. School systems, for example, should also rethink such areas as vacation scheduling, closings for inclement weather, and dealing with sickness and other emergencies where current practice is predicated on the availability of an adult at home during the day.

Governmental Interventions

Market-oriented solutions are appropriate for the majority of women who have an adequate foundation for human capital development, but poor women, lacking basic skills, need assistance from government. Roughly 3 million such women and their children are currently on the welfare rolls. As seen in Table 3.2, 13.7 percent, or about 5.3 million, of the adult women in the labor force in 1985 lacked a high school diploma. Although not a panacea, governmental employment and training programs are one approach to meeting their needs.

Employment and training programs, an important part of the government's antipoverty initiatives during the 1960s and 1970s, have fallen out of favor in the United States. Their critics generally argue that such efforts have low payoffs relative to their cost. While it is true that the measured gains of past programs have been modest, most of these studies capture only short-term gains. Moreover, evaluations of programs under the Comprehensive Employment and Training Act (CETA) during the 1970s found that women tended to gain the most from these programs.

For instance, a longitudinal follow-up study (Westat 1981) of over 6,000 CETA participants found average gains of 19 percent in postparticipation earnings for women (25 percent for minority women) compared with 4 to 5 percent for men. In another study, using 1977 data, the Urban Institute (Simms 1986) found that public service employment programs under CETA increased earnings for white women by $882 to $990 in the first postprogram year and by $1,035 to $1,144 in the second. For black women, the gains were $1,126 to $1,196 in the first year and $608 to $678 in the second. Similar gains were found for women in an on-the-job training program. For men, on the other hand, the same study found no significant gains for those who participated in the public service employment program, and a very small gain—for white men only—for those who participated in the on-the-job training program. Perhaps it is because women face special employment barriers, as discussed earlier, that the assistance provided by these programs provides payoffs for women that exceed those for male participants.

Another area for direct governmental involvement lies in the provision of child care, schooling, and other social services. Although a comprehensive approach to child care policy should have a substantial private component, there is no denying that the provision of extrafamilial child care (as well as care of the elderly and some other social services) has a large "public goods" element. The United States is the only major industrial country that has a sizable proportion of women working outside the home but lacks a national child care policy. The lack of child care and other services not only prevents working women from realizing their full potential but also—to the extent that human capital investments in children would be enhanced by improved child care—undermines the long-term potential human-capital base for tomorrow's labor force.

Summary and Conclusions

The transformation of the household economy and the changes in women's work and family roles have had an enormous impact on our society. They also present an extraordinary opportunity to expand our economy's output and productivity. Not only has it meant an unprecedented expansion in the labor force in a relatively short period of time, but it raises important human capital issues. We must ensure that women are rewarded appropriately for their work in order to provide appropriate incentives for human capital investments. Moreover, we must be vigilant to the need for increased social responsibility for human capital investments in children, now that their mothers spend fewer hours at home.

Public policy should aim at improving labor market mobility for women, thereby mitigating market failures in human capital investments. Where necessary, government should intervene directly, providing human capital investments through public programs such as employment and training programs for poor women, child care programs, and other social services.

Notes

The author is grateful for comments by Barbara Bergmann, Elizabeth Conway, and Sar Levitan.

1. This figure refers to the number of nondisabled adult females who are not in the labor force.

2. The Swedish figure is an annual figure for 1986 and is taken from Persson-Tanimura (1988). The U.S. figure is for November 1986 and is taken from the U.S. Bureau of Labor Statistics (1986: 9).

3. According to U.S. Bureau of Labor Statistics official Deborah Pisetzner Klein, the 1983 reclassification of detailed occupations into the broad categories shown in Table 3.5 moved a few formerly clerical jobs into the sales category. Consequently, the finding in the table that the proportion of the female labor force in the sales and clerical categories taken together remained stable between 1972 and 1988 suggests that the small decline in clerical employment might be at least partly due to the change in statistical definitions rather than to a movement of women out of clerical employment.

4. All data on earnings and sex composition for detailed occupational categories are from unpublished tabulations supplied by the U.S. Bureau of Labor Statistics.

References

Blau, Francine D., and Andrea H. Beller (1988). "Trends in Earnings by Gender, 1971–1981." *Industrial and Labor Relations Review* 41 (July): 513–29.

Blau, Francine D., and Marianne A. Ferber (1986). *The Economics of Women, Men, and Work*. Englewood Cliffs, N.J.: Prentice-Hall.

Congressional Caucus for Women's Issues (1987). *Update* (December 22): 1,10.

Haber, Sheldon, Enrique Lamas, and Gordon Green (1983). "A New Method of Estimating Job Separations by Race and Sex." *Monthly Labor Review* 106 (June): 20–27.

Johnston, William B., and Arnold E. Packer (1987). *Workforce 2000: Work and Workers for the Twenty-first Century*. Indianapolis, Ind.: Hudson Institute.

Klein, Deborah Pisetzner (1984). "Occupational Employment Statistics for 1972–82." In U.S. Bureau of Labor Statistics, *Employment and Earnings* 31 (January): 13–16.

Levitan, Sar A., and Elizabeth A. Conway (1988). "Raising America's Children: How Should We Care?" Washington, D.C.: Center for Social Policy Studies, George Washington University. Unpublished report.

National Center for Educational Statistics (1984). *Digest of Education Statistics 1983/84.* Washington, D.C.: U.S. Government Printing Office.

Nordhaus, William D. (1972). "The Recent Productivity Slowdown." *Brookings Papers on Economic Activity* 3: 493–536.

Norsworthy, John R., and L. J. Fulco (1974). "Productivity and Costs in the Private Economy, 1973." *Monthly Labor Review* 98 (June): 3–9.

Persson-Tanimura, Inga (1988). "Economic Equality for Swedish Women: Current Situation and Trends." University of Lund. Unpublished report.

Simms, Margaret (1986). "The Participation of Young Women in Employment and Training Programs." In National Research Council, *Youth Employment and Training Programs: The YEDPA Years.* Washington, D.C.: National Academy Press, pp. 462–85.

U.S. Bureau of Labor Statistics (1985a). *Educational Level of U.S. Workforce up Sharply over Decade.* USDL 85–355, table 1.

——— (1985b). *Handbook of Labor Statistics.* Washington, D.C.: U.S. Government Printing Office.

——— (1986). *Employment and Earnings,* vol. 33 (December).

——— (1988a). *Employment and Earnings,* vol. 35 (September).

——— (1988b). *Employment in Perspective: Women in the Labor Force.* Report no. 752.

——— (1988c). *Employment of Women in Nontraditional Jobs. 1983–88.* Report no. 758.

——— (1988d). *Labor Force Participation Unchanged among Mothers with Young Children.* USDL 88–431, table 1.

——— (1988e). "Marital and Family Characteristics of the Labor Force from the March 1988 Current Population Survey." September. Unpublished tabulations.

U.S. Bureau of the Census (1983). "Child Care Arrangements of Working Mothers, June 1982." *Current Population Reports,* ser. P-23, no. 129.

——— (1988). "Money Income and Poverty Status in the United States: 1987." *Current Population Reports,* ser. P-60, no. 161.

U.S. Congress. House. Committee on Ways and Means (1989). *Background Material and Data on Progress within the Jurisdiction of the Committee on Ways and Means.* 101st Congress, 1st session. WMCP: 101–4, March 15, 1989.

U.S. Council of Economic Advisers (1987). *Economic Report of the President.* Washington, D.C.: U.S. Government Printing Office.

U.S. Department of Labor, Employment and Training Administration (1979). *Employment and Training Report of the President, 1979.* Washington, D.C.: U.S. Government Printing Office.

U.S. Social Security Administration, Office of Strategic Planning (1987). *Fact Sheet.*

Viscusi, W. Kip (1980). "Sex Difference in Quitting." *Review of Economics and Statistics* 62 (August): 388–98.

Westat (1981). *Impact on 1977 Earnings of New FY 1978 CETA Enrollees in Selected Program Activities.* Continuous Longitudinal Manpower Survey: Net Impact Report No. 1. Prepared for the Office of Program Evaluation, Employment, and Training Administration, U.S. Department of Labor. Rockville, Md.: Westat.

4

Immigrants

Ray Marshall

Immigration has had, and will continue to have, an important impact on human capital formation in the United States. For one thing, because the United States is a nation of immigrants, a certain "immigration momentum" has built up because of the connections between residents of the United States and people in their ancestral homelands. There are, in addition, important economic forces attracting people to the United States or propelling them from other countries. During the 1980s, the United States was the destination of about half of the world's immigrants seeking permanent resettlement, and about 30 percent of our annual population growth was due to the influx of immigrants and refugees (INS 1988). Major pressures for immigration also come from the decline of the birthrate in the United States to below the replacement rate; from the slowdown in the rate of growth of the U.S. population and work force; from projected labor shortages because the demand for labor is expected to grow faster than the work force; and from a combination of technological change, domestic labor market trends, and international competition which has caused skill requirements to outrun the ability of our educational system to produce workers with those skills.[1]

This chapter stresses the human capital implications of immigration. It is concerned primarily with the effects of immigration on the quantity and quality of American workers. The quality of the work force is extremely important because it has become a major determinant of economic competitiveness, or the ability of high-wage countries like the United States to maintain and improve personal incomes and national power. This chapter therefore discusses the human capital characteristics of immigrants. It concludes with some recommendations for policies that can cause immigration to be more effectively integrated into overall economic policy and enable immigrants to develop themselves more effectively.

Immigration Policy

Overview

Immigration policy has had a strong impact on the quality and the rate of population growth in the United States. In the early days of the nation's history, there were minor efforts to control immigration, though the first serious controls came late in the nineteenth century, when Congress passed the infamous Chinese Exclusion Act. Even here, however, Congress attempted to take into account education and skill; it barred the immigration of Chinese laborers, but not teachers, students, diplomats, merchants, or tourists.

The Immigration and Naturalization Act of 1952 is, with its amendments, the basis for present immigration policy. The 1952 act raised the ceiling from the Eastern Hemisphere and reaffirmed the national origins policy, which sought to restrict immigration from non-European countries. Although this act abolished racial designations as a basis for immigration, very small quotas were established for Asian countries. The 1952 act also established a system of preferential immigration policies which stressed family unification but acknowledged the importance of human capital. Highly skilled immigrants "whose services are urgently needed in the United States," as well as their spouses and children, were assigned up to half of the visas available for each country. The other visas were assigned priorities based on kinship with U.S. citizens and legal residents. The 1952 act also contained the "Texas proviso," which exempted employers from penalties for "harboring" illegal aliens. This proviso did much to encourage the flow of illegal immigrants into the United States, especially after the end of the "bracero" program, which brought in 4.8 million temporary Mexican workers between 1942 and 1964.

The Immigration Act of 1965 represented the most significant change in American immigration policy since 1924. Among other things, the 1965 statute raised the annual quota from the Eastern Hemisphere to 170,000, with no more than 20,000 from one country, and placed a ceiling of 120,000 a year on immigration from the Western Hemisphere. In 1978 the allocation of visas was changed; the worldwide total was still 290,000, but no more than 20,000 could come from one country. This ceiling was subsequently lowered to 270,000, where it is today. It should be noted, however, that these ceilings do not define the upper limit on immigration because refugees and immediate family members (i.e., spouses, unmarried children, and parents of legal residents of the United States) come in outside the quotas.

As a practical matter, therefore, many more legal immigrants come in than the ceiling of 270,000 suggests. Largely because of the 1965 law, the flow of legal immigrants increased from about 297,000 in 1965 to 602,000 in 1987. During the 1970s, 4.5 million immigrants entered the United States legally; 2.9 million entered between 1980 and 1985; and 602,000 entered in 1987. Of these 602,000 immigrants in 1987, only 52,000 were admitted under occupational preferences—the rest were relatives of citizens and permanent residents. Of these 1987 legal immigrants, 271,135 came in under the worldwide ceilings and 330,381 under the relatives, refugees, and asylees exemptions from that ceiling (INS 1988: xiv–xvi).

A major effect of the Immigration Act of 1965 was to change the national origins policy that had prevailed for most of this century. By replacing country quotas with a preference system that favored family unification, Congress undoubtedly expected to maintain a balance between various nationalities, since priority went to existing residents, who were predominantly of European ancestry. However, the family unification provisions soon greatly increased the flow of immigrants from Asia and Latin America. At first, the immigrants from those areas were people who were eager to come to the United States under the work-related quotas at a time when tight labor markets and relatively high wages in Western Europe slowed immigration from that area. This led to so-called "chain immigration." The first Asian immigrants under the 1965 act were mainly professionals, engineers, and military spouses, but during the 1970s and 1980s Asians made full use of the relatively open family-preference system. In fact, many of the earliest Asian professionals were students who stayed on after graduating from American colleges and universities. In 1965, the four leading sources of legal U.S. immigrants were Canada, Mexico, the United Kingdom, and Germany; in 1986, the four leading countries were Mexico, the Philippines, Korea, and China.

Illegal Immigration

To these legal immigrants were added an unknown number of illegals, whose numbers are widely thought to have increased sharply during the 1970s. Siegal, Passel, and Robinson (1981: 13–40), for example, estimate that the number of illegals increased from a few hundred thousand employed mainly in agriculture during the late 1960s to between 3 and 6 million living mainly in urban areas in 1980. These estimates are much lower than the ones originally issued by the Immigration and Naturalization Service (INS) (Chapman 1975: 15–18). They also are higher, however, than the estimates by those who minimized the number of illegals, but compatible with the evidence that emerged after the legalization program in the 1980s described below. The problem is, of course, that nobody knows how many illegal immigrants there were (or are) in the United States. The problem is not only with the inherent difficulty in measuring any illegal activity, but also with defining "immigrants." One of the reasons for the wide range in estimates is that the number of people in the country at any given time without proper documents is much larger than the number of those usually classified as "immigrants" (those who have settled in the United States).

In 1986, two of the country's leading demographers concluded with respect to legal and illegal immigration:

> Annual totals of new immigrants and refugees in the U.S. may now be up to the record highs of over a million immigrants counted in six years between 1905 and 1914. Since 1979, legal immigrants have averaged 566,000 a year . . . newly arrived refugees and asylees [have approached] . . . 135,000 and the "settled" illegal immigrant population is growing by up to half a million a year, according to some estimates. Half of illegal immigrants are persons who entered the U.S. legally but then overstayed the terms of temporary visas. . . . The Census Bureau estimates that net immigration now accounts for 28 percent of U.S. population growth and will account for all growth by the 2030s if fertility stays at the current low 1.8 births per woman. (Bouvier and Gardner 1986)

The Immigration Reform and Control Act of 1986

As a consequence of the concern about illegal immigration, Congress, after years of debate, passed the Immigration Reform and Control Act (IRCA) of 1986. IRCA granted amnesty to illegal aliens who could demonstrate that they had lived continuously in the United States since before January 1, 1982 and who petitioned for legalization between May 5, 1987 and May 5, 1988. Under a Special Agricultural Worker (SAW) program, illegals who worked in a perishable crop for at least 90 days between May 1985 and May 1986 could also qualify for legal status. IRCA also provided for Replenishment Agricultural Workers (RAW), who may be admitted between fiscal 1990 and fiscal 1993 if there is a "shortage" of workers in a perishable crop. Both RAWs and SAWs are given favorable treatment in acquiring permanent resident alien status. IRCA also makes it illegal for employers to hire workers who lack the legal right to work in the United States. Violators are subject to civil and criminal penalties that increase with the number of violations.[2]

Although it is too early to assess the impact, there are reasons to believe that IRCA is unlikely to do much to stem the flow of illegals into the United States. First, neither the INS nor the Labor Department has sufficient enforcement resources, so the probability that violators will be caught is very small. Second, IRCA did not develop a secure identification system. It permits a variety of documents to be presented to prove eligibility, and relieves employers of liability for failing to verify their authenticity. There is therefore a booming market for counterfeit documents. As will be noted below, the SAW program is especially vulnerable to fraud. Third, the main sanction against the aliens themselves is deportation, and deportees often return to the United States as soon as they are deported. Chiswick (1988) suggests that such penalties as fines, detention, and administrative sanctions (denying for a time the right to reenter the United States) could improve enforcement. "Once the certainty of meaningful penalties if apprehended is established, the flow of illegal aliens, particularly across the Southern border, would decrease. . . . Unless more effective policies are implemented, illegal immigration will be a continuing feature of the American labor market and society" (Chiswick 1988: 114–15).

In fact, although it was expected that only about 350,000 would apply for the SAW program, there were over a million applicants, more than the total seasonal agricultural work forces in the places where these applicants were supposed to have worked. According to David North, a leading authority on agricultural workers and immigration, "if all California SAW applicants worked full time in California agriculture, they would have provided twice as many years of work as California used in 1987, even if no one except SAW applicants were employed in the role of farmer, unpaid farm family worker, year-round farm worker, and seasonal farm worker" (Applebome 1988: 1). Fraud under the SAW provisions is encouraged by the fact that IRCA permits loose standards of proof of residence through easily counterfeited documents. This problem is compounded by understaffed government agencies, the large number of applications, and the fact that the federal courts have given the INS the burden of proving that applications are fraudulent.

Temporary or Guest Workers

In addition to the SAW and RAW provisions of IRCA discussed earlier (which give temporary resident alien status to agricultural workers), section H of the Immigration and Naturalization Act provides for four other categories of temporary workers: (1) workers of distinguished merit and ability; (2) workers admitted if similarly skilled U.S. workers are not available; (3) trainees; and (4) spouses and children of the above.

The most widely used of these sections is H-2, which provided for about 29,000 workers in 1987, most of whom worked in agriculture. Temporary visas for distinguished merit or ability (H-1) have increased steadily, from 17,000 in 1978 to over 65,000 in 1987 (U.S. Department of Labor, International Labor Affairs Bureau, unpublished data). IRCA made it easier for employers to obtain temporary workers. As noted above, the SAW program had over a million applicants, many of whom probably will become permanent residents. The "temporariness" refers not to the length of time they stay in the country but to the length of time they remain in agriculture.

Because of the emphasis in U.S. immigration policy on family unification, 470,000 of the 500,000 nonrefugee immigrants admitted in 1986 had family sponsors. Another 65,000 immigrants entered each year between 1983 and 1986 as refugees. Only 27,000 visas per year go to professionals, and another 27,000 go to skilled and unskilled workers sponsored by their employers.

Pending Proposals

In order to give greater weight to education and skills, bills have been introduced in the Congress (in the Senate by Senators Edward Kennedy and Alan Simpson and in the House by Congressman Charles Schumer) that would shift preferences away from family unification through a point system giving greater weight to education and to English-language skills. This bill would increase legal immigration to 590,000, an increase of 80,000. Of these, 470,000 would be for family unification and 120,000 for people who meet labor market tests. Skill-related immigration would increase from 10 percent to 20 percent of the total legal immigration. This proposed legislation would, in addition, increase the number of visas available for spouses and children of U.S. permanent resident aliens but reduce the number available to such distant relatives as married brothers and sisters, in-laws, and nieces and nephews of U.S. citizens. Proponents of the Kennedy-Simpson bill believe that family unification should continue to be the overwhelming focus of U.S. immigration policy but believe that present procedures make it possible for distant relatives of U.S. citizens to crowd out skilled people who do not have close relatives in the United States. Almost half (55,000) of the 120,000 visas available for labor-market purposes would be distributed on the basis of points awarded for labor-market characteristics and English-language proficiency. There is a presumption that the English-language provision would favor Europeans, but this is not necessarily true because there are many skilled English-speaking technical and professional people in China, India, and other places who would like to come to the United States.

Table 4.1 Civilian Labor Force Participation Rates of the 1980 Total and Foreign-Born Population and of Fiscal Years 1972–1979 Legal Immigrants, by Sex (percent)

	Both Sexes	Male	Female
Total, 1980	61.6	74.7	49.8
Foreign-born, 1980, by year of immigration:			
1970 to 1980	64.2	77.6	50.8
1970 to 1974	70.3	85.0	56.7
1975 to 1980	59.6	72.3	46.2
Legal Immigrants, 1972–79[a]	53.8	77.4	34.0

Sources: U.S. Bureau of the Census 1984 (table 272); U.S. Bureau of the Census 1985; and unpublished tabulations based on the U.S. Immigration and Naturalization Service's public-use tapes for immigrants (complete enumeration) for fiscal years 1972–79.

Note: The civil labor force participation rate is the percentage of the civilian population 16 years and over in the civilian labor force.

[a]Percentage of total immigrant population, 16 years and over, who reported an occupation at entry.

The Impact of Immigration on Human Capital Formation

What is the impact of this flood of immigrants on America's supply of human capital? To answer this question, we turn here from a discussion of recent immigration patterns and policies to an analysis of the contribution immigrants are making to the supply of human capital in the country as reflected in occupational patterns, educational levels, and income.

The Composition of Employment

Employment and Unemployment

One measure of human capital is the labor force participation rate (LFPR, the percentage of the population working or looking for work) of different groups. The LFPR for the U.S. population 16 and over was 62 percent in 1980, whereas it was 53.8 percent for immigrants in that age group (Table 4.1). LFPRs were much lower for immigrants from Europe (47.4 percent), North America (50.3 percent), and the U.S.S.R. (34.8 percent) and were slightly lower for African immigrants (60.8 percent), but were higher for immigrants from Asia (62.6 percent) and Latin America (66.0 percent). Immigrants from India and the Philippines had particularly higher labor force participation rates (74.7 and 72.6 percent, respectively).

Table 4.2 Percentage Distribution of Occupations of 1987 Employed U.S. Workers and
Reported at-Entry Occupations of Fiscal Year 1985–1987 Immigrants, by Sex

Occupational Group	U.S. Employed, 1987			Immigrants, 1985–87		
	Both Sexes	Males	Females	Both Sexes	Males	Females
Managerial and professional specialty	24.7	24.9	24.4	24.8	25.2	24.0
Executive, administrative, and managerial	11.8	13.3	10.0	9.1	10.9	5.9
Professional specialty	12.8	11.6	14.4	15.7	14.3	18.1
Technical, sales, and administrative support	31.2	19.9	45.1	16.2	12.2	23.5
Technicians and related support	3.0	2.8	3.2	2.4	2.7	2.0
Sales occupations	12.0	11.3	12.8	5.2	5.0	5.7
Administrative support, including clerical	16.2	5.9	29.0	11.5	14.5	6.0
Precision production, craft, and repair	12.1	20.0	2.3	11.5	14.5	6.0
Operators, fabricators, and laborers	15.6	20.9	9.0	22.5	27.1	14.3
Service occupations	13.4	9.5	18.1	20.0	14.9	29.3
Farming, forestry, and fishing	3.1	4.8	1.1	4.9	6.1	2.9
Total number (thousands)	112,440	62,107	50,334	1,075	438	638
Civilian labor force participation rate, 1985–87	65.2	76.2	55.3	50.2	65.0	35.6

Sources: U.S. Department of Labor 1988 (tables 1, 2, and 20); U.S. Immigration and Naturalization Service 1986 (table IMM 6.6), 1987 (table 19), 1988 (table 19), and unpublished tabulations.

Note: Percentages may not add to totals due to rounding.

The labor force is divided between those who are employed and those who are unemployed. In 1980, 93.5 percent of the total U.S. labor force and a similar percentage of immigrants were employed. The lowest levels of employment were for immigrants from Latin America, especially Mexico (91.5 percent and 90.2 percent, respectively) and the highest were for those from Asia (94.6 percent) and North America (95.2 percent).

Occupations

Of the 570,000 new immigrants recorded by the INS in 1985, only 39 percent (221,873) listed an occupation. Of these, 18 percent listed "professional specialty" and 9 percent "executive, administrative, and managerial." At the other end of the scale, 22 percent were "operators, fabricators, and laborers." Immigrants from the Caribbean and Central and South America were more likely to be in the lower-paying occupations, while those from Canada, Europe, Asia, and Africa were more concentrated at the upper end of the scale (Bouvier and Gardner, 1986: 23).

Table 4.2 presents data on the occupational distribution of immigrants relative to total U.S. employment. These data show that immigrants are more likely than U.S. residents to be in the following categories: managerial and professional specialty; operators, fabricators, and laborers; service occupations; and farming, forestry, and fishing. Note, however, some differences by sex. Immigrant males are more likely than employed U.S. males to be in "administrative support, including clerical" jobs, and immigrant females are more likely than U.S. females to be in "precision production, craft, and repair" occupations.

Tables 4.3 and 4.4 show the leading occupations reported at entry for males and females who entered the United States between 1970 and 1980. These data confirm the heavy concentration of immigrants in blue-collar, service, and professional occupations. However, the professionals are mostly males—the only professional categories in which females are heavily represented are "registered nurses" and "teachers, except colleges and universities." Immigrant males are more likely than females to be physicians, engineers, and college and university teachers, though the male immigrant list is dominated by blue-collar and service occupations.

A careful examination of the employment of Asian Americans using 1980 census data provides some additional insight into their employment patterns. There is, for instance, a distinct occupational as well as geographic clustering, as has been seen with other immigrants. Vietnamese immigrants, for instance, concentrate in manufacturing; Chinese, Japanese, and Koreans in retail trade and manufacturing; and Indians and Filipinos in professional services. Asian immigrants are concentrated geographically mainly in the western states. That these occupational clusterings represent "beachheads" from which the immigrants then disperse occupationally is suggested by the fact that there is a tendency for native-born Asian Americans to move toward the national employment pattern (DeJong and Gardner 1987: 6–8).

Immigrants also are making significant inroads into some professions, especially engineering, the physical sciences, and mathematics. Between 1980 and 1987, about half of all Ph.D. degrees awarded by American universities in mathematics, science, and engineering went to foreign nationals. A study by the National Academy of Engineering (NAE) (1987) reported that about half of all engineering graduate students (but only about 10 percent of undergraduates) were from other countries, and

Table 4.3 Specific Occupations with Largest Number of the Foreign-Born Females Who Entered the United States during 1970–1980

Occupation	Number of Females	As % of all Foreign-Born Females[a] Reporting Occupations	Females as % of Foreign-Born Population[a] Reporting Occupation
Textile operatives	118,920	8.4	86.5
Secretaries	64,720	4.6	96.7
Assemblers	59,880	4.3	56.1
Registered nurses	48,420	3.4	93.9
Cashiers	46,460	3.3	74.7
Nursing aides, orderlies, and attendants	45,540	3.2	85.9
Waiters, waitresses, and helpers	42,080	3.0	63.3
Maids and housemen, except household	37,040	2.6	72.9
Clerks, general office	36,540	2.6	70.4
Teachers, except colleges and universities	32,620	2.3	70.7
Hand packers and packagers	31,300	2.2	63.7
Bookkeepers	30,640	2.2	75.7
Farm laborers	29,680	2.1	28.2
Cleaners and servants, private household	25,880	1.8	93.8
Janitors and cleaners, except private household	24,640	1.7	28.2
Office machine operators	24,160	1.7	70.5
Production inspectors	22,180	1.6	64.4
Cooks, except private household	22,040	1.6	26.5
Typists	16,940	1.2	91.9
Writers, artists, entertainers, and athletes	15,380	1.1	37.0

Table 4.3   (continued)

Occupation	Number of Females	As % of all Foreign-Born Females[a] Reporting Occupations	Females as % of Foreign-Born Population[a] Reporting Occupation
Accountants and auditors	13,740	1.0	42.3
Child care workers except private household	13,260	0.9	84.2
Dressmakers	12,820	0.9	91.2
Health technologists and technicians	12,460	0.9	63.2
Hairdressers and cosmetologists	12,220	0.9	84.6
Physicians	11,560	0.8	26.3
Electric and electronic assemblers	11,500	0.8	75.2
Bank tellers	11,320	0.8	79.4
Housekeepers, private household	10,880	0.8	97.1
Receptionists	10,700	0.8	88.9
Sales workers, apparel	10,120	0.7	75.3
Subtotal	905,640	64.3	63.7
Other occupations	503,060	35.7	27.7
Total	1,408,700	100.0	43.5

Source: U.S. Bureau of the Census, 1980 Public-Use Microdata File, A File (5% sample).

Note: Populations from the public-use file were inflated by a factor of 20. Percentages may not add to totals due to rounding.

[a] Who came to the United States to stay during 1970–80.

almost 50 percent of engineering doctorates went to foreign students. Foreigners filled an even larger share of engineering assistant professorships; the proportion of foreigners among engineering assistant professors under age 35 rose from 10 percent in 1972 to 50 to 55 percent in 1985, about three-fourths of whom had applied for American citizenship. Engineering education therefore seems to be a way for a select group of highly educated foreigners to achieve entry into the United

Table 4.4 Specific Occupations with Largest Numbers of the Foreign-Born
Males Who Entered the United States During 1970–1980

Occupation	Number of Males	As % of all Foreign-Born Males[a] Reporting Occupations	Males as % of Foreign-Born Population[a] Reporting Occupation
Mechanics and repairmen	82,160	4.5	95.6
Farm laborers	75,420	4.1	71.8
Janitors and cleaners, except household	62,820	3.4	71.8
Cooks, except private household	61,140	3.3	73.5
Engineers	52,560	2.9	93.9
Assemblers	46,900	2.6	43.9
Construction laborers, except helpers	34,180	1.9	97.2
Physicians	32,460	1.8	73.7
Engineering and science technicians	29,740	1.6	75.0
Carpenters	28,500	1.6	97.6
Truck drivers	27,920	1.5	96.5
Welders and cutters	26,440	1.4	92.7
Store owners and supervisors	26,240	1.4	73.2
Writers, artists, entertainers, and athletes	26,180	1.4	63.0
Stock handlers and baggers	25,740	1.4	84.3
Production supervisors	25,480	1.4	73.2
Waiters, waitresses, and helpers	24,400	1.3	36.7
Groundskeepers and gardeners, except farm	23,140	1.3	94.4
Teachers, colleges and universities	22,820	1.2	69.9
Busboys	20,560	1.1	82.0
Painters,			

Table 4.4 (continued)

Occupation	Number of Males	As % of all Foreign-Born Males[a] Reporting Occupations	Males as % of Foreign-Born Population[a] Reporting Occupation
construction, and maintenance	19,980	1.1	94.6
Machinists	19,220	1.1	91.0
Accountants and auditors	18,780	1.0	57.7
Textile operatives	18,560	1.0	13.5
Hand packers and packagers	17,860	1.0	36.3
Technicians, except health, engineering, and science	17,680	1.0	76.2
Cashiers	15,720	0.9	25.3
Clerks, general office	15,400	0.8	29.6
Subtotal	898,000	49.2	63.2
Other occupations	928,340	50.8	51.6
Total	1,826,340	100.0	56.5

Source: U.S. Bureau of the Census, 1980 Public-Use Microdata File, A File (5% sample).

Note: Populations from the public-use file were inflated by a factor of 20. Percentages may not add to totals due to rounding.

[a]Who came to the United States to stay during 1970–80.

States. One reason for the high percentage of foreigners among engineering graduate students is that many American students shun engineering and scientific fields in favor of such areas as law and business, which often are more lucrative and require less natural science and mathematics. The NAE report points out that these foreign engineers represent "absolutely the cream of the crop" and constitute a "terrific economic bargain" for the country, since most have completed undergraduate engineering schools in their native countries. There are some negatives: (1) foreign professors often are very deficient in English and come from cultural backgrounds that tend to discourage women and minorities from pursuing engineering careers; and (2) because of U.S. security restrictions, foreign engineers are sometimes unable to participate fully in the sensitive defense-related research that consumes a large part of U.S. research resources.

With respect to the impact of foreigners on American engineers, the NAE report concludes that there is insufficient data to answer this question but that U.S.-born engineers "have not faced appreciably diminished opportunities in industry" (cited by Walsh [1988: 455]). Moreover, "without the use of noncitizens and foreign-born engineers, both research universities and industries would have difficulties in handling the educational research, development, and technological programs that are currently supported" (Walsh 1988: 455). The report does not call for restrictions on foreign engineers but, in order to attract more U.S. applicants to engineering graduate schools, it recommended "the establishment of well-paying graduate fellowships for U.S. citizens with stipends that would be (nearly) competitive with attractive opportunities for immediate industrial employment" (Walsh 1988: 455).

Characteristics of Illegal Immigrants
The applications for legalization under the IRCA provide some additional insight into the characteristics of the illegal immigrants who entered the United States before 1982. As of December 1988, there were about 3 million applicants for legalization (2,953,582)—1.77 million under the general or "pre-1982" provisions of the act, and 1.19 million under the Special Agricultural Workers (SAW) provision. The INS collected some detailed data on the characteristics of 2.35 million of these applicants, representing 79.4 percent of the total—92.9 percent of the pre-1982 and 59.4 percent of the SAW applicants, respectively (INS, unpublished data). Of the pre-1982 applicants

- Seventy percent were from Mexico.
- Eighty percent were between 15 and 44 years of age; the median age was 30, somewhat lower than the median age of non-Hispanic whites (about 33) but higher than the median age of Hispanics (24) and the median age of 28 cited by the U.S. General Accounting Office (1988) for illegal immigrants from Mexico.
- These applicants were heavily concentrated geographically: 55 percent were in California and 18 percent were in Texas, while New York and Illinois had about 7 percent each, so that 87 percent were in these four states.
- Forty-two percent were married, and 57 percent were males.
- As might be expected, while 15 percent of these applicants were in craft and clerical occupations, most were concentrated in lower-paying blue-collar occupations. They were distributed occupationally as follows:

Laborers	24%
Service workers	21%
Students	12%

Skilled crafts persons	11%
Unemployed/retired	5%
Clerical workers	4%
Farm workers	4%
Other and unknown	19%

Thus, these data seem to confirm studies that have found illegal aliens to have had lower levels of formal schooling, fewer skills acquired on the job, and lower occupational status than legal immigrants from the same countries (Massey 1987: 236–74).

The data support the conclusion that immigrants contribute to both extremes of the occupational structure and are heavily concentrated in some professional categories and in semiskilled and unskilled occupations. Undocumented workers skew the total immigration heavily toward the unskilled occupations.

Schooling

Schooling is another important measure of the impact of immigration on the nation's aggregate human capital. The data in Table 4.5 show that immigrants have polarized levels of schooling relative to the native-born population: the percentage of individuals who are college graduates is larger among the foreign-born than among the native-born, and the percentage of individuals who have completed only elementary school is also higher among the foreign-born. Indeed, 13 percent of the immigrants who entered the United States between 1975 and 1980 had less than five years of schooling, compared with only 3 percent of natives. By contrast, 24 percent of immigrants but only 16 percent of natives had four or more years of college. Natives were more likely than were immigrants to be high school graduates and to have some college. These data suggest that in schooling, as in occupations, immigrants tend to cluster at the extremes.

The data in Table 4.6 provide some information on immigrant schooling by country of origin. The main conclusions from this table are the following.

1. Immigrants from Africa and Asia had higher levels of high school and college completion relative to both the total U.S. population and other immigrants. Asian immigrants make a particularly large contribution to the country's average levels of schooling because of their rapidly increasing proportion of the population; they were 18 percent of the foreign-born population counted in the 1980 census, but 44.4 percent of the immigrants admitted in 1985. African immigrants, by contrast, were only 1.4 percent of the foreign-born population in 1980 and 3.0 percent of those who were admitted in 1985 (Bouvier and Gardner, 1986: 8, 22).

Table 4.5 Distribution of Native-Born and Recently Entered Foreign-Born Population, Ages 25 and Over, by Sex (percent), by Years of School Completed

Years of School Completed	Foreign-Born Entered 1975–80			Native-Born Population		
	Both Sexes	Males	Females	Both Sexes	Males	Females
Elementary, grades 0–4	12.9	11.6	14.1	2.9	3.2	2.5
Elementary, grades 5–8	17.9	16.3	19.4	13.9	14.0	13.8
High school, grades 9–11	10.0	9.2	10.8	15.6	14.5	16.6
High school, grade 12	20.9	18.4	23.3	35.5	32.0	38.6
College, years 1–3	14.5	15.3	13.8	15.9	16.3	15.5
College, 4 years and over	23.8	29.2	18.5	16.3	20.0	12.9
All grades	100.0	100.0	99.9	100.1	100.0	99.9
Number	1,637,997	817,109	820,888	122,072,241	57,557,836	64,514,405
Median years of school completed	12.4	12.7	12.2	12.5	12.6	12.4

Source: Department of Labor's submission to the President's triennial Comprehensive Report on Immigration (forthcoming, 1989). Figures are from the U.S. Bureau of the Census 1983b (table 83) and 1984b (table 10).

Note: Percentages may not add to 100.0 due to rounding.

2. High school and college completion levels of immigrants from Europe and Latin America were below those of all U.S. residents. Mexican immigrants had particularly low levels of schooling—only 21.3 percent and 3.0 percent had completed high school and college, respectively, compared with 66.5 percent and 16.2 percent for all U.S. residents. In fact, over two-thirds (68.4 percent) of Mexican immigrants had no high school at all, by far the highest for any nationality group. The U.S. General Accounting Office (1988: 13) reported that illegal immigrants from Mexico averaged only four to five years of schooling. Mexican immigrants' low level of schooling is important because Mexican immigrants comprise such a high proportion of foreign-born U.S. residents; they were 15.6 percent of those counted in the 1980 census and 10.7 percent of those admitted in 1985, but they probably account for at least 40 percent of legal and illegal immigration combined.

Table 4.6 Distribution of Total U.S. Population and Immigrants Aged 25 and Over by Educational Attainment, 1980 (in Percent)

Region and Country of Birth	All Immigrants			Immigrated 1970–74		
	No High School[a]	Completed High School	Completed College	No High School[a]	Completed High School	Completed College
Total U.S.	18.3	66.5	16.2	—	—	—
All immigrants	35.6	53.1	15.8	35.5	54.3	20.3
Europe	37.8	51.2	12.1	37.2	53.8	14.9
U.S.S.R.	37.9	50.2	17.1	17.8	70.4	30.7
Africa	11.6	81.9	38.7	7.3	88.0	45.6
North America	20.4	61.8	14.3	9.1	74.4	25.5
Latin America	47.6	41.0	8.9	51.7	36.1	6.4
Mexico	68.4	21.3	3.0	72.0	17.2	2.1
Asia	18.9	73.0	35.9	14.0	78.9	43.9
India	5.6	88.9	66.2	4.0	91.3	69.9
Korea	14.0	77.8	34.2	12.8	78.8	34.2
Philippines	18.3	74.0	41.8	11.2	82.7	53.5

Source: Reprinted from Bouvier and Gardner 1986: 22–23.
[a]No more than 8 years of education.

3. Immigrants from India not only had much higher high school and college completion rates but also had the lowest proportion with no high school at all. Although low proportions of immigrants from the U.S.S.R. had attended or completed high school, a slightly higher percentage had completed college (17.1 percent as compared with 16.2 percent for all U.S. residents).

4. A general improvement in the level of schooling for immigrants is evident through time. For example, only 20 percent of those who arrived between 1970 and 1974 had completed college, compared with 24 percent for those who arrived between 1975 and 1979. This conclusion is, however, not true for Asian immigrants, and especially not for Indians. The percentage of Indians with no high school increased from 4 to 8.5 percent, and the percentage who had completed college fell from 69.9 to 56.9 percent. These numbers undoubtedly represent the Indian use of the combined family unification and occupational preference systems made possible by the 1965 INA amendments noted earlier. While family unification has lowered their average education level, Indians are still the best educated immigrants.

The Indian data thus support the so-called "wave theory" of immigration, which posits that the first immigrants or refugees tend to be the well educated from any emigrating population and that they are followed by the less well educated because of networking and family unification (Stein 1986). This theory was confirmed by a study of the parents of Indochinese students in San Diego schools (Kellog 1988: 202), which found average years of school attendance to be 9.5 years for immigrants who arrived before 1978, only 14 percent of whom spoke no English, compared with only 6.3 years for those who arrived between 1978 and 1983, a much larger 43 percent of whom spoke no English. Similarly, 80 percent of those who arrived between 1978 and 1983 had incomes below the poverty level, compared with only 34 percent of those who came before 1978.

A study of differences in the rates of assimilation of different immigrant groups by Jorge Chapa (1988) sheds further light on this issue. Using education and occupational status for first, second, and third generations, Chapa notes that for Mexican American immigrants aged 25–64 in 1979, there were substantial improvements in education for the second generation, but not much thereafter.

Table 4.7 shows the progress of immigrant groups of Asian, Mexican, and Anglo origin, as measured by education and occupational status. First-generation Asian immigrants had about twice as many years of education as Mexican immigrants. However, Asian-American educational attainment deteriorated between generations in the United States as a whole but improved in California, a state with heavy Asian and Mexican immigration. In fact, by the third generation, Asian Americans averaged

Table 4.7 Measures of Educational Attainment and Occupational Status, by Ethnic Group, Ages 25–64, California and U.S., 1979

	Asian		Mexican Origin		Anglo	
	Calif.	U.S.	Calif.	U.S.	Calif.	U.S.
Years of school						
1st generation	12.8	13.0	6.8	6.9	13.4	12.2
2nd generation	12.7	12.3	10.9	9.6	13.3	12.4
3rd generation	13.5	11.8	11.1	10.4	13.4	12.5
High school dropouts (%)						
1st generation	26.0	27.0	82.0	80.0	27.0	43.0
2nd generation	20.0	29.0	46.0	55.0	22.0	35.0
3rd generation	19.0	40.0	39.0	48.0	17.0	26.0
Occupational index[a] (100 = highest)						
1st generation	44	45	19	20	53	43
2nd generation	40	41	35	32	52	45
3rd generation	43	37	35	32	49	43

Source: Chapa 1988.

[a]Males only.

more years of schooling than did Anglos in California, but not in the United States as a whole. The assimilation of Asian Americans has clearly been more complete in California than in the rest of the country, at least as measured by the dropout rate, number of years of education, and occupational position. Indeed, the increase in the Asian-American high school dropout rate in the United States from 27 percent and 29 percent for the first and the second generation to 40 percent for the third generation is a matter that warrants careful study. It could be that Asian immigrants lose their heavy emphasis on education as they become Americanized—at least outside of California.

The indicators for immigrants of Mexican origin show a different pattern. First-generation immigrants have relatively low levels of education, but there is a significant improvement in the second generation, though not much improvement in the third generation. That the lack of educational attainment is an important factor in low earnings by third and third-plus generations of Mexican Americans is suggested by the fact that the earnings of Mexican-American high school dropout males aged 25–64 in California were only 67 percent of those of high school dropout Anglos as of 1979, down from 87 percent in 1970. By contrast, the

earnings of Mexican-American males who had completed high school
was on a par with that of Anglos (Chapa 1988).

Chapa drew the following conclusions from his detailed analysis of
Mexican Americans:

> A large part of the Mexican American population is not being as-
> similated. . . . A substantial portion of third generation Mexican
> Americans have educational levels that have shown no indication
> of converging with Anglo levels, and their earnings and occupa-
> tional status have decreased compared to those of Anglos. . . .
> Many Mexican Americans show indications of maintaining a
> separate social structure and subculture. . . . Mexican Americans
> with lower-level jobs . . . are much more likely to live in a struc-
> turally segregated society with a subculture that is different than
> Anglo culture. (Chapa 1988: 6)

In view of the fact that Mexicans comprise a large proportion of total
U.S. immigrants, this lack of assimilation of Mexican Americans warrants special attention from all who are concerned about the country's
future.

Income

For most economists, the best overall indicator of human capital is
income, though the indication may not necessarily be accurate at any
point in time. Data from the 1980 census (Table 4.8) show the median
income of full-time immigrant workers from Asia, Africa, and the
U.S.S.R. to have been above the median for all U.S. residents, while immigrants from Latin America, especially those from Mexico, had substantially lower median incomes. The absence of European statistics prevents comparison of incomes of all *full-time* workers, but the median
income of *all* workers (i.e., full time and part time) was lower for immigrants ($10,542) than for all U.S. residents ($12,192). There are, however, some differences in the patterns, reflecting a relatively lower incidence of full-time work by immigrants from the Philippines and Korea.
Note, however, that female workers from the Philippines do better relative to all U.S. residents, while the opposite is true for males. This probably reflects the high number of nurses from the Philippines working in
the United States.

Should We Rely on Immigration to Meet Our Human Capital Needs?

It is widely assumed that immigration can be used to meet a large
part of our human capital requirements, as it has for much of our history.

Table 4.8 Median Income of Immigrant Workers Aged 15 and Over, 1979

	Males		Females	
Region and Country of Birth	Median Income All Workers	Median Income Full-Time Workers	Median Income All Workers	Median Income Full-Time Workers
Total U.S.	$12,192	$17,363	$5,263	$10,380
All immigrants	10,542	—	5,094	—
Europe	12,344	—	4,850	—
U.S.S.R.	9,465	20,098	4,344	12,034
Africa	11,003	18,014	5,760	11,093
North America	13,539	21,091	5,218	12,062
Latin America	9,019	12,255	5,184	8,681
Mexico	8,192	10,809	4,442	7,408
Asia	11,412	17,557	6,328	11,384
India	18,421	22,649	7,162	13,138
Korea	12,111	17,607	6,011	10,092
Philippines	11,190	15,240	8,713	12,715

Source: Reprinted from Bouvier and Gardner 1986: 25.

This assumption is based on the belief that the slowdown in population and work force growth because of the decline in fertility of U.S. residents, the aging of our population, and the "birth dearth" that followed the 1946–64 baby boom will create general labor shortages in the 1990s and beyond. Even those who do not foresee a general labor shortage nevertheless predict shortages in particular industries and occupations that could be detrimental to the U.S. economy. Some proponents of this position advocate increased immigration and/or "guest worker" programs to meet these needs. These assumptions will be explored in this section.

Does Immigration Have Positive or Negative Effects on U.S. Labor Markets?

William Johnston and Arnold Packer (1987: 93) are among those who argue that immigrants will be needed to compensate for the slow growth in the American work force during the 1990s and beyond. These influential analysts cite evidence from an Urban Institute study of Los Angeles, discussed below, to support the conclusion that legal immigration of 450,000 to 750,000 would be beneficial and "need not overwhelm the 'carrying capacity' of the country." These authors believe that immigrants are "complementary to, rather than in competition with, native minority workers." Moreover, immigrants will be needed, they argue, because employment growth of 21 million new jobs by the end of the century will outrun projected increases in the labor force. Similarly, the Reagan administration's Council of Economic Advisers (1986: 374) believed that immigration will be good for the economy; it reported that "there is evidence that immigration has increased job opportunities and wage levels for other workers."

Most of those who argue that illegal immigration is beneficial to the country admit that it has a negative impact (usually termed "slight" or "small") on low-income workers but argue that these negatives are more than offset by the benefits to other workers. These models usually are based on very restricted assumptions and often assume that immigrants are complementary to (and not substitutes for) more highly skilled American workers. According to the principle of complementarity, the productivity of any factor increases the greater the supply of the complementary factor with which it works. As Chiswick (1988: 1,907) argues: "although one native factor loses and the other native factors gain, the overall income of the native population increases; the losses to native low-skilled labor are offset by the gains to native high-skilled labor and capital." Chiswick notes, however, that even under these restrictive assumptions, "the average income of the total population (natives and immigrants) in the immigration receiving country has declined. More importantly, perhaps, the inequality of incomes in the destination country has increased: there are more low-skilled workers and the unskilled workers have lower average income." [3]

The Rand and Urban Institute Studies

The nature of the problems involved in reaching meaningful conclusions about the impact of immigration can be illustrated by examining two studies widely cited as having demonstrated the large positive and "small" negative effects of immigration on American labor markets, one by the Rand Corporation (McCarthy and Valdez 1985), and the other (entitled *The Fourth Wave*) by the Urban Institute (Muller and Espenshade 1985). The Rand report concludes: "Overall Mexican immigration has probably been an economic asset to the state, in that it has stimulated employment growth and kept wages competitive. Potential displacement effects have been relatively minor except perhaps among low-skilled, native-born Latinos."

The two studies deal with the nature and effects of legal and illegal migration from Mexico to California, particularly Southern California. Reading the summaries, one gains the impression that the effects range from nil to beneficial, but a deeper look, particularly at the Urban Institute study, supports a different conclusion.

Extent of immigration. Using conservative approaches and relatively sturdy government statistics (largely from the census), the Urban Institute study estimates that about one-fifth of California's population in 1983 was foreign-born; about half this group of 4.7 million persons arrived in the state in the 13 years after 1970 (at a rate of about 180,000 a year). Dealing with the period 1970–80, the authors estimate some 1,868,000 census-enumerated post-1970 immigrants, of whom the majority (1,087,000) were illegally present. In addition, census undercount data suggest that another 493,000 undocumented aliens were present but missed by the census. Thus, the Urban Institute finds that there were more than 1.5 million undocumented immigrants in California in 1980, with that population rising by about 100,000 per year. This would bring the total to over 2 million in 1986 (Muller and Espenshade 1985). These are large, serious numbers, carefully handled;[4] and while the techniques used probably understate the size of the illegal immigrant population, they do give us a reasonable lower limit for the size of this population in California.

Labor market effects. Many people believe, as I do, that there are two different but related impacts of immigration on American labor markets: the *displacement* effect, in which legal residents lose their jobs (or do not secure new ones) because of competition from the undocumented workers; and the *depression* effect, in which low-productivity marginal jobs are perpetuated and legal residents work for lower wages than they otherwise would have had there been no undocumented workers.

What do these studies tell us about the impact of recent immigration from Mexico on labor markets? Both show (the Urban Institute study with stunning effect) that these immigrants depressed wages in the segments of the labor markets where they clustered. On the question of displacement, the Urban Institute points out that the newly arrived Mexican immigrants largely worked in blue-collar jobs and "although unskilled blue-collar employment expanded by only 71,000 [in Los Angeles County between 1970 and 1980], Mexicans held 116,000 such jobs and other immigrants another 52,000. Clearly the number of persons other than recent immigrants holding these jobs actually declined" (Muller and Espenshade 1985: 56).

Similarly, "net manufacturing employment [in Los Angeles County] rose by 113,000 during the 1970s but because immigrants arriving since 1970 held 168,000 manufacturing jobs in 1980, there must have been a net decline of 55,000 jobs among other workers" (Muller and Espenshade 1985: 58). Looking at the entire labor market in Los Angeles County, the report tells us that recent immigrants absorbed fully two-thirds of the 645,000 jobs added to the economy during the decade. Further, as noted subsequently (and as I had not realized), large numbers of blue-collar workers migrated out of Los Angeles County during the 1970s.

Looking beyond the numbers in these studies, unemployment rates in

Table 4.9 Comparison of Wages, Los Angeles County and the United States, 1972 and 1980

	Los Angeles Wages, 1980	Increase in L.A. Wages, 1972–80 as percentage of U.S. Wage Increase	Mexican Immigrants as percentage of All Workers, 1980
All workers	$15,594	108.8	9.9
Low-wage manufacturing[a]	5.06[b]	76.7	47.1[b]
High-wage manufacturing[c]	7.97[b]	90.7	19.5[b]
All retail	9,469	108.3	9.5
Eating and drinking establishments (restaurants, bars)	5,591	89.1	16.8
All other retail	11,196	108.4	6.6
All services	14,099	115.8	5.5
Hotels, etc.	7,312[d]	95.1	15.0[d]
Personal services	8,069	92.2	15.2
All other services	14,659	117.2	3.9
Finance, insurance, and real estate	15,590	104.4	2.6

Source: Reprinted from Muller and Espenshade 1985: table 13.

[a]Includes leather goods, apparel, textile mills, lumber and wood, and furniture and fixture industries.

[b]Hourly wages include only production workers.

[c]Includes metals, machinery, stone, clay, and glass; food; and transportation equipment industries.

[d]Estimated.

California were above the national average for 12 of the 14 years covered by the Urban Institute study (1970–83), sometimes by more than 2 full percentage points (Statistical Abstracts of the U.S., various years). While factors other than international migration undoubtedly played a role, those data are at least compatible with the conclusion that there was some displacement.

Both reports agree on the second labor-market effect, the depression of wages, with the Urban Institute's *The Fourth Wave* presenting new and convincing data on this point. The Urban Institute has measured the apparent impact of heavy migration on Los Angeles County in an interesting way. The first of the two following tables (Table 4.9), reprinted from *The Fourth Wave*, shows that in low-wage manufacturing, Los Angeles

County workers received only 76.7 percent of the wage increase recorded nationally; furthermore, in this sector immigrants from Mexico accounted for a remarkable 47.1 percent of the county's work force. In contrast, when dealing with all Los Angeles County workers vis-à-vis all U.S. workers, county wages increased 8.78 percent faster than those of the nation at large. In the county as a whole, recent Mexican immigrants constituted only 9.9 percent of the labor force.

Examining the data another way, the report states: "Relative average wages of unskilled workers in the Los Angeles manufacturing sector have declined dramatically—from 2 percent *above* the U.S. metropolitan average in 1969 and 1970 to 12 percent *below* the average a decade later" (Muller and Espenshade 1985: 110).

The direct relationship between relative wage increases in Los Angeles County and the percentage of Mexican immigrants in a given sector of the labor market is shown in an adaptation of the *Fourth Wave* table presented by Frank Loy of the German Marshall Fund (1986). Loy's recasting (in Table 4.10) shows that as the percentage of Mexican immigrants in a labor market sector falls, the wage increases rise to meet, and then pass, the national average. In this instance at least, the more immigrants, the lower the wage increases.

While factory workers' wages were lower in California than in the nation on average, this does not seem to indicate that their productivity was comparably lower. The Urban Institute report says that the rate of wage increase for low-wage Hispanic factory workers in Los Angeles was 16 percent less than the national average for all workers but that worker productivity was only 6 percent less than in the nation as a whole, so Los Angeles employers secured more for their wage dollar than their competitors elsewhere in the nation (Muller and Espenshade 1985: 113).

Rand's report concludes that "overall, the immigrants provide economic benefits to the state, and native-born Latinos may bear the brunt of competition for low-skill jobs" (McCarthy and Valdez 1985: vii). A little later the Rand study continues: "Our evidence suggests that Mexican immigrants may actually have stimulated manufacturing employment by keeping wage levels competitive" (p. 20). This leads to the next point.

Effects on the Industrial Mix of California and the Nation

According to the Rand report, "in the United States as a whole, manufacturing employment grew modestly during the 1970s—significantly less than in California or in its principal manufacturing center, Los Angeles. Although several factors may have contributed to California's and Los Angeles' superior performance, one factor that certainly played a

Table 4.10   The Higher the Percentage of Mexican Immigrants in a Los Angeles Labor Market, the Lower the Increase in Wages, 1972–1980

Category	Mexican Immigrants as Percentage of All Workers, 1980	Increase in L.A. Wages, 1972–80, Compared to U.S. Wage Increase[a] (%)	Los Angeles Wages, 1980
Low-wage manufacturing	47.1	−23.3%	$ 5.06/hr
High-wage manufacturing	19.5	− 9.3%	$ 7.97/hr
Eating and drinking establishments	16.8	−10.1%	$ 5,591/yr
Personal services	15.2	− 7.8%	$ 8,069/yr
Hotels	15.0	− 4.9%	$ 7,132/yr
All workers	9.9	+ 8.8%	$15,594/yr[b]
All retail	9.5	+ 8.3%	$ 9,469/yr
All other retail	6.6	+ 8.4%	$11,196/yr
All services	5.5	+15.8%	$14,099/yr
All other services	3.9	+17.2%	$14,659/yr
Finance, insurance, and real estate	2.6	+ 4.4%	$15,590/yr

Source: Reproduced from Loy 1986. For full original text, sources, and footnotes, see Table 4.9 above.

[a]The second column in this table is expressed as deviations from the U.S. norm of wage increases in the period 1972–80, and is derived from the second column of the *Fourth Wave* table.

[b]This number, the average wage level, appears to be considerably higher than one would expect from reading the other numbers; Loy has explained, however, that several high-wage sectors of the labor market (such as construction and transportation) were not included in the original table, which makes the average wage shown here plausible.

significant role was slower wage growth" (McCarthy and Valdez 1985: 20). If manufacturing, particularly apparel and furniture, have grown rapidly in Los Angeles while shrinking elsewhere, there is at least a suspicion that someone has been hurt: the workers, managers, and owners of the firms that had formerly operated outside California.

As Vernon Briggs (1975) and others have pointed out, illegal immigration shapes labor markets as well as responding to them. In fact, illegal immigration restructures the very nature of the local and national economy, distorting, for example, the investment decisions made in labor-intensive industries such as the garment industry, tilting investment towards Los Angeles and away from the rest of the country. In the short run the winners would seem to be the Los Angeles factory owners who are getting the de facto wage subsidies from the presence of the undocumenteds; but in the long run the situation does not bode well for healthy economic growth in the nation, the state of California, the county of Los Angeles, and perhaps even the firms now relying on the illegal immigrants. These investment decisions retain, temporarily, some marginal low-wage jobs in the United States that otherwise might disappear or move to the Third World. It is, however, very unrealistic to assume that the United States can compete in even minimum-wage jobs in those products where wages constitute the principal source of competitive advantage. The only hope for competitiveness in the international market on terms that will maintain American living standards is to improve productivity and quality through mechanization, skill upgrading, or improved management and production systems, all of which are discouraged by a steady flow of illegal, low-wage migrants.[5]

Internal migration. One may have the image of Southern California, generally, and Los Angeles, specifically, as the magnet for Americans living in less blessed places. The Urban Institute study suggests that this is only partly accurate: that blue-collar workers, both non-Hispanic white and Hispanic, presumably largely legal residents, are leaving Los Angeles in droves, apparently largely because of competition from the newly arrived immigrant workers.

The Fourth Wave reports that while in the five-year period 1955–60 there was a net migration to California from other states of more than 1,122,000, in the 13-year period 1970–83 the net migration to California fell to a statistically insignificant 11,000. Who was leaving? During this time there were, among other movements, a net inflow of 205,000 white-collar workers and a net loss of 134,000 blue-collar workers. The report concludes: "The similarity between the socioeconomic characteristics of the people leaving California and the characteristics of Mexican immigrants suggests that the flow from Mexico may have substituted for internal migration" (Muller and Espenshade 1985: 53).[6]

Taxpayer costs. Both reports deal with the taxes paid by and the public services used by immigrant households. (The Urban Institute's careful analysis was, more precisely, of Los Angeles County households headed by Mexican immigrants, with the understanding that some to many members of such households are native-born children of such immigrants.)

The Rand report concluded: "In general, immigrants contribute more to public revenues than they consumed in public services; however, the youthfulness of the population, their low incomes, the progressiveness of the state income tax structure and the high costs of public education produce a net deficit in educational expenditures" (McCarthy and Valdez 1985: vii). But, as Roger Conner has noted, "saying that illegal aliens contribute in taxes more than they use in benefits 'except for education' is like saying the U.S. budget is balanced except for defense spending" (FAIR 1986: 1).

Using a variety of data sources, the Urban Institute study estimated the costs incurred and the taxes received by state and local governments during 1980 for Mexican immigrant households in Los Angeles County. They found the following:

	State	County	Total
Revenues	$1,425	$1,172	$2,597
Expenditures	3,204	1,638	4,842
Fiscal gap	−1,779	−466	−2,245

These data do not take into account substantial amounts of federal funds passed through state and local government. Even so, as the report says, "benefits received outweighed taxes paid by a factor of nearly 2 to 1" (Muller and Espenshade 1985: 143).

Impacts on Hispanic and Black Workers

While both reports indicate that because of the heavy immigration, resident Hispanic workers—particularly those with blue-collar jobs— were paid less than they would have been otherwise, the Urban Institute study suggests that this statement could not be extended to blacks. The explanation offered is that many blacks had moved into clerical jobs, where there is relatively little competition from Mexican immigrants. The report's analysis of labor force participation rates of black adults and teenagers shows few adverse effects from immigration; similarly, the rates of wage increases for Los Angeles County blacks were close to the national norms (over the period studied), unlike those of Hispanics, which were often only 60 percent or so of the country-wide averages (Muller and Espenshade 1985: 96).

I would argue, however, from the Urban Institute's data, that black blue-collar workers suffer indirect displacement because of the extensive international migration to Los Angeles County. The in-migration rate of blacks to California slowed, according to *Fourth Wave* statistics, and those migrating were highly self-selected to deploy in the white-collar sections of the labor market still unencumbered by Mexican immigrants.[7] Elsewhere in the United States, moreover, blacks are well represented in some of those industries that employ large numbers of undocumented workers in Los Angeles. While many of those industries are in decline elsewhere in the nation (e.g., textile manufacturing in the Carolinas), blacks are not often candidates for these jobs when the work, in effect, moves to Southern California. Illegal Mexican immigration has thus foreclosed an option for unemployed black, blue-collar workers.

Impact of Legal Status

Some analysts make the very questionable assumption that legal status makes no difference in labor market impacts. There are, however, at least four levels of legal status which bear heavily on the impact of immigration on California:

- At the bottom are the illegal aliens, who have few rights in the labor market and who cannot legally draw welfare benefits.
- Next are the legal (green-card) immigrants, with many labor market rights and, after a few years, full rights to welfare benefits.
- Then there are the refugees, with the same labor market rights as the immigrants, but even more complete access to welfare than citizens.
- Finally, there are the citizens, both native-born and naturalized, who have full access to welfare systems and more access to jobs than anyone else (in that they are the only class that can work in government offices and in defense plants, which are numerous in California).

One of the reasons blacks living in California have apparently been less harmed than resident Hispanics by the massive immigration to Southern California is their legal status. Virtually all blacks are citizens. They can and do work in government offices—federal, state, and local—and in defense factories, and they vote, join unions, and otherwise attempt to protect their rights. Mexican nationals, on the other hand, are much less likely to seek naturalization than other immigrants. Hence, many of them cannot compete for jobs in the public sector. That the blacks are English-speaking is, of course, another advantage.

Conclusions on Labor Market Impacts

In any discussion of immigration, it is very important to distinguish between legal and illegal immigration. Whatever its economic effects, there is no justification for *illegal* immigration in a society that believes in the rule of law. If immigration is in the national interest, it should be done legally.

There can be little doubt that immigration displaces workers, though not on a one-to-one basis. The degree of displacement clearly depends on the looseness or tightness of labor markets, the ratio of immigrants to nonimmigrants in those markets, and the nature of those markets. When unemployment is very low, as during World War II or in engineering and other professional fields in the 1980s, there is less displacement. In fact, it could be argued that in very tight labor markets, or where the immigrants have skills not available among unemployed legal residents, immigration facilitates economic growth. In loose markets, by contrast, there is little question that immigrants displace other workers, as both the Urban Institute and Rand studies show.

As noted, however, no study of the economic effects of immigration is able to hold everything else constant. This makes it very difficult for standard economic and labor market analytical techniques to factor out the independent effects of immigration. In particular, there is evidence that some employers prefer immigrants because they are, at least for a time, less likely than are long-time residents and citizens to be dissatisfied with wages and working conditions that, however bad by U.S. standards, are likely to look good relative to those in their home countries. It is understandable that many employers prefer the foreign workers who have limited options and therefore are more easily forced to work scared and hard. However, we must consider the basic policy question of whether or not legal residents and refugees should be subjected to this kind of competition. I do not think they should be. It is, moreover, very hard to protect labor standards in situations where workers are afraid to complain. For that reason, I favor vigorous enforcement of labor standards as well as tighter controls of illegal immigration.

Elementary economics suggests that in labor markets with high unemployment, increased labor supplies depress wages and reduce employment opportunities for legal residents, unless you assume, unrealistically, completely segregated labor markets. Advocates of continued illegal immigration often argue that the immigrants only take jobs legal residents will not accept. There are several things wrong with that argument. First, there are no such jobs—there is no job category in the United States filled entirely by illegal immigrants. Second, employers have other options—they can raise wages, mechanize, go offshore, or go out of business. In the long run, marginal industries can only be competitive if they are subsidized by American workers or (if we decide to protect them from international competition) by consumers. Improving productivity is particularly important. The United States has done fairly well in job creation, but, as noted later, we have not done as well relative to other countries in maintaining productivity and real wage growth. We will not be able to reverse this situation so long as we perpetuate marginal industries that depend on easily exploitable people for their existence.

Some try to justify illegal immigration on the grounds that illegal immigrants pay more taxes than they burden public revenues. Some studies suggest that for selective public programs this might be true, but the more careful Urban Institute work described above suggests that this is not so, at least for Los Angeles County. Moreover, even those studies that do show net positive fiscal effects miss two important points: the effects of displacement and depressed wages on legal residents, and the dynamic nature of the immigration process. Studies assuming that illegals always will be young, unmarried people without families have a strange view of human behavior and demographics—people will start families and grow older, and many illegals will be legalized. So, a snap-shot at any time misses this dynamic. But from my perspective, this argument misses the main point: it is *not* whether or not illegals produce net fiscal benefits, but whether people use the services they need. It is not at all comforting to be told that because of their illegal status, undocumented workers are afraid to use public services. This is one of the reasons there is absolutely no justification for illegal immigration. If people come into the United States they should do so legally, with the full legal rights of residents.

We also should note the differential impact of immigration on different groups in the receiving country. Employers are the clear gainers, at least in the short run. In the long run, it is questionable that employers who depend on wage subsidies will be competitive. I believe they would be better off mechanizing those operations that depend on subsidized labor. The clear losers are those workers in the developed countries who compete most directly with the immigrants. These ordinarily are other recent immigrants and other workers in secondary labor markets, usu-ally women, minorities, and young workers with limited skills. Consum-ers in receiving countries could conceivably gain, but here again we must consider the alternatives. Consumers probably would be at least as well off importing many of these products from low-wage countries. Whether the country as a whole is better off with immigrants depends on whether the social benefits of immigration outweigh the social costs. I believe that the social benefits of *legal* immigration have in general outweighed the costs, but that more explicit immigration and human capital strategies could see to it that immigration is a mutually beneficial process. For reasons discussed below, I do not believe policies that cause the costs of immigration to be borne mainly by low-wage American workers or that assume unlimited immigration, legal or illegal, are in the national interest.

Finally, we should note that some defend illegal immigration because of their concern about the welfare of Mexican and other workers who are compelled by conditions in their home countries to come to the United States illegally. I fully share this concern and believe that the United States and other developed countries should pay much more attention to this problem than they do. (For a development of this point, see Marshall 1988a.) The United States should work with the developing countries to produce the kind of economic development that is in our mutual interests, which generally means a full-employment, human-resource development strategy. A broader view of our own self-interest requires that we support efforts to improve economic growth, fight job-lessness, and improve working conditions in these countries. But this should be done through national and international economic institutions; it definitely should not be done at the expense of those low-wage American workers who can least afford to extend aid to these developing countries.

Immigration and Economic Competitiveness

Beyond its impact on various groups within a country, immigration must also be judged in the context of its broader implications for the competitiveness of the U.S. economy. This issue, too, is very much in dispute, but there is growing evidence that key facets of traditional U.S. economic practice and immigration policy must change if the United States is not to lose its competitive position further in the years ahead. Space will not permit a detailed discussion of the circumstances requiring changes, but they might be outlined as follows.

The United States is now a high-wage country, and the traditional mass production system is much less viable in high-wage countries. This system stressed economies of scale, oligopolistic pricing, the use of natural resources, standardized technology, fragmented work assignments, an authoritarian management system, and relatively unskilled workers. It was originally made possible in the United States by a large internal market and abundant natural resources. Unionization and the adversarial bargaining system made it possible for workers with limited formal educations to share in oligopolistic profits and economies of scale and to achieve relatively high (middle-class) incomes. Favorable economic circumstances also made it possible for the United States to absorb large numbers of relatively uneducated immigrants and refugees, as well as others whose human capital endowments were higher than the U.S. average.

Internationalization and technological change have made the traditional system obsolete. Oligopolistic pricing made U.S. firms vulnerable to companies in other countries that gave more attention to quality, productivity, price competition, and flexibility. Technological change made it possible to practice flexible manufacturing, permitting companies to target markets. A new system has developed, which is predominantly market driven, while the traditional system was predominantly producer driven. The opening of the U.S. markets to producers in Japan and other countries made it difficult for mass producers to continue to achieve economies of scale in the large internal U.S. market. The Japanese and others who emulated early U.S. policies acquired the advantages of mass production by restricting access to their own markets (thus making it possible to achieve more economies of scale) while penetrating American and other relatively open markets. The greater mobility of technology caused standardized production processes to move to suitable low-wage places that could use that technology. The ideological commitment to free trade made it difficult for the United States to use access to the U.S. market as a means of opening the Japanese and other relatively closed markets. Technological change also increased output-to-natural resource ratios, improving the terms of trade of resource-poor countries like Germany and Japan relative to the United States and resource-oriented Third World countries.

Competitiveness, within the new system, can take many forms. As noted, competition can be in terms of wages; for a high-wage country, such competition implies a decline in individual income. The alternative is to compete by increasing productivity, finding market niches, improving quality, and being more flexible. The evidence also suggests the importance of developing and using leading-edge technology.

Therefore, the United States can either improve its competitive position by improving productivity, quality, flexibility, and efficiency through better management and improved technology; or it can compete by reducing wages. There is, moreover, growing agreement that marginal low-wage industry using standardized technology will not be viable in the United States and other high-wage countries. We must therefore be adaptable (i.e., shift resources from noncompetitive to more competitive activities) as well as flexible (i.e., provide for rapid response to demand within companies). Countries that have adapted quickly, like Japan, Sweden, and most of the Pacific Rim countries, have been able to rapidly improve productivity by moving into more productive industries. Similarly, the most competitive firms are those that have had the internal flexibility to quickly adjust to shifting demand.

The development and use of leading-edge technology will require a work force with higher-order thinking skills than were required for the more stable and static mass production system, where much work was routine. Moreover, the pervasiveness of the information technology means that a much larger proportion of the work force must have higher-order thinking skills. This means that workers will have to learn to deal with change, be more self-managed, be able to analyze the greater amounts of data made possible by the information technology, communicate with considerable precision, and be able to deal with abstract thinking. Much of the routine work will be done by machines or shifted to lower-wage countries and places.

The immigration of people into the United States legally and illegally who have very low levels of education works in the opposite direction. As noted earlier, illegal immigration and the heavy emphasis on family unification, especially of distant relatives, combine to reduce the nation's human capital pool.

Conclusions and Recommendations

While our data and analysis are necessarily rough, they nevertheless support several conclusions about immigration and human capital.

Positive Effects of Immigration on Human Capital Formation

First, immigration has a number of positive implications for human capital formation:

1. Immigrants, especially the first waves and generations, seem generally to be highly motivated.
2. Immigrants add to the diversity of the American population, which is an important factor in creativity, innovation, and the quality of life.
3. The immigration of highly skilled, highly educated people makes it possible for the United States to acquire the social returns from education without having paid the costs. In fact, immigration has played a very important, if not critical, role in the scientific preeminence of the United States and the world class quality of many of our research and higher education institutions (Hamburg 1985).
4. Where there are labor shortages, immigration can promote growth and improve productivity and total output.
5. Immigration reduces the average age of the American population and therefore helps increase the ratio of workers to retirees.
6. The immigration of highly skilled, educated, motivated people improves our human capital pool.
7. Immigrants have made major contributions to American arts and entertainment and have greatly improved the quality of life in America.

Negative Effects of Immigration on Human Capital Formation

Immigration can also have some negative effects on capital formation, however.

1. The importation of uneducated, unskilled people and their families can depress wages, and perpetuate poverty among immigrants and others in secondary labor markets.
2. Dependence on cheap foreign labor could retard the adjustment of human and physical resources out of industries whose viability depends mainly on low wages, making it more difficult for these people to acquire the human capital they need to maintain and improve their incomes in a more highly competitive, internationalized, knowledge-based economy.

3. As our data on education, income, and occupations suggest, immigration contributes to the growing polarization of income in the United States, which already has wider extremes in wealth and income than any other major industrial country.

4. Immigration could exacerbate political and social divisions over language, race, religion, and ethnicity. Fragmentation makes it very difficult for the political process to promote educational equity and human capital formation. Racial and ethnic conflict leads to such elitist myths as "achievement is mainly due to innate ability," which makes it difficult to generate support for human capital investments.

5. Immigrants with low levels of education, skill, and English-language proficiency could burden already strained educational resources, especially since immigration is highly concentrated geographically. Immigration could therefore make it much more difficult to achieve educational equity and school reform.

6. The emigration of highly educated, skilled, and motivated people from other countries, especially in the Third World, could cause financial drains on those countries (because they pay for, but do not receive, the returns on their human capital investments) and could impair the economic, social, and political development of those countries. Some Mexican immigration experts have concluded that the flow of undocumented workers out of Mexico into the United States has shifted from a "safety valve" for Mexico to a "labor force drain" (Bustamente 1987). Francisco Alba (1985) concludes, however, that the migrants have more education than the average Mexican laborer and often some job training, but do not constitute a "brain drain."

Balancing the Positives and Negatives: Recommendations for Action

Immigration Policy

There is no way—without better information and analysis than we now have—to tell whether or not the positives or negatives predominate. But based on my reading of the evidence, my conclusions and recommendations are as follows.

There probably will be some selective labor shortages for the rest of this century. The Bureau of Labor Statistics expects employment to grow at about 1.3 percent a year while the work force expands at an annual rate of 1.2 percent, implying tighter labor markets, especially of educated and skilled workers. Given present rates of legal and illegal immigration, foreign workers will fill over 20 percent of these new positions. It is highly unlikely, however, that there will be shortages of unskilled labor. The American labor force has always been extremely resilient. We should, however, give high priority to preventing the growth of (and re-

ducing the size of) the large underclass of young people who are generally outside our legal economy. Dependence on highly motivated—even
docile—foreign workers provides very limited incentive for business or
political leaders to address this very serious problem. It would be in the
nation's long-term interest to create shortages of unskilled labor.

Expanded immigration should not be allowed to interfere with the
urgent business of reforming American schools and providing educational equity for immigrants and members of minority groups. Un-
checked immigration of illegals and distant family members with low
levels of human capital could overburden the system, which already will
have great difficulty generating the resources to provide high-quality education for all legal residents.

With proper policies, the United States probably could continue to
absorb the present flow of immigrants. However, we should maintain the
following safeguards.

First, labor market tests should be applied to more workers, and improved methods should be devised to protect U.S. workers. Applying
labor market tests to prevent damage to residents of the United States is
the best way to see to it that the positive effects of immigration outweigh
the negative, but so far our labor market test procedures for doing this
have been cumbersome, inefficient, fraudulent, and unfair.

Second, we should avoid large guest worker programs. The United
States' main experience with temporary foreign workers on a large scale
was the "bracero" program, mentioned earlier, which resulted from a
wartime agreement between the United States and Mexico. This program
continued in various forms until 1964, and not only resulted in widespread abuse of the braceros and adverse effects on U.S. workers but also
contributed to increased illegal immigration after the program was ter-
minated in 1964. Similar experience abroad led the Select Commission
on Immigration and Refugee Policy to vote down, by a large majority, a
proposal that measures to curb illegal immigration should be accompanied by a large-scale foreign-workers program. Conversations with labor
ministers in Western Europe disclosed that most of them wished they had
never adopted such programs. Moreover, discussions with officials of
many sending countries revealed that they had rarely realized the benefits
expected from guest worker programs. The younger, better-educated
workers tend to emigrate permanently, and returning migrants do not
increase productive investment because they usually have heavy preferences for expensive consumer durables, and return when unemployment
already is high. The main advantage of these programs is temporary help
with balance of payments while the sending countries' citizens work in
the receiving countries. The sending countries also began to realize that
emigration tended to deplete their human capital resources, since they
were losing some of their most productive people, in whom they had

invested scarce capital. There is therefore general agreement that it would be a mistake for a country to take in large numbers of workers who would have inferior legal and labor market status. If workers are needed, it would be much better to bring them in as immigrants with full legal status.

Third, enforcement of IRCA should be strengthened by closing the identifying-documents loopholes, preventing fraud in the SAW program, and strengthening the penalties against the illegal immigrants themselves. Without these changes, it is highly doubtful that the IRCA will do much to halt the flow of illegal immigrants into the United States.

Fourth, a point system should be developed—similar to the Kennedy-Simpson bill—that would give more weight to occupational preferences and put an overall cap on immigration until we can improve the present system and get a better assessment of its impact.

Fifth, U.S. immigration policy should be careful not to impede the economic development of the developing countries by encouraging a "brain drain" or even a drain of workers who can find adequate employment with reasonable policies in their home countries. Not only is it in our interest for Third World countries to develop; we are not likely to have sustained economic growth and prosperity unless these countries restore the kind of growth they had in the 1970s (Marshall 1988a). Our economic policies should be designed to achieve the restoration of growth, through trade, investment, and the creation of institutions and policies conducive to an open and expanding international economy. Our immigration policies should support these policy objectives. At the same time, treating immigration as a "safety valve" weakens the necessity for Third World leaders to develop the kinds of policies that will provide balanced employment growth in those countries.

A Human Capital Strategy for Immigrant Groups

In addition to measures to ensure greater attention to the human capital endowments of immigrants before they come to the United States, U.S. policy should stress measures to improve the human capital development of immigrants who are already here. This is important because immigrants, especially Hispanics, will be a rapidly growing proportion of our total work force. The number of Hispanics will probably double between 1985 and 2020—from 16 million to 31 million. This will happen whether or not we bring illegal immigration under control. By 2020 there will be 91 million minority group members in the United States, 3 million more Hispanics than blacks; they will be 34 percent of our population, up from 17 percent in 1987. A second reason for greater attention to the human capital needs of minorities is their importance for economic competitiveness. As Schultz has demonstrated, people will either be assets or liabilities. Educated, healthy, motivated people will be unlimited assets (Schultz 1988). Moreover, Schultz and others have demonstrated that the returns to human capital are higher than the returns to physical capital. And, as Berlin and Sum (1988) have demonstrated, low educational achievement is closely correlated with such social pathologies as crime, teenage pregnancies, high dropout rates, drug and alcohol abuse, low incomes, and unemployment. This means, of course, that failure to address the human capital needs of immigrants will be very costly to nonimmigrants in terms of quality of life as well as economics. It would therefore be very unwise to deny education, health care, or other social services to immigrants.

A human capital strategy for immigrants should be based on the following considerations.

First, policies should be targeted, because different groups have different needs. Asians, for example, seem to be more quickly assimilated into the work force and population than other groups, as Jorge Chapa (1988) has demonstrated. Among immigrants, Mexicans have particularly serious problems. Special efforts should therefore be made to develop policies to assimilate Mexicans into the U.S. work force more effectively. While all of the reasons for the disadvantages Mexican immigrants face are not clear, language is clearly a major factor. Present resources to provide language instruction to adult immigrants are grossly inadequate, mainly because of inadequate federal funding for this purpose. Efforts also should be made to work with Hispanic organizations to strengthen adult education for immigrants.

Second, special attention needs to be given to the health and education of immigrant children. These measures should start with early childhood and prenatal programs, such as Head Start and the Special Supplemental Food Program for Women, Infants, and Children, both of which are high-yield public investments that serve only about 20 to 50 percent of those who are eligible (CED 1987). Education programs at every level should be sensitive to the special problems of immigrant children—many of whom have serious emotional and physical problems, as well as language problems. Schools and teacher-training institutions should train teachers and counselors to deal with the special problems immigrant children face. Language policies, especially, should be guided mainly by what is required to help immigrant children learn English and other subjects most effectively. It makes sense to allow basic subjects to be taught in students' native tongue while they are learning English. Other subjects (art, physical education) should be taught only in English. Moreover, experience suggests that parental involvement is important to student learning, and some immigrants would not be able to help their children unless they were able to study in their native languages.

Third, those responsible for implementing school reforms currently under way should be particularly alert to avoid damage to immigrants.

The development of standardized achievement tests has sometimes been particularly detrimental to Hispanics and blacks. There is a special need to see to it that immigrant children have teachers they can relate to and regard as role models. Special efforts therefore should be made to have teachers or teachers' aides who speak the immigrant children's language and understand their culture. Schools and community organizations should develop approaches that reduce racial and cultural conflict and cause students to appreciate differences.

Fourth, more needs to be done to reduce the dropout rate of Mexican-American students. Although a number of approaches have been developed to reduce these rates, they are still the highest of any major group. Giving teachers and schools greater flexibility and autonomy to improve educational achievement would help all students, especially those with special learning problems. This is particularly likely to be true if progress with immigrants and other students with special problems were made a specific area by which teachers and schools would be judged in a performance-based system.

Fifth, a national youth service program could help immigrant children by providing more human capital services to them and allowing them to become more involved in working with nonimmigrant students in joint service activities. The Intercultural Development Research Association's (IDRA) Valued Youth program in San Antonio demonstrates the potential of one approach. This program was funded by the Coca-Cola Company and implemented by IDRA. The basic objective was to encourage learning in a population of Hispanic-American children with a dropout rate of about 45 percent. High school and junior high school students who were at risk of dropping out were used to tutor elementary school students, who also were at risk of dropping out. The first year of the program, there were 100 tutors and only 6 dropped out. The next year, there were 150 tutors and none dropped out. The learning of both the tutors and those tutored improved. National service, whether military or civilian, should have educational entitlement attached, making it possible for immigrant participants to finance higher education.

Sixth, immigrant human capital formation could be enhanced by "second-chance" learning systems for the non-college-bound. National service is one such program. Another valuable program is the Job Corps, which has developed especially efficient English, reading, mathematics, and job skill development programs. These activities have been particularly beneficial to immigrants. The Job Corps should therefore be doubled in size, and special efforts should be made to apply the lessons learned in the Job Corps to other groups.

Because the education of immigrants is likely to be more costly than that of nonimmigrants, there will be a temptation to avoid these targeted approaches. This would be a huge mistake. Efficient learning systems for immigrants can be high-yield public investments, and these investments therefore should be made. Policies to reverse the growth of America's underclass are urgently needed. Human capital activities for immigrants could prevent them from becoming members of the underclass.

The Challenges

The challenges for the United States are thus immense. In meeting these challenges, demographic changes will present the nation's policy-makers with some advantages and disadvantages. A major advantage until 2010 will be the maturing of the baby boom generation. This has been the best educated, most advantaged generation in U.S. history. Since they will be fully absorbed into the work force during the 1990s, the baby boomers should greatly improve productivity and innovation. As noted, moreover, immigration presents the United States with some important advantages. The immigration of younger, highly motivated, better-educated people whose early development costs have been borne by other countries represents a net gain for the American economy.

Unfortunately, both demographic changes and immigration could create some serious problems for America during the 1990s, but especially after 2010 when the baby boomers start retiring. Other problems will be created if immigration adds to the nation's growing underclass, which—without major policy shifts—is not likely to be prepared for jobs requiring higher-order thinking skills. As noted, minorities and women, many of whom have serious human capital disadvantages, will constitute almost all of the growth of the nation's work force over the next 50 years. Demographics will create a real challenge for the United States after 2010, when the economic burdens of the aging baby boomers and a growing proportion of people over 85 will greatly burden U.S. economic resources. This aging process will produce higher proportions of workers to nonworkers. In 1988 there were about five workers for each nonworker; in 50 years, this ratio will be five to two.

The extent to which these changes result in marked declines in national power and personal welfare depends heavily on how we strengthen our international competitiveness during the 20-year period between 1990 and 2010, when the demographics will be favorable. By 2010 the U.S. population probably will shrink to less than 4 percent of the world's total. If other countries' productivity overtakes ours—as many surely will at present trends—their total production will be commensurate with the size of their work force. The only way the United States can maintain its relative position and meet the burdens of an aging population is to give heavy emphasis to improving the competitiveness of our economy. Competitiveness, in turn, will depend heavily on the quality of our work force. During the 1990s we must make the human capital and physical capital investments to meet the challenges of the twenty-first century. We have particularly serious problems with school reform and providing high-quality education for minorities. Immigration policy should support these objectives. This means relying more on labor market tests and controlling the admission of immigrants who will make it more difficult for us to erode our large and growing underclass and provide quality education for all of our people. If we do not meet these challenges in the next 25 years, the economic, political, and social outlook for the United States in the twenty-first century is not bright.

Notes

1. For further detail on these developments, see Chapter 2 in this volume, by Arnold Packer.

2. Civil penalties range from $250 to $2,000 per illegal alien. Criminal penalties for a "pattern or practice" of violation may range up to $3,000 per alien and imprisonment for up to six months.

3. There have been a number of studies of the impact of immigrants on local labor markets, almost all of which conclude that immigrants depress the wages of low-wage workers in the United States, but some of which argue that other people gain more from immigration than low-income workers lose (Maran 1980; Vazquez 1981; Miller 1981). Similarly, studies using larger data bases have generally concluded that illegals reduce the wages of low-wage workers in the United States, especially those of other immigrants (McCarthy and Valdez 1985; Smith and Newman 1977: 51–56; USGAO 1986; North and Houston 1976).

Studies using aggregate quantitative techniques generally conclude that while the evidence on displacement is not clear, immigration tends to have negative effects on earnings, especially for immigrants (Borjas 1987: 382–92). One interesting study of legal and illegal immigrants cited by Bean, Telles, and Lowell (1988: 21) concluded that while undocumented workers had little impact on other groups, the supply of legal Mexican workers had a negative effect on female earnings, whereas undocumented Mexican workers had a positive effect on female earnings. This suggests that undocumented workers are complementary to legal women residents but that legal immigrants compete with them. In other words, legalization might do more to reduce the wages of legal residents than illegal immigration. A National Bureau of Economic Research study concluded: "While there is evidence that increased immigration adversely affects some wage rates, virtually all of this burden falls on immigrants themselves. Labor market effects for nonimmigrants appear to be quantitatively unimportant: the wages and employment of natives are not very sensitive to immigration. In short, this research implies that immigrants are rather easily absorbed by the American labor market. There is little in this research to indicate that the redistributive effects of immigration should be a major concern" (Topel 1988: 21).

4. As opposed to the often casual use of statistics by the leadership of the INS, which, for example, persists in not figuring out how many people it apprehends each year, while telling us that the number of apprehensions is rising to more than 1.5 million per year.

5. The extent of our wage competition problem is suggested by a 1986 report

on Korean wages (CFEE 1986b). In a modern VCR factory near Seoul, Korea, relatively well educated Koreans work 12 hours per day, 7 days per week, with two days off per year for $3,000 a year.

6. The outmigration of workers from Los Angeles County in the 1970s to other parts of California and to other states is estimated at 372,000 by the Urban Institute.

7. In fact, many immigration impact studies suffer from making longitudinal inferences from cross-sectional data. If cross-sectional data show more blacks (or native whites) in higher-paying jobs *after* the immigrants come in, analysts are more likely to conclude that immigrants and natives are complements and have moved up the occupation ladder as a result of increased immigration. The assumption is that the same native workers are involved. Unless migration of natives is controlled for and the same native workers are followed through time, this conclusion is not warranted.

References

Alba, Francisco (1985). *Migrant Workers, Employment Opportunities, and Remittances: The Pattern of Labor Exchange between Mexico and the United States.* Washington, D.C.: Georgetown University, Center for Immigration Policy and Refugee Assistance. Working Paper.

Applebome, Peter (1988). "Farm Law Abused by Illegal Aliens." *New York Times.* November 17.

Bean, Frank D., Edward E. Telles, and B. Lindsay Lowell (1988). *Perceptions and Evidence about Undocumented Immigration in the United States.* Paper no. 10.01. Austin, Tex.: Population Research Center.

Berlin, Gordon, and Andrew Sum (1988). *Toward a More Perfect Union: Basic Skills, Poor Families, and our Economic Future.* New York: Ford Foundation.

Borjas, George (1987). "Immigrants, Minorities, and Labor Market Competition." *Industrial and Labor Relations Review* 40(3): 382–92.

Bouvier, Leon, and Robert W. Gardner (1986). "Immigration to the U.S.: The Unfinished Story." Washington, D.C.: Population Reference Bureau, *Population Bulletin* 4 (4): 1–51.

Briggs, Vernon (1975). *Mexican Migration and the U.S. Labor Market.* Austin, Tex.: Center for the Study of Human Resources.

Bustamente, Jorge A. (1987). "Mexican Immigration to the United States: A Bilateral Perspective." Paper presented at the Pan American Economic Leadership Conference, June 14–16.

Carnegie Forum on Education and the Economy (CFEE) (1986a). *A Nation Prepared: Teachers for the Twenty-first Century.* New York: CFEE.

———— (1986b). *Report of the Task Force on Teaching as a Profession.* Washington, D.C.: CFEE.

Chapa, Jorge (1988). "The Question of Mexican American Assimilation: Socioeconomic Parity or Underclass Formation?" *Public Affairs Comment* 35(1): 1–6.

Chapman, Leonard F., Jr. (1975). "Illegal Aliens: A Growing Population." *Immigration and Naturalization Reporter,* vol. 24.

Chiswick, Barry R. (1988). "Illegal Immigration and Immigration Control." *Economic Perspectives*. Summer.

Committee for Economic Development (CED) (1985). *Investing in Our Children*. Washington, D.C.: Committee for Economic Development.

Council of Economic Advisers (1986). "The Council of Economic Advisers on Immigration." *Population Bulletin*. June.

DeJong, Gordon F., and Robert W. Gardner (1987). "Asians in American Industry." *Population Today*. May.

Federation for American Immigration Reform (FAIR) (1986). *News Advisory*. February 5.

Hamburg, David (1985). "The Scientific Community, Technology and Peace." Statement to the American Association for the Advancement of Science, November 7.

Immigration and Naturalization Service (INS) (1988). *The 1987 Statistical Yearbook of the INS*. Washington, D.C.: U.S. Department of Justice.

Johnston, William B., and Arnold E. Packer (1987). *Workforce 2000: Work and Workers for the Twenty-first Century*. Indianapolis, Ind.: Hudson Institute.

Kellog, John B. (1988). "Forces of Change." *Phi Delta Kappan*. November.

Loy, Frank (1986). Presentation to the Ninth Annual Conference of the Center for Migration Studies, Washington, D.C., March 20.

McCarthy, Kevin F., and R. B. Valdez (1985). *Current and Future Effects of Mexican Immigration in California*. Santa Monica, Calif.: Rand Corporation.

Maran, Sheldon L. (1980). "Hispanic Workers in the Garment and Restaurant Industries in Los Angeles County." Working Paper in U.S.-Mexican Studies No. 12. San Diego: U.S.-Mexican Studies.

Marshall, Ray (1988a). "Jobs: The Shifting Structure of Global Employment." In John Sewell and Stuart Tucker, eds., *Growth, Exports, and Jobs in a Changing World Economy: Agenda 1988*. New Brunswick, N.J.: Transaction Books.

——— (1987). *Unheard Voices: Labor and Economic Policy in a Competitive World*. New York: Basic Books.

Massey, Douglas S. (1987). "Do Undocumented Migrants Earn Lower Wages than Legal Immigrants?" *International Migration Review*. Fall.

Miller, Michael V. (1981). "Economic Growth and Change along the U.S.-Mexican Border: The Case of Brownsville, Texas." University of Texas—San Antonio: Human Resources Management and Development Program. Working Paper.

Muller, Thomas, and Thomas Espenshade (1985). *The Fourth Wave: California's Newest Immigrants* Washington, D.C.: Urban Institute Press.

National Academy of Engineering (NAE) (1987). *Foreign and Foreign-Born Engineers: Infusing Talent, Raising Issues*. Washington, D.C.: NAE.

North, David S., and Marion F. Houston (1976). *The Characteristics and Role of Illegal Aliens in the U.S. Labor Market: An Exploration Study*. Washington, D.C.: Lunton & Co.

Schultz, Theodore W. (1988). *Investing in People: The Economics of Population Quality*. Berkeley: University of California Press.

Siegal, Jacob S., Jeffrey S. Passel, and J. Gregory Robinson (1981). "Preliminary

Report on Existing Studies of the Number of Illegal Residents of the United States." In Select Commission on Immigration and Refugee Policy, *Immigration Policy and the National Interest,* appendix 5, *Papers on Illegal Migration to the United States.* Washington, D.C.: United States Government Printing Office.

Smith, Barton, and Robert Newman (1977). "Depressed Wages along the U.S.-Mexico Border." *Economic Inquiry* 15, no. 1.

Stein, Barry (1986). "Understanding the Refugee Experience: Foundations for a Better Settlement System." *Journal of Refugee Settlement,* vol 1.

Topel, Robert (1988). "The Impact of Immigration on Local Labor Markets." In Richard B. Freeman, ed., *Immigration, Trade, and the Labor Market.* New York: National Bureau of Economic Research.

U.S. Bureau of the Census (1984). *1980 Census of the Population.* Detailed Population Characteristics, United States Summary, Section A: United States.

———— (1985). *1980 Census of the Population.* Foreign-Born Population in the United States. Microfiche.

U.S. General Accounting Office (USGAO) (1988). *Studies of the Immigration and Control Act's Impact on Mexico.* Washington, D.C.: U.S. Government Printing Office.

———— (USGAO) (1986). *Illegal Aliens: Limited Research Suggests Aliens May Displace Native Workers.* Washington, D.C.: U.S. Government Printing Office.

Vasquez, Mario (1981). "Immigrant Workers in the Apparel Industry in Southern California." In Antonio R. Bustamente, ed., *Mexican Immigrant Workers in the U.S.* Los Angeles: UCLA Chicano Research Center.

Walsh, John (1988). "Foreign Engineers on the Rise." *News and Comment.* January.

William T. Grant Foundation (1988). *The Forgotten Half: Pathways to Success for America's Youth and Young Families.* Washington, D.C.: William T. Grant Foundation.

5

The Poor

Sheldon Danziger

In any year, individuals who have completed a greater number of years of schooling are likely to have higher earnings and lower rates of unemployment and poverty than those who have less education. Over the past 40 years, the rising educational attainment of the population has been a significant factor in the historical trend toward lower poverty rates. As a result, policies that enhance basic skills and increase educational attainment—for example, by reducing the high school dropout rate—have a continuing role to play in antipoverty policy.

In recent years, however, the levels of individual earnings and family income have stagnated and poverty rates have risen, especially for the young, in all educational categories. This experience stands in sharp contrast to that of the two post–World War II decades, when living standards increased rapidly and poverty rates fell for all demographic groups. The poverty rate increases have been greatest for those who have not completed any schooling beyond high school. Those who have a high school diploma are still much less likely to be poor than those who do not. But a high school diploma no longer protects against low earnings to the extent it did 20 years ago.

One implication of this disturbing trend is that increasing the human capital of the poor is now a less effective antipoverty strategy than it was in the past. Policies that enhance human capital through investments in health and education are thus necessary, but they are not sufficient to significantly raise earnings and reduce the current high poverty rates of many demographic groups. Additional policy interventions, such as an expanded Earned Income Tax Credit, a refundable Dependent Care Credit, and child support reforms are also needed to supplement low family incomes. In fact, stronger antipoverty measures can contribute to the next generation's educational gains and thus can have a cumulative impact on poverty.

In the next section, I briefly review the history of antipoverty policy in the period since 1965. Then I present some original tabulations from the censuses of 1950 through 1980 and the March 1987 Current Population Survey that show how the relationships among earnings, poverty, and educational attainment have changed over time for persons categorized by age, race, and gender. The final section offers some antipoverty policies that are consistent with both the policy history and the empirical trends.

A Brief History of Antipoverty Policy

Twenty-five years ago, in his first State of the Union address, President Johnson declared an "unconditional" war on poverty. Shortly thereafter, he transmitted to Congress the *Economic Report of the President* (U.S. Council of Economic Advisers 1964), which presented the conceptual foundation on which the War on Poverty was based and outlined a set of antipoverty initiatives. Included in this broad range of policies were maintenance of full employment, acceleration of economic growth, reduction of discrimination, improvements in regional economies, rehabilitation of urban and rural communities, improvements in labor market functioning, expansion of educational opportunities, enlargement of job opportunities for youth, improved health, promotion of adult education and training, and assistance for the aged and disabled. The report recognized the complexity of the poverty problem and cautioned that no single program could meet the needs of all of the poor.

The primary focus of the attack on poverty was to help the young achieve better employment opportunities and higher earnings. Policies to foster full employment and economic growth would increase the demand for the labor of the poor, while education and training programs would increase the quantity and the quality of the labor the poor supplied. The poor would then escape poverty in the same manner as the nonpoor—through the private labor market.

This emphasis on the provision of opportunity rather than on the direct provision of public jobs or income-maintenance benefits was reflected in Johnson's remarks of August 1964 when he signed the Economic Opportunity Act: "We are not content to accept the endless growth of relief rolls or welfare rolls. We want to offer the forgotten fifth of our people opportunity and not doles" (Johnson 1965: 988).

This optimistic vision—that poverty could be virtually eliminated within a generation through informed policies (Lampman 1971)—seemed to be borne out as the official poverty rate for all persons declined from 17.3 percent in 1965 to 11.1 percent in 1973. Optimism faded, however, after the 1973 oil price shock, as economic growth and productivity lagged and consumer prices and unemployment rates increased. The official poverty rate changed little during the rest of the 1970s and jumped after the next oil price shock to 13.0 percent in 1980.

By 1981, the presidential perspective was one of pessimism. Government policies in general and antipoverty policies in particular were blamed for what now seemed to be intractable poverty. According to President Reagan, "in 1964, the famous War on Poverty was declared. And a funny thing happened. Poverty, as measured by dependency, stopped shrinking and then actually began to grow worse. I guess you could say, 'Poverty won the war.' Poverty won, in part, because instead of helping the poor, government programs ruptured the bonds holding poor families together" (Reagan 1986).

The "Reagan Experiment" cut taxes for the well-to-do and cut social spending for the poor on the assumption that if government did not intervene, productivity and economic growth would increase and prices, unemployment rates, and poverty would fall. In 1989, six years into a sustained economic recovery, the experiment appears to be a success from a macroeconomic perspective but a distributional failure. In addition to its atypical length, this recovery has had atypical distributional effects—poverty and income inequality in 1989 are higher than in 1979, the previous business cycle peak. Although poverty has fallen somewhat from its peak of 15.2 percent in 1983, the 1989 rate, about 13 percent, exceeds the 11.7 percent rate of 1979. And the rates for minority children, white[1] children living in single-parent families, the minority elderly, elderly white widows, and those without a high school diploma all exceed 20 percent.

This distributional experience—that poverty declined less during the recovery than it rose during the recession—demonstrates that a growing economy is necessary, but not sufficient, to reduce poverty. The concern that antipoverty policies would be needed even during periods of economic growth is not a new one, as it was expressed by the Council of Economic Advisers when the War on Poverty was declared. Indeed, this recovery's modest antipoverty effect can be viewed as the outcome of a "natural experiment" that disproves the Reagan-era view that explicit antipoverty policies need not be emphasized or expanded in a growing economy.

The Bush administration, in advocating a "kinder and gentler" nation, has implicitly rejected the view that antipoverty policies are responsible for the continuing high poverty rate and therefore cannot contribute to its solution. The juxtaposition of a robust economic recovery with the hardships of the poor, the medically uninsured, inner-city residents, and the homeless has shifted public opinion to favor increased government intervention. And concerns about foreign competition and the private sector's needs for a better-educated work force have produced numerous reports from the business and philanthropic communities that advocate increased government support for human capital investment strategies to raise productivity and living standards (see, for example, Committee for Economic Development 1987; William T. Grant Foundation 1988).

There is now a consensus among the public and the policymakers that government must initiate or expand policies to aid the poor in a number of areas that were targets of the Reagan budgetary retrenchment, particularly child health and nutrition programs and federal aid to education. This consensus was reflected in the Tax Reform Act of 1986 and the Family Support Act of 1988. Both bills garnered bipartisan support and provided substantial additional resources to poor families with children.

It is clear that now, 25 years after the War on Poverty was declared, attention and resources must once again be directed to the problem of poverty. It is also clear that the initial motivation of the War on Poverty was correct—no single program or policy can deal with this multifaceted problem. Both increased income supplements, such as those discussed below, and a variety of human capital investment strategies will be needed to alleviate poverty and address its causes for the able-bodied. What James Tobin stated in 1965 remains true today:

> In the national campaign to conquer poverty there are two basic
> strategies. . . . The structural strategy is to build up the capacities
> of the poorest fifth of the population to earn decent incomes. The
> distributive strategy is to assure every family a decent standard
> of living regardless of its earning capacity. In my opinion both
> strategies are essential; correctly designed, they are more comple-
> mentary than competitive. (Tobin 1965: 31)

The Impact of Educational Attainment on Poverty

Conventional wisdom about the ability of increased education and training to reduce poverty mirrors the same pattern of development: optimism first, then pessimism, and now, hopefully, realism. According to Henry Aaron, the view of education's impact on income and poverty changed "from its high point in the early 1960s as an all-powerful transformer of economic potential to its low point in the early 1970s as an ineffective instrument that had few, if any, predictable consequences" (1978: 65).

In a recent review of the literature on the antipoverty impacts of targeted education and training programs, on which the federal government spent almost $300 billion (1986 dollars) between 1963 and 1985, Isabel

Sawhill concluded that "overall, the results from investing in the human capital of the poor present a mixed record. Certainly not everything that has been tried has been successful, although there are programs that appear to have worked. . . . Thus, both the skeptic and the true believer can find support for their positions" (1988b: 1096–97). Sawhill estimates that the poverty rate for all persons in 1985 would have been from 0.4 to 2.2 percentage points above the actual rate of 14.0 percent in the absence of this human capital investment.

Today the conventional views on the importance of education and the economic returns of education are remarkably different from those of the mid-1970s. In 1976, Richard Freeman, alarmed by the "sudden collapse" in the job market for the college educated, wrote *The Overeducated American* (1976). Freeman wrote at a time when the "college premium," the difference between the average wages of a high school and a college graduate, had been falling for five years. Then, it seemed that a high school degree was sufficient to escape poverty and that investment in college education produced minimal monetary returns.

> The figure shows the college premium dropping substantially from 1969 to 1974. Among all men in 1969, college graduates earned 53% more than high school graduates and 99% more than grade school graduates; in 1974, the premiums stood at 35% and 74% respectively. . . . The sharp decline in the college income premium was not anticipated by conventional economists. . . . Overall, the period of severe "overeducation" is likely to last for about a decade, to be followed by a period of market balance at a lower plateau. . . . Income distribution is likely to become more egalitarian as a result of the relative surplus of the educated. (Freeman 1976: 13–14, 188–89)

Figure 5.1 extends Freeman's data forward from 1974 to 1986 and shows that what occurred during those years was not what Freeman had anticipated. The top graph shows the ratio of the annual income of college graduates to that of grade school graduates; the bottom, the income ratio for college graduates relative to high school graduates. These premiums stopped declining after 1974 (coincidentally, the last year of data available when Freeman was writing his book) and then jumped dramatically in the 1980s. By 1986, they were almost identical to those in 1969—college-educated men earned 53 percent more than high school-educated men and 96 percent more than grade school-educated men. And income inequality has also increased dramatically, both because of the greater differences in earnings between men in different educational categories and because inequality increased within most educational categories.

Today, public and academic discussions are focused on the "under-

Figure 5.1   Income of males employed full time, aged more than 25, by years of school completed, 1969–86.

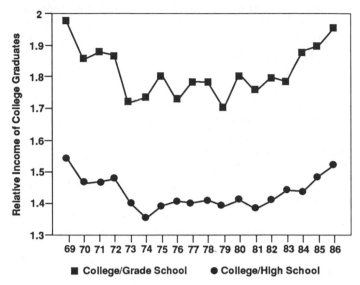

   ■ College/Grade School   ● College/High School

educated" American and the large and growing gap between the incomes of those with greater and lesser amounts of education (see, for example, Blackburn, Bloom, and Freeman 1989, and Murphy and Welch 1989). I now turn to a review of the evidence that emphasizes the relationships among educational attainment, earnings, and poverty.

Measuring Poverty

The official definition of poverty is a function both of family income and of family size. In 1986, the poverty line varied from $5,701 for a nonelderly single person, to $11,203 for a family of four, to $22,497 for a family of nine or more. A family of a given size is counted as poor if its cash income from all sources during a calendar year falls below its poverty line. Income, summed over all related persons in the family, includes wages and salaries, net income from self-employment, Social Security and other social insurance benefits, cash welfare benefits, interest, dividends, net rental income, private pensions, child support, alimony, and so forth.

The official poverty measure does not include capital gains, imputed rents, or noncash government or private benefits (e.g., food stamps, housing subsidies, Medicare benefits, employer-provided health insurance). Nor does it subtract taxes, although all of these omitted items affect a family's living standard. The U.S. Bureau of the Census (1988) has published data on poverty rates for the period since 1979 that reflect these more comprehensive sources of income. They show less poverty in any year than the official measure but reveal similar trends over time, and similar differences for persons classified by education, race, or gender. Because I focus on the past 40 years, I am not able to account for noncash income in the empirical work that follows.

The official poverty lines are updated yearly to account for changes in the Consumer Price Index so that they represent the same purchasing power each year. In its publications, the Bureau of the Census has extended the lines forward from the mid-1960s, when the current definition was adopted, and backward to 1959. In this analysis, I extend the official lines back to 1949 in the same manner (see Ross, Danziger, and Smolensky 1987, for a discussion). The poverty line in current dollars for a family of four was $2,417 in 1949, $2,955 in 1959, $3,714 in 1969, $7,355 in 1979 and $11,203 in 1986.

Because real family income grew rapidly between 1949 and 1969, the poverty line, which is adjusted only for price changes, fell relative to average family incomes. Since 1969, however, because family income has not grown much faster than prices, the poverty line as a fraction of the mean family income has remained roughly constant. In 1949 the poverty line for a family of four was about 80 percent of mean family income for all households, whereas in 1986 it was about 40 percent of the mean.[2]

The Concept of Low Earnings

Because the most direct impact of education is on earned income, I begin my analysis with a measure of "low earnings" that compares an individual's own earned income (the sum of wages, salaries, and self-employment income) to a fixed real amount—the official poverty line in a given year for a family of four.[3] A person with low earnings does not earn enough to keep a family of four out of poverty. While most of those with low earnings are among the "working poor," some do not work at all, and others work only sporadically during the year. In other words, some low earners work full time, year-round, but at a low wage rate, while others earn a "good wage rate" but work too few hours to raise their earnings above the poverty line because of voluntary or involuntary unemployment.[4] In addition, a low earner may not be poor, as officially measured, if her or his family size is less than four and/or there are other earners in the family and/or the family has sufficient amounts of income from other sources.[5] Likewise, some persons who are not low earners, that is, those who earned more than $11,203 in 1986, may be officially classified as poor if they live in families of more than four persons.

In the next section, I focus on all males between the ages of 25 and 54. They are most attached to the labor force and are the group for

Table 5.1 Distribution of Men Aged 25–54, by Years of School Completed, 1949–1986 (percent)

	Years of School Completed				
	0–8	9–11	12	13–15	16+
White[a]					
1949	38.4	20.4	23.3	8.8	9.2
1959	27.2	21.2	28.2	10.7	12.7
1969	16.1	18.1	34.4	13.2	18.2
1979	8.1	11.1	35.2	19.6	26.1
1986	4.2	8.2	38.0	20.0	29.7
Black[a]					
1949	71.0	15.0	8.5	3.4	2.1
1959	56.2	20.7	14.4	5.2	3.5
1969	35.0	26.3	26.2	7.2	5.3
1979	16.1	20.7	35.2	17.4	10.6
1986	7.1	17.0	43.9	18.8	13.2
Hispanic					
1949	68.4	14.6	10.7	3.5	2.9
1959	61.0	17.1	13.3	5.5	3.1
1969	44.7	19.9	22.1	9.1	4.2
1979	36.3	15.2	24.3	16.3	8.0
1986	28.9	14.5	30.4	15.9	10.4

Source: Computations by author from computer tapes of the 1950–80 Censuses of Population and the March 1987 Current Population Survey.

Note: Totals may not add to 100.0 due to rounding.

[a]Non-Hispanic.

whom the relationship between education and earnings should be most evident. These men are classified into 15 mutually exclusive groups— three racial-ethnic groups classified by five categories of educational attainment. After examining the incidence of low earnings and the official poverty rate for these men, I turn to the data for women in this age group.

The Relationship between Education and Low Earnings among Men

Table 5.1 shows the educational attainment of white, black, and Hispanic men in 1949, 1959, 1969, 1979, and 1986. For each group, there has been a dramatic increase in educational attainment over time. In 1949, those who had completed no more than eight years of schooling

were by far the largest category: about 38.4 percent of whites, 71.0 percent of blacks, and 68.4 percent of Hispanics. By 1986, these percentages
had fallen to 4.2, 7.1, and 28.9 percent, respectively. While majority-
minority differences in attainment have narrowed, they remain substantial—in 1986, 12.4, 24.1, and 43.4 percent of white, black, and Hispanic
men, respectively, had not completed high school.

The percentage of men with advanced education has also increased
dramatically. High school graduates were the modal category for whites
by 1959, for blacks by 1979, and for Hispanics by 1986. In 1986, 29.7
percent of whites, 13.2 percent of blacks, and 10.4 percent of Hispanics
were college graduates.

Table 5.2 shows the percentage of men in each of the 15 categories
whose earnings were below the poverty line for a family of four in the
selected years between 1949 and 1986. In every year, and for each of the
three groups, those with more education are much less likely to have low
earnings than those with less education. Figure 5.2 shows the dramatic
decline in the percentage of men with low earnings as education increases
for the three racial-ethnic groups in 1986. While more than half of white
men with eight or fewer years of schooling earned less than $11,203,
only 10.6 percent of white college graduates earned less than this
amount. At every education level, black men have the highest rate of low
earnings, followed by Hispanics and then whites. The percentage point
disadvantage for blacks is smallest for college graduates: 22.7 percent of
blacks, 18.7 percent of Hispanics, and 10.6 percent of whites had low
earnings.

The data in Table 5.2 for the post-1969 period do not show the kind
of economic progress that Americans in the immediate post–World War
II decades came to expect. For example, between 1949 and 1969 the
incidence of low earnings declined dramatically. For all white men, it
declined from 40.1 to 11.8 percent; for blacks, from 79.7 to 32.0 percent; for Hispanics, from 67.8 to 26.3 percent. Large declines occurred
for men in each of the five educational categories. Most of this large
decline was due to the rapid growth in the level of earnings. Between
1949 and 1969, mean earnings (in 1986 constant dollars) for all men
between the ages of 25 and 54 more than doubled, from $10,353 to
$24,125 (data not shown), so the poverty line for a family of four as a
percentage of this mean fell from 107 to 46 percent. However, the incidence of low earnings also fell because inequality decreased over these
two decades—those at the bottom experienced more rapid earnings increases than those at the top (see Danziger and Gottschalk 1988).

In 1986, the mean earnings for all men aged 25 through 54 was
$24,288, virtually the same as it had been 17 years earlier. The incidence
of low earnings, however, holding education constant, increased dramatically for all the groups. In 1986, 20.6 percent of whites, 42.2 percent of

Table 5.2   Low-Earnings Rates for Men Aged 25–54, by Years of School
Completed, 1949–1986 (percent)

| | Years of School Completed | | | | | |
	0–8	9–11	12	13–15	16+	All Men
White[a]						
1949	53.2	37.8	30.0	31.0	24.5	40.1
1959	34.4	17.7	13.2	13.1	10.6	19.6
1969	24.5	12.7	8.3	9.7	7.9	11.8
1979	36.5	24.0	15.3	15.3	10.9	16.8
1986	52.8	38.3	22.6	17.9	10.6	20.6
Black[a]						
1949	85.0	70.4	63.4	66.4	52.8	79.7
1959	65.0	45.9	36.7	29.5	18.2	53.5
1969	46.0	32.3	20.0	18.0	16.4	32.0
1979	53.6	44.9	34.0	28.2	17.1	36.6
1986	73.7	55.5	42.7	30.6	22.7	42.2
Hispanic						
1949	76.0	53.2	46.4	—[b]	—[b]	67.8
1959	57.2	24.6	22.7	23.4	—[b]	43.9
1969	37.7	18.4	16.4	18.4	12.2	26.3
1979	42.7	31.7	26.7	18.4	16.7	31.3
1986	60.9	47.4	35.9	28.3	18.7	41.8

Source: Computations by author from computer tapes of the 1950–80 Censuses of Population and the March 1987 Current Population Survey.

Note: A man is classified as having low earnings if his earned income from wages, salaries, and self-employment is below the poverty line for a family of four—$2,417, $2,955, $3,714, $7,355, and $11,203 in 1949, 1959, 1969, 1979, and 1986, respectively.
[a]Non-Hispanic.
[b]Cell size below 75 men.

blacks, and 41.8 percent of Hispanics had earnings below the poverty line for a family of four, representing increases of 8.8, 10.2, and 15.5 percentage points over their respective levels in 1969, despite the higher education levels of 1986. Thus this period was disappointing both because of the stagnation in mean earnings and because inequality increased. Those at the bottom earned less than in 1969, while those at the top earned more.[6]

The increases in low earnings were particularly dramatic for less-educated men. For example, in 1986, men with a high school degree were substantially less likely to have earnings in excess of the poverty line for a family of four than similar men in 1959! The rate of low earnings for high school graduates increased between 1969 and 1986 by 14.3, 22.7,

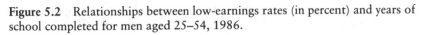

Figure 5.2 Relationships between low-earnings rates (in percent) and years of school completed for men aged 25–54, 1986.

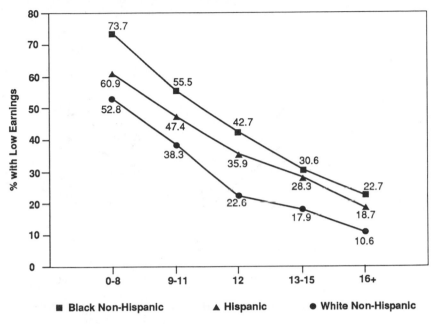

and 19.5 percentage points for the three racial-ethnic groups.[7] High school graduates in 1986 had a rate of low earnings similar to that of men with eight or fewer years of school in 1969.

This deterioration in earnings was even greater for younger men. Their experience emphasizes the relationship between education and earnings for recent labor market entrants and demonstrates the economic hardship facing those who go no further than high school.[8] Figure 5.3 shows the incidence of low earnings in each of the five years for men aged 25 through 34 who graduated from high school but completed no additional years of schooling. The percentage of young white high school graduates who were low earners increased from 8.6 to 25.6 percent between 1969 and 1986, with the 1986 level substantially exceeding 14.8 percent, the level of 1959.[9] For minorities, the percentage point increases after 1969 were even greater—from 15.6 to 40.2 percent for Hispanics, and from 19.9 to 49.6 percent for blacks.

The data in Table 5.2 clearly show that high school graduation is an economic necessity—the percentage point differences between low-earnings rates for high school graduates and those less educated have never been greater. The recent experience also demonstrates, however, that policies to increase the high school graduation rate, while necessary, are not sufficient to significantly reduce poverty. In fact, the low-earnings

Figure 5.3 Low-earnings rates (in percent) of male high school graduates aged 25–34, 1949–86.

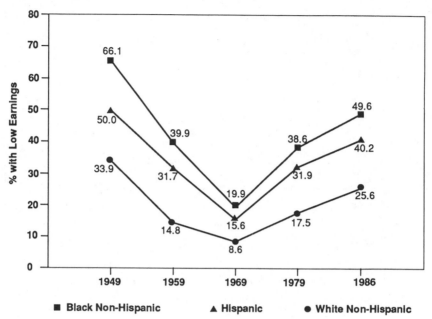

rates of college graduates in 1986—10.6, 22.7, and 18.7 percent, for whites, blacks, and Hispanics—are somewhat higher than those for high school graduates in 1969—8.3, 20.0, and 16.4 percent, respectively.

Several recent studies (Blackburn, Bloom, and Freeman 1989; Levy and Michel 1988; Murphy and Welch 1989) have focused on the declining real earnings of high school graduates and the growing gap between the mean earnings of high school and college graduates, which can be seen in Figure 5.1. They all attribute the changes, particularly since 1979, to differential shifts in the demand for labor. The causes of these demand shifts have not been resolved. As Murphy and Welch conclude,

> Although the data suggests a rapid rise in demand for educated workers in the 1980s, we have yet to identify the precise cause or causes of this rise. Possible explanations include changing patterns of international trade and international competition, structural change in the domestic economy (such as the shift in employment from manufacturing to the services) and changes in production technologies within industries (such as the shift to flexible production and the increased use of computer-aided technologies). (1989: 26)

Table 5.3 Decomposition of the Trend in Low-Earnings Rate for Men Aged 25–54, 1949–1986

	White[a] (%)	Black[a] (%)	Hispanic (%)
Actual rates of low earnings			
1. 1949	40.1	79.7	67.8
2. 1969	11.8	32.0	26.3
3. 1986	20.6	42.2	41.8
Hypothetical rates			
4. 1949 education distribution and 1969 rates of low earnings	15.5	40.2	31.2
5. 1986 education distribution and 1969 rates of low earnings	9.5	23.1	22.7
6. 1949–69 percentage point change (row 2 minus row 1)	−28.3	−47.7	−41.5
7. Due to changes in education-specific low-earnings rate (row 4 minus row 1)	−24.6	−39.5	−36.6
8. Due to educational changes (row 2 minus row 4)	− 3.7	− 8.2	− 4.9
9. 1969–1986 percentage point change (row 3 minus row 2)	+ 8.8	+10.2	+15.5
10. Due to changes in education-specific low-earnings rate	+11.1	+19.1	+19.1
11. Due to educational changes (row 5 minus row 2)	− 2.3	− 8.9	− 3.6

Source: Computations by author from data shown in Tables 5.1 and 5.2.

[a]Non-Hispanic.

None of these studies, however, has focused on the rising rate of low earnings of college graduates.

Table 5.3 presents a demographic standardization that decomposes the observed changes in the percentage of men with low earnings into two components—one reflecting changes in educational attainment, and the other reflecting changes in the education-specific rates of low earnings. This decomposition assumes that the changes in the education-specific rates of low earnings were not affected by the increasing educational attainment over this period. To minimize the effects of such interactions between educational attainment and the education-specific rates, the approximate midpoint year, 1969, is used as a benchmark. One can view the decomposition as a "thought experiment" that holds all aspects of the labor market constant at their 1969 values and then asks how the low-earnings rates for the three groups would have differed if only their educational distributions had been different.

The decomposition begins by computing two hypothetical rates of low earnings based on the 15 low-earnings rates for 1969 that are shown in Table 5.2 and the corresponding educational distributions for 1949 and 1986 shown in Table 5.1. Row 4 of Table 5.3 shows the rate for each of the three racial-ethnic groups that would have existed in 1969 if men had the same educational attainment as in 1949 but the low-earnings rates of 1969. Row 5 shows the rates that would have existed in 1969 if men had the 1986 distributions of educational attainment and the low-earnings rates of 1969.

Consider the 1949–69 period (rows 6 through 8). For each group, there were very large declines in the incidence of low earnings—28.3, 47.7, and 41.5 percentage points for whites, blacks, and Hispanics, respectively. Most of these declines can be attributed to the declining rates of low earnings (row 7). Increasing educational attainment accounted for 3.7, 8.2, and 4.9 percentage points of the declines in the rates for the three groups (row 8).

The 1969–86 period of rising rates of low earnings would have been even worse had it not been for the continuing increase in educational attainment. During this period, rising education (row 11) offset some of the increasing economic hardship—2.3, 8.9, and 3.6 percentage points for the three groups. For blacks, for example, the rate of low earnings increased by 10.2 percentage points (row 9), from 32.0 (row 2) to 42.2 (row 3) percent. If the education-specific rates of low earnings had not increased between 1969 and 1986, the low-earnings rate for all blacks in 1986 would have fallen instead to 23.1 percent (row 5). This 8.9-percent decline (row 2 − 5) is attributable to rising educational attainment. Rows 3 and 5 are both based on the 1986 educational distributions; the difference between them is 19.1 percentage points (row 10) and is attributable to the rising rates of low earnings. Thus, the low-earnings rate would have been 51.1 percent (row 10 + row 2) in 1986 if educational attainment had not increased.

Educational attainment for minorities—especially blacks—has converged toward that of whites, leading to substantial reductions in their incidence of low earnings. However, the low-earnings rate among minorities would remain significantly higher than that for whites even if their educational distributions were identical. The impact of factors other than education is shown in Table 5.4, which uses the data in Tables 5.1 and 5.2 to perform another demographic standardization.

The standardization shows what low-earnings rates would have been if minorities changed only their educational distributions. This exercise reveals that if black men had the same educational distribution as white

Table 5.4   The Effect of Race Differences in the Education Distribution on Low-Earnings Rates, 1986

	Black[a] (%)	Hispanic (%)
1. Actual 1986 rate	42.2	41.8
2. Basis for comparison (1986 rate for whites[a])	20.6	20.6
3. Percentage point difference	21.6	21.2
4. Due to educational differences[b]	5.5	10.5
5. Due to other factors	16.1	10.7

Source: Computations by author from data in Tables 5.1 and 5.2.
[a]Non-Hispanic.
[b]If minority educational distributions were the same as those for whites, and all else did not change, the rates of low earnings for blacks would be 36.7 percent (42.2 − 5.5 = 36.7); for Hispanics, it would be 31.3 percent (41.8 − 10.5 = 31.3).

men in 1986, but had their own education-specific low-earnings rates, their low-earnings rate would have been lower by 5.5 percentage points (row 4)—36.7 instead of 42.2 percent. The black-white gap would still have been 16.1 percentage points (row 5). Similarly, for 1986, the 21.2-percent difference between Hispanics and whites can be divided into a 10.5-point educational component (row 4) and a 10.7-point component due to other factors (row 5).

It is beyond the scope of this discussion to evaluate the basis for these differences between whites and minorities in the education-adjusted rates of low earnings. A complete analysis would have to consider age, regional, and work-effort differences, and differences in the quality of education received by whites and minorities. It would also have to account for the effects of discrimination in occupational entry and advancement and wage rates.[10]

The standardizations of Tables 5.3 and 5.4 document that rising educational attainment in the post–World War II period has been a powerful factor in holding down the rate of low earnings and in reducing the gap between whites and minorities. If high school graduation rates could be increased further and if the educational attainment of minorities could be raised to that of whites, then the rate of low earnings would fall and the racial gap would be narrowed even more. Even if these educational advances could be achieved, however, the 1986 low-earnings rate for white high school graduates remained more than 10 percentage points above its 1969 level, and the 1986 rate for minority college graduates remained about 10 percentage points above that year's level for white college graduates (Table 5.2). Clearly programs and policy changes beyond educational improvement are needed.

Table 5.5 Percentage of Men Aged 25–54 Living in Poor Families, by Years of School Completed, 1959–1986

	Years of School Completed					
	0–8	9–11	12	13–15	16+	All Men
White[a]						
1959	21.0	9.1	6.3	5.0	4.2	10.5
1969	12.4	5.4	3.6	3.2	2.5	5.1
1979	14.6	8.6	4.8	4.6	3.2	5.5
1986	18.8	13.7	5.9	4.3	2.0	5.6
Black[a]						
1959	47.4	29.3	21.1	14.5	7.2	36.8
1969	29.1	16.9	9.8	7.6	5.9	18.1
1979	24.7	20.7	13.6	10.6	5.7	15.5
1986	36.9	22.6	13.2	8.2	6.8	14.7
Hispanic						
1959	49.6	17.0	14.5	14.0	—[b]	36.0
1969	30.8	13.8	8.8	8.9	7.3	19.6
1979	25.5	16.1	10.2	6.1	5.2	15.6
1986	33.6	20.8	10.6	5.5	3.3	17.2

Source: Computations by author from computer tapes of the 1960–80 Censuses of Population and the March 1987 Current Population Survey.

Note: The poverty line varies for each man according to his family size. In 1986, the poverty line ranged from $5,701 for a single man to $22,497 for a man living in a family of nine or more persons. The 1950 Census utilized a sample frame that differs from those of the other years. As a result, family income was not available for all persons.
[a]Non-Hispanic.
[b]Cell size below 75 men.

The Relationship between the Low-Earnings Rate and the Income Poverty Rate among Men

By comparing the earnings of men to a fixed poverty standard—the poverty line for a family of four—the analysis thus far has presented a picture that is gloomier than analyses of poverty based on the official definition. Table 5.5 presents the official poverty rates for men in 1959, 1969, 1979, and 1986. Because the 1950 Census of Population used a different sample frame to gather data on the earnings of persons than it used to gather family income, poverty rates based on family income for all men are not available for 1949. For every cell in the table, these rates are lower in each year than the rates of low earnings shown in Table 5.2 because they include the man's income from other sources (e.g., property

Figure 5.4   Difference between low-earnings rates (in percent) and official poverty rates (in percent) for men aged 25–54, 1959–86.

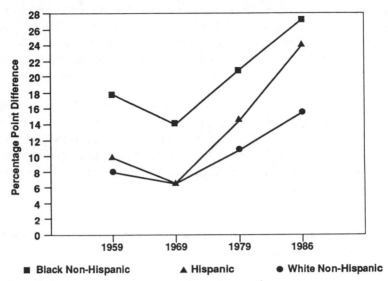

■ **Black Non-Hispanic**   ▲ **Hispanic**   ● **White Non-Hispanic**

income, government transfer benefits) and from other family members and because they reflect the man's actual family size, which is typically smaller than four persons.

Although these rates are lower than the low-earnings rates, their relationship with educational attainment is also very strong. A white high school dropout, for example, is more than six times as likely to be poor as a white college graduate—the respective poverty rates are 13.7 percent and 2.0 percent. And minority high school dropouts have official poverty rates that exceed 20 percent.

The official poverty rates declined by about half between 1959 and 1969, and then increased somewhat. The official poverty rates increased after 1969 by a much smaller amount than the corresponding rates of low earnings, primarily because family size declined and the contribution of working wives to family income increased (see Danziger, Gottschalk, and Smolensky 1989). Rising income transfers also played a role before 1979.

The percentage point gaps between the rate of low earnings and the official poverty rate for all men aged 25 through 54 for each of the three racial-ethnic groups for the four years are shown in Figure 5.4. Each curve shows a slight decline between 1959 and 1969 and then a rapid increase to 1986. For example, for blacks, the rate of low earnings increased by 10.2 percentage points between 1969 and 1986 (from 32.0 to

42.2 percent, from Table 5.2). The official poverty rate for blacks actually declined by 3.4 points (from 18.1 to 14.7 percent, from Table 5.5). The percentage point gap between the two rates, shown in the Figure 5.4, increased from 13.9 to 27.5 points between 1969 and 1986. Thus, declining family size and increasing earnings of wives have tended to keep the poverty rate from reflecting most of the dramatic declines in the ability of men to earn an income above the poverty line for a family of four.

In sum, the recent period has been characterized by decreases in the ability of prime-age males to earn an amount sufficient to raise a family of four above the poverty line and by approximately constant male poverty rates. Those with the least education have the highest poverty rates in any year and have experienced the greatest deterioration in their economic status over time.

The Relationships among Education, the Low-Earnings Rate, and the Income Poverty Rate among Women

Table 5.6 presents the distributions of educational attainment for all women aged 25–54 in each of the racial-ethnic groups. The pattern of dramatic increases in schooling over time is as true for women as for men. The largest educational difference by gender for any racial-ethnic group is that white women are less likely to have completed college than are white men—22.5 versus 29.7 percent (compare Table 5.6 with Table 5.1). As a result, majority-minority differences in educational attainment are somewhat smaller for women than for men.

Women have a greater attachment to nonmarket work in the home and a lesser attachment to paid employment. As a result, the rates of low earnings for all women, shown in Table 5.7, are much higher than those for men. Even if the data had been restricted to employed women, their rate of low earnings would exceed that of comparable men because employed women earn much less on average than employed men. Women's labor force participation rates have increased significantly over time. Thus, their rates of low earnings—in contrast to those of men—have continued to fall over time.

The low earnings rates for women also decline as educational attainment increases. For example, 85.0 percent of black women who had completed only some years of high school earned less than $11,203 in 1986, while the rate was 22.3 percent for college graduates. In part because of the convergence in wage rate differentials for minority and majority women, and in part because black women have a higher employment rate than white or Hispanic women, there are much smaller

Table 5.6 Distribution of Women Aged 25–54, by Years of School Completed, 1949–1986 (percent)

	Years of School Completed				
	0–8	9–11	12	13–15	16+
White[a]					
1949	33.8	20.6	29.9	9.5	6.2
1959	23.0	22.0	37.2	10.8	7.1
1969	13.4	19.9	44.6	12.2	9.8
1979	6.2	13.0	44.8	18.8	17.1
1986	3.2	8.3	45.3	20.7	22.5
Black[a]					
1949	66.6	16.8	10.5	3.4	2.7
1959	48.9	24.9	17.7	4.7	3.8
1969	28.2	31.8	28.2	6.7	5.1
1979	12.2	23.9	37.1	16.8	9.9
1986	6.2	18.2	43.8	19.5	12.2
Hispanic					
1949	68.8	13.4	13.7	2.5	1.6
1959	62.4	17.5	14.6	3.4	2.2
1969	49.9	19.5	21.8	5.9	2.9
1979	37.7	18.3	27.5	10.9	5.6
1986	28.5	14.9	33.5	14.5	8.6

Source: Computations by author from computer tapes of the 1950–80 Censuses of Population and the March 1987 Current Population Survey.

Note: Totals may not add up to 100.0 owing to rounding.

[a]Non-Hispanic.

differences between white and minority women in the incidence of low earnings than there are between men.

Table 5.8 shows the official poverty rates for women. Here the pattern is similar to that of men—declines from 1959 to 1969, and little change thereafter. Figure 5.5 plots the official rates for all men and women aged 25 through 54 for the three racial-ethnic groups in 1959, 1969, 1979, and 1986. If all men and women were married, there would be no male-female differences, as the official poverty rate is based on the income of all family members. Thus, the rates differ to the extent that the poverty rates of unmarried women are higher than those of unmarried men. This is the case for two main reasons. First, women earn less than men. Second, women tend to retain custody of children after a marriage dissolves; thus, even if single men and women earned the same

Table 5.7 Low-Earnings Rates for Women Aged 25–54, by Years of School
Completed, 1949–1986 (percent)

	Years of School Completed					
	0–8	9–11	12	13–15	16+	All Women
White[a]						
1949	96.7	95.1	90.6	86.8	74.5	92.2
1959	91.5	86.9	82.2	77.6	62.5	83.5
1969	84.7	80.1	73.5	70.2	54.4	74.0
1979	84.4	80.4	68.6	59.9	46.7	65.8
1986	89.0	81.2	65.5	53.5	37.3	58.7
Black[a]						
1949	98.8	97.9	94.9	90.1	72.1	97.3
1959	96.5	92.4	84.6	76.1	42.7	90.4
1969	90.8	82.1	67.6	53.9	22.2	75.5
1979	84.6	78.6	61.6	49.7	23.0	62.7
1986	92.7	85.0	65.6	48.1	22.3	62.1
Hispanic						
1949	97.9	92.8	92.4	—[b]	—[b]	96.1
1959	96.6	90.5	81.9	—[b]	—[b]	91.7
1969	92.1	83.5	47.8	64.0	—[b]	84.0
1979	90.5	84.5	68.7	59.6	38.7	77.1
1986	91.1	86.5	68.4	50.1	40.4	72.5

Source: Computations by author from computer tapes of the 1950–1980 Censuses of Population and the March 1987 Current Population Survey.

Note: A woman is classified as having low earnings if her earned income from wages, salaries, and self-employment is below the poverty line for a family of four—$2,417, $2,495, $3,714, $7,355, and $11,203 in the five years. All women, including those who do not work outside the home, are included in the table.
[a]Non-Hispanic.
[b]Cell size below 75 women.

amounts, the official poverty rate for women would be higher due to their larger family size.[11] The male-female gap has grown over time as a greater percentage of women have become heads of families.

Implications for Antipoverty Policy

I have emphasized the relationships among educational attainment, the rate of low earnings, and the official poverty rate. Because these rates fall as education rises for every demographic group, further increases in educational attainment can significantly reduce economic hardship.

Table 5.8 Percentage of Women Aged 25–54 Living in Poor Families, by Years of School Completed, 1959–1986

	Years of School Completed					
	0–8	9–11	12	13–15	16+	All Women
White[a]						
1959	24.1	13.1	8.1	6.9	5.9	12.6
1969	18.1	9.4	5.3	4.8	3.2	7.6
1979	19.7	13.1	6.3	5.6	3.8	7.5
1986	31.8	22.7	8.4	6.2	2.4	8.5
Black[a]						
1959	58.6	45.2	30.5	21.7	8.6	46.6
1969	44.2	31.5	18.9	12.8	3.4	28.8
1979	41.0	36.7	22.6	15.9	5.0	25.4
1986	54.3	48.3	29.8	16.7	4.9	29.1
Hispanic						
1959	50.0	23.6	15.1	—[b]	—[b]	38.2
1969	35.5	20.2	10.0	7.2	3.3	24.3
1979	31.6	24.2	10.4	11.9	7.2	20.9
1986	41.2	35.9	18.8	9.6	4.6	25.2

Source: Computations by author from computer tapes of the 1960–80 Censuses of Population and the March 1987 Current Population Survey.

Note: The poverty line varies for each woman according to her family size. In 1986, the poverty line ranged from $5,701 for a single woman to $22,497 for a woman living in a family of nine or more persons. All women, including those who do not work outside the home, are included in the table.
[a]Non-Hispanic.
[b]Cell size below 75 women.

However, because low-earnings rates are high for all persons without a college education, and official poverty rates are high even for blacks and Hispanics who have high school diplomas, additional policies to supplement low incomes are needed.

The poor are diverse, and no single program or policy can deal with the entire range of poverty problems. The poverty problem of the elderly widow differs from that of the family whose head seeks full-time work but finds only sporadic employment; the poverty of the family head who works full time but at low wages differs from that of the family head who receives welfare and either cannot find a job or does not find it profitable to seek work. Because the emphasis here is on the relationship between education and low earnings, I focus in this section on income-supplementation policies that seek to raise the earnings of working poor families with children. In 1986, about 40 percent of the household heads

Figure 5.5 Official poverty rates (in percent) for men and women, by race, 1959–86.

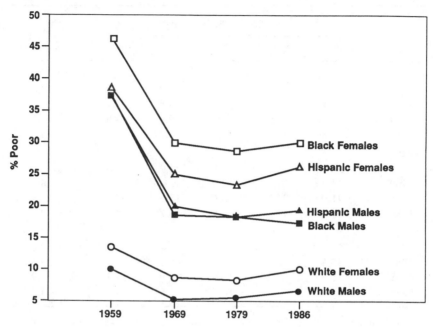

between the ages of 25 and 54 whom I classify as low earners worked at some point during the year and had dependent children. About one-third of the total official poverty population lives in households with a child present where the head works at some point during the year and is neither aged, disabled, nor a student. I do not discuss either welfare or work strategies for those who do not work.

The kinds of income-supplementation policies I have in mind can be viewed as indirect human-capital-enhancing policies because they are likely to raise the educational attainment of the next generation. Since most human capital strategies are focused on children or young adults, income-supplementation policies are an important strategy for aiding poor prime-age workers. For example, human capital strategies may have little to offer a 45-year-old family head with a high school degree who works full time, year-round, in an industry with competitive wages that are too low to raise his or her family above the poverty line. Supplementing this family's income, however, may increase the educational attainment of the children, since achievement is quite responsive to family income.

According to Richard Murnane, "it is important to keep in mind that the roots of the low achievement of many American children lie in the circumstances of poverty in which they live. Consequently, educational policy changes not accompanied by policies that significantly reduce the poverty that dominates many children's lives will have only modest influences on their academic achievements" (1988: 229). In other words, human-capital-enhancing strategies seek to directly raise the productivity of the young, while income supplementation policies—by alleviating current hardship in their families—make it easier for them to remain in school and to gain more from the education and training programs that serve them. There is some evidence that the Negative Income Tax experiments of the 1970s, which provided experimental families with income supplements that exceeded those available from existing welfare programs, had just such effects. Eric Hanushek reviewed the Negative Income Tax literature and concluded that the schooling "effects appear quite large and significant. For example, Mallar (1976) estimates the probability of completing high school for families on a 'middle' negative income tax plan to be 25 to 30 percent higher. . . . Venti and Wise (1984) find an 11 percent increase for youth in the Seattle-Denver experiments" (1987: 112–13).

The kinds of income supplementation policies I advocate do not extend welfare programs; rather, they involve the expansion of two provisions in the federal personal income tax, the Earned Income Tax Credit (EITC) and the Dependent Care Credit (DCC), and further reforms of the child support system. The proposed expansions build on the Tax Reform Act of 1986, which eliminated the personal income tax liability of most poor families with children, and the Family Support Act of 1988, which made important changes in the child support system.

The EITC is a refundable tax credit targeting low-income families with children. In 1989, the credit is 14 percent for each dollar of earned income up to $6,520, where it reaches its maximum value of $913. The credit remains at $913 until earnings reach $10,000, after which it is reduced by 10 percent of additional earnings, phasing out at $19,300. According to congressional estimates (U.S. Congress 1988), the provisions of the Tax Reform Act of 1986 increased the number of families receiving the credit each year from about 6.3 million to 13.8 million between 1986 and 1990 and increased the amount of the credit from $2.0 billion to $7.5 billion per year over the same period.

The DCC allows working single parents and couples, when both spouses work, to partially offset work-related child care costs. The credit begins at 30 percent of expenses for families with incomes below $10,000 and falls to 20 percent for those with incomes above $50,000. Because the credit is nonrefundable, and because the Tax Reform Act of 1986 eliminated the income tax liability of many of the poor, only a very small percentage of poor and low-income families now receive any DCC. On the other hand, higher-income taxpayers receive credits of up to $960 if they have more than one child and if they spend at least $4,800 on child care.

Several proposals have been introduced in Congress to expand the EITC by making the credit an increasing function of family size. Under current law, the EITC provides a constant amount per family, whereas the income necessary to bring a family above the poverty line increases as the number of children does. The Family Living Wage Act, sponsored by Congressman Thomas Petri (Wisconsin), the Toddler Tax Credit, sponsored by Congressman Richard Schulze (Pennsylvania), and the Employment Incentives Act, sponsored by Congressman Thomas Downey (New York) and Senator Albert Gore (Tennessee), among other bills, would provide larger credits for families with more children. The Downey-Gore bill, for example, would raise the maximum EITC in 1990 to $1,430 for families with one child and $2,043 for families with two or more children.

President Bush has proposed a refundable credit for families with children under the age of four, which he labels "child care assistance" but which is essentially a second earned income tax credit. Like the EITC, the credit equals 14 percent of wages up to $7,143, where it reaches the proposed $1,000 maximum. It then remains at $1,000 until wages reach $8,000, after which the credit is reduced by 20 cents for each additional dollar earned, so that it phases out at $13,000. The phase-out range would be increased to between $15,000 and $20,000 by 1994. For families with several children under the age of four, this plan is similar to an EITC that provides greater subsidies to larger families.

The Bush proposal would allow a family that had child care expenses that were reimbursable under the new child care assistance credit to receive both the concurrent EITC and the new credit, or the EITC and the DCC. The Bush proposal would also make the DCC refundable. The family would not be able to receive both the new child care assistance credit and the DCC. The Bush plan would apply only to families with children under the age of four because of budgetary constraints. But to increase its antipoverty impact, the new credit should be made available to all families with children, not just those with children younger than four.

In addition, the DCC should be expanded and made refundable. One could combine the Bush proposal, revised to benefit all families with children, with the proposed Expanded Child Care Opportunities Act of 1989 (ECCO), sponsored by Senators Bob Packwood (Oregon) and Daniel Patrick Moynihan (New York). ECCO expands the DCC by raising the maximum subsidy rate—the percentage of child care expenses that can be credited—from 30 to 40 percent and by making the credit refundable. The bill leaves unchanged the maximum amount of child care expenses that are eligible for the subsidy—$2,400 for one child and $4,800 for two or more children—so the maximum DCC would increase to $960 for one child and $1,920 for two or more children.

One could combine an expanded Bush proposal with ECCO to provide additional aid for working poor and low-income families and recoup some of the additional budgetary costs of these proposals by phasing out the DCC for higher-income taxpayers. For example, under ECCO, the child care subsidy rate falls from 40 percent at $10,000 to 20 percent at $27,500, after which it remains constant. An alternative would be to have the subsidy rate continue to fall in the same manner so that it was phased out for families with incomes above $45,000. Alternatively, one could follow the plan of the Downey-Gore bill, which would pay for itself by raising the marginal tax rate in the personal income tax for the highest-income taxpayers.

Because female-headed families have such high poverty rates, and because poor female-headed families have incomes that fall further below the poverty line than poor male-headed families, additional strategies are necessary. The Wisconsin Child Support Assurance System (Garfinkel 1988), for example, would provide uniform child support awards financed by a percentage-of-income tax on the absent parent, which would be automatically withheld from his or her earnings. If this amount were less than a fixed minimum level because the absent parent's income was low, then the support payment would be supplemented up to the minimum by government funds.

The three policies highlighted here target the working poor with children. Various combinations and permutations of these and other current policy proposals, such as extensions of medical care coverage for the uninsured, and a variety of education and training proposals, including the expansion of work/welfare programs such as those recently implemented in California, Massachusetts, New Jersey and other states are all necessary components of a comprehensive antipoverty strategy (see Ellwood 1988 for one example of such a strategy).

The experience of the 25 years since the declaration of War on Poverty has shown that no single program or policy can aid all of the poor. Yet the new realism requires us to confront the facts that all of these proposals have budgetary costs, and that we do not even have model programs to address some aspects of the poverty problem, let alone solutions that could be implemented on a nationwide basis. While we do not know how to eliminate some of the causes of poverty, we know how to alleviate most of its effects. And we certainly know that without a refocused antipoverty strategy and additional antipoverty funds, the rates of low earnings and poverty will remain unacceptably high.

Notes

This research was supported in part by grants from the U.S. Department of Health and Human Services and the Russell Sage Foundation. Greg Acs, Tom Donley, and Jon Haveman provided computational services. Cindy Brach, Steve Garasky, Deenie Kinder, William Prosser, and Elizabeth Uhr provided valuable comments on a prior draft. Any opinions expressed are those of the author and not of any sponsoring institution or agency.

1. In this chapter, *white* refers to white non-Hispanics and *black* refers to black non-Hispanics.

2. When poverty is measured by an absolute poverty line such as the official measure, the poverty rate will generally fall as real incomes rise. For example, consider the case in which the real income of each family doubles over a 20-year period. Income inequality and relative poverty will be unchanged, as the relative distance between the rich and poor has remained constant. Absolute poverty, however, will decline significantly, because it is measured by comparing a family's income, which has now doubled, to a poverty line that has remained unchanged in real terms.

The poverty rate, as officially measured, is thus likely to decline over long periods, such as 1949–69, marked by rapid growth in real incomes. With a relatively constant mean, the poverty rate will fall only if the income of poor families grows more rapidly than the mean. If the incomes of the poor grow less rapidly than the mean, the poverty rate can increase even if the mean increases. In this case inequality, relative poverty, and absolute poverty are increased. Such a situation characterizes the 1979–87 period (see Danziger, Gottschalk, and Smolensky 1989).

3. Any choice of a fixed cutoff with which to compare earnings is arbitrary. Levy and Michel (1988), in evaluating whether or not a job is a "good" one, use a cutoff of $20,000. David Ellwood (1988: 87) uses a normative definition: "I believe that in a two-parent family, the earnings of one person working full year, full time (or the equivalent number of hours of combined work by a husband and wife) ought to be sufficient for a family to reach the poverty line." Ellwood's norm implies a cutoff that varies, like the official poverty line, with family size. The measure used here is similar to Levy and Michel's in that it does not take into account the person's family size or structure, but it is similar in level to Ellwood's. Berlin and Sum (1988) use the poverty line for a family of three as their benchmark in an analysis of male earnings in 1973, 1979, and 1984.

4. Sawhill (1988a) uses a classification of the poor that would subdivide my category of low earners into three groups—the "underemployed poor" who report themselves as unable to find work; the "hard-working poor" who work full time year-round; and a residual category of students, early retirees, and others who do not report difficulty in finding work and who either do not work at all or work only sporadically. In the empirical work that follows, this third group is mostly eliminated by my restriction of the analysis to persons between the ages of 25 and 54. To reduce the number of tables, I do not distinguish between "the underemployed" and the "hard-working" low earners.

5. Most low earners are, in fact, not officially poor. The connection between low earnings and poverty has weakened over the past 40 years because of

changes in family size and sources of income. Mean family size has declined over time and is now less than four; and the percentage of families with two earners and with income from government transfers has increased.

6. Levy and Michel (1988) examine changes between 1973 and 1987 in the percentage of men who earn less than $20,000 per year in constant 1987 dollars. Their results are similar to those reported here—substantial increases in the percentage of men earning less than a fixed threshold. They also report increased inequality, with a greater proportion of men earning above $60,000 in 1987 than in 1973.

7. This increase in the low-earnings rate of men reflects mainly lower real earnings, not reductions in work effort. The mean number of weeks worked for men aged 25 to 54 with exactly 12 years of schooling was 46.32 in 1949, 45.75 in 1979, and 44.13 in 1986. Levy and Michel (1988) also find that falling real earnings between 1973 and 1987 are mostly due to declining weekly wages.

8. *The Forgotten Half* (William T. Grant Foundation 1988) is devoted to the economic problems of those who graduate from high school but do not go on to college. Also, see Berlin and Sum 1988 for a discussion of the relationship between educational attainment and ability.

9. A comparison of high school graduates over the entire 40-year period is problematic because of the educational upgrading that took place. For example, for whites, a high school graduate in 1949 was among the top 40 percent in educational attainment, while in 1986 he was in the bottom half of the educational distribution. However, over the seven-year period between 1979 and 1986, there was relatively little change in the educational distribution, and, as Figure 5.3 shows, there was a dramatic decline in the ability of young high school graduates to avoid low earnings. The changes in the returns to schooling between 1979 and 1986 are much too large to be explained by changes in the quality of schooling. For a more complete discussion, see Murphy and Welch 1989.

10. For a comprehensive discussion of changes in the socioeconomic status and educational attainment of blacks, see Jaynes and Williams 1989.

11. Of course, differences in the economic status of formerly married men and women would not be as large if noncustodial parents paid more in child support.

References
Aaron, Henry (1978). *Politics and the Professors: The Great Society in Perspective.* Washington, D.C.: Brookings Institution.
Berlin, Gordon, and Andrew Sum (1988). *Toward a More Perfect Union: Basic Skills, Poor Families, and Our Economic Future.* New York: Ford Foundation.
Blackburn, McKinley, David Bloom, and Richard Freeman (1989). "Why Has the Economic Position of Less-Skilled Male Workers Deteriorated in the United States?" Photocopy.
Committee for Economic Development (1987). *Children in Need: Investment Strategies for the Educationally Disadvantaged.* New York: Committee for Economic Development.

Danziger, Sheldon, and Peter Gottschalk (1988). "Increasing Inequality in the United States." *Journal of Post-Keynesian Economics* 11 (2): 174–95, Winter.

Danziger, Sheldon, Peter Gottschalk, and Eugene Smolensky (1989). "How the Rich Have Fared, 1973–1987." *American Economic Review* 79 (2): 310–14.

Ellwood, David (1988) *Poor Support: Poverty in the American Family.* New York: Basic Books.

Freeman, Richard (1976). *The Overeducated American.* New York: Academic Press.

Garfinkel, Irwin (1988). "The Evolution of Child Support Policy." *Focus* 11 (1): 11–16. (Madison, Wis.; Institute for Research on Poverty).

Hanushek, Eric (1987). "Non-Labor-Supply Responses to the Income Maintenance Experiments." In Alicia Munnell, ed., *Lessons from the Income Maintenance Experiments.* Boston: Federal Reserve Bank of Boston, pp. 106–21.

Jaynes, Gerald, and Robin Williams, eds. (1989). *A Common Destiny: Blacks and American Society.* Washington, D.C.: National Academy Press.

Johnson, Lyndon (1965). *Public Papers of the Presidents of the United States, 1963–64.* Book 2. Washington, D.C.: U.S. Government Printing Office.

Lampman, Robert (1971). *Ends and Means of Reducing Income Poverty.* Chicago: Markham Publishing.

Levy, Frank, and Richard Michel (1988). "Education and Income: Recent U.S. Trends." Washington, D.C.: Urban Institute, December. Research Paper.

Mallar, Charles (1976). "Educational and Labor Supply Responses of Young Adults in Experimental Families." In Harold Watts and Albert Rees, eds., *The New Jersey Income Maintenance Experiment.* Vol. 2. New York: Academic Press, pp. 163–84.

Murnane, Richard (1988). "Education and the Productivity of the Work Force: Looking Ahead." In Robert Litan, Robert Z. Lawrence, and Charles Schultze, eds., *American Living Standards: Threats and Challenges.* Washington D.C.: Brookings Institution, pp. 215–45.

Murphy, Kevin, and Finis Welch (1989). "Wage Premiums for College Graduates: Recent Growth and Possible Explanations." *Educational Researcher* 18 (May): 17–26.

Reagan, Ronald (1986). "Radio Address by the President." Office of the Press Secretary, February 15. Photocopy.

Ross, Christine, Sheldon Danziger, and Eugene Smolensky (1987). "The Level and Trend in Poverty, 1939–1979." *Demography* 24 (November): 587–600.

Sawhill, Isabel (1988a). "Poverty and the Underclass." In Isabel Sawhill, ed., *Challenge to Leadership.* Washington, D.C.: Urban Institute Press, pp. 215–52.

——— (1988b). "Poverty in the U.S.: Why Is It So Persistent?" *Journal of Economic Literature* 26 (September): 1073–1119.

Tobin, James (1965). "The Case for an Income Guarantee." *Public Interest,* No. 4, pp. 31–41.

U.S. Bureau of the Census (1988). *Measuring the Effect of Benefits and Taxes on Income and Poverty: 1986.* Series P-60, No. 164-RD-1. Washington, D.C.: U.S. Government Printing Office.

U.S. Congress. House Committee on Ways and Means (1988). *Background Material and Data on Programs within the Jurisdiction of the Committee on Ways and Means.* Washington, D.C.: U.S. Government Printing Office.

U.S. Council of Economic Advisers (1964). *Economic Report of the President.* Washington, D.C.: U.S. Government Printing Office.

Venti, Steven, and David Wise (1984). "Income Maintenance and the School and Work Decisions of Youth." Cambridge, Mass.: Harvard University. Photocopy.

William T. Grant Foundation Commission on Work, Family, and Citizenship (1988). *The Forgotten Half: Pathways to Success for America's Youth and Young Families.* New York: William T. Grant Foundation.

PART TWO

Components

6

Elementary and Secondary Education

Ernest L. Boyer

In 1957, the Soviets hurled a 184-pound satellite into space. America was stunned. The nation's confidence was shaken, and our very survival seemed threatened. Jolted by Sputnik, the United States was determined to recapture its leadership and pride. Of all the steps we took, the one most revealing of our national character was our renewed commitment to public education.

Education is in the headlines once again. The president and all fifty governors have established national education goals because of the deep, bipartisan conviction in America today that, if this country is to be economically productive and competitive in world markets, every young person must develop knowledge that is global as well as national in scope. Thirty years ago, school reform was driven by a military threat. This time the fear is economic.

Today, the world's 190 independent nations are economically related. High interest rates in the United States hurt Common Market countries; bad harvests in the Soviet Union help Canadian farmers; a Middle East oil glut means recession in Houston; a robotics breakthrough in Tokyo makes a difference in Detroit.

Education and the national economy are inextricably connected. Mind power is the key to tapping America's full potential. More knowledge and more skills will be required in all areas—civic, professional, and cultural—but especially in the workplace. Language proficiency, problem solving, and numerical reasoning are crucial.

The Bureau of Labor Statistics reports that very few new jobs will be created for those who cannot read, follow directions, and use mathematics. To revisit briefly a point made by Arnold Packer earlier in this vol-

Figure 6.1   Trends in college entrance examination scores: the SAT and the ACT.

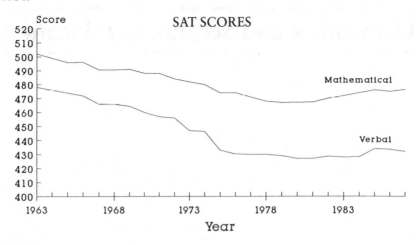

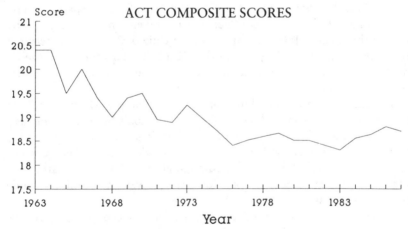

(Reprinted from National Center for Education Statistics, U.S. Department of Education, *The Condition of Education—Volume 1* [Washington, D.C.: U.S. Government Printing Office, 1988].)

ume, the fastest-growing job categories will be in professional, technical, and sales fields requiring the highest education and skill levels.

Responsibility for providing an educated work force is concentrated largely in the nation's schools, and since 1983 the United States has been working hard to strengthen public education. Academic standards have been raised in almost every state. Teacher training has improved, and the salaries of teachers have increased at twice the inflation rate.

Figure 6.2 Percentage of in-school 17-year-olds at or above various reading levels.

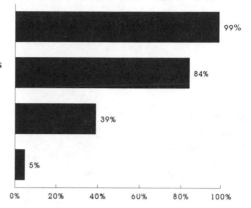

Basic: Find information in a short paragraph — 99%

Intermediate: Recognize paraphrases of lengthy passages — 84%

Adept: Analyze moderately complicated passages about topics studied in high school — 39%

Advanced: Extrapolate ideas in specialized documents common in professional and technical work — 5%

(Reprinted from National Assessment of Educational Progress, *The Reading Report Card* [Princeton, N.J.: Educational Testing Service, 1986].)

While college entrance scores on the Scholastic Aptitude Test (SAT) and the American College Test (ACT) show little improvement after years of decline (Fig. 6.1), test data show that black and Hispanic students are performing better. In city after city, business leaders have formed partnerships with schools, and the nation's top corporate executives have become leading advocates for public education.

Despite spotty gains, however, we still do not have in the United States a public school system capable of preparing a top-quality work force. While a small percentage of America's schools—10 to 15 percent, perhaps—offer the finest education in the world, the majority of our students attend schools where quality ranges from good to mediocre. And, for a disturbingly large group of America's young people—perhaps 20 to 30 percent—the school experience is a failure.

Each year, almost 700,000 students drop out of school. And according to one estimate, the cost of each year's class of dropouts is more than $240 billion in lost earnings and forgone taxes (Committee for Economic Development 1987: 3). Of those who do stay in school, fewer than 50 percent read at levels adequate to carry out even moderately complex tasks (Fig. 6.2). And while most students can complete simple arithmetic assignments such as addition and subtraction, the majority cannot apply mathematical knowledge to more complex questions (Table 6.1).

In science, our dilemma is no less great. A survey by the International Association for the Evaluation of Educational Achievement (1988: 3) revealed that ten-year-olds in the United States ranked in the middle

Table 6.1 Percentages Performing At or Above Each Level of the Mathematics Scale, Age 13

	Add and Subtract	Simple Problems	Two-Step Problems	Understand Concepts	Interpret Data
Level:	300	400	500	600	700
Korea	100	95	78	40	5
Quebec (French)	100	97	73	22	2
British Columbia	100	95	69	24	2
Quebec (English)	100	97	67	20	1
New Brunswick (English)	100	95	65	18	1
Ontario (English)	99	92	58	16	1
New Brunswick (French)	100	95	58	12	<1
Spain	99	91	57	14	1
United Kingdom	98	87	55	18	2
Ireland	98	86	55	14	<1
Ontario (French)	99	85	40	7	0
United States	97	78	40	9	1

Source: Reprinted from LaPointe et al. 1989, by permission of Educational Testing Service, the copyright owner.

Note: Jackknifed standard errors for percentages range from less than .1 to 2.4.

when compared to their counterparts from 15 other participating countries. Fourteen-year-old students ranked 14th out of 17 countries. And in the upper grades of high school, advanced science students in the United States ranked last in biology and performed far behind students from most countries in chemistry and physics (Table 6.2).

Computer competence is also disappointing. While today's young people should know more about word processing and spreadsheet programs, most students, according to a recent National Assessment (Martinez and Mead 1988: 70), do not have such skills, nor are they getting the information necessary to develop them.

The nation's schools have been particularly unsuccessful in preparing young people for the world of work. A high school diploma modestly enhances job prospects, regardless of the courses taken, but the capacity of vocational courses to help students become employed is largely disappointing. Indeed, job prospects for students specializing in vocational education—auto mechanics, secretarial studies, metal shop, wood construction, and the like—are not much better than they are for those in the general education program (Osterman 1980: 28).

Table 6.2 Rank Order of Countries for Achievement at Each Level

	10-yr.-olds Grade 4/5	14-yr.-olds Grade 8/9	Grade 12/13 Science Students		
			Biology	Chemistry	Physics
Australia	9	10	9	6	8
Canada (English)	6	4	11	12	11
England	12	11	2	2	2
Finland	3	5	7	13	12
Hong Kong	13	16	5	1	1
Hungary	5	1	3	5	3
Italy	7	11	12	10	13
Japan	1	2	10	4	4
Korea	1	7	—	—	—
Netherlands	—	3	—	—	—
Norway	10	9	6	8	6
Philippines	15	17	—	—	—
Poland	11	7	4	7	7
Singapore	13	14	1	3	5
Sweden	4	6	8	9	10
Thailand	—	14	—	—	—
U.S.A.	8	14	13	11	9

Source: Reprinted from International Association for the Evaluation of Educational Achievement 1988.

Furthermore, few schools can offer a full range of vocational courses to match the changing job market. According to Bureau of Labor Statistics projections, data processors, machine mechanics, and computer systems analysts, operators, and programmers will be among the fastest-growing job categories during the 1990s. But most high schools are ill-equipped to prepare students for such occupations. Another problem is that vocational students are often academically short-changed. Students in work-related programs frequently are offered a less challenging curriculum and less effective teaching. At graduation, they often do not have the verbal and intellectual tools needed to do productive work.

Thus, after years of school reform, this nation is still not preparing students adequately for the world of work. We are simply not developing the human capital required. Where did we go wrong? Why does the United States still seem unable to achieve academic excellence for its schools? Although the problem is enormously complex, there is strong evidence to suggest that we're losing ground for three interlocking reasons:

1. In spite of all the talk about better schools, America is not responding to the school crisis with the sense of urgency required. Reforms are succeeding in schools that are already working fairly well, but our most troubled institutions are standing still or getting worse. The commitment—especially to save urban schools—simply is not there. When hundreds of our students are economically and socially unprepared year after year, the crisis is not met with either outrage or urgent action. There seems to be a feeling that the problem is so complex and the responsibility for action so diffused that action is endlessly deferred.
2. Education in this country continues to fail because our approach to school reform is piecemeal rather than coherent. We have loads of reports but no comprehensive plan. "Magnet schools" and "model schools" are being promoted—all of which is helpful—but what about the other schools? Today's reform movement is not systematic; it's best described as a strategy of "excellence by exception."
3. There is confusion about goals, and in a country where local control has been the preferred tradition, no one is held accountable for results. Since we don't know where we're going, it's impossible to know if progress has been made. Thus, the reform movement is failing not just from lack of overall direction but also from confusion about how to measure the results adequately.

For the reform movement to succeed, we don't need more model schools; we don't need a rash of new reports to describe effective education. What the reform movement does need is a comprehensive strategy for renewal. In the remaining sections, a six-point approach to school improvement is defined, one in which all levels of education can work together to achieve commitment, coherence, and accountability, as well.

The Mandate: Excellence for All

First, to achieve better schools, we must agree that all students can and will succeed. We need a national commitment to the proposition that every child, regardless of background, must have a high-quality education and must be given full opportunity to become socially and economically empowered.

Today many people simply do not believe this objective can be reached. Year after year, about one out of every four students leaves school before receiving a diploma—and for minority students, high school completion rates are even worse (Fig. 6.3). Especially disturbing is the crisis in the cities, where the U.S. Department of Education reports an average attrition rate of 50 percent. And independent studies of drop-

Figure 6.3 High school completion rates, by race and Hispanic origin.

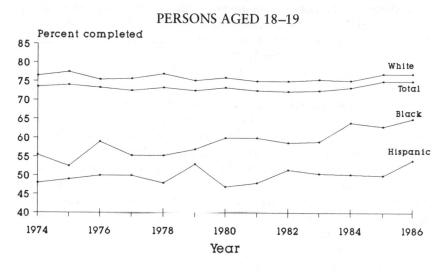

PERSONS AGED 18–19

PERSONS AGED 25–29

(Reprinted from National Center for Education Statistics, U.S. Department of Education, *The Condition of Education—Volume 1* [Washington, D.C.: U.S. Government Printing Office, 1988].)

outs in some Chicago schools and in New York City report even higher rates: 63 percent and 68 percent, respectively (Education Commission of the States 1988: 37).

A recent Carnegie Foundation report (1988a: xiii) revealed that 75 percent of the high school freshmen in Chicago had reading test scores below the national average, and only 229 of the 1,918 students at one

Los Angeles high school scored at grade level in reading. For the nation as a whole, the National Assessment of Educational Progress reports a 22-point gap between the average reading scores of disadvantaged urban 17-year-olds and the average scores of all 17-year-olds in 1984 (Council of the Great City Schools 1987: 9).

A particularly sobering appraisal was offered by the Citywide Educational Coalition in Boston, which concluded: "Not only do 44 percent of [Boston's] high school students drop out before they reach 12th grade, over 40 percent of those who do reach 12th grade score below the 30th percentile on a standardized reading test. They may graduate, but they are functionally illiterate" (Carnegie Foundation 1988a: xiii).

Clearly, many of the nation's schools still are in deep trouble, and yet we accept this failure as a way of life. It is significant, for example, that 21 percent of today's teachers believe that schools cannot expect to graduate more than 75 percent of those enrolled. Still more sobering, about 30 percent of urban high school teachers feel this way (Carnegie Foundation 1988b: 49).

If snow was piling up on city streets, if we had heaps of garbage on the curbs, if a health epidemic was striking one fourth of our children in this country, the president, governors, and mayors would declare a national emergency. They would bring together all appropriate officials in a round-the-clock crisis session, and no one would be dismissed until an appropriate plan of action had been shaped. But when students' lives are wasted, when hundreds of thousands of our children leave school educationally and socially unprepared, public officials do not act with the sense of urgency—and persistence—the emergency requires. The very language of the current school reform movement tells a revealing story. We hear much talk these days about "model schools" and "magnet schools" and "essential schools." The focus is on a handful of privileged institutions that are "showcased," as educators like to say. This strategy, which might best be described as "excellence by exception," benefits the "lighthouse" institutions, while the rest struggle on their own.

The United States, if it is to remain an economically vital nation, cannot tolerate a system that divides the winners and the losers. The satisfactory completion of 12 years of schooling must be viewed as the right of every student. We must ensure that all children, even those from the most difficult backgrounds, will have available to them the conditions to assure that they will succeed academically and socially. The goal must be quality for all.

Developing a Curriculum with Coherence

Second, we must agree on goals. Educators should define, with clarity, what it means to be an educated person, and agree upon the content to be studied. Tomorrow's curriculum surely must provide something more than the disconnected courses and the minimalist fragmentation of information that exist today. Since 1983, states have made significant additions to the core of courses mandated for high school graduation (Fig. 6.4). Forty-two states increased their mandates in mathematics, and science curriculum requirements have gone up in 36 states. All but 11 states now make four years of English a requirement for graduation. Five states have increased their foreign-language requirements.

Even with these gains, the school curriculum still has neither quality nor coherence. We have added "Carnegie units," which measure time in class, requiring students to complete another course in "history," or "science," but we have failed to ask, "What's behind the labels?" The curriculum, in most states, is still shaped more by textbooks and lesson plans than by a national consensus of what is most worth knowing.

But is there a core curriculum appropriate for all students? If so, how should it be defined? The first priority is to teach proficiency in the written and spoken word. Twenty-first-century workers must think critically and communicate with clarity and precision. They must have strong computational skills as well. In its appeal to strengthen mathematics education, the National Research Council (1989: 1) noted that high-quality education in mathematics is essential for a healthy economy because workers in the twenty-first century must be prepared to absorb new ideas, adapt to change, cope with ambiguity, and solve unconventional problems.

Clearly, high school students who plan to enter the job market, no less than those who prepare for college, should have a command of English and mathematics. A survey of basic skills in the work force (Center for Public Resources 1982: 5, 19, 20, 23), found that more than 65 per cent of companies questioned said that poor basic skills are a barrier to job advancement among their high-school-graduate employees. And 35 percent were forced to offer their own remedial programs. Half the companies identified writing as a problem, and more than half reported that speaking and listening were serious problems, too. Employees were unable to follow verbal instructions. They could not express ideas effectively.

In addition to learning verbal and numerical skills, all students—through a study of history, literature, geography, civics, and the arts—should be introduced to a core of common learning. In such a general education sequence, they should study Western thought and learn about our own traditions. But in an increasingly interdependent world, students also should become familiar with languages and cultures other than our own. Today's youth will be living in a world that is economically, politically, and ecologically connected, and students need a perspective that is not only national but global as well.

Figure 6.4   Changes in high school graduation requirements, by subject area, 1980–1987.

SUMMARY OF CHANGES IN HIGH SCHOOL SUBJECT AREA REQUIREMENTS—1980–1987

Mathematics

Math requirements were increased in 42 states. In 1987:

11 states require 3 years	5 states have no requirements
2 states require 2 or 3 years	(1 state recommends 2 years and 1 state
31 states require 2 years	recommends 3 years)
2 states require 1 year	

Science

Science requirements were increased in 36 states. In 1987:

3 states require 3 years	5 states require 1 year
2 states require 2 or 3 years	5 states have no requirement (2 of these
34 states require 2 years	recommend 2 years)

Language Arts/English

English or Language Arts requirements were increased in 18 states. In 1987:

30 states require 4 years	5 states have no requirement (2 recom-
7 states require 3 years	mend 4 years)

Social Studies

Social Studies requirements were increased in 29 states. In 1987:

1 state requires 4 years	1 state requires 2 or 1.5 years
2 states require 3.5 years	2 states require 1.5 years
24 states require 3 years	1 state requires 1 year
3 states require 2.5 years	1 state requires 0.5 year
14 states require 2 years	2 states have no requirement

Physical Education/Health

Health and Physical Education requirements were increased in 7 states. In 1987:

1 state requires 4.5 years	18 states require 1 year
1 state requires 4 years	9 states have no requirement
1 state requires 2.5 years	1 state requires 0.5 year of health only
9 states require 2 years	1 state requires 1 year of physical educa-
9 states require 1.5 years	tion only
1 state requires 1.25 years	

Foreign Language

Foreign Language requirements or electives were added in 5 states. In 1987:

1 year is required in the District of Co-	4 states emphasize as an optional elective
lumbia	1 year

Computer Science

Computer Science requirements or electives were added in 7 states. In 1987:

4 states require 0.5 year	1 state emphasizes as an optional elective
2 states emphasize computer science as	2 years
an optional elective 1 year	

(Reprinted from Education Commission for the States, *Clearinghouse Notes* [Denver, Colo.: ECS].)

All students also must discover their connections to the natural world and, through science, understand the interdependent nature of our planet. Not every student is a budding scientist. But being a responsible citizen in the twenty-first century means becoming scientifically literate and understanding more fully the interdependent world in which we live. The American Association for the Advancement of Science, for example, in its "Science for All Americans" curriculum, recently called on educators to move away from memorization toward a more integrated approach that helps students see the larger picture and better understand the structures of our universe and the interdependence of our world.

Furthermore, the core curriculum should include a seminar on the meaning of work. Work is a universal experience. Except for a handful of individuals, no one can choose not to work, and a course on the meaning of vocation should be a part of the required core. Included in such a study would be an introduction to career options, an occasion in which students would be given detailed information about job alternatives and meet with adults in the various career fields.

We also suggest that the new curriculum include an apprenticeship experience. During the last two years of high school, students should have an opportunity to work closely with a mentor at the work site, learning firsthand about career options. In such a setting, the student would understand the importance of good work habits—showing up on time and completing a task once it has been started.

Finally, there is an urgent need for all students to see connections between what they learn and how they live. Today it is possible for American teenagers to finish high school yet never be asked to participate responsibly in life in or out of the school, never be encouraged to spend time with older people who may be lonely, to help a child who has not learned to read, to clean up litter on the street, or even to do something meaningful at the school itself.

In *High School* (Boyer 1983: 209), a new Carnegie unit was proposed. We suggested in that report that all students complete a voluntary service term, one in which the student might serve in a hospital, nursing home, or art gallery, or tutor other kids at school. Students urgently need to relate what they learn to how they live.

Many school districts, Detroit and Atlanta for example, now require community service for graduation. And in Tennessee, 85 schools are now participating in the Governor's Study Partner Program, which enlists student volunteers to serve as tutors for their at-risk peers. This project, whose participants have already demonstrated gains on test scores and improved school attendance, is supported by South Central Bell, which wants these "future workers to stay in school" (Grasso 1988: 5).

The school should be viewed, then, not as an isolated island but as a staging ground for action. Developing human capital—a rather remote term, perhaps—should not remain a vague abstraction. Empowering the nation's youth means helping them to become proficient in the written and the spoken word, learn to think quantitatively, acquire a core of essential knowledge, develop the capacity to think creatively, and in the end, relate activities in the classroom to the realities of life. This is the investment in human capital schools must make. It is an investment that will secure the civic and economic future of the nation.

Building a Good Foundation in the Early Years

Third, to assure that all children are educationally well prepared, a solid foundation must be laid. Since the growing child requires a diet rich in protein, vitamins, and minerals, any concern about good school performance must begin with children's basic nutritional requirements, which precede schooling and even birth itself. While health matters may appear to be far off the reform agenda, the evidence is overwhelming. Educational problems cannot be divorced from the problems of the poor. Undernourishment restricts the physical and intellectual growth of children and, in time, affects their ability to succeed in school.

The Physicians' Task Force on Hunger in America (1985: 101) reported that a child deprived of adequate nutrition during critical years of brain growth risks "cognitive deficits" that restrict learning later on. In a Louisiana study, poor children who received nutritional supplements were compared to those who had been nutritionally denied. The children receiving good nutrition had a higher IQ, a longer attention span, and higher grades in school.

The harsh truth is that most mothers in poverty are not adequately nourished. Malnutrition affects almost a half-million children in this nation. Compensatory help for disadvantaged mothers and small children is required. Specifically, support for the federally financed Special Supplemental Food Program for Women, Infants, and Children should be increased. This program is cost-effective. It provides nutritional supplements and prenatal care to low-income, at-risk mothers and babies, yet it serves half of those needing help. Funding for this program should be increased significantly. Expectant mothers and young children must have good nutrition if good education is our goal.

Many poor children are not just nutritionally deprived; they are intellectually undernourished, too. "Kids grow up with little interest in school," said Everett J. Williams, the school superintendent in New Orleans. "They come to school not able to count to ten, not knowing their colors, not knowing where they live, and some not even knowing their names. At the beginning of their careers in school they are already students at risk" (Carnegie Foundation 1988a: 18).

Table 6.3 Percentage of Teachers Reporting Significant Student Health Problems

Conditions Reported	Urban Teachers	Other Teachers
Abused and/or neglected children	41	36
Undernourished children	25	13
Poor health among children	29	16

Source: Carnegie Foundation 1988a.

There is special poignancy in the fact that over one-third of all teachers and nearly half the urban teachers surveyed by the Carnegie Foundation said that the neglect of children is a problem at their school. Twenty-five percent of teachers in the cities described poor nourishment as a serious matter, and nearly 30 percent said that poor health is a problem, too (Table 6.3).

The Perry Preschool Project in Ypsilanti, Michigan, makes a strong case for educational intervention during the first years of life. This long-term program provided daily preschool education and weekly home visits for economically disadvantaged three- and four-year-olds. When followed up over time, children in that program were found to have better grades and a greater likelihood of high school graduation than did a comparable control group. Furthermore, it has been estimated that for every $1,000 invested in the two-year preschool program, almost $4,000 has been or will be recouped in lower educational, prison, and welfare costs later on (Parnes 1986: 20).

Thus, investing successfully in human capital means early intervention. To be sure, the first obligation rests with the family, but outside help also is needed for the growing number of poor families that cannot make it on their own. This means full funding of Head Start, a program described by Marian Wright Edelman in Chapter 10 of this book, and Chapter I of the Elementary and Secondary School Improvement Act. It is a national disgrace that 20 years after Chapter I was created, only half the eligible children are being served (Children's Defense Fund 1988: 146).

Chapter I remedial programs have successfully improved the reading and math skills of millions of elementary school students. A 1985 report by the House Select Committee on Children, Youth, and Families found that for every $500 invested in a year of compensatory education, $3,000 could be saved in the cost of repeating a grade. And new accountability and parental-involvement requirements included in the 1988 five-year reauthorization of Chapter I make this program even more effective in helping the educationally deprived catch up with their more advantaged peers (Committee for Economic Development 1987: 6).

One final point: to strengthen early education, the primary school program must be altered. If a child does not have a good basic education, it is almost impossible to compensate fully for the failure later on. To give all children a solid educational foundation, school districts may wish to reorganize the first years of formal education into a Basic School, a unit that would include kindergarten through grade three. The goal would be to assure that every child, by grade four, reads with understanding, writes with clarity, and speaks and listens effectively.

In the Basic School, rigid grade levels should be blurred. Teachers in the early years should not fret over whether a beginning student should "fail." Some children develop more slowly than others, and whether a student is in "first grade" or "second grade" is inconsequential. What is important is not age, but linguistic progress.

The most efficient investment in human capital occurs when a solid foundation is laid during the first years of formal education. A good beginning will assure that students will succeed academically, be productive in the work place, and be prepared to adapt to rapid changes. These must be the educational objectives for every child.

Governance: Restructuring the Schools

Fourth, there must be a restructuring of public schools. In recent years, we have had a top-down approach to school improvement. Educators at the local level are caught in a system often more preoccupied with paperwork than with learning. Principals are robbed of authority to act, and teachers have little control over the key elements of education. They are held responsible for the bureaucratic, rather than the educational aspects of their work.

Especially disturbing is the rigidity of large urban schools. In these schools, teachers are three times as likely as their counterparts in nonurban schools to feel uninvolved in setting objectives and in selecting books and materials, and they are twice as apt to have no control over course content (Table 6.4).

The real work of education takes place at the local school and in classrooms where teachers meet with students every day. School-based management is urgently required. Day-to-day decisions about textbooks, teaching schedules, and the like should shift to the local school. Teachers and principals must be given freedom to work creatively toward overall objectives. Furthermore, they should be held accountable for outcomes, not hassled by entangling red tape that focuses on procedures.

At the same time, schools must be held accountable for their work.

Table 6.4   Percentage of Teachers Reporting "No Control" over Decision Making

Decisions Made	Urban Teachers	Other Teachers
Setting goals	17	6
Selecting course content	29	14
Selecting textbooks and materials	36	12

Source: Carnegie Foundation 1988a.

This nation cannot move forward with a disconnected educational arrangement in which 83,000 schools and 16,000 districts go their own separate ways. We need criteria by which progress can be measured. Currently, we have a hodgepodge of isolated items—SAT scores, occasional international comparisons, and the like—but, in the end, these random efforts often confuse rather than clarify the issue. The president has a Council of Economic Advisors to keep track of financial trends, but we have no way to measure, in timely fashion, trends in education.

The time has come to fix accountability in education. For the first time in its history, the United States must strike a balance between local control and national results. Specifically, I suggest that a panel of educators and distinguished citizens be organized to evaluate the progress of the states—using criteria that range from school finance, to teacher morale, to student achievement. This body—called, perhaps, the National Council on Education Trends—should report periodically to the president and to the nation on how the states are doing, separately and collectively, in fulfilling their mandate to provide, for all students, a quality education.

Beyond state-by-state accountability, we also need to evaluate educational success at the local school. While teachers assess the progress of each child using more subtle measures, the public deserves to see some indication of the results. Specifically, each school should submit annually a report card to the state measuring its effectiveness against statewide and national standards. Such an assessment should be prepared by teachers and local school officials and should respond to questions about the performance of both the student and the school. The yardstick used might include items such as the following:

A School Report Card

- Does the school have clearly defined goals that include the guarantee of an effective education for every student?

- What evidence is there that students are developing their ability to communicate in both the written and spoken word?
- Does the school have a core curriculum for all students? What is the general knowledge of students in such fields as history, geography, science, mathematics, literature, and the arts? Is such knowledge appropriately assessed?
- What are the number and types of books being read by students?
- Is the school organized into small units to overcome anonymity among students and provide a close relationship between each student and a mentor?
- Is there a program that encourages students to take responsibility for helping each other learn and helps make the school a friendly and orderly place? How well is it succeeding?
- What teaching innovations have been introduced during the preceding academic year? Are there programs to reward teachers who exercised leadership?
- Does the school have a plan of renewal for teachers and administrators?
- Is the school clean, attractive, and well equipped? Does it have adequate learning resources such as computers and a basic library? Can the school document that these resources are used by students and teachers to support effective learning?
- Are parents active in the school and kept informed about the progress of their children? Are there parent consultation sessions? How many parents participate in such programs?
- What are daily attendance and graduation rates at the school?
- What changes have occurred in the dropout rate and in students seeking postsecondary education and in getting jobs after graduation? What is being done to improve performance in these areas?
- What percentage of the students go to college? What is their record of performance?
- What percentage of the students go directly to the work place? What do employers say about their productivity and skills? What is their record of performance six months or a year later?

In developing a framework of accountability, one additional point must be considered. If the local school, for whatever reason, is unable to provide the conditions for effective education, public officials have an obligation to intervene. Specifically, if a school is failing to educate its students, the state should appoint a school evaluation team to review the school's performance.

The proposed team of evaluators should conduct on-site visits and have access to school records. Team members also should observe classes and conduct interviews with the principal, teachers, students, and parents. Upon completion of its visit, the team should identify strengths and weaknesses and prepare a specific plan for school improvement, outlining steps that the state, the district board, and the local school should take.

The California Department of Education has introduced a statewide assessment plan for its secondary schools. The California plan—a joint review conducted by the Western Association of Schools and Colleges and the State Department of Education—has three goals: to assure that the curriculum meets established criteria for quality, to assist high school students in meeting requirements for graduation and postsecondary admissions, and to provide an opportunity for professional growth. A main feature of the California assessment is the assigning of specialists, one for each academic subject area, to consult with the teachers on professional development and to help in the preparation of the self-study.

Other states have proposed or enacted legislation dealing with "academic bankruptcy" or "failed" districts, including Arkansas, Georgia, Illinois, Kentucky, New Jersey, New Mexico, Ohio, South Carolina, and Texas. While the results of this legislation are largely untested, local districts are being called upon to undergo periodic evaluation relating to such "input" measures as fiscal resources, number of library books and programs, and organizational, pedagogical, and curricular practices—as well as "output" measures ranging from academic achievement to attendance and dropout rates.

There is, in short, a need for both input and output in assessment. The focus must be not just on means but also on ends. While overall objectives (output) at the state and local level must be established, great flexibility and resources (input) must be given to each school in the pursuit of these goals. Such a restructuring will breathe new life into a suffocating system and increase America's confidence that public education can, in fact, prepare good workers with good skills.

Investing in Teachers

Fifth, we can strengthen our schools by promoting excellence in teaching. The quality of education in this country can be no greater than the dignity we assign to teaching, and we urgently need in the United States a national crusade to attract the brightest and the best into the classrooms. Interest in teaching as a career declined in the late 1970s and dipped to its lowest level in 1982. Since 1983, it has rebounded slightly, sparked perhaps by publicity about the need for good teachers, as well as by higher salaries, which have gone up at nearly twice the inflation rate. Still, a teacher shortage is expected due to an increase in the number of teachers nearing retirement age and a decrease in the number of college freshmen planning to become teachers (Office of Technology Assessment 1988: 54–55). In fact, many school districts face a situation in which half of their teachers may have to be replaced by the end of the decade. Between 1986 and 1992, 1.3 million new teachers will be hired (Carnegie Forum 1986: 31).

The harsh truth is, the nation's ablest students most often do not choose teaching. The National Commission for Excellence in Teacher Education (1985: 5) reports that high school seniors who said they planned to enter teaching scored in the bottom quartile of all those taking the American College Test. The National Science Board Commission on Precollege Education in Mathematics, Science, and Technology finds that many of the teachers in elementary schools are not qualified to teach mathematics and science for even 30 minutes a day, and a significant fraction of secondary school teachers are called upon to work in subjects for which they were never trained (Carnegie Forum 1986: 39).

To attract better students into teaching, working conditions must improve. This means higher salaries (Fig. 6.5) and a systematic program of renewal. When the Carnegie Foundation recently surveyed teachers on the impact of school reform, we found little evidence of improvement in the area of teacher renewal: 17 percent said that special awards for teachers have either not changed or gotten worse; about 7 teachers in 10 said that the amount of money available to support innovative ideas has not improved; and 87 percent said that money for teacher travel has not gotten better.

The need for professional renewal is especially great in math and science, where new technologies and research breakthroughs are being discovered every day. Corporate America understands the importance of renewal programs for employees because such expenditures pay off at the bottom line, and in medicine and law such programs are taken for granted. Teachers, too, need formal opportunities for professional development. We cannot expect a teacher trained 20 years ago to prepare students to live 40 years into the future without a program of renewal.

President Dwight Eisenhower's response to Sputnik, the National Defense Education Act, provided summer fellowships for teachers and sent a powerful signal to the nation, declaring that teachers were part of the solution, not the problem. Today we need a new version of that initiative—a Teacher Excellence Act—that would, among other things, establish teacher institutes in every region of the country and provide fellowships to thousands of teachers from all 50 states, allowing them to spend time in libraries, in laboratories, and with other teachers—the simple things that college professors take for granted.

The new legislation could also include a distinguished teaching fel-

Figure 6.5 Starting salary of teachers compared to starting salaries of engineers and mathematicians in industry.

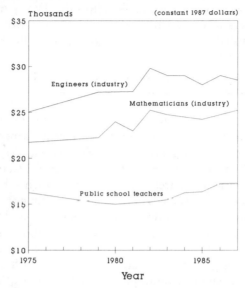

(Reprinted from Office of Technology Assessment, *Elementary and Secondary Education for Science and Engineering* [Washington, D.C.: U.S. Government Printing Office, 1988].)

lows program in which master teachers in each state would spend a year moving from school to school, holding seminars with colleagues. A model is the Yale–New Haven Institute, which enables teachers from the New Haven schools to study with senior members of the faculty at Yale during the summer, based on a curriculum teachers themselves have put in place. Teachers say the program has been a key factor in persuading them to stay in teaching.

Colleges also might organize "conversations in the disciplines," bringing together teachers with college colleagues. Often, teachers feel isolated and have little contact with peers beyond their own schools. To keep intellectually renewed, they need a stronger sense of developments in their disciplines.

Recruiting better teachers is one of the greatest challenges America now confronts, and the federal scholarship program for gifted high school students who plan to enter teaching should be expanded. After all, we have a Peace Corps to send gifted Americans overseas; why not attract the best and brightest to teach the rural poor and the disadvantaged in our inner cities here at home?

Finally, the president himself should give priority to teaching and convene a dinner in the East Room of the White House for the 50 men and women designated by their states as teachers of the year. On this occasion, the president, as host, could affirm the dignity of teaching and invite the teachers to discuss the inspiration of their work. To heighten the impact of this event, it should be televised, prime time.

Creating Partnerships for Excellence

Sixth, we must realize that schools cannot do the job alone. Partnerships with parents are urgently required. In a recent Carnegie Foundation survey, teachers overwhelmingly reported that parents do not participate sufficiently in their children's education. Overall, 9 teachers in 10 said that lack of support from parents is a problem at their schools (Carnegie Foundation 1988b: 36). Today's parents have less time to foster the educational progress of their children. Parent education and parent conferencing must begin early and must continue throughout all the years of formal education. For this to be accomplished, however, more time will be required, and employers must allow parents time off periodically for school conferences and consultations. Schools also must be responsive to the new realities and schedule evening and Saturday opportunities for parents to meet with teachers.

The role of parents in improving U.S. education has been largely overlooked. But if this country is truly concerned about the quality of schools, we must recognize that parents are still the first and most essential teachers. Ways must be found to build new partnerships between home and school. In addition to permitting flexible work schedules, America's corporate executives also have an obligation to be leading advocates for public schools. During the past five years, leaders in business and industry have spoken out aggressively for better schools. They have testified before congressional committees in support of programs to help the disadvantaged. Corporate leaders should continue to use their "bully pulpit" to link education to the economic vitality of the nation.

Finally, industry also should help strengthen human resources in the schools by providing scholarships for future teachers and by sponsoring institutes for principals and teachers. Examples are Kraft's support for the federal Leadership in Education Administration program and Polaroid's move to encourage teachers on sabbatical leave to join the company's paid work force and see how mathematical and scientific concepts are put to use in industry.

Again, schools cannot do the job alone. Partnerships between the family and the school must be strengthened, and corporate America—which truly has a vested interest in the outcome of education—must continue to be a strong advocate for better schools and for better teachers, upon whom the success of any school reform effort ultimately depends.

Conclusion

Since 1983, this nation has been engaged in the most serious and most sustained commitment to school renewal in its history. Encouraging progress has been made, and the Education Summit at the start of the 1990s signals a great opportunity for the new decade. Now we face the really tough agenda. The new, national initiative is most timely because we must now move beyond the scattershot approach to school reform and develop a more coherent, more systematic strategy for action. This means a program committed to educating effectively all students, not just the most advantaged. It also requires a curriculum with coherence, early intervention, a new governance arrangement, excellence in the classroom, and partnerships with other institutions.

Sweeping improvements in the nation's schools can and must occur, but change will come only when the nation wills it. Without good schools, none of America's hopes can be fulfilled. The quality of our education will determine the strength of our democracy, the vitality of our economy, and the promise of our ideals. It is through the schools that this nation has chosen to pursue enlightened ends for all its people. And it is here that the battle for the future of America will be won or lost.

References
Boyer, Ernest L. (1983). *High School.* New York: Harper & Row.
Carnegie Forum on Education and the Economy (1986). *A Nation Prepared: Teachers for the Twenty-first Century.* New York: Carnegie Corporation of New York.
The Carnegie Foundation for the Advancement of Teaching (1988a). *An Imperiled Generation.* Princeton: Carnegie Foundation for the Advancement of Teaching.
——— (1988b). *The Condition of Teaching.* Princeton: Carnegie Foundation for the Advancement of Teaching.
——— (1988c). *Report Card on School Reform.* Princeton: Carnegie Foundation for the Advancement of Teaching.
Center for Public Resources (1982). *Basic Skills in the U.S. Work Force.* New York: Center for Public Resources.
Children's Defense Fund (1988). *A Children's Defense Budget FY 89: An Analysis of Our Nation's Investment in Children.* Washington, D.C.: Children's Defense Fund.
Committee for Economic Development (1987). *Children in Need.* New York: Committee for Economic Development.

Council of the Great City Schools (1987). *Results in the Making.* Washington, D.C.: Council of the Great City Schools.

Education Commission of the States (1987). *Clearinghouse Notes.* Denver, Colo.: Education Commission of the States.

—— (1988). *Renewing Urban Schools.* Denver, Colo.: Education Commission of the States.

Grasso, Christopher (1988): "Peer Tutors Help At-Risk Students Stay in School." *Education Daily,* December 1.

International Association for the Evaluation of Educational Achievement (1988). *Science Achievement in Seventeen Countries.* Oxford: Pergamon Press.

Lapointe, Archie, Nancy Mead, and Gary Phillips (1989). *A World of Differences: An International Assessment of Mathematics and Science.* Princeton: Educational Testing Service.

Martinez, Michael, and Nancy Mead (1988). *Computer Competence: The First National Assessment.* Princeton: National Assessment of Educational Progress, Educational Testing Service.

National Assessment of Educational Progress—Arthur Applebee et al. (1986). *The Writing Report Card.* Princeton: Educational Testing Service.

National Center for Education Statistics, U.S. Department of Education (1988). *The Condition of Education—Volume 1, Elementary and Secondary Education.* Washington, D.C.: U.S. Government Printing Office.

National Commission for Excellence in Teacher Education (1985). *A Call for Change in Teacher Education.* Washington, D.C.: American Association of Colleges for Teacher Education.

National Research Council (1989). *Everybody Counts.* Washington, D.C.: National Academy Press.

Office of Technology Assessment, Congress of the United States (1988). *Elementary and Secondary Education for Science and Engineering.* Washington, D.C.: U.S. Government Printing Office.

Osterman, Paul (1980). *Getting Started: The Youth Labor Market.* Cambridge: MIT Press.

Parnes, Herbert S. (1986). "Developing Human Capital." Columbus, Ohio: National Center for Research in Vocational Education.

Physicians' Task Force on Hunger in America (1985). *Hunger in America.* Middletown, Conn.: Wesleyan University Press.

7

Higher Education

Donald M. Stewart

Historical Evolution of the American System of Higher Education

The First 300 Years

In the United States today, more than 1.5 million students from 25,000 high schools are matriculated each year in over 3,000 colleges and universities. There are 12.5 million students enrolled in undergraduate, graduate, and professional higher education, 80 percent of whom are in public institutions. These diverse institutions of higher education (e.g., public and private, two-year and four-year, teaching and research, liberal arts and vocational-technical) were established over time to meet the diversity of student interests and societal needs of a pluralistic nation. There is an absence of central control and no common nationwide curriculum at either the secondary or postsecondary levels of education. Yet, beginning with the founding of Harvard College in 1636, there have been certain common expectations about what students ought to know and be able to do in order to make a successful transition from high school to college, as well as to exit from a college or university as an "educated person" capable of assuming a role in the world of business, government, the arts, or the voluntary sector. Harvard was patterned after Emmanuel College at Cambridge University in England, and in the seventeenth century its principal function was the training of clergymen and later of teachers, doctors, and lawyers. Harvard's curriculum provided a "pious education in good letters and manners, and was designed for a numerically small elite in early British America" (Stewart 1988).

In the early eighteenth century, America's model for medical education came from Scotland, and along with it as a by-product came a model for the undergraduate college in the form of programs in the natural sciences and laboratory research. The French added to the Scottish contribution in the late eighteenth century by adding undergraduate science, professional education such as teacher training, and foreign languages to the American college curriculum. Throughout the first half of the nineteenth century, religious denominations created numerous sectarian institutions, but higher education remained essentially a small and elite enterprise. It was not until the promulgation and implementation of the two Morrill Acts in the last half of the nineteenth century (1862 and 1890) that American higher education at last came loose from its elitist moorings in order to meet the emerging new manpower needs of a nation already well into an industrial revolution.

Through the creation of state land-grant institutions that stressed training in the agricultural and mechanical arts, the Morrill Acts promoted the idea that advanced education could provide for practical and social needs as well as public service. Thus education did not have to be based solely on the traditional and classical mode. Today's massive state systems of higher education have evolved from the nineteenth-century land-grant institutions. Also to be included among the significant educational changes of the late nineteenth century are the "separate but equal" 1890 institutions of higher learning for former slaves, which, along with the private colleges for black citizens created by liberal white church missionaries after the Civil War, are today's approximately 120 historically black colleges and universities.

At the close of the nineteenth century, American higher education went through its last major structural change by grafting onto the American college the German university model, with its emphasis on graduate research and training in specialized fields of knowledge. The German model was pioneered by Presidents Daniel Gilman of Johns Hopkins University and Charles Eliot of Harvard. As the nineteenth century came to a close, America's "mixed economy" of public and private higher education was distinctive, as was the American college (which stressed teaching of undergraduates and the liberal arts) and the graduate school (which stressed research, scholarship, and advanced learning). The graduate school influence encourages intellectual depth in a given field, while the liberal arts college tradition encourages intellectual breadth and growth based on a common learning experience. The many curricular permutations since the founding of Harvard University notwithstanding, the creation of an educated work force to meet the needs of the American economy remains one of the principal and enduring roles of our colleges and universities.

Early in the twentieth century, industrialization, urbanization, improved transportation and communications, as well as the impetus for social change brought about by World War I forced a redefinition of the roles and responsibilities of the nation's colleges and universities. The higher education system would need to expand in order to produce the trained middle-class professional and technical cadres that would develop and run many new forms of human enterprise. New fields of knowledge and intellectual inquiry were introduced. Old assumptions about preparation for college, about standards, and about curricular content were challenged. Increased opportunities were provided for students from diverse backgrounds to participate in and benefit from higher learning, and academia ceased to be an elite preserve of the wealthy and the socially prominent.

The twentieth century brought forth a new concept of college education: a form of education appropriate even for the masses, based upon meritocratic standards of individual talent and achievement. Educational and psychological testing became widely accepted and practiced. Meritocratic standards of student selection prevailed in American higher education until the end of World War II and the passage of the Servicemen's Readjustment Act (the GI Bill of Rights). That legislation sparked a broad democratization of access and choice, ushering in the current egalitarian period of American higher education. There was a significant growth in student population in public colleges and universities, and community colleges began to offer educational opportunities to people who had never dreamed that higher education would be possible for them.

The Federal Role in Contemporary Higher Education

Along with "democratization" and the use of meritocratic standards, the most significant change in the world of higher education following World War II was the burgeoning presence of the federal government. The pursuit of national goals with regard to scientific research, student aid, and admissions policies has resulted in a complex network of federal programs that are highly visible. They have profound consequences for the economics of higher education and its ability to meet the labor needs of the American economy in the future. Terry Sanford, senator from North Carolina and former president of Duke University, has observed that while federal funds are "the glamour money," the federal government supplied slightly less than 25 percent of all revenues to higher education in 1985 (Gladieux and Lewis 1987: 2). State governments, which have the basic responsibility for higher education (indeed, for all education), supplied over 40 percent of the revenues in 1985. "Over the past two centuries, the states have moved with varying speed to create and expand public systems of higher education and, more recently, to assist private colleges and universities or to purchase educational services from them" (Gladieux and Lewis 1987: 2). In addition, local governments supply about 4 percent and private sources about 31 percent. Federal money assumes a special importance in that it is the source of funding for meeting national objectives.

The GI Bill, designed to reward veterans for service and compensate them for lost opportunities, and the National Defense Education Act (NDEA) of 1958, enacted in response to Russia's launching of Sputnik, are good examples of such federal initiatives. Both programs served to enhance America's supply of educated workers. As strategies for the development of human resources, both programs were successful as measured by the increase in the number of college and graduate degrees granted during the 1940s, 1950s, and 1960s. America's economy grew stronger and expanded during this postwar period, well fueled in part by an increasingly better educated work force (Stewart 1988).

Since the early 1960s, federal student aid has served as an instrument of social policy—a means to increase educational opportunity and enhance social mobility for the poor and disadvantaged. The federal government's student assistance policies grew out of factors including the disenchantment in the early 1960s with scientific research as the key to solving all of society's problems, the lessening of international tensions, the apparent success of the GI Bill, the changing economic conditions, and a new political consensus. While many critics complained that the United States had reached the moon but could not solve the problems of the inner city, government policies encouraging universal higher education and open admissions seemed to offer some hope.

The Economic Opportunity Act and Civil Rights Act of 1964 set the egalitarian tone for the 1960s. The Higher Education Act of 1965 reinforced this emphasis with the inclusion of an Education Opportunity Grants (EOG) program, under which students with "exceptional financial need" could receive up to $1,500 in federal aid to be matched by institutional support. Eligibility for this financial aid assistance was often determined by the need analysis calculations made by the College Scholarship Service (CSS) of the College Board.

Other federal assistance programs designed for low-income students were created during the 1960s. Talent Search and Upward Bound (part of today's TRIO programs), incorporated from the War on Poverty into the Higher Education Act, were designed to identify disadvantaged young people able to profit from higher education and prepare and motivate them to take advantage of college opportunities. The GI Bill itself, because of the changing demographic composition of the armed services, came to resemble a program of special benefit to minorities and the disadvantaged. The College Work Study programs (CWS), part of the 1965 Higher Education Act, could be classified as student aid or institutional support. Two loan programs, NDSL (National Defense Student Loan program, authorized by the National Defense Education Act in 1958) and GSL (Guaranteed Student Loans, authorized by the Higher Education Act of 1965) complemented the federal student assistance framework. The former (known today as Perkins loans) provided low-interest loans through institutions, while the latter (known today as Stafford loans) provided federally insured loans and subsidized interest payments through third parties such as banks and credit agencies.

In 1966 and 1968, Congress amended the Higher Education Act of 1965, each time increasing the funds earmarked for the poor and disadvantaged. Simultaneously, Congress reduced the funds earmarked for the academically excellent under the National Defense Education Act (NDFA), National Aeronautics and Space Administration (NASA), National Science Foundation (NSF), and other federally sponsored training programs, particularly in the sciences.

By the end of 1972, total federal support for higher education amounted to $8 billion. In that year, Congress and the Nixon administration presented similar legislative proposals that resulted in a significant expansion of the federal commitment to student assistance. Characterized as an "educational incomes strategy," the 1972 amendments to the Higher Education Act clearly put the emphasis of federal policy on student-based financial assistance as opposed to general aid for institutions, which had been advocated by the higher-education establishment. The new legislation represented an effort to reform higher education by making colleges and universities more "market oriented." Targeting aid directly to the neediest students, rather than to institutions, it encouraged greater sensitivity to the needs of applicants before enrollment.

Federal support for higher education continued to grow significantly through the 1970s, totaling $18 billion by the end of the decade. This included support for middle-income families through the Middle Income Student Assistance Act (MISAA), which was approved by President Jimmy Carter as a political strategy to head off a tax-credit scheme for middle-income families that was gaining momentum in Congress. The Middle Income Student Assistance Act raised the family income ceiling on eligibility for grants and loans, thereby permitting many families to benefit from federal student aid whose incomes—although moderate—had previously disqualified them.

In the 1980s, during the presidency of Ronald Reagan, federal support for higher education was severely threatened and would have been reduced significantly had Congress not resisted the administration's proposed budget cuts. In real dollar terms, the value of federal student support during the 1980s increased only slightly, but (as will be discussed

later in this chapter) the character of federal student aid has been seriously altered by a major shift from grants to loans. The change in policy
was signaled by the first Reagan budget, in 1981, which repealed key
parts of the Middle Income Student Assistance Act and tightened eligibility for Pell grants and Stafford loans.

In a change from the strong bipartisan support that had characterized
federal policy toward higher education since the close of World War II,
the tone of the relationship between the federal government and higher
education during the Reagan years grew negative and adversarial. In
large measure to help justify proposed cuts in federal aid to higher education, a process that was stimulated as the federal deficit mounted, institutions were pictured as being overpriced, inefficient, and out only to
get as many federal dollars as possible. At the same time, from then
Secretary of Education William Bennett's "bully pulpit," they were portrayed as being of dubious academic quality with faint-hearted faculty,
low standards, and little appreciation for Western values and culture.
Caught up with the same fervid questioning that has engulfed public
primary and secondary education since Terrel H. Bell (Bennett's prede-
cessor) published *A Nation at Risk* in 1983, higher education, too, was
portrayed as contributing to the "rising tide of mediocrity." Students, the
secretary asserted, no longer performed real college-level work and were
not imbued with strong academic discipline or values.

As the nation enters the last decade of the century, attitudes toward
higher education are mixed. On the one hand, concern about costs
(which will be examined shortly) and the negative image promulgated by
the Reagan administration linger in the public mind and in the press. On
the other, we hear that in order to be more competitive, America must
educate more of its citizens beyond high school—particularly minorities,
who will make up one-third of the nation's population by the year 2000.
All of this is in anticipation of new knowledge and technological sophis-
tication that will be required if the United States is to compete successfully in the economy of the next century.

The Challenges for the Last Decade of the
Twentieth Century

It is tempting to say that recent challenges to academia are the consequence of the ending of the long growth period that higher education
enjoyed after World War II. The fact that the growth of higher education
reached a plateau in about 1980 has been an influential factor. In reality,
however, there have been many reasons for the growing intrusion of
worldly concerns. Speaking abstractly, colleges and universities are feeling the impact of economic, social, political, and technological changes

of a profound nature. Speaking more concretely, the factors that have created or will continue to create pressure include *changes* in

- The number, age, and attitudes of students
- The age and attitudes of faculty
- Public policy (including the decline of federal support)
- Technology, particularly the rise of computers
- The status of the United States (from looming economic and political leader to peer group member confronted by the new economic prowess of the Pacific Rim and Europe)
- The demography of the labor market
- The economy (from heavy-industry manufacturing to high-technology and service industries)
- The relationships with governmental and corporate funders of basic research and research and development
- Competitive pressures for endowment dollars and students
- The performance of the stock market and the U.S. economy (needed to sustain the necessary levels of endowment return and charitable giving)
- Public support for established standards of testing and admissions
- The academic preparation of students from kindergarten through twelfth grade
- The cost of academic materials and infrastructure renewal
- The purchasing power of the American family in comparison with cost of attending college
- The role of trade schools and the size of the population they serve.

While this is only a partial listing, it serves to underscore the array of pressures with which higher education must contend. In addition, it demonstrates the significant level of interdependence between the "ivory tower" and the mainstream economic and social environment, both national and global. One study foresees "profound changes in the nature and quality of the skills demanded in the economy, the labor supply, and the institutional mechanisms by which this country tries to create the human capital that the economy needs. . . . [As a result] two among the most powerful human capital pressures on the economy [are] the ability of workers to deal with discontinuity—the need for 'adaptability' or 'flexibility' . . . [and] the quality of the labor supply" (Berryman 1987: 1).

It is possible to simplify this view by using the basic model of supply and demand. Using this approach, we see that the *demand* for the outputs of higher education is as high, if not higher, than it has ever been. Leaders in government and business are calling for more and better-educated graduates, new scientific and technological products to undergird the economy, and constant intellectual discovery. What has undergone change is the *supply* of human and financial resources, and of supportive federal policy necessary to sustain the academic enterprise in order to meet the new demands. Moreover, the change is occurring at a time when the marketplace of higher education itself has become dramatically more competitive. Institutions are being constrained to develop, pay for, and undertake marketing programs that would have been unthinkable a decade ago. They must restructure the way they pursue students, endowment funds, research grants, and legislative support in order to maintain the quality of their programs and, in some cases, in order to survive.

The Demand for Higher Education

With regard to the demand side of the equation, it should be noted that higher education has long played a major role in the training of the work force, even if all the questions about appropriate curricula are not (and may never be) fully resolved. Traditional institutions of higher education have provided more courses of study for both professional qualification (in business, law, medicine, architecture, etc.) and for upgrading professional and managerial skills for the American work force than have all noncollegiate institutions combined. According to a report from the Bureau of Labor Statistics, in 1985 academic study led to professional qualification for 16.1 million workers, and professional upgrading for 5.5 million workers (Carnevale and Gainer n.d.: 11). These statistics seem to indicate that higher education is inherently suited to meet higher levels of demand for adequately prepared human resources.

There has been some question as to whether what students learn in an academic setting is what is needed for success in the workplace. As the United States moves into a period of intense international competition, we need to understand exactly "what it is about more education that helps produce this ability to adapt in the face of transitions and breakdowns (such as we expect in the future from the economic and political environment). We can surmise that more education provides students with more alternative ways to think about the unfamiliar" (Berryman 1987: 5).

Debates about the relevance of curriculum, and especially about fields of study, to success in the marketplace have not been resolved. Over the last 20 years, students have made very different choices. Between 1970 and 1986, the number of bachelor's degrees in the arts and sciences dropped by some 75,000, while degrees in technical and professional fields such as business, marketing, communications, computer programming, and engineering rose by almost a quarter of a million. Whereas the number of degrees in these two categories were almost equal in 1970, in

1986 professional and technical diplomas outnumbered those in the arts and sciences among undergraduates by a 2:1 ratio (Stern 1988: 20). Moving counter to this trend is an emerging understanding of the sustained, long-term value of a liberal arts degree in an economy based on fast-changing technology. As the liberal arts include mathematics and the sciences as well as the social sciences, students who pursue these studies are less vulnerable to dislocations in the workplace caused by sudden advances in technology than students with narrower technical training. In the short run, of course, training in specific technologies provides opportunities for employment as long as technological change does not make the specific industrial processes obsolete.

If the following are taken together:

- The essential contribution of higher education to the professions, business, science, and engineering;
- The reports of the increasing levels of learning needed for participation in the workplace of the future (as Packer showed in Chapter 2 of this volume, the proportion of all jobs requiring education beyond high school will rise from 50 percent in mid-1985 to over two-thirds by 2000), and
- The increasingly desperate straits of illiterate Americans who until recently could find a productive place in the work force (between 1979 and 1985, the United States lost 1.7 million jobs in the manufacturing sector [Steinbruner 1989: 33]),

it seems fairly clear that college and university study is needed for success in the emerging economy.

I believe that there will not necessarily be a significant "net change" in the organizational or curricular shape of American colleges and universities, nor will their role in the larger society alter significantly in the coming several decades. On the contrary, the fundamental structure and character of the higher education enterprise is strong. (As we shall see below, the maintenance of this strength will be determined in the near future by our response to a number of key issues.) Over the past 350 years, as the earlier part of this chapter has proposed, higher education has evolved in a way that permits it to enjoy continuity even while coping with pressures from many directions. Moreover, the increase in demand for its output exerts a stabilizing force even in the face of other negative forces.

If we agree that what is needed is an increase in the quantity and quality of what academia currently produces (e.g., an educated work force, research, and intellectual discovery), then the basic question is: will the academy be able to handle all the pressures on it, especially those on the "supply" side of the equation?

The Supply to Higher Education

One of the aspects of American higher education that makes it unique in the world is its enormous diversity. The United States enjoys an array of great research universities; public and private colleges; comprehensive urban universities; vast land-grant state systems; small, elite colleges; a multitude of religiously affiliated, special-purpose private institutions; as well as the growing and increasingly important community college systems. Each of these prepares differing populations in differing ways for different roles in the economy. In this diversity, we see not only a tremendous variety in academic programs and purposes but also an enormous range in bureaucratic and economic organization. It is simply impossible to count on a unified "corporate culture" among institutions of higher education. This factor alone is one reason that effecting change in higher education is a monumental task. Problems and even desired outcomes can be defined, but bringing them about in such a highly decentralized and polyvalent environment is much more complicated. Moreover, relatively modest changes in the human, financial, and policy resources can have a significant impact due to the complexity of the system itself. Respecting this complexity, it can be said, nevertheless, that the future of higher education depends on the answers to the following questions:

- Will educational reform in the primary and secondary schools be effective enough to give American students from every background adequate precollegiate preparation?
- Will higher education be able to recruit, retain, and graduate a greater number of minority students and students from socioeconomic groups that have not traditionally gone to college?
- Will the large number of faculty retiring in the next two decades be replaced by a suitable and appropriate new professoriate?
- Will price and competitive pressures be dealt with successfully so that high-quality learning environments are maintained?
- Will financing be available for those academically qualified students unable to pay the price at many institutions?
- Will the relationship with corporate sponsors of research protect the intellectual and academic freedom necessary for the pursuit of knowledge?
- Will federal policy preserve the diversity of academic institutions and the range of options for students of limited financial means?

Each of these questions must be answered in the affirmative in order for the academy to be able fully to supply the nation with the highly trained work force and the prepared citizenry that it desperately requires. However, there is no guarantee that any or all of them will be so answered.

Preparation of Students for College

The question of educational reform in the primary and secondary schools demands an analysis beyond the scope of this chapter. This issue is treated in the excellent contributions of Ernest Boyer (Chapter 6) and David Hornbeck (Chapter 13). As they note, all recent assessments of national achievement indicate that students in the United States are not performing well enough. These include the National Assessment of Education Progress and several multinational studies. These facts create serious "pipeline" problems.

We lose one-quarter of all students as dropouts; in many urban school systems, as many as 50 percent. School success rates for minorities and those for whom English is not a first language are particularly miserable. "In 1980, one of five black male teenagers was unable to read at the fourth grade level" (Gibbs 1988). Nancy Barrett, elsewhere in this volume, has noted the inadequate preparation of young women. Those facts are crucial, of course, in the light of Packer's data demonstrating that only 15 percent of the new entrants into the labor force between 1985 and 2000 will be white, American-born males. Those facts also underline the "pipeline" problem for higher education.

Though the task of real reform is enormous, it is not surprising that business leaders around the country, through their trade associations such as the Business Roundtable and the Committee on Economic Development, as well as in the context of individual states, are organizing to improve the quality of precollegiate education and of children's health care and nutrition.

Fortunately, there is an emerging attitude among business leaders, politicians, and educators that whatever has caused the problems in the past simply must be overcome in the future. Pilot projects and new approaches in Atlanta, Boston, New York City, and Los Angeles, among other cities, and stories like that of teacher Jaime Escalante's use of the Advanced Placement Calculus program to transform the lives of his students in East Los Angeles, are providing hope and useful models for others to follow.

Problems of Recruitment and Retention

Strictly speaking, the problems for the enterprise of higher education only begin at the end of high school. Since the passage of the Higher Education Act of 1965, colleges and universities have been making greater efforts to recruit minorities, an effort that had its greatest success in the 1970s. Individual institutions such as Stanford University, Boston University, Xavier University, Beloit College, Ramapo College, Connecticut College, and Arizona State University are working to increase the preparedness of minority students by intervening directly in the local school systems. Some of these programs start as early as seventh grade and continue through the college years. Too often, however, colleges are competing for the same small segment of highly qualified minority students. Moreover, too many of the minority students who do go on to postsecondary education are tracked into for-profit training schools, two-year vocational programs, and community colleges.

Three factors make the question of equitable admissions practices a serious challenge: (1) the diversity of institutions of higher education; (2) the increasing diversity of the demographic environment [by the year 2010, 40 percent of school-aged children will be from minority groups, and six of the nine most populous states (representing half of the U.S. population) will have a "minorities majority" among school-aged children (Hodgkinson 1985: 21)], (3) the enormously decentralized network of 25,000 high schools. Even though the vast majority of colleges, particularly community colleges, are not selective and admit almost all of their applicants, the "common yardstick" represented by standardized admissions tests such as the SAT (Scholastic Aptitude Test) has provided, as many commentors have noted, an important democratizing influence. Without such a national standard, it is reasonable to suppose that colleges would have to revert to a system of admissions based on an elite subset of secondary schools—the system that characterized higher education in the late nineteenth and early twentieth century, when its students were primarily well-to-do white males.

The most inefficient aspect of the admissions process is not in recruitment at all, but in retention. While only half of all white college students graduate within six years after entering college, barely 25 percent of all successfully recruited minority students do so. This same situation also holds true for minority students in graduate school; their rate of retention is 50 to 75 percent lower than that of white graduate students (Benderson 1988: 3). Some preliminary studies seem to indicate that the situation has not changed much in the last 10 years. Students are dropping out, not just "stopping out." Moreover, given that 90 percent of all adult students are white (Aslanian and Brickell 1988: 23), it is clear that minorities do not return to higher education once they leave.

The first step in increasing the efficiency with which higher education provides career preparation to students from socioeconomic groups that do not traditionally go to college is to recapture a large portion of the 75 percent of successfully recruited students who do not get their degrees. In order to do this we must

- Immediately develop programs to increase minority students' level of comfort and identification with the institution
- Increase the number of minority faculty and administrators
- Emphasize the multicultural aspects of curricular materials within courses

- Develop ongoing mechanisms on campus to insure the fulfillment of these goals.

"You can't have a world-class university in America," states Donna Shalala, chancellor of the University of Wisconsin, Madison, "unless it truly comprises a diverse student body, faculty and staff, and the curriculum reflects that fact" (Barry 1988). While many colleges and universities are beginning to move toward greater diversity, Dr. Shalala's assertion provides the basis for a tangible, well-defined initiative, the "Madison Plan," a $6.3-million, three-year effort whose goals and components are

- A doubling of minority enrollment within five years
- New mechanisms of financial aid that will limit the debt burden of low-income students
- A substantial increase of minority faculty and staff
- A new ethnic studies course required of undergraduates.

In a similar vein, Stanford University is actively involved in evaluating and implementing 120 recommendations made by the University Committee on Minority Issues in the report it submitted in the spring of 1989. According to Stanford's president, Donald Kennedy, "We accept the basic design of a multicultural community [at Stanford]" (Kennedy 1989). This model is founded on the principles of

- *Pluralism* as opposed to assimilation
- *Inclusion* of differences among students as part of a multicultural mainstream, rather than special pleadings of diverse minority groups for recognition by the majority group
- *Partnership* involving everyone in the implementation
- Active *leadership* on the part of the university and its constituent parts.

Wisconsin and Stanford provide but two examples of similar initiatives happening at institutions around the country, but they are indicative of the magnitude of the effort required to create a truly multicultural environment in higher education. The overlap between economic disadvantage and minority background, however, should not obscure the fact that there are a substantial number of white youngsters who are also economically disadvantaged and whose families have not traditionally participated in higher education. It is just as important to bring them into the educational mainstream as it is to include minority youngsters, and for the same reasons.

By contrast, the success story in recruitment and retention in higher education is the adult student. Students 25 years of age and older will make up a full 50 percent of the undergraduate population by the year 2000. Their primary motivation, career change (Aslanian and Brickell

1980) also demonstrates the considerable efficacy of higher education in turning out graduates adequately prepared for the work force once a sufficiently prepared and motivated supply of students is directed to their institutions. This represents yet another confirmation that the essential problem is one of supply.

The Vulnerability of the Professoriate

Along with the issue of the preparation of students in the pipeline and the problems of minority retention, higher education must contend with major changes in the composition of the professoriate in the coming decades. In the 15 years between 1985 and the end of the century, almost one-third of the nation's full-time and part-time faculty, numbering more than 700,000 individuals (Snyder 1988: 177), will have to be replaced (Heller 1986: 25), assuming current enrollment levels. This figure reflects the retirement of faculty members who were appointed between 1950 and 1969, when new appointments to faculty jumped from 50,000 (from 1950–54) to 200,000 (from 1965–69) to address the enormous expansion in higher education (especially at the state and community college level) brought about by the need to educate the children of the baby boom (Bowen and Schuster 1986: 176). As Bowen and Schuster remind us in their study *American Professors: A National Resource Imperiled*, academic faculty are not only responsible for educating 30 to 50 percent of all young people, but they "train virtually the entire leadership of the society in the professions, government, business, and to a lesser extent, the arts." In addition, the professoriate conducts a significant amount of basic research in scientific and public policy fields, and incidentally provides the administrative leadership for higher education itself (Bowen and Schuster 1986: 3).

As was predicted by Allan Cartter, the number of faculty appointments was sharply exceeded by the supply of Ph.D.'s in the mid-1970s in most disciplines (Breneman and Young 1988: 201). While the number of faculty appointments fell back to below 150,000 during the five years from 1980 to 1984, the number of Ph.D. degrees awarded has leveled off at about 30,000 per year. The demographic composition of the advanced degree candidates has changed substantially, moreover, with a decline in the number of white and especially black students earning both master's and Ph.D. degrees between 1977 and 1985, and a substantial surge in both Hispanic and Asian-American students, the latter jumping more than 60 percent in the number of Ph.D. degrees received, and both groups increasing more than 75 percent in the number of first professional degrees awarded. Overall, the number of blacks in graduate school dropped almost 20 percent between 1976–77 and 1984–85, while the number of women climbed almost 8 percent, to the highest levels in American history. In 1955 women were awarded Ph.D. degrees at perhaps a tenth the rate of men; 30 years later, they received Ph.D. degrees at 50 percent the rate of men, with their trend line rising and that for male Ph.D.'s falling (Bowen and Schuster 1986: 178). In 1985, only 909 black Americans received the Ph.D. degree, compared with over 20,000 white Americans.

Another new development is that over 43 percent of all Ph.D.'s now work outside of an academic institution. The salary levels in higher education are not commensurate with what can be earned in industry, particularly in fields such as physics or the natural sciences (Bowen and Schuster 1986: 177). Within academia, faculty salaries fell precipitously during the 1970s. The average salary for a full professor in a public university fell from $50,000 to $40,000 in inflation-adjusted dollars (Stern 1988: 45). And while salaries began to recover in 1980, they have yet to reach 1972 levels. Bowen and Schuster estimate that the annual rate of faculty appointments will go from as low as 30,000 between 1990 and 1994 to as many as 180,000 ten years later, depending on a variety of economic and demographic assumptions. While strong demand for faculty will no doubt stimulate a positive response (as it did in the 1950s and 1960s), historically the supply of qualified Ph.D.'s has always been out of phase with the market, given the several years "lag-time" needed to complete advanced degrees (Breneman and Young 1988: 202). Undoubtedly, there will be an insufficient supply of minority faculty, especially black faculty members, at a time when the demographic composition of the student body will be moving toward a situation in which no single group is a majority. In view of the tremendous demographic and economic shifts the nation is about to experience, an overriding concern must be whether the professoriate will be able to deliver the quantity and quality of teaching, learning, and research that will be needed in the decades immediately ahead.

In the near term, William Bowen, president of the Andrew W. Mellon Foundation, and his coauthor Julie Ann Sosa surprised the academic community by predicting particularly severe shortages in the humanities and social sciences, not the natural sciences, between 1997 and 2002 (Bowen and Sosa 1989: 2). According to their study, there will be 1.6 new candidates for each available faculty post between 1987 and 1992. Over the five-year period between 1997 and 2002, however, this ratio will fall to 0.83 as the number of new faculty members drops below the number of openings in the professoriate. And the situation will worsen slightly at least until 2007. These changes are due not to faculty retirement, death, or decision to leave the academy for other reasons "but rather to known population trends that will affect enrollment in the late 1990s" (Bowen and Sosa 1989: 2).

Their suggestion that government-sponsored stipends are needed to boost the number of faculty members in the humanities and social sciences has, however, met with some criticism (Cheney 1989). The debate demonstrates the complexity of this issue, which is due to many unknowable factors such as projections of demographic change, the behavior of new and previous Ph.D.'s in a labor market that includes both higher education and outside employment, and campus decisions such as what constitute desirable student-faculty ratios. Whatever the complexity, it is clear that to meet the need, we must now initiate government-sponsored stipends, increase the allure of doctoral programs through higher and targeted scholarship programs, create mechanisms to lead qualified persons in the private sector to change careers and enter the college classroom, and/or undertake other imaginative initiatives that will close the professoriate gap. Once again it is clear that the challenges facing higher education, in this case with regard to faculty, are a function of the "supply" side of the equation.

The Price of Higher Education to the Consumer

In addition to concerns about the number and quality of faculty, concerns about the rising cost of college and university tuition have also been expressed. Over the past decade and a half, institutions of higher education have been asked to incorporate significant increases in "academic technology" including broader recruitment efforts; improved teaching; computerization; increased levels of research; or better health, psychological, and academic counseling for students. At the same time, we have entered an economic downswing characterized by

- Declining family purchasing power
- Declining federal support in real dollars for higher education
- Increases in college price outstripping the Consumer Price Index.

If one compares the Consumer Price Index (CPI) supplied by the Bureau of Labor Statistics with the College Entrance Examination Board's statistics about tuition increases, one sees that since 1980 the rate of tuition increase has been substantially higher, leveling off to about 8 percent per year, while the CPI has increased at about 4 percent per year. With college costs rising at twice the rate of other goods, it is not surprising that higher education has suffered considerably from what the automotive industry calls "sticker-price" shock.

For 1989/90, the average cost per year of tuition and fees at a four-year private college has been estimated at $8,737, whereas the average cost at a public four-year college has been estimated at $1,695 (Gams 1989). Colleges themselves are actively helping families to bridge the tuition gap through college-funded financial aid. However, highly publicized projections that the price of a full *four* years of college at the most expensive schools may be as high as $100,000 by the end of the century—and over $300,000 by the time those born in the late 1980s get to college—send waves of panic through American families.

Again, the issues here are many and complex. First, a student paying full tuition and fees, even at the most expensive institutions, is still paying less than the cost of his or her education, with subsidies coming from endowment and other sources. High as it may appear to be, the price to the student is still less than the cost to the institution. Second, from the point of view of what is expected from higher education, vis-à-vis adequately prepared human capital, these rises in price may simply be the reality of providing quality education. According to President Harold T. Shapiro of Princeton University, "from a wide variety of sources, intellectual and economic, there are a series of emerging forces that are raising the cost structures of existing institutions of higher education. Indeed, there seems to be no alternative to these rising costs if we are to operate on the frontier of scholarship and education and within existing institutional commitments and forms" (Hanson and Meyerson 1989: 5). Third, a further cost pressure is exerted by the significant jump in the amount of financial aid which institutions themselves must contribute to fill the void left by declining federal support in constant dollars (Hauptman 1989a). Thus, as Deidre Carmody put it in the New York Times, "colleges [are] caught in a tuition-student aid squeeze" in which the cost of equality is added to the cost of quality (Carmody 1989).

Fourth, the feeling that the price of a college education is too high is as much psychological as economic in origin. In part, this perception is the result of declining real family income, which has led to the phenomenon known as the cost squeeze for the middle class. Between 1949 and 1969, median family income increased by about 30 percent in constant dollars (Levy 1989). It collapsed and then recovered during the 1970s and the oil-embargo–inflation crisis, but it has remained virtually unchanged over the past decade, during which all costs have increased, college costs have increased sharply, and the value of federal student aid has declined in real dollars. The overall effect on middle-class families and those less economically favored is chilling.

By contrast, however, between 1973 and 1986 the earnings gap between a high school graduate and a college graduate jumped from 16 percent to 50 percent. Moreover, according to Bureau of the Census statistics for 1986, as the level of educational achievement rises (for all students, but especially for minorities) there is a significant decrease in the unemployment rate. The unemployment rate nationally for black high school dropouts is almost 25 percent, whereas that of black college graduates is only 4 percent. For Hispanics the numbers are 17 percent and 3 percent, and for white students, 13 percent and 2.5 percent (Hayes-Bautista 1988: 4). It appears that a college education is becoming economically more valuable at precisely the time it appears to be economically more difficult to achieve.

While these numbers should be effective in motivating students to pursue further studies, in terms of consumer behavior (especially for families from demographic groups who have not traditionally gone to college) the "sticker price" of attending college, and the recent strident publicity about it, can have a depressing effect on the number of students even considering college attendance. This situation is not helped by the widening socioeconomic gap in our society. Between 1978 and 1987, "the poorest fifth of the American families became eight percent poorer, and the richest fifth became 13 percent richer. This leaves [the former] with less than 5 percent of the nation's income, and [the latter] with over 40 percent" (Reich 1989: 23). Young people as a category, especially young people from certain minorities and newly immigrated groups, have now become the poorest segment of the nation. Unfortunately, these are exactly the children to whom America now desperately needs to give a college education.

Fifth, the sheer complexity of the commodity called higher education makes it difficult to compare it to similar commodities. Essentially, no similar commodity exists.

The five preceding points lead one to conclude that, although we may not like what we pay for a year at college, especially in an era of declining purchasing power, the forces leading to these prices may well be of a macroeconomic nature, and not the fault of the "manufacturers." A contrasting point of view has been mounted by those who feel that some colleges at the upper end of the tuition scale have become too aggressive in their marketing and are arbitrarily raising prices to position themselves as "leaders" in order to attract students and families who will equate high cost with high quality and prestige. In order to put the question of the price of a college education in a larger perspective, two basic points must be understood. The first is that there are many factors driving the cost of higher education which have nothing to do with marketing. These can be said to be the basic forces determining price levels within all of higher education. Certain institutions, however, may be arbitrarily raising tuition in an attempt to reposition themselves. The effect of this, however, is relatively marginal compared with the basic forces driving college costs up.[1]

A confirmation of this can be seen from a recent analysis of prices (Hauptman 1989b) in which the CPI is shown to be an inappropriate indicator for higher education. The Higher Education Price Index (HEPI) more closely mirrors the real expenditures. Rises in the price of colleges have been only 12 percent higher than HEPI over the past several years, as opposed to twice the CPI. This difference may, to some degree, reflect the "marketing" push on tuition levels. It may also be a function of the roughness of the indicator itself in a sector as diverse as American higher education.

Unfortunately, the variety shown by institutions of higher education in terms of programs, control, and financial structure—one of the unique strengths of American higher education—also causes a problem of perception with regard to price. Lower-priced state institutions admit any student who qualifies for admission, regardless of financial need. The assumption is, therefore, that state systems are serving the needs of less affluent families, while higher-priced private institutions are the preserve of those families with financial resources. This is not necessarily the case. In the state of Washington, for example, one study has shown that the average family income of students at state colleges and universities is actually higher than those at private institutions (Dent 1987). Furthermore, while state institutions usually have lower tuition, there is little financial aid for other costs. In some cases, a student from an economically disadvantaged background can only afford to go to a private institution, since along with financial aid for tuition, an aid package is also available to cover living expenses.

Finally, the situation is further complicated by the fact that even the most gifted economists will admit privately that they are unable to compute accurately what it *costs* to educate a student. The intricate organizational structure, the overlapping and varied functions of the faculty and the administration, and finally the wide variety of student programs requiring very different levels of resources, together add up to a systemic complexity that defies exact economic analysis.

Lower, tax-subsidized tuition at state colleges also make it difficult for the consumer to understand the issue of college prices clearly, since the difference in "sticker price" of tuition would seem to indicate a difference in expenditure made by the institutions themselves. This is not the case, as the background tables used by the U.S. Department of Education to prepare the *Digest of Education Statistics, 1988* show. These tables divide education and general expenses incurred by institutions into nine categories: instruction and administration, student services, research, libraries, public service, operation and maintenance, transfers, and student aid. In 1985/86, student aid at four-year private schools was, on the average, 12 percent of the budget, whereas it was only 3 percent at four-year public colleges. Except for student aid, however, there is a remarkable similarity in the percentages allocated to each of the nine categories at public and private universities.

In summary, cost structures are similar in public and private education, although sticker prices are very different, reflecting the significant "subsidies" which state tax dollars represent. Based on the HEPI, the increases in college prices seem to reflect the real costs of providing quality education. Therefore we should take a more reasoned view of the question of the cost to consumers. In fact, it might be said that the psychological distress felt by the middle class at the cost of college could itself be used as a barometer of the lack of economic health of the nation as a whole. If, due to our negative comparative position in terms of economic competitiveness, national debt, trade deficit, declining gross national product (GNP), defense spending, and so forth, college prices are now "painful," it is a sign that our economy is not functioning as well as it once did. We should not, therefore, place the blame solely on higher education for the economic realities that cause tuition and fees to be as high as they are. Instead, we should realize that, although the price of higher education is high, it cannot—under present conditions—be lowered without sacrificing quality. If our goal is to maintain the highest standards of education in order to ensure our global competitiveness, and if in so doing we must broadly include students from socioeconomic groups for whom the price of tuition and fees can be daunting, then policies that support meaningful and effective student aid for lower- and middle-income students without enormous debt burden are an absolute necessity.

Student Financial Aid

As was previously stated, financial aid adds a new dimension to the issue of the "price" of higher education. After grants, loans, scholarships, and work-study are deducted, the "net price" of a college education can be significantly different from the "sticker price." Unfortunately, in the last decade, federal support for financial assistance has become fragmented and clouded by financial constraints and ideological biases.

Need-based aid, where financial support is awarded based principally on the financial resources of student and family as opposed to academic merit, is a relatively new concept. Proposed in the early 1950s by John Monro, then dean of students at Harvard College, the concept was developed by the College Entrance Examination Board into a workable system based on a calculation of a family's or student's "ability to pay." It has become the basis of a $25-billion "industry" as of 1988, when 75 percent of financial aid comes from federally supported programs, and 19 percent from states and institutions themselves. This comes to an average of $2,000 per year per student, were it simply divided evenly among all 12 million postsecondary students. In reality, only about half of these 12 million students receive any financial aid, and many receive only modest amounts. As of 1987/88, over 50 percent of this aid was in the form of loans (Gams 1988). Although the amount of student aid has risen nominally over the past decade, due to cuts made by the Reagan administration, it fell in inflation-adjusted dollars and only recovered in 1987/88, rising 6.5 percent over the level of aid in 1980/81, due to the significant increase in student loans (Lewis 1988: 2).

There has been considerable discussion of the effects of this switch in the kind of federal aid. Between 1976 and 1986, when tuition slightly more than doubled, the amount of aid in the form of grants increased by less than 20 percent, while the amount of aid in the form of student loans increased almost 600 percent (Hansen 1987: 6–9). Between 1980 and 1988, according to College Board estimates, the value of all student aid in the form of grants actually fell from $10.7 to $9.6 billion in constant 1982 dollars, while aid in the form of loans jumped from $7.8 billion to $10.3 billion. In part, concern about the jump in student loans is due to the tremendous increases in the rates of indebtedness of students upon graduation, and in part it is due to a default rate that now stands at $2 billion per year. Potential indebtedness appears to discourage students from low-income families from even considering higher education (Kirschner and Thrift 1987).

In light of the decrease in federal support in constant dollars over much of the decade, as well as the shift toward loans as opposed to grants, institutions of higher education have significantly increased the student aid they provide by some 120 percent between 1980/81 and 1987/88, from $2 billion to over $5.5 billion. This is 20 percent more than the value of the federal Pell grants for the same years, although at the beginning of the decade, Pell grants exceeded institutionally awarded aid by $380 million, or just over 11 percent (Lewis 1988: 6).

As reasoned economic analysis and the spirit of a "kinder and gentler" nation have again made their way to the Department of Education, the real economic issues have resurfaced. How can we provide higher-quality education for students from a middle class with shrinking economic capability, and for a growing pool of students who come from families with slender if any means at all? Currently, in a nation whose gross national product exceeded $5 trillion in 1988, and whose federal budget exceeded $1 trillion in the same year, support for students in higher education represents less than 3 percent of the budget and barely 0.6 percent of the GNP. This does not seem to reflect the importance that is now being given to the development of adequate human capital. A more aggressive federal policy with bipartisan backing is needed if we are to develop effective, long-range programs of financial support to permit access to higher education for economically disadvantaged students.

Support for Research

The needs of World War II generated the first major federal sponsorship of scientific research and development on university campuses. Over the next two decades, cold war tensions and the launching of Sputnik ensured continued federal interest and heavy investment in academic research. The rate of growth in federal research funding has slowed considerably in the 1970s and 1980s, but the federal government remains by far the largest patron of academic research, accounting for roughly $6 billion of the $9.5 billion in research and development expenditures at colleges and universities in 1985.

However, the level of federal support has not kept pace with the costs of doing significant investigation at the frontiers of the scientific disciplines. Although the economic and scientific successes of the 1950s, 1960s, and early 1970s were undeniable, by 1983 it was clear that the United States was slipping in its competitive advantage vis-à-vis other industrialized nations in terms of expenditures for plant and equipment, productivity, and funding for research and development. Research and development funding, as well as the number of graduates in scientific and high-technology fields and the number of patents applied for and granted are important indicators of national strength. In the "privatizing" spirit of the 1980s, universities began to develop highly publicized linkages with corporations, especially those in fields such as chemistry, the biosciences, and pharmaceuticals. Companies such as Pfizer, IBM, Dow, General Foods, Merck, Eastman Kodak, and Monsanto are just a few of the corporate giants involved in corporate-academic cooperation. However, analysts do not see this involvement growing to more than 6 percent of the total research budget in higher education. As the chief scientist of Monsanto commented: "Monsanto invests a great deal in universities, but the sums are a drop in the bucket. For example, Washington University has a $100 million research budget, of which we contribute $8 million. I cannot conceive of our relative contribution exceeding eight percent" (Brown and Samore 1987: 46).

With the prospect of significant royalties accruing for important breakthroughs, universities have become very protective of the discoveries of their faculty through ownership of patents. The confusion about a breakthrough in cold fusion at the University of Utah in March 1988 (which could not be confirmed) represents an example of how intensely the ownership of "intellectual property" is being pursued, and how vulnerable traditional university procedures are to the intrusion of powerful marketplace forces. In this new environment, the complexities of preserving both academic freedom and appropriate "arms-length" financial relationships, whether the funding comes from government or from private industry, are far from being resolved. Extensive protocols for sponsored research agreements, licensing agreements, and instructions for principal investigators are being put in place at major American research universities in an attempt to manage this complex processing of contract research and development while maintaining educational integrity and intellectual objectivity (Office for Sponsored Research 1988).

If the question of national competitiveness, which is highly dependent on research output, is of paramount importance to the nation's future, however, the federal government will have to continue to play the leading role in financing academic research. If this is to be the case, levels of appropriations for research must be raised so that they reflect the current costs of doing sophisticated scientific research in all strategically important areas, whether they be advanced computer science or biotechnology.

Higher Education's Integral Connection to Economic Performance

Overall, the health of higher education and its ability to create human capital remain complex issues. Furthermore, there are many variables that link the strength and economics of higher education to the national economy. The direction these variables may take in the future is hard to predict. If the economy were to move into a depression, all institutions would suffer, but higher education would be particularly affected since it is dependent on the ability of the national economy to maintain the necessary levels of tuition, charitable giving, and government appropriations. Assuming relative stability in the economic sphere, and thus relative stability of state appropriations and programs (which are certainly under pressure at the close of the 1980s, especially in certain states such as Louisiana and Texas), the strength of higher education will be maintained. Nonetheless, this analysis shows the extreme sensitivity of college finances to the overall financial health of the nation. The national economy and higher education form a balanced, interlocking system: the national economy must remain strong in order to provide adequate support for the educational system, which will provide the nation with the commodities most essential to its success in a competitive global society: a well-educated work force and the results of scientific research. If the economy begins to falter, it will result in the underfunding of higher education—particularly for the task of bringing new groups (minorities) into the higher educational mainstream. This will lead eventually to work force shortages and greater expenditures for social services.

Higher education, fortunately, continues to enjoy a special relationship with American society, and the American economy. Contemplating the uncertainties of the future, President Derek Bok of Harvard observed: "If we are resourceful enough there will be many ways for us to adapt and many unanticipated events that may change the picture. In the end, perhaps our greatest protection lies in our growing importance to the society that sustains us. So long as this trend continues, society may find it more difficult, rather than less, to allow our institutions to decline in quality" (Hanson and Meyerson 1989: iii).

Conclusion

Seen as a $100-billion economic sector, higher education enjoys and will continue to enjoy strong demand for its products as the United States moves into the twenty-first century. In fact, there are those in government who now believe that protecting our national security has become an economic rather than a military issue.

The vulnerabilities facing higher education with regard to meeting this demand have to do with the changes in the supply of human, financial, and policy-support resources that undergird our highly pluralistic and decentralized system of postsecondary study. More specifically, these changes in supply are represented by

- A profound change in U.S. demographics
- A sustained rise in the cost of educational materials and trained personnel (both faculty and administration)
- A decade of skepticism and reduced federal support based on an ideological shift
- A significant change in the performance of the American economy since 1980, with the emergence of the United States as the world's leading debtor nation.

If our national security depends upon economic prowess, and if economic prowess in a competitive, high-technology global economy depends on a work force armed with an advanced education, then U.S. colleges and universities are crucial to the nation's well-being.

Reviewing this entire prospect, an analysis of higher education in an economic as well as historical context leads us to several observations that have policy implications. First, as we approach the twenty-first century, it may no longer make sense to speak of "minorities" but rather of a complex "demographic diversity" that will characterize the U.S. population—and that entire population, even the sectors previously underrepresented in the colleges and universities, must receive the finest higher education possible. Second, while it is the responsibility of the federal government to maintain the structure of student aid so that even the economically least-advantaged from among this demographic diversity can attend a college of their choice and appropriate to their ability, it is up to our institutions of higher learning to create an environment in which much closer to 100 percent of these students (not 25 percent, as is currently the case with nonwhite students) achieve a college degree. And many of these must be encouraged to return to the academy as faculty. Finally, while corporations will join with academia to fund research and new technologies, it will remain predominantly the responsibility of the federal government to increase support for the research efforts taking place on America's campuses.

Notes

The author wishes to acknowledge with deepest appreciation the collaboration and assistance of his College Board colleagues James Lichtenberg and Lawrence E. Gladieux.

1. I acknowledge but do not address the launching in 1989 of a Justice Department probe of alleged "price fixing" among some thirty leading institutions. Whatever legal implications may or may not exist, they have little to do with the cost of higher education for the vast majority of American students.

References

Aslanian, Carol B., and Henry M. Brickell (1980). *Americans in Transition: Life Changes as Reasons for Adult Learning.* New York: College Entrance Examination Board.

———— (1988). *How Americans in Transition Study for College Credit.* New York: College Entrance Examination Board.

Barry, Paul (1988). "Toward the Model University: Donna Shalala Charts the Courts." *College Board Review* 149: 4–9, 29–30.

Benderson, Albert, ed. (1988). *Minority Students in Higher Education: FOCUS.* Princeton, N.J.: Educational Testing Service.

Berryman, Sue E. (1987). *Breaking Out of the Circle: Rethinking Our Assumptions about Education and the Economy.* Presentation at the 43d National Conference and Exposition of the American Society for Training and Development, "Human Resource Development: The Strategic Investment," June 21–26, 1987. New York: National Center on Education and Employment, Teachers College, Columbia University, July.

Bowen, Howard R., and Jack H. Schuster (1986). *American Professors: A National Resource Imperiled.* New York: Oxford University Press.

Bowen, William B., and Julie Ann Sosa (1989). *Prospects for Faculty in the Arts and Sciences.* Princeton: Princeton University Press.

Breneman, David W., and Ted I. K. Young (1988). *Academic Labor Markets and Careers.* New York: Falmer Press.

Brown, James K., and Evelyn Samore (1987). *Getting More out of R & D Technology.* New York: Conference Board.

Carmody, Deidre (1989). "Colleges Caught in Tuition-Student Aid Squeeze." *New York Times,* April 5.

Carnevale, Anthony P., and Leila J. Gainer (n.d.). *The Learning Enterprise.* Alexandria, Va.: American Society for Training and Development and the U.S. Department of Labor Employment and Training Administration.

Cheney, Lynne V. (1989). "The Phantom Ph.D. Gap." *New York Times,* September 28.

Dent, Richard (1987). *Student Financing of Higher Education in Washington State, 1985–86.* Olympia, Wash.: Council for Post-secondary Education.

Gams, Janice (1988). "College Board Finds Student Aid Reached over $24.5

Billion in 1987–88, While Borrowing for College Set Record." Press Release from the College Entrance Examination Board, New York, September 9.

——— (1989). "College Board Survey Shows College Students Will Pay an Average of 5 to 9 Percent More for Tuition and Fees in 1989–90." Press release from the College Entrance Examination Board, New York, August 5.

Gibbs, Jewelle Taylor (1988a). "Young, Black, in Critical Condition." *Los Angeles Times,* May 29, p. 1.

———, ed. (1988b). *Young, Black, and Male in America: An Endangered Species.* Dover, Mass.: Auburn House.

Gladieux, Lawrence E., and Gwendolyn L. Lewis (1987). *The Federal Government and Higher Education: Traditions, Trends, Stakes, and Issues.* New York: College Entrance Examination Board, October.

Hansen, Janet S. (1987). "Paying for College: Who Should be Responsible?" Presented at Panel Session at Education Commission of the States Annual Meeting, July 10.

Hanson, Katharine H., and Joel W. Meyerson (1989a). *Higher Education in a Changing Economy.* New York: Coopers & Lybrand.

——— (1989b). *Higher Education in a Changing Economy.* New York: American Council on Education and the Association of Governing Boards.

Hauptman, Arthur M. (1989a). *New Ways of Paying for College.* New York: Ace/Macmillan.

——— (1989b). "Why Are College Charges Rising?" *College Board Review* 151 (Summer): 10–17.

Hayes-Bautista, David (1988). "Shifting Demographics: Implications for the Community and Higher Education." In *Economic Development in a Multicultural Society.* Washington, D.C.: National University Continuing Education Association.

Heller, Scott (1986). "Women Flock to Graduate School in Record Numbers, but Fewer Blacks Are Entering the Academic Pipeline." *Chronicle of Higher Education,* September 10.

Hodgkinson, Harold L. (1985). *All One System.* Washington, D.C.: Institute for Educational Leadership.

Kennedy, Donald (1989). "Report to the Academic Council." Unpublished draft. Palo Alto: Stanford University.

Kirschner, Alan H., and Julianne Still Thrift (1987). *Access to College: The Impact of Federal Financial Aid Policies at Private Historically Black Colleges.* Washington, D.C.: United Negro College Fund and National Institute for Independent Colleges and Universities.

Levy, Frank (1989). "Paying for College: A New Look at Family Income Trends." *College Board Review* 151 (Summer): 18–21.

Lewis, Gwendolyn L. (1988). *Trends in Student Aid: 1980 to 1988.* Update from the Washington Office of the College Board. New York: College Entrance Examination Board.

Office for Sponsored Research (1988). *Principal Investigator's Handbook.* Cambridge, Mass.: Harvard University.

Reich, Robert B. (1989). "As the World Turns." *New Republic,* May 1, p. 23.

Snyder, Thomas D. (1988). *Digest of Education Statistics.* Washington, D.C.: National Center for Education Statistics, U.S. Department of Education.

Steinbruner, Maureen (1989). *America Tomorrow: The Choices We Face*. Washington, D.C.: Center for National Policy.

Stern, Joyce D. (1988). *The Condition of Education*, vol. 2: *Post-Secondary Education*. Washington, D.C.: National Center for Education Statistics, U.S. Department of Education, Office of Educational Research and Improvement.

Stewart, Donald M. (1988). "American Undergraduate Education: A Time for Reflection and Reform." *International Journal of Educational Research* 12 (2): 221–26.

8

Science and Technology

Daniel S. Greenberg

In addition to a broad range of other skilled workers, modern countries need multitudes of scientists, engineers, and technicians. The work they do basically defines the modern nation. Furthermore, in an era of anxiety about productivity, technically trained people are an indispensable part of every national growth strategy. Mere numbers, however, are no measure of the value that these specialists bring to a nation's economy and culture. The quality of their education is of critical importance, as are the conditions in which they work and the capacity of the economy to make use of their skills. When working conditions are poor, the practitioners of science, engineering, and related fields frequently join the transnational "brain drain"—a testimonial to their mobility and the good sense of the countries welcoming their skills.

The United States is blessed with great numbers of excellently trained scientists and engineers; it continues to produce many more and to attract others as immigrants. But demographic trends, along with the maturation and institutional inertia of the U.S. research enterprise, raise serious concerns about the long-term strength of our nation's science and technology. The concerns are intensified by inflexibility in responding to the new era of intense high-tech industrial competition. The problems can be distilled to a few basic issues: Are we producing enough scientists and engineers with training suitable for the economic needs of the country? Are they in large measure fruitfully employed? Are the nation's resources effectively employed along the spectrum of research activities, from basic science (the quest for fundamental knowledge) to the incorporation of that knowledge into products and services? And if the United States is not doing well in these matters, what remedies should be pursued?

The argument of this chapter is that we are not doing well, that we are squandering the potential of an immensely valuable national resource. This is happening because of a number of failings: neglect in educating the next generation of scientists and engineers; excessive emphasis on military research at a time when the greatest threat to national security is on the economic front; failure to adapt an aging research enterprise to the economic needs of the nation; and insufficient attention to applied research—the middle ground of activity between basic science and useful goods.

Background

America's Research Strengths

Before we proceed, however, it is useful to recognize America's great present strengths in science and technology, terms that are often interchanged with research and development (R & D). The United States has long set the standard for the rest of the world with its superbly well developed, generously financed, and sensitively managed scientific and technical enterprise. In its most visible forms, this enterprise comprises university laboratories and training programs, industrial research organizations, and government R & D facilities and projects. Many of these are the very best, or among the best, in the world.

Throughout most of the postwar years, R & D has been a heavily favored sector of the American economy, a status arising from a mixture of cultural enthusiasm for science, cold war anxieties, and carefully calculated business decisions that reflect confidence in the profit-making value of R & D. Despite the impression created by recently sounded alarms, the R & D enterprise retains that favor—if anything, both financial and political support have actually increased—and its scientific and engineering sectors remain highly productive. These strengths are worth bearing in mind to avoid overreaction when seeking remedies for the many real problems, whether current or looming, in the academic, government, and industrial sectors, and in the interrelationships among them.

The United States produces about one-third of the world's scientific, technical, and biomedical literature—far more than any other nation. The sheer bulk of research papers can be a misleading measure of scientific and technical prowess, but it is by and large a revealing sign, particularly when citation studies show that the majority of the world's scientists overwhelmingly take their leads from research produced in the United States (National Science Board 1985: 7).

The number of employed scientists and engineers in the United States, at all degree levels, rose from 2.6 million in 1978 to 5.4 million in 1988. Of those, more than 800,000 are employed in research and development. The latter number is twice the size of Japan's R & D work force and is slightly greater than the combined totals of Japan, West Germany, France, and Great Britain.[1] The United States also leads the non-Communist world in expenditures for R & D: $104 billion (in 1986) for the United States, $36 billion for Japan, $18 billion for West Germany, and about $13 billion each for France and Britain (National Science Foundation 1988b: 37–39). The Soviets claim to outspend the United States in R & D, but *glasnost* has confirmed the widely held impression that the Soviet R & D enterprise is remarkably backward. The few exceptions are confined to national security areas, such as space-launching capacity, and several theoretical fields that are not dependent on sophisticated research apparatus.

Even the supposedly frugal Reagan era brought sizable increases in support for R & D. Most of the growth was concentrated in the national security area, but even so, the budget of the National Science Foundation—which primarily supports academic basic science—rose 73 percent between 1980 and 1988. In the same period, the budget of the National Institutes of Health rose 134 percent (*AAAS Observer* 1989: 11).

Nonetheless, the final years of the Reagan administration also brought increasing expressions of uncertainty and concern about the internal health of the R & D enterprise and its relevance to industrial competitiveness as well as the technical quality of the work force. Though the United States remained strong and productive in scientific research, Japan took the world lead in the design, manufacture, and sale of many products embodying scientific knowledge—a great deal of which had originated in the United States.

For perspective on this problem, however, it is useful to note that as important as the research enterprise might be, its performance was probably the least of many factors contributing to the difficulties confronting American industry. As Frank Press, president of the National Academy of Sciences, told the Senate Budget Committee on March 9, 1989, "Our [research] system has delivered. The problems we face are not those of science and technology, our national laboratories, our research universities." Rather, he said, the nation's economic failings are mainly attributable to other factors, including high capital costs, "the litigious nature of our relationships," and "the short-term view of American management" (U.S. Congress. Senate. Budget Committee 1989).

Nonetheless, science and engineering are so critical to economic success that serious questions must be asked about their condition and their relevance to national needs. Research in the United States must face up to a paraphrase of that old barroom taunt: If you're so smart, why aren't we richer?

Institutional Inertia

The problems of the R & D enterprise have evolved in what is now a mature institutional setting, with rooted interests, alliances, congressional and other political ties, and old habits of doing business. Though research decisively affects the future, the institutional framework of research in America is very much a holdover from the past. The federal organizational table for research and development has remained virtually unchanged since the establishment of NASA and the White House science office 30 years ago. In the academic sector, the list of the top 100 universities in research expenditures has changed little over the past 25 years. Ten states receive nearly 65 percent of all federal R & D funds, according to the U.S. General Accounting Office (1987: 48). Call it stability, stultification, or a reaffirmation of the rule that the rich get richer, but the patterns of distribution of federal R & D funds have proved extremely frustrating to the have-not states.

One consequence of the lopsided distribution of R & D funds is the arrival on Capitol Hill of "pork barrel science"—the quest for appropriations for laboratories back home. Another is bootstrap efforts in many states to build up their scientific and technological resources. In both cases, the motive forces are faith in the power of science and technology to confer economic growth and disappointment with federal interest in local needs. But these developments are appended to, rather than integrated into, the national research enterprise. They are potentially so important, however, that in 1988 the Congress directed the National Institute of Standards and Technology (formerly the National Bureau of Standards) to make what is apparently the first comprehensive survey of state R & D activities. A preliminary estimate placed state expenditures in this area at $500 million per year, with most of that money leveraged by a factor of two or three through support from industry, the federal government, and community resources.

The basic cause of the durability, and rigidity, of the R & D system is that postwar dominance of the U.S. economy stood as an endorsement of the American way of science and technology. It worked, and change was not necessary. The system has its own special characteristics, matched in some respects by the R & D enterprises of other nations, but in toto it is uniquely American. Even in the face of markedly changed economic and technological conditions, it endures with little change.

Within the system, programs are segregated into government and industry sectors on the assumption that it is the proper, and unique, role of federal agencies to support research whose economic benefits cannot be captured by the organization performing the research. Thus the federal government finances academic basic research, which is openly published, and "big science"—space research and research in high-energy physics, for example, for whose products scientists are the only consumers. R & D related to national security has received huge annual increases over the past decade, and it prospers among industrial contractors, in government's own laboratories, and, to a limited extent, in universities. Government contracts out a good deal of its R & D tasks to industry, but the selection of the projects belongs to the government, as do the results. Industry, meanwhile, in using its own funds, selects its R & D targets for the purpose of making profits.

There is a big hole in this division of responsibilities: commercially oriented applied research—the middle range of activities between pure science and product development. Applied research of that type is not a government responsibility, though basic research, heavily supported by government, is the fundamental feedstock for applied research. The policy assumption is that out of natural self-interest, industry will rake over the results of basic research and exploit their commercial potential. To some extent, of course, it does—an excellent current example being biotechnology. Federal funds supported the basic research, and corporate laboratories, large and small, undertook the task of translating the results of that research into pharmaceutical and agricultural products. By and large, however, the gap between basic research and commercial product development tends to be regarded as a high-risk area by American firms. And if the likelihood of marketplace payoff is too distant, they are reluctant to proceed.

In contrast, according to a recent analysis by the Science Policy Research Division of the Congressional Research Service (CRS), "One of the primary factors in the ability of foreign firms to compete with U.S. industry is their government's support for technology development activities." In numerous cases, the CRS continues, "governments in these countries actively promote commercial technology advance and application as a component of economic growth. . . . This is a contrast to the United States, where technological considerations are not well integrated into economic policy decisions; where the responsibility for technology development, if present, is diffused across agencies, and where cooperation generally has been limited to [basic] research" (Congressional Research Service 1988: 12). Furthermore, though our entire system requires a large and continuing supply of scientists and engineers with advanced training, its personnel requirements are left to a faith in the marketplace combined with relatively skimpy federal fellowship programs.

In recent years, in response to the competitive difficulties of U.S. industry, serious attention has been directed at the federal share of the R & D enterprise, simply because it can be affected most directly by national policy making. This introspection revealed that while the R & D organizational patterns and the supporting educational structure served reasonably well through the earlier part of this decade, they were increas-

ingly inappropriate for the problems of the late 1980s and the foreseeable problems of the next decade.

Let us now examine the grounds for these concerns, starting with the
increasingly wobbly educational underpinnings of the American scientific and engineering enterprise.

The Crisis in Science Education

Education, particularly in the sciences and in mathematics, has received intense public attention in recent years. The effects of its failings
conspicuously pervade society, put a drag on the economy, and easily stir
media, public, and political concern. Nevertheless, despite the many
knowledgeable studies and reports that have decried the decrepit condition of elementary and secondary education, few improvements have
been made. The average science and mathematics test scores of U.S. students are shameful in comparison to those of students from other industrialized nations. According to a recent report by the Educational Testing
Service (1988: 5), after years of reform efforts the "average science proficiency across the grades remains distressingly low." Recent surveys document a widespread lack of trained teachers and of classroom and laboratory equipment.

The crisis reports from the science and mathematics classrooms are
so numerous and so unanimous that it is difficult to choose among them.
The Educational Testing Service (1988: 5) notes that between 1983 and
1988 "as many as 100 national reports have been issued calling for
greater rigor in science education and suggesting numerous reforms"—
without significant effect. *Physics in the High Schools,* a report by the
American Institute of Physics (1988) chronicles a wasteland of neglect
for the scientific discipline that is central to modern industry. The survey
found that while 96 percent of secondary school students attend schools
where some sort of physics course is available, only 20 percent study
physics. A major reason, obviously, is that physics is shunned as a difficult subject—but the difficulties are surely aggravated by the inappropriate educational background of a large majority of those assigned to
teach physics. Only one-fourth of those surveyed held a degree in that
subject, and only 13 percent of the physics teachers specialized in teaching physics (American Institute of Physics 1988: 16–17). The survey also
reported that "the budget available to physics in public schools for supplies and equipment varies over a wide range and averages about $300
per physics class"—a grossly inadequate sum (American Institute of
Physics 1988: 7). A survey respondent, identified in the physics study
only as "a teacher trained in England," provided a suitably despairing
observation: "I am appalled at the lack of science education [in the

United States] just in terms of the number of years that a subject is taken. How can physics be taught in a year to any depth? Worse is the fact that so many U.S. students pass through high school and into the world with no idea of physics" (American Institute of Physics 1988: 51).

The former director of the National Science Foundation (NSF), Erich Bloch, has repeatedly expressed concern that a shortage of scientists and engineers is a certainty unless more students, particularly women and underrepresented minorities, are encouraged to seek careers in these fields. There is no sure formula for doing that, but a necessary first step would be an improvement in the intellectually and materially tattered condition of science education. The funds available for curriculum development, in-service teacher training, and equipment remain insufficient—even the funding from NSF, which is the principal agency for the support of innovation in science education. The education and research community and its allies in science and industry consistently complain, with little effect, about science education's low standing in NSF budget priorities—$171 million of NSF's $1.8 billion in fiscal year 1989 went to science education. For example, in testimony on April 6, 1989, to the Senate Committee on Labor and Human Resources, Professor Lewis M. Branscomb of the Kennedy School of Government at Harvard, formerly chief scientist of IBM, lamented the effects of education's low standing at NSF:

> Those dependent on NSF for research support in science often note that the NSF education budget is too small in comparison with the $22 billion DoEd [Department of Education] budget or the $150 billion spent by the states to have much effect. I disagree. I have seen so many state reform efforts slowed or sidetracked for want of a small sum of risk money for an educational experiment, or an inducement to bridge institutions or communities, I am sure an activist approach by NSF would bear fruit. (U.S. Congress. Senate. Committee on Labor and Human Resources 1989)

Why the relatively low standing of science education, even in the face of the NSF leadership's own expression of concern about science education? Through its staff and advisory mechanisms, NSF functions as an extension of the physical and natural sciences research community, with education as an afterthought. As Jerry A. Bell, director of the Institute of Chemical Education at the University of Wisconsin, told the Science, Research, and Technology Subcommittee of the House Science, Space, and Technology Committee on March 9, 1989: "We need only look at NSF's budget over the years to see that the immediate interests of the research community are, understandably, their own research grants, not the educational system that at some time in the future produces new scientists and enlightened citizens" (U.S. Congress. House. 1989).

The long-term personnel supply problem, or the "pipeline" problem, as it is referred to, has in recent years come to be regarded as one of the most pernicious difficulties confronting the science and engineering professions and threatening their ability to serve the country. There are skeptics who respond that many past warnings of impending serious shortages of trained personnel have been confounded by events. Thus, the Congressional Office of Technology Assessment (OTA) argued in a report in 1985 that variables such as career choice, market incentives, professional mobility, and so forth are so numerous and poorly understood that dour forecasts "should be treated with considerable skepticism" (Office of Technology Assessment 1985: 5).

OTA's optimism was a rare event in a field dominated by gloom, but its cheerful conclusions were derived from little more than a mixture of hopefulness and the fact that we have more or less muddled through in the past. "It is entirely possible," OTA stated, "that the supply of trained people in science and engineering will not decline at all, despite the drop in the college-age population." The demographic shortfall, it suggested, could be covered if a larger proportion of the college-age population went into science and engineering; if women and minority groups were encouraged to increase their relatively low participation in these professions; and if market forces pulled specialists into shortage areas. OTA pointed out that "the Manhattan Project in World War II, the Apollo program in the 1960s, the environmental and energy programs of the 1970s and the rapid buildup of the semiconductor and computer industries all relied successfully on the importation of scientific and technical talent from related fields. Many analysts consider the mobility and adaptability of the Nation's scientific and engineering workforce to be one of its greatest strengths" (Office of Technology Assessment 1985: 6).

By 1988, however, OTA had tempered its optimism on the likelihood that minority-group recruitment would help to counter the effects of the demographic decline on science and engineering enrollments. In a follow-up to its 1985 report, OTA noted "a continued drop in the number of minority high school graduates who enter college, due to the increased attractiveness of the Armed Forces and disillusionment with the value of a college degree in today's job market" (Office of Technology Assessment 1988: 7).

Today, the prospects for the 1990s and the early years of the next century must be regarded with apprehension. Rescue may possibly result from unplanned factors such as professional mobility, immigration, and a greater proportion of students opting for careers in science and engineering. But the available data do not support those possibilities.

A cogent report by Richard C. Atkinson, chancellor of the University of California at San Diego, plausibly argues that a major shortage of Ph.D.'s in science and engineering is currently in the making for the turn of the century. Without forceful countermeasures, Atkinson contends, the shortage will reach a peak in 15 years, when there will be a demand for about 18,000 of these Ph.D.'s per year and a supply of only 10,500 (Atkinson 1989). The basic numbers cited by Atkinson are as follows: Hirings of new science and engineering Ph.D.'s in the United States now total about 12,500 a year—5,000 by universities, 6,000 by industry, and the remainder by federal, state, and local governments. Assuming that the annual number of new positions in industry remains approximately constant—which it has since 1977—a coming surge of retirements will raise industrial demand to 9,500 science and engineering Ph.D.'s annually by 2004.

Meanwhile, the rate of retirement of academic Ph.D.'s is projected to rise from 2,000 per year in 1988 to 4,500 per year in 2004. During the greater part of the 1990s, the rising number of retirements will coincide with a decline in the traditional college-age population, thus removing some pressure from faculties thinned by retirements. But, Atkinson points out, around the year 2000 the size of the college-age population will increase substantially. "Assuming that the percentage of the age group entering college does not change appreciably," he states, "and assuming current faculty/student ratios, academic demand for new Ph.D. scientists and engineers will almost double between 1988 and 2004 to about 8,000 per year" (Atkinson 1989).

On the demand side, that adds up to 18,000 Ph.D.'s per year early in the twenty-first century. The supply forecast is not reassuring. Since 1971, the total U.S. production of Ph.D.'s in natural sciences and engineering has fluctuated within a narrow range—from 13,500 in 1971 to 11,000 in 1978, when it began a steady growth to the 1989 level: 14,500. The latter total includes 5,000 foreign citizens who received Ph.D. degrees, comprising 30 percent of the Ph.D.'s in the physical sciences, 50 percent of those in mathematics, and 60 percent of those in engineering.

Based on the current rate of 2.25 Ph.D.'s per 1,000 U.S. citizens aged 30, and assuming that foreign enrollments remain constant, Atkinson notes that Ph.D. production in these fields will fall to 12,000 per year in 2004. Some 70 percent of foreign Ph.D.'s now remain in the United States, but, Atkinson points out, "as working conditions improve in other countries, a decreasing percentage of foreign-born Ph.D.'s will remain in the United States to make up the shortfall between demand and supply" (Atkinson 1989). According to a recent report in the *Wall Street Journal,* a small reverse tide long flowing between the United States and South Korea has been accelerating rapidly. "The [South Korean] science ministry estimates that it has brought back some 1,200 expatriates to government labs and universities since 1968, most of them since 1982," the report states, adding that "the ministry has its eye on the 6,000 Korean scientists and engineers it estimates are still in the United States (Yoder 1989).

The upgrading of master's degree holders to positions usually occupied by Ph.D.'s was a saving strategy in meeting the surging personnel needs in the past. But here, too, the work force in several key disciplines has experienced either only slight growth or some decline over the past decade. In the physical sciences, the number of master's degrees awarded rose from 5,485 in 1976 to 5,910 in 1986. In the life sciences, it fell slightly, from 9,823 to 8,572. In engineering, it rose from 16,170 to 21,314. The only case of major growth was in the category of the mathematical and computer sciences, in which the number of degree recipients roughly doubled, to 11,241, over the decade (National Science Foundation 1988b: 30).

In engineering and several other fields, universities have become heavily dependent on foreign-born faculty, mainly because more Americans with bachelor's and master's degrees are going directly to work rather than pursuing the Ph.D. degree. The concerns that arise from this trend are complex and controversial. Some argue, quite plausibly, that the availability of qualified foreigners for teaching is a blessing and a source of strength for American science and technology. But at a minimum, questions can be raised about the condition of an essential national enterprise that must rely on foreigners for a large proportion of its key personnel.

Another increasingly grave shortcoming concerns the expensive facilities required by the colleges and universities for training scientists and engineers. Federal research agencies financed the great wave of campus laboratory construction that followed Sputnik. These facilities were used to train much of the personnel for the Apollo moon landing and the arms buildup that began late in the Carter administration and accelerated through the Reagan years. Fifteen years ago, however, federal aid for building and renovating campus laboratories was severely curtailed; it now accounts for about 6 percent of current spending in this area. Other sources—principally bond issues, state support, and public fund drives—have partially filled the gap. But amid some laboratory splendor in academe, there are also many rundown and inadequate facilities, and even some squalor. A survey conducted for the National Science Foundation found that nearly 40 percent of campus laboratories were in need of repairs, and there was a good deal of overcrowding and a considerable reliance on that bane of sound financial planning, deferred maintenance (National Science Foundation 1988c).

Clearly, science and engineering education in the United States—all along the personnel pipeline—is afflicted by deficiencies that pose grave dangers to our chance of meeting the productivity requirements of the next decade. Many useful remedies await serious application. They will be discussed in the final section of this chapter, but next we will examine the financial and institutional context in which American science and technology function.

The Financial and Institutional Context

As noted above, total U.S. spending on R & D far exceeds the R & D spending of our industrial competitors. Amid the usual clamor for more money, it should be recognized that quantity is not the problem. Rather, attention and corrective measures should be applied to the misdirection of much of the vast sum that the United States devotes to research and development.

The Focus on Defense

A central fact of American R & D is that, in an era in which the military threat to American security has been at least equalled by economic threats, a huge share of the resources is still commanded by the Department of Defense (DOD) and other national security agencies. R & D funding over the past decade swung heavily to the military, which receives about 65 percent of all federal R & D spending, or some 30 percent of total national R & D funds (Table 8.1). Japan devotes about 2 percent of its R & D spending to military purposes, West Germany about 10 percent (National Science Foundation 1985: 8).

The dominance of military R & D spending in the United States has been accompanied by stringencies in many other fields of R & D that rely on federal support—the environment, education, energy, transportation, and the space sciences. Spinoff from defense to civilian areas has diminished as military needs become more exotic. Defense, more concerned with performance than with cost or marketplace acceptance, tends to be an unwholesome influence on the scientific enterprise. Because of its ample resources, it dominates certain fields, prominent among them artificial intelligence research in universities.

John Gibbons, director of the Congressional Office of Technology Assessment, summarized a widespread misgiving about the military share of federal R & D resources when he observed: "My concern for the academic enterprise is that we may be unduly influencing students and professors to work on essentially defense-related projects. . . . I think the shifting ratio of defense versus civilian sector research is going to impact to some degree on the academic enterprise. And I say unduly influencing. Because that old saw—that defense R & D spending spins

Table 8.1 Trends in Federal R & D Spending (obligations in billions of dollars)

Year	Defense	All Other
1980	15.1	14.7
1981	17.8	15.3
1983	22.1	14.3
1984	28.3	14.9
1985	33.4	16.1
1986	36.5	16.2
1987	38.4	17.6
1988	39.5	19.3
1989	41.3	21.7
1990 (est.)	44.0	23.3

Source: Office of Management and Budget, special analysis, budget of the United States Government, fiscal year 1990.

out and feeds the civilian economy—is definitely debatable" (Garfield 1988: 9).

Lack of Institutional Base for Applied Research

Of equal concern is the absence of a federal government organization specifically responsible for the support of engineering and applied industrial research. Basic science across the disciplines is the charge of the National Science Foundation. NSF notes that its charter extends to engineering, and it claims to do right by that discipline—within the parameters defined by NSF's limited resources. But the support of engineering research accounts for about only 12 percent of NSF's funds, with the bulk of the remainder going for research in the basic sciences.

Most of DOD's R & D funds are allocated to weapons development. Though DOD excels at applied research, principally through the Defense Advanced Research Projects Agency, the work there is tightly focused on military needs. The National Aeronautics and Space Administration for many years made a serious effort to transfer aerospace technology to broad sectors of the commercial economy, but even before the *Challenger* disaster, budget stringencies restricted that role. After the disaster, NASA was so heavily burdened by the costs of reviving the shuttle program that activities not directly essential to that goal were severely crimped. "Between 1976 and 1986," according to NSF, "Federal applied research performance had diminished by 20 percent in real terms, mainly because of cutbacks at NASA, where spending decreased by one-half in constant dollars" (National Science Foundation 1988a: 18).

The research laboratories of the U.S. Department of Agriculture (USDA) are a model of a research institution tied to the needs of the customer—the farmer. Many contend that USDA science is too tightly tied—site specific, as it's called—and pays insufficient attention to the new frontiers of the genetic sciences. In any case, agriculture is a rare success story of modern American productivity. The USDA's venerable system of extension agents—locally based experts who assist with technical advice—is regarded as a model for government to emulate in assisting technology transfer to the manufacturing realm.

The National Institutes of Health (NIH) concentrate on the basic biomedical sciences, feeling confident, with justification, that the pharmaceutical industry will diligently tend to the process of turning the knowledge that NIH produces into commercial products. The linkup between NIH and the pharmaceutical industry is unique, however, in that it is the only case in which an industry hovers over a federal research establishment to acquire usable knowledge. Elsewhere, the laboratories of the federal government—mostly concentrated in the Departments of Defense, Energy, and Agriculture, as well as NASA—have traditionally gone about their work with little or no attention to economic productivity or the marketplace.

Since these so-called national laboratories absorb about one-third of all federal R & D spending, they naturally have drawn covetous attention from other organizations seeking federal support for research, and have been the target of budget cutters simply on the prowl for whatever is accessible. But as major employers, they command the support of their congressmen and senators. The protected status of these facilities was starkly revealed at a hearing on March 9, 1989, before the Senate Budget Committee. Robert M. Rosenzweig, president of the Association of American Universities, a consortium of institutions strong in research, stated that "some national laboratories have come to occupy the same status as military bases, justified not for what they do to advance a mission, but for what they contribute to the local economy." Noting that the politically aloof device of a national review commission had been employed to eliminate unneeded military bases, Rosenzweig proposed a similar approach to eliminating unneeded federal laboratories.

A blunt response came from Senator Pete V. Domenici, Republican of New Mexico, site of the Los Alamos National Laboratory and other federal research facilities. Agreed, said the senator, if the same review process is applied to universities (U.S. Congress. Senate. Budget Committee 1989).

The Reagan administration achieved some success in cutting spending on the national laboratories, mainly by reducing research in the Department of Energy on solar energy and other renewable resources. Overall, however, laboratories have been politically untouchable. Efforts to orient them toward civilian industrial needs have received a good deal of political support, including an executive order by President Reagan that directed the laboratories to give industry access to their research results and specialized equipment. Ironically, according to many reports, representatives of foreign firms have responded to the opening of the laboratories in far greater numbers than have their American counterparts.

The absence of a clearly defined institutional link between industry and government-supported research has led to many proposals to establish a National Technology Foundation along the lines of the National Science Foundation. But the proposals have foundered on academic fears of a diversion of support from basic research. Several years ago, academe successfully countered a proposal to rename NSF the National Science and Technology Foundation.

By default, the DOD has, in effect, become the nation's Department of Technology. With no other federal agency authorized and financed to promote applied research and the development of technologies to the precompetitive stage, DOD has quietly assumed the role. Thus, it provides $100 million a year for Sematech, the industrial consortium for research on semiconductor manufacturing techniques. It subsidizes research in high-definition television, otherwise neglected by American firms. Moreover, DOD is a major source of support for research in robotics and other advanced technologies.

The suitability of this role for DOD is open to serious doubt, some of which has been expressed by the president of the National Academy of Engineering, Robert M. White. "The Department of Defense," he said in an address to the Academy's 1988 annual meeting, "has become the nation's de facto Ministry of Technology and Industry by default. While we need to be thankful that some agency is taking the initiative, the Defense Department is not where it should be. I find it interesting," White continued, "that the recent budget proposals of the Japanese Ministry of International Trade and Industry (MITI) targeted such fields as artificial intelligence, superconductivity, and hypersonic planes among others for concerted attention. And where are the analogous initiatives in the U.S. government? Largely in the DOD" (White 1988).

Why not DOD? The answer is that the technology of defense is focused on high performance to suit one customer—with broad market acceptance of no concern and cost a matter of marginal interest. The managers of defense research are so steeped in these criteria that some managers of civilian industry regard military R & D experience with wariness in hiring scientists and engineers. White did not state those concerns in his address, but it is likely that they contributed to his disapproval of DOD as the American answer to MITI.

Congressional dissatisfaction with the applied-research gap in federal

R & D affairs led to the remodeling, late in 1988, of the National Bureau of Standards. Retitled the National Institute of Standards and Technology (NIST), it was given responsibility for a wide range of activities focused on promoting industrial research and economic productivity. Unfortunately, this responsibility was not accompanied by the wherewithal to finance these activities. In fact, the departing budget of the Reagan administration trimmed some $3.5 million from the sum appropriated to NIST for fiscal year 1989.

Big Science

The money issue—eternally vexing in science and technology, where bright ideas inevitably exceed available resources—demands special scrutiny of the growing number of projects that come under the heading of "big science." The current science and technology agenda contains several projects that are so exceptionally costly that their financing, in a general atmosphere of constraints on federal funding, could seriously affect other fields of research, both financially and in terms of specialized personnel. The projects include the Superconducting Super Collider (SSC), the space station, the hypersonic aircraft, and human genome research. Taken together, they would require perhaps an additional $3 billion or $4 billion per year in federal R & D spending.

International cost sharing was a stated goal of the Reagan administration for the SSC, the space station, and the genome project. But it was determined to proceed, with or without foreign partners. In all cases, the main financial burden remains with the United States. Given the large costs and the widely distributed benefits of high-technology scientific enterprise, rhetorical court has been given to the importance of foreign collaboration and sharing of the costs. In fact, however, very little cost sharing has been achieved, mainly because a nationalistic spirit remains strong among the managers of American science and their political supporters. But it is long past the time when this nation can economically tolerate that tunnel-visioned approach. The scientific and technical merits of these projects, strongly argued by their advocates, are difficult to assess in advance. The costs, however, are so enormous that international cost sharing should be considered essential for proceeding.

A Strategy for the Future

Remedying the current and incipient ills of American science and technology is in part difficult and in part easy. The most essential step concerns R & D resources, currently dominated by obsolete national security concerns, which consume some 65 percent of federal R & D spending. As the Soviet military menace receded in the late 1980s, and economic concerns continued to rise on the national political agenda, the balance began to shift toward federal support of nonmilitary R & D. The final Reagan budget, endorsed by the Bush administration, contained greater growth for civilian than for military R & D—although the Pentagon is still far ahead by a lopsided amount: $44 billion proposed for defense R & D, $23.3 billion for civilian R & D.

The deficiencies of elementary and secondary education are too deeply embedded in broad societal upheavals and failings for any quick fix to produce major improvements. Nonetheless, intelligently devised curricula and teaching techniques are an essential ingredient for drawing children's attention to science and mathematics and encouraging them to proceed with these subjects. Trained teachers—and retrained teachers— are obviously important. The National Science Foundation has compiled an impressive record in supporting good work in all these areas of education. What it lacks is money to do the job on a scale that can make an important difference nationally. The remedy here is obvious, and cheap, given the economic value of scientific and technical competence. Now financed at about $250 million per year, NSF's educational activities should quickly be expanded far beyond that sum.

Chancellor Atkinson of the University of California at San Diego calculates that if in 1992 an additional 63,000 high school seniors enter college with plans to major in science or engineering, "the number of Ph.D.'s derived from that additional cohort would bring the 2004 production up to the 1988 level" (Atkinson 1989). He also proposes creation of a National Fellowship Program for graduate students, with 3,000 four-year fellowships of $25,000 per year. The cost would be $300 million per year, trivial in comparison to the approximately $150 billion that the United States will be expending annually on R & D early in the present decade.

University-based training in science and engineering requires proper buildings and equipment—both increasingly expensive as research becomes more reliant on sophisticated apparatus. In 1988 federal legislation was enacted authorizing a renewal of support for building and renovating university laboratory facilities. The good intentions were not accompanied by money, however. Funding of the facilities bill deserves a high priority.

Along with assuring an adequate supply of scientists, engineers, and other technically trained people, attention must be directed toward improving the conditions in which research is conducted and the organizational mechanisms that help bring its results into the economy.

Above all, we must assure that good use is being made of the scarce funds supporting the research enterprise. In this regard, the organizational pluralism and diversity of American science and technology are strengths that argue strongly against centralization. But given the federal government's enormous financial presence and regulatory authority in R & D, the present system of independent departments and agencies setting and pursuing their own goals is too uncertain and too wasteful to be tolerated in an era of continuing budget crises.

Off and on, proposals have been raised to create a Department of Science that would embrace a number of major federal research agencies, including the National Science Foundation, the National Institute of Standards and Technology, the Office of Energy Research in the Department of Energy, and the basic science functions of NASA. The wisdom of establishing a Department of Science is difficult to assess. It should be sympathetically and carefully examined, however, if only because the federal way of doing science and technology has retained the same organizational format for over three decades, during which dynamic changes in science and society have occurred.

There should be no doubt, however, about the need for rejuvenating the science-advisory function at the presidential level. Reveries derived from C. P. Snow's romantic tales of science and politics distort the realities of science and politics, American style, in the late twentieth century. Though their works have figured large, scientists have actually figured little in the major political decisions of the postwar era—nostalgic accounts of the Kennedy era notwithstanding. But there needs to be an entity in the federal system which would collect essential information about the health and performance of the R & D enterprise, attempt to look over the scientific horizon for the "hot" areas of the future, and pay close attention to the institutional barriers to moving research from the laboratory to the marketplace. That role was written into the 1976 legislation that revived the White House Science Office. (President Nixon had wiped it out in 1973 because, he felt, the scientists there lacked loyalty to the goals of his administration.)

However, the restored office has never fulfilled its potential, not out of failings on its part but simply because recent presidents and their inner White House circles have not felt that they suffer from lack of science advice in political or technical matters. A revival of White House science advice has occurred in the Bush administration, but its effectiveness remains to be seen. When science policy is a low-priority item on the presidential agenda, Congress has characteristically moved in to assert its authority. The transformation of the National Bureau of Standards into the National Institute of Standards and Technology—with added responsibilities for industrial competitiveness—was mainly a Congressional initiative. But Congress, with its fragmented committee structure, is ill-suited to prescribe broad national science policies. The task can be performed only by the presidency.

Recognized or not, issues of science and technology policy intrude themselves on the national agenda, and they require resolution if we want science and technology to contribute in full measure to our national productivity. It could be costly to leave these issues untended in hopes of muddling through.

The derelict state of science education cries for correction. Major international cost-sharing should be regarded as a necessity in undertaking "big science" projects. The one-third share of federal R & D funds going to the government's own laboratories should be reassessed in terms of relevance to industrial competitiveness and domestic social needs such as environmental cleanup and the training of scientists.

Science and technology can be powerful contributors to the improvement of productivity, but only if their ranks are filled with well-trained and properly supported practitioners. Sensible choices must be made in choosing research goals. And in the new era of industrial accomplishment, our complex research enterprise must be orchestrated in the difficult task of translating knowledge into wealth.

The United States is needlessly neglecting its position as the world's leading scientific and technological power. The steps required to maintain that position are neither mysterious nor terribly expensive. What has been lacking so far is the political determination to take those steps.

Note

1. Doubts have recently been expressed about the criteria used by the National Science Foundation for tabulating scientific and engineering personnel (National Academy of Sciences 1989). But the numbers cited above have, at least until recently, been widely accepted as accurate.

References

AAAS Observer (1989). January 6.

American Institute of Physics (1988). *Physics in the High Schools: Findings from the 1986–87 Nationwide Survey of Secondary School Teachers of Physics.* New York: American Institute of Physics.

Atkinson, Richard C. (1989). "Supply and Demand for Science and Engineering Ph.D.'s: A National Crisis in the Making." Unpublished remarks to the Regents of the University of California, February 16.

Congressional Research Service, Science Policy Research Division (1988). *The Europe 1992 Plan: Science and Technology Issues.* Washington, D.C.: Congressional Research Service.

Educational Testing Service (1988). *The Science Report Card: Elements of Risk and Recovery.* Princeton, N.J.: Educational Testing Service.

Garfield, Eugene (1988). "Science/Technology Policy." *Current Contents,* November 21, pp. 3–10.

National Academy of Sciences (1989). *Surveying the Nation's Scientists and Engineers: A Data System for the 1990's.* Washington, D.C.: National Academy Press.

National Science Board (1985). *Science Indicators.* NSB 85-1.
National Science Foundation (1985). *International Science and Technology Update.* Washington, D.C.: National Science Foundation.
——— (1988a). *National Patterns of Science and Technology Resources 1987.* NSF 88-305. Washington, D.C.: National Science Foundation.
——— (1988b). *Science and Technology Data Book.* NSF 88-332. Washington, D.C.: National Science Foundation.
——— (1988c). *Scientific and Engineering Research Facilities at Universities and Colleges.* NSF 88-320. Washington, D.C.: National Science Foundation.
Office of Technology Assessment (1985). *Demographic Trends and the Scientific and Engineering Work Force.* Washington, D.C.: Office of Technology Assessment.
——— (1988). *Elementary and Secondary Education for Science and Engineering.* Washington, D.C.: Office of Technology Assessment.
U.S. Congress. House. Science, Space, and Technology Committee. Subcommittee on Science, Research, and Technology (1989). Hearings. March 9.
U.S. Congress. Senate. Budget Committee (1989). Science, Technology, and Strategic Economic Policy Hearings. Vol. 3, 101–83, March 9.
U.S. Congress. Senate. Committee on Labor and Human Resources (1989). Hearings. April 6.
U.S. General Accounting Office (1987). *University Funding: Patterns of Distribution of Federal Research Funds to Universities.* Washington, D.C. U.S. Government Printing Office.
White, Robert (1988). Address to 1988 Annual Meeting, National Academy of Engineering.
Yoder, Steven Kreider (1989). "Reverse Brain Drain Helps Asia but Robs U.S. of Scarce Talent." *Wall Street Journal,* April 18.

9

Employment and Training

Marion Pines and Anthony Carnevale

Improvements in formal schooling, whether at the elementary, secondary, or postsecondary levels, are critically important, but in themselves they will not suffice to meet the continuing human capital investment needs of the future. For one thing, unless there are dramatic and sustained changes in the holding power of schools, far too many potential employees will drop out of formal education before they are adequately prepared for productive employment. For another, rapid changes in the nature of work require almost constant skill upgrading that goes well beyond what formal education or private employers currently provide. To complicate matters further, demographic changes will require more intensive and sustained human capital investments to meet the expected demand for labor in the decade ahead. For these and other reasons, an effective human capital investment strategy must involve more than "fixing" the public education system. It must involve a broad and continued commitment to employment and training initiatives geared to equipping and reequipping the labor force with the skills, behaviors, and expectations needed to enter and remain productive in a rapidly changing economy.

Education and skill training—on and off the job—have always been the most effective means of improving individual opportunity and institutional competitiveness, both in the United States and around the world. They account for most of the differences among Americans in terms of earnings and the ability to choose how and where to earn a living (Lillard and Tan 1986).

The context and the language surrounding employment and training policy have undergone a dramatic change over the last 25 years. Central to this change is the growing recognition, documented more fully by Arnold Packer in Chapter 2 of this volume, that recent demographic, economic, and technological forces are driving this nation toward a major human capital deficit. Recognition of these trends demands a new agenda for employment and training policy in both the public and private arenas. Without that, the competitiveness of our economic institutions is threatened, and many Americans' opportunities for productive lives will be seriously jeopardized.

The purpose of this chapter is to explore what this new agenda should entail and to show how this relates to the evolution of employment and training policies. To set the stage for this analysis, we begin by exploring the basic forces that make greater attention to employment and training so urgent.

The Context

Work Force Trends

The first of these basic forces is an important change in the makeup of the American work force. From the point of view of employment and training policy, the most salient facts are these:

- According to the Bureau of Labor Statistics, more than 80 percent of those now working will still be in the work force in the year 2000. Because of rapidly changing work force demands, former secretary of labor Elizabeth Dole estimated that as many as 30 million of these current workers would have to be retrained during the next 11 years.
- Changing birthrates have slowly reduced the number of new workers available to employers. This trend is expected to continue, leaving employers with an older, less flexible work force, more resistant to requisite changes. At the same time, older workers with critical technical skills will be retiring at an increasingly rapid rate. Case in point: the average age of the nation's 300,000 machinists is 58.
- Since 1982, the black labor force has been growing at almost twice the rate for whites. This trend is expected to continue at least until 1995. The black population is beset by a multiplicity of social and economic ills (e.g., high dropout rates and low labor-market participation rates), symptomatic of historically deficient human resource investments by existing institutions.
- Women will account for two-thirds of the labor force growth during the next decade. Based on projections by the Bureau of Labor Statistics, the participation rate of women in the labor force will grow from 57 percent in 1988 to 62 percent by the year 2000. This phenomenon can be attributed to many factors. Rising costs of living, inflation,

and changing mores have made families with two working parents a social norm at every level of society. In addition, however, the erosion of the traditional family structure has produced a phenomenal growth in female-headed households over the past 20 years, with the accompanying economic necessity for the head of household to seek work (or public aid).

- Immigration—both legal and illegal—will become a major factor in the competitive race for entry-level jobs. Problems are most evident along the southern border and in the Far West, where undocumented workers agree to wages and working conditions below traditional U.S. standards. This has the potential for creating social unrest in many communities around the nation, as demonstrated by the January 1989 riots in Miami.

The cumulative effect of these factors is clear. If the economy grows at even a moderate pace, employers will find it difficult to fill entry-level jobs and will need to dip increasingly into the more at-risk segment of the employment pool, comprising the poor, the dependent, dropouts, minorities, and immigrants.

Workplace Trends

In addition to changes in the work force, a second set of changes has significantly altered the character of the workplace. The remarkable shift in the American economy from manufacturing to service has been well documented. One statistic sums up the story: of the over 28 million new jobs created during the decade from the late 1970s to the late 1980s, 85 percent were in service and information industries (Personick 1989). It is too optimistic to imagine that large numbers of service jobs will remain available to workers who are unskilled and ignorant of technology.

Today, employers are creating new organizational structures which recognize that:

- New technologies have increased the autonomy both of individual employees and of working teams.
- Accelerating economic and technical changes demand organizational flexibility rather than traditional top-down hierarchical and centralized structures.
- Frontline employees need technical capabilities, resources, and authority to customize products and services in order to meet customers' demands for high quality and timely service.
- Employees at all levels of the organization need to be involved in decision making in order to shorten the "cycle time" (the time it takes to get innovations to the marketplace).

One might ask, what does this have to do with training? New efficiencies, new structures, quality improvements, new applications, and innovations come from refinements during the production phase, as well as customer feedback from the use of a product or service. This suggests the need for decentralized training systems throughout the production process extending to the point of sale and interface with customers, where communication and decision making skills become critical.

Employers are flattening and decentralizing institutions to make them more flexible and efficient. They are also reducing the size of their "permanent" work forces—keeping a minimal core work force on the payroll and utilizing suppliers, contractors, and part-timers—"contingent workers"—to respond to temporary changes in the needed quantity or mix of workers (Belous 1989). As a result, the traditional implicit commitment between employer and employee is in decline.

Thus, in the new workplace environment, employees will not only need new and better skills to perform on the job, they will need new and better skills to get and keep a job. At the same time, more and more U.S. workers will become responsible for their own career development. If they are to shoulder this responsibility successfully, they will need a range of fairly sophisticated employability skills—the skills necessary to get a job—and career development skills—the skills necessary to keep a job and manage a career. This mandates access to a continuum of job-related training accompanied by access to the newer employee benefits involving child care, care of the elderly, parental leave, and new "social adjustment" products such as portable pensions and portable health care, especially important for workers with a strong permanent attachment to the labor force.

It is not so much that all jobs will become "high tech" but rather that technology will irreversibly alter the way jobs are performed as well as the very nature of the workplace. It is this *upskilling* of work in America, driven by technological changes, innovation, and world competition that undergirds the need to adjust employment and training policy.

A few examples may help to illustrate the point. Today, the fast-food industry is among the nation's largest employers. It has become a traditional point of entry for young workers, welfare mothers, and others seeking part-time, flexible schedule employment. Today fast food is a very labor-intensive, hands-on industry. Its employees range from order takers, cashiers, and servers to short-order cooks turning out the quarter-pounders. Yet over the next four years at least one of the giants in the industry is projecting a market increase in productivity coupled with a staggering decrease in employment (Daggett 1989). Technological advances will permit computerized equipment to take orders, transmit the orders to trigger electronic preparation of food, and convey the food to the customer. Instead of the large numbers of relatively unskilled workers now employed, only skilled technicians (to solve equipment glitches) and human relations specialists (to keep the customers happy) will be needed in each retail outlet.

Another familiar job already in marked transition is that of bank teller. Competition and new technologies have already had a profound effect on the structure, organization, and management of banks. A new customer-service philosophy demands that traditional institutional and professional specialties give way to a "one-stop-shopping" approach for financial services. The bank teller was traditionally a processor whose primary role was to perform a series of repetitive tasks (checks in, money out, reconciling). Competitive pressures to satisfy customers' desires for one-stop shopping have expanded this role to include providing advice to consumers on a wide range of customized financial services. The teller, now privy to an array of information previously reserved for midlevel managers, is empowered to advise customers and charged with making judgment calls "on the line." Moreover, since the teller is linked with data sources via a computer terminal, a new range of skills is required to operate the equipment and access relevant data on demand.

The Issue of Basic Workplace Skills

For employers, the issue of basic workplace skills has been coming into focus slowly. Reading, writing, and math deficiencies were the first to surface, but, increasingly, attention has been directed toward skills such as problem solving, listening, negotiating, and knowing how to learn. "The dexterity of the mind will be as important as the dexterity of the fingers" asserts a major clothing maker (Mitchell 1990). In the 1990s, deficiencies in many of these basic workplace skills will be significant barriers for entry-level workers, dislocated workers, and even experienced employees attempting to adapt to economic and technological change within employer institutions.

Obviously, employers' interest in improving basic skills is driven by economic concerns. When deficiencies affect the bottom line, employers have two alternatives: training or replacement. But replacement, the time-honored choice, is becoming less practical because, as the section on "Work Force Trends" reveals, the supply of new workers is shrinking. As a result, the imperative for providing training in basic workplace skills is growing.

However, employer and worker adjustment problems will continue to escalate beyond the problem of competence in basic skills. As technology performs more tasks, employers are combining many jobs into fewer jobs with broader responsibilities. These new, consolidated jobs require workers who have broader and more advanced skills and who will use technology to handle repetitive tasks. The new technology itself

requires more advanced computational skills for operations, maintenance, and control, as well as higher literacy skills for reading complex
manuals and taking directions from computer screens. The available evidence tells us that skilled labor and technology are ultimately complementary and do not substitute for one another. A greater proportion of
educated employees and a higher incidence of training on the job are
found where the technical content of work is the highest (Lillard and Tan
1986).

Workers are being challenged as never before. For those already employed, deficiencies in basic workplace skills threaten adaptation and
short-circuit successful job transitions and career growth. The ground
under them is shifting as the range of skills needed to participate successfully in this economy expands. They are less often supervised and more
often called upon to identify problems and make crucial decisions.

Perhaps the most devastating impact of deficiencies in basic workplace skills falls upon the disadvantaged who are outside the economic
mainstream, struggling to get in. For those attempting to enter the work
force and those who have been displaced from their jobs, such deficiencies inhibit entry into productive and well-paying work. Thus it is clear
that those who are already disadvantaged will remain at the bottom of
the economic heap unless there is a redirection of the major public systems—education and employment and training—and a greater involvement of private employers.

Needed: A New Approach to Employment Policy

In our view, it is the inflammable mixture of technical, economic, and
demographic forces described earlier that provides the impetus for new
strategies for developing human resources in and around the workplace.
Employers who used to be able to "cream" the most qualified workers
from an oversized labor pool increasingly will have to *make* rather than
buy skilled employees. These same forces are redefining our notions of
the role of public human resources policies. Public policy makers are
now concerned with increasing the size of the labor pool to meet demand, increasing access to the workplace for those at the margins, and
increasing productivity to benefit all Americans.

In summary, the changing workplace is ordering up a new kind of
U.S. worker. And this new worker will be expected to have the broad set
of skills and judgment previously required only of supervisors and management personnel. Placing this set of new worker specifications alongside the changing demographic profile of workers described earlier illuminates the painful mismatch that employment and training policy and
programs must address. Major symptoms of this mismatch are evidenced

by massive functional illiteracy (affecting approximately 25 million people) and welfare dependency (3 million recipients of working age), and by an excessive number of school dropouts (almost 1 million per year).

Public Policies

No discussion of restructuring employment and training efforts would be complete without looking at the recent history of public activities in this field to understand the motivations and missions of the policies that are the underpinning of the current debates.

Early Origins

Since 1917, the federal government has expressed concern about maintaining the availability of a skilled work force necessary in order to sustain economic growth. At the same time governmental policies have attempted to provide opportunities for people with barriers to employment to obtain the education and skill training needed to enter the mainstream economy. In 1917 Congress passed the Smith-Hughes Act to encourage states and local areas to build a vocational education system to prepare the work force needed at that time. During the Great Depression of the 1930s, this initiative was joined by two new programs—Unemployment Insurance and the U.S. Employment Service—which were designed in tandem not to develop skills but to preserve workers' incomes during temporary bouts of unemployment caused by economic forces beyond their control and to provide a labor exchange mechanism to help return them to work following cyclical economic shifts. Because both these initiatives were financed through taxes on employers, both had a built-in employer constituency. Laid-off employees were obligated to accept alternative employment (if suitable) when it was offered or risk losing their unemployment insurance benefits, and the U.S. Employment Service depended on employer notification to identify jobs that needed to be filled.

Other Great Depression initiatives were mostly counter-cyclical in nature—the Civilian Conservation Corps (CCC) and the massive job creation efforts of the Works Progress Administration (WPA) and Public Works Administration (PWA). Although the vocational education system was eventually modified to create modest set-asides targeted to various disadvantaged populations, neither the Unemployment Insurance nor the Employment Service program was designed to address the problems of the structurally unemployed or those lacking basic workplace skills. Yet, prior to the 1960s, these were the initiatives that formed the heart of national employment policy.

The 1960s

By the 1960s the inadequacies of national employment policies were becoming increasingly apparent. The civil rights movement, the "redis-covery" of poverty, and the urban ghetto riots all graphically portrayed the existence of a sizable cadre of people effectively locked out of the nation's labor market yet untouched by existing employment policies. This combination of social and political forces resulted in the creation of a variety of new programs and institutional machinery designed not just to return the temporarily unemployed to their jobs but to address the far more serious skill and training gaps and discrimination barriers facing the structurally unemployed.

The Job Corps, the Neighborhood Youth Corps, New Careers, Community Action Agencies, Model Cities, and the Concentrated Employment programs were programmatic responses to these needs. In every case, the major emphasis of these various *federally* designed programs was on outreach and training *based on economic disadvantage*—a direct outgrowth of the consciousness raising produced by the civil rights movement.

In the beginning, the actual training provided was varied and often improvisational (despite the prescribed "categorical" federal packages) accompanied by a marked degree of "on-the-job" training taking place among the policymakers and service providers at every level of public life. Since then, the major training strategies have more or less been set, although the skills to be taught and the institutional context have varied. Thus, employment and training as an "industry" typically includes basic skills remediation and functional occupational skill training delivered in classroom settings; subsidized work experience, either part-time or full-time, delivered in the workplace with public or private employers; and a set of activities to improve access to the workplace, such as job clubs, job coaching, job-search training, and subsidized on-the-job training with private employers. These activities are increasingly accompanied by varying degrees of assessment, counseling, case management, and motivational incentives to encourage use of the appropriate service mix, and continued participation.

The need to develop new educational techniques to reach and teach at-risk youth and adults who were functioning dramatically below their age levels became apparent early on, as well as the need to create incentives to keep people enrolled long enough to derive lasting benefit from the programs. These needs, which continue to the present—outreach, effective training, support services, and motivational incentives—have produced over time some responsive new networks, partnerships, and institutional arrangements. The neighborhood-based community action agencies and other indigenously staffed community-based organizations created and enfranchised by the Economic Opportunity Act of 1964 provided the necessary outreach to the poor, and offered literacy, child care, health, and referral services. They became a significant local and national advocacy voice for the poor. The skill training programs usually were run by proprietary schools, community colleges, and a variety of contractual providers. The training divisions of many major corporations, such as Singer, RCA, Control Data, and General Electric, detecting the emergence of new markets, used some of the federally funded training programs, principally the Job Corps, to test and develop new educational materials and computer-assisted instruction programs. These early investments have been widely replicated, and have spawned a new industry targeted at remediating educational deficits within school systems, in youth and adult training programs, and in the workplace.

It is interesting to note that as early as the mid-1960s, the publicly funded labor exchange, the U.S. Employment Service, was not perceived by social advocates as an effective system for outreach, referral to training, or job placement for the poor.[1] This led to the establishment of neighborhood-based service centers, usually run by community action agencies or community-based organizations. Although some observers claim that public money was being wasted by the creation of duplicate and parallel systems for intake, referral, and job placement, advocates justified the expenditures by claiming that functions and services delivered in neighborhood-based, hospitable settings were more responsive, flexible, and effective.

It is probably fair to characterize the employment and training policy environment of the 1960s by its recognition of the need to create new opportunities for human development among the economically disadvantaged and the need to foster activities and new institutions that would provide those opportunities. In these "early" days there was remarkably little public policy or programmatic attention paid to the demand side of the issues—the needs of employers or local labor markets—with the exceptions of the U.S. Employment Service and the Manpower Development and Training Act (MDTA) of 1962.[2]

There was also a certain lack of enthusiasm on the part of employers for the newer groups of trainees produced by the federal antipoverty programs. In fact, employers made little use even of the U.S. Employment Service, despite a federal executive order requiring government contractors to list their job orders with the Employment Service, and despite the introduction of a much-heralded computerized job bank. (The somewhat anachronistic Employment Service structure still persists—federally funded, state managed, but located in local labor markets. It is resistant to change).

The 1970s

By the 1970s, the body of experience with and knowledge about employment and training had grown, as had the recognition of the increasingly obvious need to match the needs of disadvantaged trainees to the needs of local labor markets. These factors contributed to the passage in 1972 of the Comprehensive Employment and Training Act (CETA), which dramatically expanded and changed the funding relationships and the training system. The federally designed categorical training programs, such as the Neighborhood Youth Corps, New Careers, and the Concentrated Employment Program, which had been prepackaged and contracted by the federal government directly to local community-based service providers, were replaced by a decategorized, decentralized system. Under CETA the federal government gave formula grants directly to *units of local government* and charged them with devising training programs for the economically disadvantaged *to meet local labor market needs.*

The two most controversial elements in the public training schemes of the past 25 years have been large-scale job creation and the payment of participant wages, both of which carry hefty price tags and some negative political baggage. The practice of paying millions of enrollees the minimum wage during all their hours of enrollment in training activities began with the War on Poverty programs and continued under CETA, enacted in the early Nixon years, but it came to an abrupt end early in the Reagan years. This led to the oft-quoted satirical remark of Sar Levitan, noted labor market economist: "The poor cannot eat training" (Levitan and Gallo 1989: 26).

Public Service Employment (PSE), which reached its zenith in the Carter years under CETA, is an antirecessionary public policy tool that traces its roots to the Great Depression job creation programs. Its critics claim that it is usually ill-timed, legislated when a recession is perceived but implemented when the cycle is turning up, and that it provides little training and creates only "make-work" jobs. Its advocates see public service employment as a significant job creation strategy with multiple benefits: immediate jobs and purchasing power for the needy, important work experience for those who lack it, and public benefits realized through productive work and services in local hospitals, schools, housing projects, and communities. For many disadvantaged groups facing the barriers of discrimination and lack of experience, public service employment has provided the critical entry point and track record needed for success in the labor market. To a sagging economy, public service employment provides undergirding support to purchasing power and tax revenues. Nevertheless, public service employment was effectively killed with the demise of CETA in the early 1980s and the implementation of the Job Training Partnership Act in 1982.

A significant legacy of CETA was the formalization of the involvement of the private sector. Building on the tradition of the advisory councils used by vocational education and the labor-management committees used by some forward-looking communities, Congress legislated employer input with the 1978 amendments to CETA. The Private Industry Councils created by these amendments grew in authority and scope under the Job Training Partnership Act and are now the major public-private policy instrument for local employment and training initiatives.

The 1980s

The Job Training Partnership Act of 1982 (JTPA) created still another delivery system for publicly funded job training in the United States, though it was accompanied by a significant drop in the job training resources made available. JTPA is funded at approximately a $3.5-billion level, compared to a $20-billion level under CETA, in today's dollars. Under JTPA, switching direction again, the federal government granted these reduced formula funds to *states* to pass through to local "service-delivery areas" (presumably labor market areas—usually large, single jurisdictions or consortia of political jurisdictions), which are governed by Private Industry Councils (PICs). The Private Industry Councils include community and public agency members but by law are business dominated. Thus, in less than 20 years, the locus of control for public job-training programs has gone from the federal government to community-based organizations under the Office of Economic Opportunity, to local governments under CETA, and to states and Private Industry Councils under JTPA. Most participant wages and public-service employment, the big-ticket items of the 1960s and 1970s, are gone. Employers, through membership in Private Industry Councils and the state counterparts—State Job Training Coordinating Councils—are bringing to the table both a growing awareness of training as a critical part of a national work force investment strategy, and a new insistence on accountability for results as contrasted with the greater process or input orientation of the 1960s and 1970s.

This insistence on accountability helped create one of the most forward-looking elements of JTPA, which is the system of performance standards undergirding it. No longer content to focus only on measurements of inputs, the JTPA job-training system developed nationally determined performance expectations including measures for competencies gained, job placements, wage rates, and job retention. It must be remembered that JTPA was enacted in the middle of a recession (1981–82). Congress and the administration wanted a lean program that emphasized training (70 percent of funds had to be spent on training) leading to job placement. The system did what it was asked to do. This has resulted in a 68 percent job placement rate, unequalled by prior training programs. This development has earned the system high marks, especially among elected officials and their business partners in the Private Industry Councils, for its "bottom-line" approach to doing business. However, critics charged that performance standards and the strong role of business interests encouraged the training of the most employable, leaving the harder-to-serve last in the queue. Partly in response to critics, but more in response to changing labor market conditions described earlier in this chapter, most of the recommendations for legislative amendments to JTPA offered in 1989 stressed enrolling people in training who have more serious barriers to employment, and adjusting performance standards so that local areas are not penalized for doing so.

The late 1980s also brought a stronger policy and program response to the continuing problems created by worker dislocation. Title III of JTPA was rewritten to become the Economic Dislocation and Worker Assistance Act (EDWAA), with additional funds authorized (although not fully appropriated) to provide retraining for workers laid off because of changes in technology or plant closures. EDWAA also mandated a change in membership in the State Job Training Coordinating Councils, increasing the role of organized labor.

Another recent addition to the public job-training program arsenal was authorized by Congress and signed into law in October 1988, effective July 1, 1989. Focusing on the growing numbers in the population dependent on Aid to Families with Dependent Children (AFDC)—and the exploding expenditures connected with public assistance—the Family Support Act of 1988 authorizes federal funds (matched with state funds) to be expended on targeted subgroups of the welfare population for education, job training, and job placement. While there is admirable language in the act that speaks to human capital investment, there is also a clear emphasis on welfare savings, with mandates for enrolling fixed (and growing) percentages of the case load each year.

In addition to the explicit employment and training programs, the federal government also operates a wide range of other programs that seek to assist the poor. In fact, a 1986 White House report identified 59 "major public assistance programs" (Executive Office of the President 1986). Two years later, the Congressional Research Service listed 46 antipoverty programs. "Allowable activities" under most of these programs include components of employment and training strategies: counseling, assessment, remediation, skill training, job development, and so forth. Eighteen congressional committees authorize and appropriate funds for these programs, and 12 federal departments administer them. Each program has its administrative counterparts at state and local levels, its own eligibility rules, its own data collection requirements, and often ill-identified or murky outcome expectations. People in need of services often need to "shop" at a dozen separate organizations in order to put together a reasonable mix of needed services. As the White House report concluded: "Each program began with its own rationale, representing the intent of public officials to address a perceived need. But when the programs are considered as a system, they amount to a tangle of purposes, rules, agencies and effects. . . . As a system, they constitute a confusing cacophony" (Executive Office of the President 1986: 50).

Against this backdrop, the enfranchisement of state governments under JTPA is a potentially significant development. As mentioned above, states are the direct recipient of the federal JTPA funds and are mandated to pass through 78 percent of the dollars by formula, to local Private Industry Councils. The state is also the recipient of funds from title II of the Family Support Act: Job Opportunities and Basic Skills (JOBS). The governor of each state, through the legislatively mandated State Job Training Coordinating Council (with a strong private sector presence) has clear policymaking authority for JTPA and the U.S. Employment Service within that state. The State Council has implicit potential for expanding its mission and scope to include the development of interagency policies, programs, and strategies with other human resource development systems within the state, such as vocational education programs and the welfare-to-work programs, in order to make the best use of funds coming from disparate pipelines. The challenge is to create a coherent human capital investment strategy in every state. This will be explored further in this chapter.

An Assessment: Strengths and Weaknesses of the Public System

During the past 20 years, the Department of Labor has funded a modest program of research and demonstration in an attempt to learn more about training strategies and thereby to raise the quality of service across the increasingly decentralized delivery system. Some of the research has focused on programs targeted to specific groups such as youth, welfare mothers, teenage fathers, and criminal offenders. Other studies have examined the impact of various training strategies such as classroom training, on-the-job-training, and work experience. For example, the Supported Work experiment conducted by the Manpower Demonstration Research Corporation (MDRC) of New York tested the impacts of well-run work-experience programs operated in several sites and serving a variety of target groups: dropout youth, drug addicts, ex-offenders, and long-term welfare recipients. These small-scale, voluntary programs were designed to provide peer support, close supervision, and gradually increasing responsibility. Yet little or no post-program earnings effects were noted for any group, except for the welfare recipients, who did experience statistically significant gains (Taggart 1981).

Studies of classroom training under CETA, conducted under the auspices of the Department of Labor, concluded that the net impact of participation in training was determined by the duration of participation and by job placement. This conclusion was buttressed by the finding that the estimated annual earnings gains of classroom trainees participating between 1 and 20 weeks were only one-sixth as great as those of enrollees staying 40 weeks or more (Taggart 1981: 103).

Unfortunately these research findings are neither widely understood nor widely disseminated, nor is there a national capacity-building system to assist local areas to replicate "proven" models effectively. However, research findings do make their way into legislation. The studies describing the limited impact of work experience led directly to a legislative limitation on extensive use of work experience as a training strategy in JTPA. Recent MDRC studies of welfare-to-work pilot programs authorized by the 1981 Omnibus Reconciliation budget bill have shown modest impacts for welfare participants (over a followup period of three years) from interventions that are short-term and of low-to-moderate cost, combining job search and work experience. These impacts are measured in terms of increased earnings of $300 to $500 per year. However, the difference in earnings is not enough to move people out of poverty and keep them out; this fact is what pushes welfare advocates and other policymakers to favor more intensive developmental programs (MDRC 1988).

There is still a great deal that we do not know from definitive research studies, so that much of the system is driven intuitively. (That may not be all bad!) For example, as Judith Gueron, president of MDRC, stated in recent correspondence (1989) to the authors:

> There is no clear evidence that higher-cost programs lead to
> larger impacts than low-cost ones, although there is some evi-
> dence that this may be the case. (The reason the evidence isn't
> clear is that the studies are hard to compare, since the services
> have been delivered to different groups, with the expensive ser-
> vices usually provided to volunteers.) This is *the* major unan-
> swered research question: i.e., the incremental return to spending
> more. It will be very important to get information on this subject,
> and will require carefully structured tests.

We have no comparable knowledge base for the rest of the JTPA population: i.e., youth groups and male adults. The available information for youths (less rigorous than that on AFDC women) suggests that job search alone does not have a long-term effect. For males, we have no evidence that anything much works consistently, and not even strong evidence on what doesn't work.

Clearly, a more rigorous research agenda is needed across the range of policies and programs for human resource development.

However, relatively stable and well-tried arrangements (with both public- and private-sector participation) are in place for planning, policymaking, and delivery of employability-related services that have measurable outcomes. This is no small achievement. These institutional arrangements now exist at both the state and local level and are improving in breadth of knowledge, experience, professionalism, perception of mission, and results. Despite considerable programmatic diversity and still a fair degree of organizational chaos, there is a new and growing *recognition* of the interrelatedness of the efforts and resources directed to vocational education, dropout prevention, moving people from welfare to work, providing remedial education for those lacking basic skills, providing training for those facing serious barriers to employment, and providing retraining for those displaced from their jobs by plant closure, technology, or foreign competition. There are promising initiatives in several states (e.g., Maine, New Jersey, Washington, Michigan, and Maryland) that go beyond recognizing the need for collaborative efforts and are addressing the turf issues. They are trying to combine available resources in order to develop integrated and effective human capital investment systems that have a market-driven outcome focus.

Private-Sector Training

Lately, there has been a growing recognition of the importance of employer-based training, both to avoid employee dislocation and to encourage U.S. economic competitiveness. Dislocated employees rarely end up better off, even after conscientious former employer and public efforts to help them. Many observers, therefore, have concluded that policies for dislocated employees provide too little, too late. Continuous training on the job would discourage dislocation, or at least provide the kind of job-related learning that would be most helpful in the event dislocation is unavoidable. Employer-based training can also serve the public interest by improving the nation's competitiveness and the development prospects of state and local economies.

The Private Sector's Stake in Training

During most of the postwar period, the private sector was blessed with favorable demographics, a fairly healthy economy, and the growing development of world markets. Most of corporate America's efforts concentrated on improving productivity through investments in equipment, in communication systems, and in research and development activities. Because, during most of the past 40 years, there has been an ample supply of labor ready and willing to fuel the productivity needs of the country, employers saw no compelling need to develop formal strategies for human capital investment. The one notable exception is the apprenticeship system, created by the Fitzgerald Act of 1937, which has been in place for over half a century. Apprenticeship is a labor- and management-sponsored hierarchical training system for some 415 different trades, concentrated mostly in the construction field. Usually apprenticeship programs accept applications on a limited basis and require both a high school diploma and written and oral examinations for admission. Despite some attempts in the 1970s to improve outreach, the proportion of women and minorities in apprenticeship programs has remained low. However, apprenticeship is getting new attention as a school-to-work transition strategy and the decade of the nineties may well see both expansion and increased flexibility.

Not until the predictions of the demographic prophets of *Workforce 2000* (Johnston and Packer 1987) became a growing reality; not until advertisements for workers produced 1,100 applicants of whom 6 might be employable; not until minimum wage levels for entry-level service jobs had to be doubled to attract workers; not until the low literacy levels of current employees became a serious impediment to installing new plant technology; not until the full force of the changing nature of the work force and workplace hit corporate America has the need for a sustained human capital investment strategy been perceived and acknowledged and some actions started.

The Current Role of the Private Sector: Strengths and Limitations

Employer-based training, accompanied by a system of selection, appraisal, and rewards, is one of the human resource management systems found in employer institutions. The principal objective of the employer-based training system is to serve the strategic goals of the employer institution through two different kinds of training: formal job-related course work and informal on-the-job training. Currently, employers spend about $30 billion for formal training and estimates range anywhere from $90 billion to $180 billion for informal training (Carnevale and Gainer

1989). Informal training is the principal means by which technical, economic, strategic, and regulatory changes are gradually integrated into the workplace, especially among the nation's small employers. In the case of formal training, employers either provide their own or buy it from outside vendors.

In the past, the employer's interest focused on measuring the skills of prospective employees and selecting from among the applicant pool those who were most suitable for hiring. But as we have indicated, times are changing. Employers are beginning to see that if they are to remain competitive, they must assist their potential and current workers to achieve competence in workplace basics and in coping with technological changes. This newly assumed sense of responsibility is grounded in economic realities and is compelling employers to invest in workplace basic skills and more advanced training programs.

Technology creates both opportunities and problems for employers. Its very transferability has leveled the worldwide playing field. The employer's competitive edge is increasingly reliant upon how effectively and efficiently workers and machines are integrated and move smoothly through the production cycle. Successful integration is dependent upon how quickly veteran workers acquire new skills. Obviously, the acquisition of new skills is facilitated when a worker has a solid grounding in the basics.

A combination of good schooling, a work-oriented attitude, and learning on the job will help an individual to qualify for a job, get promoted, and leverage earnings and job security. Learning on the job, especially formal learning, is a powerful determinant of future earnings. People who get formal learning on the job enjoy a 30-percent earnings advantage over those who do not (Lillard and Tan 1986). That finding creates two imperatives. The first is to increase access to the labor market—to help people to "get a foot in the door." That is one of the principal missions of the preemployment public training system. The second is to build on the growing awareness and commitment of the nation's employers, who must assume the major role in providing training to upgrade employees' skills on the job. Although employees have always learned on the job, the training process has changed substantially in form. The fundamental dynamic has been a consistent shift from informal toward formal learning.

Much of the current employer-based training effort lacks cohesiveness and presence and therefore is largely invisible. This shadow educational system is delivered by no single institution, is the subject of no law or policy, and functions and grows quietly, a silent postscript to the employee's formal education. Even now, executives, managers, supervisors, and others train without the direction or the assistance of training professionals. For the most part they do not recognize that they are part of a training system.

Whether formal or informal, most training is, and ought to be, provided at the work site, where changes in learning requirements have their first impact. Employers provide more than two-thirds of their formal training themselves and buy the rest of their formal training from outside providers, mostly from colleges and universities (Carnevale and Goldstein 1985).

Small employers (those with fewer than 500 employees) account for roughly half of all jobs in the U.S. economy and 40 percent of new jobs being created (Hamilton and Medoff 1988). Small employers are important potential trainers, both because they create so many new jobs and because they tend to draw their employees from populations and industries that will need employer-based training the most. Employees in small businesses tend to be younger and less well educated than those selected by larger businesses. Small businesses also tend to hire more Hispanic employees (but fewer black employees) than larger employers.

Since small employers have relatively few employees, their employees tend to have jobs characterized by broad areas of responsibility. Technologies also tend to be less specialized in small businesses than in larger businesses. The lack of specialization enables both the employees and the employers to be more flexible and provides a more generic learning experience that facilitates career transitions. At the same time, however, because small employers do not have many employees, they usually cannot afford the time lost from work required for formal training during working hours. As a result, employees in small businesses tend to get less formal training than their counterparts in larger business organizations.

The significance accorded employer-based training increases dramatically with the size of the firm. Large employers tend to pay for a larger proportion of the training taken by their employees outside of the workplace. Data indicate that employers with fewer than 100 workers pay for only 23 percent of the training taken outside the workplace while employers with more than 100 workers assume almost 40 percent more of the training costs taken outside the workplace (Carnevale and Gainer 1989).

Our analysis of the available data and case studies of individual employers leads us to conclude that formal training has a relatively low status and low frequency in the U.S. workplace and that employers' current commitments to formal training and human capital development are insufficient. The $30 billion that U.S. employers now expend on formal training and development represents only 1.4 percent of the national payroll. Many of the nation's large companies spend 2 percent of payroll on training and development, and some employers with the most substantial commitments to training and development spend 4 percent (Carnevale and Gainer 1989).

In Japan and in Europe, by comparison:

- Training is accorded a higher standing in the operations of the national economies. In both Europe and Japan, training is utilized by employer institutions as a proactive tool for responding to strategic change and is an integral component of the selection, appraisal, and reward systems for job seekers and employees.
- Higher-quality academic preparation and workplace learning are provided for other non-college portions of the work force. As a result, while the United States is good at producing white-collar and technical elites to develop new ideas, the Europeans—the Scandinavians and Germans in particular—are better at getting new ideas to the marketplace quickly, as well as developing cost efficiencies, quality improvements, and new applications of existing products.
- A substantial infrastructure for training in the workplace has been created. European employers train in partnership with public schools through their apprenticeship system. Japanese employer-based training systems, although more informal, are deeply embedded in the cultures of individual employer institutions through their appraisal and award systems. (Ergas 1987)

In summary, partnership between public educators and employers are much stronger in both Europe and Japan than in the United States.

An Agenda for the Future

A Coherent Human Resource System

More than ever, business and government leaders are joining in an effort aimed at damage control: how to meet the challenge of widespread basic skills deficiencies before the problem grows even larger. The language of their dialogue has changed since the 1960s. Increasingly this dialogue speaks of employment and training initiatives not as social programs to prevent social dynamite from exploding throughout our land, but as human capital investments to increase productivity and improve the competitive position of the United States. Underlying this new economic imperative is the *universal recognition that we need to add workers to the labor force and we need lifelong training systems that will add enduring value to these workers.* Former secretary of labor Ann McLaughlin stated the case succinctly at a December 1988 Washington, D.C. seminar: "We need to raise general awareness of the importance of human capital to our economic future. Workers are far more than a means of production and must be seen as a strategic resource and as stakeholders in any organization."

The recently issued report of the Ford Foundation project on Social Welfare and the American Future gave strong support to the same theme: "We ought to invest in human capital with the same entrepreneurial spirit and concern for long range pay-offs that venture capitalists bring to investments in new enterprises" (Ford Foundation 1989). While all these "truths" are broadly acknowledged, the dialogue is taking place in an environment in which the federal deficit and the need to control federal spending dominates.

While pressure must continue for expanded public investments in human capital development, particularly in view of likely reductions in the defense budget, there is a need to examine the structure and use of existing resources to determine if more bang can be had for the existing bucks. We contend that a greater return on existing investments can be realized and more humane and rational delivery systems can be put in place. This will require a sense of vision, strong leadership, and unprecedented interagency collaboration at both a policy and resource commitment level. We recognize that tradition and turf protection die hard. But times are changing, and the ways we organize to do public business need to change. We can no longer afford stand-alone human development systems. A sustained effort must be mounted to overcome some of the longstanding barriers that prevent the disparate systems from functioning as an effective part of a more comprehensive whole.

One approach to consider, recommended in Scott Fosler's chapter in this volume and in the recent reports of the national JTPA Advisory Committee,[3] is to build on and expand the State Job Training Coordinating Council and the Private Industry Council model created by JTPA. This model is private-sector dominated but involves participation by all significant public agencies as well as community-based organizations. Replicating this model and broadening its mission at the state and national levels could create the institutional undergirding needed to build and deliver a more coherent human-resource service delivery system. The partnership institutions described above should be empowered by elected officials to develop broad policy, make recommendations on key work force investment goals, and foster and facilitate more integrated systems for work force development at every level. Coordination for the sake of coordination is not a reasonable imperative. But coordination to reduce administrative expenses and provide more rational service delivery to clients makes sense. We acknowledge the numerous legislative, regulatory, and historical obstacles that exist. However, the fact that business leaders serving on state and local advisory councils have shown impatience with the existence of parallel public training systems with seemingly common missions—for example, vocational education (Carl Perkins Act), welfare-to-work (Family Support Act of 1988), employment service (Wagner-Peyser Act), job training (Job Training Partnership Act)—is creating added pressure for change. And encouraging signals of possible change are taking place. A recently passed House of Representatives bill (H.R. 7) reauthorizing vocational education renamed the program "Applied Technology Education" and suggested replacing each state's advisory groups for vocational education, employment service, vocational rehabilitation, adult education, and job training with a "State Human Investment Council."

Former secretary of labor Dole, in recent Senate testimony, stated:

> Our JTPA proposal and these welfare reform and vocational education provisions will provide the legislative framework to build *new, closer program relationships* at the Federal, State and local levels. I have met with Secretaries Sullivan and Cavazos to establish the basis for that working relationship. Our senior-level staff are now meeting regularly to put that relationship into operation even before new legislation is enacted. (U.S. Congress 1989: 10)

In addition, the administration's 1989 legislative proposals for amendments to JTPA put dollars on the line as an incentive to governors to develop human resource policy and program coordination. As proposed, these funds would go only to states that identify their human resource development goals and that pledge to link resources, both public and private, in pursuit of their goals with defined measurable benchmarks. This approach, if legislatively enacted, holds the promise of turning rhetoric into reality by bringing reluctant actors to the table to help solve the problem of self-sufficiency for the persistently poor. Time will tell.

Moreover, to the extent that employers come to rely more on training as a strategic tool, stronger partnership relationships will evolve between employers and the education and training community outside the workplace. Employers are more likely to be customers and advisors to a system that is not fragmented by bureaucratic turf struggles. But in addition to changing the partnership institutional arrangements described, significant changes and improvements are needed in both the public and private-sector initiatives now under way.

Needed Improvements in Public Policies and Programs

The JTPA System

The national JTPA Advisory Committee, convened in July 1988 by former secretary of labor Ann McLaughlin to contribute to the formulation of job training policy for the 1990s, has recommended that

- the majority of JTPA resources reserved for adults should be targeted to those lacking basic skills or to the long-term dependent;
- the majority of JTPA resources reserved for youth should be targeted to the out-of-schools, largely dropout population lacking basic skills and work experience;
- significant JTPA youth resources should be expended in collaborative efforts between the employment and training system, schools, and other community resources for dropout prevention strategies;
- individualized and intensified development training must be provided to meet both the needs of the less job-ready individual and the more demanding workplace; and
- one-half billion dollars in additional funding should be appropriated to support the youth initiatives. (National JTPA Advisory Committee 1989a)

Refocusing the mission of the JTPA system in the fairly directive manner suggested above is a bold step for a decentralized public policy initiative. After all, as stated earlier, this employability development system is currently placing 68 percent of its trainees in jobs, a record unequaled by other job training programs. Yet the current JTPA system is serving less than 5 percent of the eligible population. At current appropriation levels, providing more intensive (more costly) services to population cohorts with greater barriers to employment means that even fewer may be trained. Yet the recommendations flow from the changing nature of the work force and the workplace described earlier. There is a labor shortage that is predicted to worsen and therefore there is a real need to reach out to harder-to-serve populations that require more intensive and costly human capital investments, in order to enter and remain in the workplace.

Vocational Education
The Carl T. Perkins Act, which authorizes vocational education, is the updated version of the Smith-Hughes Act of 1917. Its required authorization in the 1989–1990 session created another opportunity for bringing federal program resources in line with new policy directions sensitive to the changing workplace. Our own recommendations run contrary to the traditionalist view of vocational education. Investments in equipment that will be outdated before it is paid off should be replaced with investments in retraining staff and developing new curricula. Vocational education must change its basic orientation: from providing instruction in manual tasks to teaching the applications of computers in the workplace. In general, we favor a single educational track, particularly through the middle-school years, that integrates academic and applied learning for all students but permits students to tailor the mix of

academic and applied learning to their own needs as they progress through secondary school. In this way, all students, college bound and work bound, will have the benefit of some applied technology training.

Based on the increased demands of the workplace, all students will benefit from mastering a set of skills including keyboarding, data manipulation, problem solving, decision making, technology systems, applied math and science, and resource management. The New York State vocational education innovator who dared to move in these new directions was rewarded with 10,000 telegrams asking for his removal! Fortunately, his supervisors did not capitulate, and the New York State educational system is moving toward an integrated educational track in its middle schools.

Our recommended changes represent a redirection of the vocational education system toward stronger linkages with proprietary schools, community colleges, and the state and local job training systems funded by JTPA and JOBS. There has been substantial growth in technical proprietary schools funded initially by reimbursements under the GI Bill, and more recently by Pell grants. Ostensibly their curriculum is market driven, but since the funding undergirding them is tied to enrollments and not to results, it is difficult to accurately assess their effectiveness. Yet they have some good potential for training out-of-school clients. Their claim to students is based on allegations of past success and they offer flexible schedules, and entry and exit to classes not tied to academic semesters. Linking vocational secondary school programs with more advanced community college programs also needs to be promoted. Often referred to as 2 + 2 activities, these linked activities have the potential of creating effective training systems for many entry-level technical jobs in hospitals, labs, and industry.

In addition, our recommendations reflect the conviction that we should avoid our competitors' mistakes. The European model, with its heavy emphasis on occupation-specific learning, can reduce the flexibility of the labor force. There is convincing evidence, for instance, that the European specialization in the mechanical arts through rigorous apprenticeship systems slowed the shift of European industries to electronics-based technologies, resulting in major losses in market shares to the Japanese (Ergas 1987: 213).

The Family Support Act: Job Opportunities and Basic Skills (JOBS)

For almost 20 years, social and economic policymakers, most visibly Senator Pat Moynihan of New York, have been seeking alternatives to the dependency-reinforcing nature of the current welfare system, particularly the part known as Aid to Families with Dependent Children (AFDC). Their efforts culminated in October 1988 with the passage of the Family Support Act, the much heralded welfare reform effort. Title II of the Act—Job Opportunities and Basic Skills (JOBS)—targets developmental services mainly to young mothers with limited education and to long-term dependents. Zeroing in on these target groups is appropriate employment and training public policy in view of the need to add more workers to the labor force and increase their potential productive value. JOBS's emphasis on educational remediation and on sustained child and health care (for one year after unsubsidized employment) provides the potential for increasing human capital by strengthening and stabilizing the multiproblem family. We hope that state and local governments will take advantage of these new opportunities and new funding to also deliver parenting education, life-skills training, and early childhood development training in an effort to prevent another cycle of failure and dependency. Unfortunately, the Family Support Act is silent on the absent father, except for title I, which addresses him only in terms of child support enforcement. A better answer to stabilizing these families and creating self-sufficient units is to also link the father to employment and training programs and thus bring two wage earners into the household, as well as two parent role models to share family and financial responsibilities. Much work remains to be done in this area. One of the most disturbing aspects of the Family Support Act is the potential for creating a second employment and training system by the state welfare agency parallel to the JTPA system, furthering the "confusing cacophony" referred to earlier. We would hope that governors, State Job Training Coordinating Councils, and state welfare agencies will seize the opportunity to forgo turf protection and will organize these two major human capital investment resources into a coherent system of local training activities.

The Economic Dislocation and Worker Adjustment Assistance Act (EDWAA)

Experienced employees who become unemployed after several years on the job also have a high-priority claim on federal work force investment resources. The same personally and economically destructive processes are at work for the dislocated as for the disadvantaged. The disadvantaged tend to start out and end up at the bottom of the economic heap. The dislocated experience an economic loss that rarely results in persistent poverty but probably involves an equal amount of suffering—not so much because of where they land as because of how far they fall. Given the widespread and continuing changes in the workplace, dislocation is probably here to stay. The harsh reality is that a fair trading system and new technology will inevitably benefit the nation as a whole but harm some individual citizens. In the end, practical necessity and compassion suggest the need for policies to mitigate dislocation.

Fortunately, most program strategies for the dislocated are not expensive. The almost $1 billion authorized (but not yet fully appropriated) in the new title III of JTPA should be sufficient to pay for effective programs to retrain and get new jobs for the approximately 1 million experienced American employees who are dislocated each year. In addition, current proposals for expanding the uses of the $30-billion unemployment insurance system beyond its original purpose of income maintenance are worthy of consideration. This unemployment insurance system, funded by employers, is designed to protect workers by providing income support during periods of temporary or permanent layoff. Unfortunately, as presently designed, its provisions to encourage those workers to seek retraining or new jobs before their payment support system runs out in 13 or 26 weeks are not very effective. We suggest three policy principles to follow in crafting programs for the dislocated.

1. Set a higher hitch in the safety net for dislocated employees—that is, increase support payments, particularly in the early weeks of dislocation and unemployment. Government should help dislocated employees avoid a free fall from middle-class status to official poverty.
2. Help employees before they become dislocated. Training to upgrade job skills, prior notification, counseling, job search assistance, and outplacement should be provided while employees are still on the job.
3. Above all, help dislocated employees find jobs. Give dislocated employees counseling and intensive job search assistance before exposing them to new training. Help dislocated workers relocate, by providing some lump sum payments of unemployment insurance.

Needed Changes in Private-Sector Activities

Important as public programs are in meeting the employment and training needs of the country, they are not the whole story. As we have described, the private sector also has a vital role to play, particularly with respect to the retraining of current workers. Contemporary workplace trends will make that role increasingly critical.

Accountability between learning systems and employers is a two-way street. To be served most effectively by U.S. education and training, employers must: make educators and trainers aware of new knowledge and changing skill requirements as they accumulate in the workplace; give more weight to educational attainment and achievement in hiring decisions so that students will learn to see the values of education; and work with trainers to develop and provide relevant curricula for job-related training.

We agree with other analysts who have concluded that the human capital strategies of the European nations and Japan have contributed substantially to their economic success and that our performance has fallen short. How much employer-based training do we really need? We cannot say precisely. Moreover, the training needs of every employer are different. There is no single level of human resource development appropriate to all employers. Overall national targets could be pegged to the levels of human resource development characteristic of most of the nation's more successful enterprises. We recommend that overall national targets should be increased in two phases.

- An interim target of 2 percent of payroll nationwide, or an increase of $14 billion over current expenditures, would increase total commitments to $44 billion and expand coverage from the current 10 percent to almost 15 percent of employed Americans.
- An ultimate goal of 4 percent of payroll nationwide, or an increase of $58 billion over current commitments, would increase employers' spending to $88 billion. This would mean that 3 in every 10 workers would benefit from training rather than the current 1 in 10. (Carnevale and Gainer 1989)

In addition to increasing their resource commitments to formal training, employers will need to integrate human resource development into their organizational culture and structure. If the critical processes of teaching and learning are to gain more standing in the American workplace, they will have to be embedded in everyday management and supervision and connected to performance-based selection, appraisal, rewards, and career development systems. Managers need to select new employees on the basis of their preparation both to do the job and to learn on the job. Each appraisal should conclude with a learning plan for improving individual performance. Learning and new ideas should be rewarded. Finally, managers need to be able to advise employees on strategies for using learning to enhance employment security and career advancement.

Four factors are essential to integrating human resource development into the employer institution.

- Leadership—the chief executive officer must make training a priority
- Commitment of resources—staff and budget need to be assigned, and the training and development executive must be a full member of the senior management team
- Outreach—line managers throughout the institution must be responsible for training and developing their subordinates
- Accessibility—training must be available to all employees, not just to the white-collar and technical elite

One of the manager's new roles is as a master teacher—responsible for crafting learning experiences for individual employees and for working teams so as to improve performance and overall productivity. The manager also serves as a listener to capture new ideas generated on the job that may result in improvements in efficiency and quality, as well as new applications for existing technologies, products, and services.

Successful techniques for workplace training exist. The Armed Services and corporations such as IBM and Motorola are leading the way. To replicate successful training, employers need to:

- Create an environment that actively encourages human resource development as a strategy to promote efficiency, quality improvements, new applications, and innovations
- Account for training costs and evaluate the effectiveness of training
- Share the costs of basic research on adult learning as well as the development and delivery costs of training materials and technologies with other employers, public authorities, educators, and equipment suppliers.

Employers will need not only to strengthen training systems inside their own institutions but also to build stronger linkages with networks of other employers and with external education and training institutions.

Policies to encourage more and better employer-based training are conspicuously absent from the nation's investment portfolio. One suggested device for expanding employer training—"homemade" and purchased—would be some form of investment incentive for employers to increase their expenditures on training. Much of the focus of the private sector is on short-term results that are reported on quarterly profit and loss statements. Investments in training unfortunately do not make a positive contribution to that profit and loss report as compared to equipment depreciation schedules. Therefore, we propose:

- Establishing incentives for employers to provide more training, preferably through the tax code. Tax credits should be based on specific expenditure categories such as design of training programs, development of training materials, and payments to third parties that provide education and training services
- Encouraging state-based policies to provide incentives for employers to provide "homemade" or purchased training for their own employees. Such policies might include providing matching funds, outstationing government training staff, and providing low-cost loans for start-up training costs
- Encouraging state-based policies to provide customized training for employers, particularly if linked to hiring disadvantaged groups or preventing layoffs
- Public funding of research and development in workplace training as well as dissemination of best practices.

Conclusion

- Human capital investments delivering quality employability training both outside and inside the workplace should be utilized to promote individual opportunity and institutional competitiveness.
- Government policies should encourage more effective use of existing scarce resources, including the integration of existing programs at the point of delivery and the development of closer ties among the nation's public and private providers of human capital development.
- The government should pursue both supply-side strategies that improve the capacity of public and private institutions to provide education and training and demand-side strategies that encourage employers and individuals to invest more resources in education and training.

The economically and educationally disadvantaged should have the first claim on public attention and public resources. Public resources should be provided to make every American capable of getting and holding a job, because people unable to get work disappear from the community, drop out of the political system, and fall into the underground economy. If predictions of economic growth are not fulfilled, a stand-by policy (and suitable appropriations) for public service employment should be in place.

Providing human capital development for the disadvantaged would do more than honor commitments to equal opportunity: it would also pay off in dollars and cents. Investments that endow the disadvantaged with the necessary skills to make them economically independent will reduce the costs of public dependency. In addition, with the decline in the number of entry-level workers, the nation—to remain economically competitive—now needs all its young people on the job.

The growing concern with the nation's economic competitiveness has resulted in a relatively new public interest in the quantity and quality of the nation's learning systems, and in the growing recognition that training must be viewed as a life-long learning process. We hope this new interest will energize the public-private partnerships needed to make the investments, coordinate the resources, and demand the accountability required to meet these challenges.

Notes

1. For a critique of the Employment Service system see Levitan and Carlson 1985.

2. MDTA was enacted in response to a premature perception of economic dislocation due to widespread automation. That perception is certainly true to-

day, in 1989; it was premature in 1962, and the early alarm may have blinded some to the harsh realities of the present.

3. *Working Capital: JTPA Investment for the 90's* and *Working Capital: Coordinated Human Investment Directions for the 90's,* reports of the National JTPA Advisory Committee, March 1989. The National JTPA Advisory Committee comprises 38 public and private leaders who were appointed by former secretary of labor Ann McLaughlin in July 1988 and were asked to examine the system and make recommendations for the job training and other human capital investment policies in the decade ahead.

References

Belous, Richard (1989). "How Firms Adjust to the Shift toward Contingent Workers." *Monthly Labor Review,* March, pp. 13–20.

Carnevale, Anthony, and Lei Gainer (1989). *The Learning Enterprise.* Washington, D.C.: U.S. Government Printing Office.

Carnevale, Anthony, and Harold Goldstein (1985). *Survey of Participation in Adult Education.* Washington, D.C.: U.S. Census.

Carnevale, Anthony, and Janet Johnston (1989). *Job-Related Learning: Private Strategies and Public Policies.* Washington, D.C.: U.S. Government Printing Office.

Daggett, William (1989). Lecture on "Vocational Education." Morgan State University, Baltimore, Maryland.

Ergas, Henry (1987). "Does Technology Policy Matter?" In Bruce Guile and Harvey Brooks, eds., *Technology and Global Industry: Companies and Nations in the World Economy.* Washington, D.C.: National Academy Press, p. 213.

Executive Office of the President (1986). *Up From Dependency: A New National Public Assistance Strategy* Supplement 1, Volume 1. Washington, D.C.: U.S. Government Printing Office, December.

Ford Foundation Project on Social Welfare and the American Future (1989). *The Common Good.* New York, N.Y.: Ford Foundation, May.

Hamilton, James, and James Medoff (1988). "Small Business, Monkey Business." *Washington Post,* April 24.

Johnston, William B., and Arnold H. Packer (1987). *Workforce 2000: Work and Workers for the Twenty-first Century.* Indianapolis, Ind.: Hudson Institute.

Levitan, Sar, and Peter Carlson (1985). *Policy Statement on the U.S. Employment Service.* National Council on Employment Policy, May.

Levitan, Sar, and Frank Gallo (1989). *A Second Chance: Training for Jobs.* Kalamazoo, Mich.: W. E. Upjohn Institute for Employment Research, p. 65.

Lillard, Lee A., and Hong W. Tan (1986). *Private Sector Training: Who Gets It and What Are Its Effects?* Rand Corporation, R-3331-DOL/RC, March.

Manpower Demonstration Research Corporation (MDRC) (1988). *Subgroup Impacts and Performance Indicators for Selected Welfare Employment Programs.* New York: Manpower Demonstration Research Corporation, August.

Mitchell, William O. (1990). "New Task for the Computer: Making Clothes." *New York Times,* January 24.

National JTPA Advisory Committee (1989a). *Working Capital: JTPA Investments for the 90's.* Washington, D.C.: U.S. Department of Labor.

National JTPA Advisory Committee (1989b). *Working Capital: Coordinated Human Investment Directions for the 90's.* Washington, D.C.: U.S. Department of Labor.

Personick, Valerie A. (1989). "Industry Output and Employment: A Slower Trend for the 90's." *Monthly Labor Review,* November, p. 26.

Taggart, Robert (1981). "A Review of CETA Training." In Sar Levitan and Garth Mangum, eds., *The T in CETA: Local and National Perspectives.* Kalamazoo, Mich.: W. E. Upjohn Institute.

U.S. Congress. Senate. Committee on Labor and Human Resources (1989). Testimony by Elizabeth Dole, Secretary of Labor, before the Subcommittee on Employment and Productivity, May 11, p. 10.

10

Social Services

Marian Wright Edelman

Our children are our future. For most of our nation's history, that axiom has been a statement of hope. Today it is a warning. Unless our nation reassesses its priorities and begins to invest more resources in our human capital, particularly our children, our nation's economic future is in jeopardy.

A statistical snapshot of today's children shows that

- One in five is poor (CDF 1989c: 113)
- One in five is at risk of becoming a teenage parent (CDF 1989c: 90)
- One in five has no health insurance (CDF 1989c: 6)
- One in seven is at risk of dropping out of school (CDF 1988a: xi)
- One in two has a mother in the labor force but fewer than half of the children of working mothers attend affordable, good-quality child care (CDF 1988a: xi).

These children will be the nation's young labor force in the decades ahead. Yet those who have grown up in poverty, without adequate nutrition, housing, health care, or education, probably will not be prepared to do the jobs that will be waiting for them—jobs that require high-level reading, writing, problem-solving, and math skills.

There was a time when the United States had more than enough skilled workers to meet its needs. But not anymore. By 1995 there will be almost 5 million fewer 18- to 24-year-olds than there were in 1985, reducing the potential young labor force by 14 percent (CDF 1989c: 115–16; Johnston and Packer 1987: 75–90). And more young workers will come from minority groups that are now disproportionately poor, unhealthy, and educationally disadvantaged. As Arnold Packer noted in Chapter 2 of this volume, about one-third of those who join the work force between 1985 and 2000 will be minorities. Thus, while advancing technology will demand greater numbers of well-educated workers, both the relative size of the young work force and the proportion of workers likely to be skilled will be shrinking. If recent trends in poverty, education, and teenage pregnancy are allowed to continue, in the year 2000 the potential work force will get an even poorer start in life than it does today. For example,

- One in four children will be poor (CDF 1989c: 115)
- One in four will have a single parent (CDF 1989c: xix)
- One in five 20-year-old women will be a mother, and more than four in five of these will not be married (CDF 1989c: xvi)
- Only six in ten of these young, unmarried mothers will have a high school diploma (CDF 1989c: xix).

At the very time when our society will need all of its increasingly scarce young people to be skilled and productive, fully one-quarter of our children may grow up poor, undereducated, and unprepared to be effective workers, parents, and citizens.

Yet demographics need not dictate destiny. Attitudes, leadership, values, and public policies make a difference. By choosing now to invest wisely and significantly in *all* of its children, this nation can nurture and educate a future work force that is qualified to meet the economic challenges of the twenty-first century. To produce a skilled work force for the future, the nation must, over the next decade, increase its investment at the national, state, and local levels in cost-effective programs to develop our human resources fully. If we neglect our human capital, the loss will be twofold. We will jeopardize future economic growth and productivity, and later we will have to invest even more in our welfare and criminal justice systems and in other crisis intervention programs such as drug abuse treatment programs. As we shall see later in this chapter, the ultimate cost of neglect will be far higher than the cost of prevention.

The best way to make sure our children grow up to be productive workers and citizens is to focus on strengthening families, because families are the providers and the caregivers—the cradle—for the next generation. If the cradle is strong, children will grow up to be good citizens, workers, and parents. If the cradle cannot adequately protect and support its young charges, the next generation will be stunted and unproductive.

The Challenge: Weakened Families Threaten Our Children

A growing number of America's young families—those headed by someone younger than 30—are in economic trouble. Between 1973 and

1986, the median income of young families with children fell by 26 percent (CDF 1988d: 32), and poverty rates for young families with children almost doubled—to 30 percent (CDF 1988d: 39). The reasons are several. Many young workers are taking home smaller paychecks since employment has shifted from the higher-paying manufacturing industries to the lower-paying service sector, where many employers offer only part-time work and few benefits. Lower hourly wages accounted for more than 90 percent of the drop in annual earnings between 1979 and 1986 among employed men who headed young families (CDF 1988d: viii).

Young families have also lost buying power because the minimum wage has not kept up with inflation. In 1979, full-time, year-round work at the minimum wage kept a family of three above the federal poverty line. In 1989, a parent supporting a family of three on those wages found they left the family nearly 30 percent below the federal poverty line (CDF 1988d: 29). The 1989 minimum wage bill, which will increase the minimum hourly wage from $3.35 to $4.25 over two years, will restore some lost purchasing power to minimum wage workers. But in 1991 the inflation-adjusted value of the minimum wage still will equal only about 80 percent of its 1981 value.

Another change that has increased the vulnerability of young families is the growing number headed by single teenage mothers. Teenage mothers are not a new phenomenon; in fact, teenage birthrates are not rising (see CDF 1988c: 10–11). What is new, however, is that half of all teenage mothers now raise their children as single parents—and they and their children are likely to face years of poverty. Half of all young women who give birth before age 18 do not have a high school diploma by their mid-twenties and are therefore virtually shut out of the job market (CDF 1989c: 90–91).

Government action has made matters worse for many young families by exacerbating the consequences of recent economic and social changes. For example, median rents in this country rose twice as fast as median incomes between 1970 and 1983, requiring one in four households with incomes of less than $15,000 to spend more than 60 percent of its income for rent. Instead of responding by providing more housing assistance and building more low-income housing, the federal government reduced all funding for low-income housing by 81 percent in real dollars between 1980 and 1988. As a consequence, families are now the fastest growing segment of the homeless population, and the National Academy of Sciences estimates that 100,000 American children go to sleep homeless each night (CDF 1989c: 28–29, 32)

Aid to Families with Dependent Children—which along with Unemployment Insurance and Social Security, was intended to provide a safety net for poor families—also has been permitted to unravel. In the absence of a federal requirement to index benefits to inflation rates, the states allowed the average real value of AFDC benefits for a family of four to drop by 18.5 percent between 1979 and 1986 (U.S. Congress 1989: 14). In July 1988, AFDC payments for a family of three were less than one-half of the federal poverty level in fully 31 states (CDF 1989c: 20). In 1979, nearly one in every five families with children that otherwise would have been poor was lifted out of poverty by cash benefit programs such as AFDC, Social Security, and Unemployment Insurance. By 1986, however, these programs rescued from poverty only one in every nine families with children (CDF 1989c: 18).

Also during this decade, many families have watched their private health care insurance—especially for dependents—shrink and disappear. Between 1982 and 1985, the number of uninsured Americans grew by 15 percent and the number of uninsured children increased by 16 percent (CDF 1988a: 70). If private insurance coverage continues to decline at recent rates, by 2000 less than half of America's children will be privately insured.

Medicaid, the public health insurance program for the poor, has never been available to most working poor families and thus has failed to fill the gap left by the erosion of the employer-based insurance system. In 1981, at the very time employer-based insurance began shrinking, the federal government restricted even further the Medicaid financial eligibility standards for working poor families (Edelman 1987: 40–43). Although Medicaid coverage for pregnant women and young children has expanded since 1984, only about one-half of all poor children now have Medicaid coverage (U.S. Congress 1989: 37).

To help pay the family bills, many mothers have gone to work outside the home, creating a huge unmet demand for decent, affordable child care. Although the number of working mothers with children younger than six increased from 6.9 million in 1981 to 8.9 million in 1987 and hundreds of thousands of children are on waiting lists for subsidized child care, neither the states nor the federal government has responded to the child care crisis. Taking inflation into account, virtually the same amount of combined state and federal money was available to low-income families for child care in 1988 as in 1981 (CDF 1988b: 1–5).

The federal government's failure to mitigate the effects of all of these economic changes has strained and weakened families and caused more and more American children to slip into poverty. In 1979 there were 10.3 million poor children in this country. By the late 1980s, almost 13 million children were growing up in poor families (CDF 1989c: 113). In human capital terms, the consequences are enormous. Children whose lives are plagued by cold, hunger, untreated illness, frequent moves, homelessness, and sporadic or inadequate education cannot gain either the educational or the emotional foundation for productive work lives.

Sheldon Danziger, in Chapter 5 of this volume, underlines the fact that poverty tends to hinder educational achievement. Not only are poor children likely to be unprepared for entering school, but they generally attend substandard schools. As a result, more than three-quarters of all poor youths are below average in their ability to read and do math (CDF 1988a: 137). Regardless of race, poor teenagers are about three times more likely than nonpoor teenagers to drop out of school (CDF 1989c: 70).

Beyond that, there is an established relationship between poverty, poor academic skills, and early parenthood (CDF 1987a: 5). White, black, or Hispanic, about one teenager in five aged 16 to 19 with below-average academic skills and a family income below the poverty level is a parent. In contrast, only about one teenager in twenty in the same age group who has average or better skills and a family income above the poverty line has a child (CDF 1989c: 93). When teenagers become parents too soon, they tend to perpetuate the cycle of low-level skills, poverty, and dependence by raising another generation of children ill-prepared to join the work force of the twenty-first century.

What Can Be Done: An Investment Approach to Human Services

Key Principles

Fortunately, in the past two decades we have gained some critical insights about the effects of poverty on children and how to combat those effects. Our policymakers have not yet chosen to put what we have learned into large-scale practice, but the principles are there, waiting to be applied. For example:

- We have learned without a doubt that poverty's damage begins before birth if pregnant women do not receive adequate nutrition and pre-natal care.
- We have learned that poverty generally results in physical and developmental deficits in young children; unmitigated, these are extremely difficult to overcome in later childhood.
- We have learned that preventive help is almost always more effective and less expensive than corrective help.
- We have learned that lasting change is most likely for individuals when the entire family unit is strengthened.
- We have learned that most vulnerable families have multiple, inter-related problems, and that effective help must be defined by each family's unique constellation of needs, not by rigid bureaucratic categories.

• We have learned that family support services are most effective when they are comprehensive, gathered under one roof, emphasize outreach and follow-through, and offer consistent case management and help in practical problem solving.

Throughout this country there are social support programs that are firmly grounded in these principles. They work, and they have proven cost-effective. It is true that many of these programs are relatively small-scale efforts, which means that the task of widening their scope is the challenge awaiting us in the coming decade.

What follows is an outline of the basic preventive investments this nation must make in children and families to ensure a healthy, skilled work force in the future. To continue to expand economically and remain competitive, our nation must immediately put more money into health care, child care, early childhood education, after-school and summer programs for teenagers, and supportive family services. And to get the most for our money, we will want to begin changing the way we deliver many of these services to reflect the principles of cost-effective intervention outlined above.

Health Care

Health Care for Mothers and Children

Physical and mental fitness greatly improve children's chances to become productive workers. Strong bodies and minds depend on good prenatal care and on preventive pediatric health care throughout childhood. Yet our nation's progress in assuring maternal and child health slowed during the 1980s. In some areas, such as immunization and early prenatal care, we even lost ground. If these trends are allowed to persist, they will claim a devastating toll on the size, health, and productivity of the nation's work force.

If pregnant women do not receive prenatal care that begins in the first trimester and continues throughout pregnancy, their babies are five times more likely to die in infancy than those whose mothers receive adequate care (U.S. Congress 1989: 39). Yet in 1986 a smaller percentage of mothers received early prenatal care than in 1980. The year 1986 was the seventh year in a row in which the percentage of babies born to mothers who received late or no prenatal care either increased or showed no improvement (CDF 1989a: xi). Rising poverty among young families, declining private health insurance coverage, reduced support for public health programs, and a growing shortage of obstetrical providers have all contributed to the negative trend.

One consequence is this country's high rate of infant mortality. In 1986, the United States' infant mortality rate of 10.4 deaths per 1,000 live births placed it eighteenth in the world, behind all the industrialized countries of Western Europe and behind Spain, Singapore, and Hong Kong. When the rate for black infants (18.0 deaths per 1,000 live births) was compared with other nations' overall rates, the United States ranked twenty-eighth, behind such nations as Cuba and Bulgaria (CDF 1989a: 12–14). Unless the nation improves access to prenatal and infant health care, in the year 2000 alone, more than 15,000 infants will die before they reach their first birthdays.

But a high rate of infant mortality is only part of the human capital cost of inadequate prenatal care. Another is that more babies are born at low birthweight—less than 5½ pounds. These tiny babies die more frequently than other babies, and those that live are far more likely to have lifelong disabilities such as cerebral palsy, autism, vision and learning disabilities, and mental retardation. Children with these conditions often require expensive long-term care and as adults may not be able to participate fully in the work force. If access to prenatal care does not improve, more than 3.6 million low-birthweight babies will be born between 1986 and 2000.

In addition to adequate prenatal care, infants need good nutrition, regular pediatric care, and immunization against preventable childhood diseases in order to grow into healthy adults. The federal government provides food supplements, nutrition education, and counseling to low-income pregnant and postpartum women, infants, and children through the Special Supplemental Food Program for Women, Infants, and Children (WIC). WIC participation reduces premature births among high-risk mothers by 15 to 25 percent (Schorr 1988: 129) and saves up to seven lives for every 1,000 women and infants participating in the program (CDF 1989c: 12). Yet WIC funding has been so inadequate that in 1988 the program served less than half of the eligible population (CDF 1989b: 20).

As family poverty rates have increased and public health programs have eroded in the 1980s, there has been a decrease in the proportion of preschool-aged children who are immunized against major childhood diseases such as polio, measles, rubella, mumps, diphtheria, pertussis, and tetanus. For some age groups, immunization rates are now below 80 percent, which means that many children are needlessly vulnerable to diseases that can permanently cripple them physically or mentally. In 1986, the Centers for Disease Control reported that 83 percent of the 1,200 cases of measles among preschoolers could have been prevented through adequate immunization (CDF 1989a: 62–64). The Head Start program, described below, provides nutritional supplementation, health screening, and immunizations to participating preschoolers, but it covers only a small fraction of those eligible.

Low-income children are more than three times as likely as other children never to have received a preventive health exam (CDF 1989a: 61), and health care professionals estimate that as many as 80 percent of low-income children suffer from one or more untreated medical conditions. Anemia, for example, which slows physical development and contributes to inattentiveness and conduct disorders, is three times as prevalent in poor children as in their more affluent peers (Schorr 1988:88). Poor health hinders a child's ability to learn, and learning problems are often the precursors of teen pregnancy, delinquency, and dropping out of school. The diminished lifetime productivity of children left physically or educationally disabled by preventable causes costs this nation dearly.

By investing more resources in health care for poor families, we will be investing in a healthy future work force. We will also save millions of dollars in medical costs for treatment that could have been avoided. For example, each $1 spent under the WIC nutrition program saves the nation more than $3 during a child's infancy by reducing the costs associated with prematurity and low birthweight. Every $1 the nation spends on immunization saves $10 in later medical expenses (U.S. Congress 1988a: 6). And children who receive ongoing preventive pediatric care through Medicaid and other publicly financed programs have annual health care costs that are nearly 10 percent lower than children who do not receive preventive care (CDF 1989a: 69).

Prenatal care may well be the biggest money-saver of all health programs. Every dollar the nation spends on prenatal care saves $3.38 in hospitalization costs of low-birthweight babies (U.S. Congress 1988a: 6) and $11 over a child's lifetime, taking into account the medical, social, and educational costs and the lost earnings of children born at low birthweight (CDF 1989c: 12).

Prenatal care is so effective in reducing the incidence of low birthweight and prematurity that the congressional Office of Technology Assessment recently reported that the cost of expanding Medicaid to cover all poor women's maternity care would be more than offset by subsequent savings to the federal Medicaid program (CDF 1989a: 69). In California alone, it costs $70 million to care for the 10,000 to 13,000 premature babies admitted to newborn intensive care units in the state each year (U.S. Congress 1988a: 17).

If we do nothing to improve pregnant women's access to adequate prenatal care, the nation can expect to spend approximately $6 billion between now and the year 2000 just in first-year health care costs for low-birthweight infants (CDF 1989a: xiv). Six billion dollars invested in reducing the incidence of low birthweight by expanding preventive health programs for pregnant women and children would be a far wiser investment in our human capital.

As a result of congressional action since 1984, Medicaid covers all pregnant women and children younger than six living in families with incomes below 133 percent of the federal poverty level. In 1990 Congress enacted legislation to extend Medicaid in stages to children older than six who live in families with incomes below the federal poverty level. Under that expansion schedule, however, it will be 2002 before all children younger than 19 in such families will be covered. And millions of other children and hundreds of thousands of pregnant women still will be without health insurance because their family incomes are just above the Medicaid eligibility level but are too low to buy private health insurance. We must further expand Medicaid so that by 1996 all families with incomes below 200 percent of the federal poverty level will have public health insurance.

Congress must also gradually increase funding for the WIC program so that by 1994 it can provide nutrition services to all eligible women and children who need them.

Our nation is likely to get an even healthier return on these investments if policymakers encourage some fundamental changes in the way we deliver basic health services. Our current delivery system, which is typically decentralized and highly specialized, relies on consumers to seek out the services they need. In general, the burden is also on the consumers to ask questions of health care providers and to educate themselves about health issues. Many adults, however, have never been taught to use such health services effectively. In addition, the lack of transportation is often a barrier to using scattered services. Many families would make better use of health services if they were centralized in one accessible location, if they emphasized education and outreach, and if health care professionals were consistently sensitive to lifestyle and other factors that affect health but are not strictly biological.

Our community and migrant health centers, which deliver services primarily in medically underserved areas, are a good model for comprehensive health care delivery that emphasizes education and outreach. Sociologist Paul Starr, evaluating our health care policy for the poor, notes that the community health centers have enjoyed a "decidedly positive record" of providing better health care at lower cost. And yet the health centers have never received adequate acclaim or policy support (Schorr 1988: 133). Health care policy that encourages the development of community clinics offering nutritionists, social workers, and community outreach workers along with dentists, physicians, and other health care professionals would increase the accessibility of services and thus allow us to obtain greater benefit from our health care dollars.

Client-friendly preventive health care for all of our mothers and children will save this country the billions of dollars we will otherwise spend in trying to ameliorate the effects of low birthweight, inadequate nutrition, untreated childhood disease, and teenagers' special vulnerability to drug and alcohol abuse, suicide, and other health-related risks. What's more, by keeping our children healthy, preventive health care will contribute hundreds of thousands of additional healthy citizens and workers to an economy that desperately needs good minds and sound bodies.

Health Clinics for Adolescents

Teenagers especially can benefit from comprehensive services that are easy to use, for they have unique needs and problems related to health care. Like all other children, teenagers need care for common illnesses and medical conditions. But teenagers also need special care that takes into account the reproductive, emotional, and developmental changes they experience during adolescence. Alcohol and drug abuse, violent behavior, suicide, pregnancy, and mental health problems all strike particularly hard at teenagers, whatever their family income. And these are factors that contribute to performing poorly in school, dropping out, and failing to make a successful transition to adulthood and the world of work.

Despite teens' special health care needs, they now use health care services less than any other age group. More than 28 percent of children between the ages of 12 and 18 do not see a health care provider even once during a year (CDF 1986a: 7–9). Accessibility and cost are the two main barriers.

Comprehensive adolescent health clinics that offer broad, low-cost services geared toward adolescent health issues have been remarkably successful in reaching teenagers. Where model clinics operate in schools, student participation runs between 70 and 90 percent (CDF 1986a: 11). Adolescent health clinics do not necessarily have to be at schools to be effective, but they should have most of the following key characteristics:

- Accessible location in public housing projects, community service centers, or schools
- Convenient hours and available services without long waits for appointments
- Low-cost or free services
- Staff from several professional backgrounds, interested in delivering services to teenagers and trained to look for and address nonmedical as well as medical concerns
- Availability of an array of services on-site and the ability to refer clients to other appropriate services
- Integrated health education, so teenagers know both what to do and why
- Confidentiality.

There is great variation in the range of services that adolescent health clinics provide. Some offer only health exams and basic follow-up care. Others provide sex education and counseling, contraceptive services, prenatal and postpartum care, nutrition counseling, alcohol and drug abuse counseling and treatment, and mental health counseling. All of these services improve teenagers' health. During the first two months of operation of a Chicago school-based clinic, for instance, the students made nearly 500 visits and received treatment for serious health problems that never had been previously diagnosed, such as diabetes, high blood pressure, and vision problems (CDF 1986a: 11).

Clinics that offer a wide range of services are effective in addressing problems of alcohol and drug abuse, school absenteeism and dropout, and teenage pregnancy. For example, Kansas City high schools with health clinics showed the greatest decline in absenteeism in the school district. Within the first two years of the clinics' operation, substance abuse among students in schools with clinics decreased. The proportion of youths who never or seldom used alcohol increased by 14 percent, and the proportion who seldom used marijuana increased by 12 percent. Not one student who completed the treatment program for alcohol and drug abuse, which was substituted for suspension from school, was cited again for substance-related disciplinary action (CDF 1986a: 12).

Although adolescent health clinics that provide contraceptive services and prenatal care raise fears in some communities that these services will encourage teenagers to be sexually active, there is evidence that girls who are served by school-based clinics may in fact postpone sexual activity. In a Baltimore demonstration program, for example, the proportion of girls who became sexually active by age 14 went down by 40 percent after a teen health clinic was established (CDF 1986b: 10), and the median age at which girls began sexual activity rose by seven months (Schorr 1988: 53).

Kansas City's Adolescent Resources Corporation reports that the local adolescent health care program did not change the proportion of teenagers who had ever been sexually active, but among those who were active there was a 29-percent increase in the proportion of teenagers who used contraception whenever needed and a 25-percent drop in the percentage of students who never used contraception (CDF 1986a: 12). Whether or not adolescent health clinics provide contraceptive services, however, these clinics are vital to achieving a healthy and productive young work force.

Prenatal care for pregnant teenagers is one of the most important and cost-effective services teen clinics can provide because, as we have noted, prenatal care reduces the incidence of low birthweight. Currently, only about half of all teenage mothers seek early prenatal care, and for girls aged 15 or younger, the figure is even worse: 34 percent (CDF 1986a: 4).

The result is predictable. In 1986, one infant in five born to mothers younger than 15 and one infant in eight born to mothers aged 15 to 19 was born at low birthweight. In contrast, one infant in fourteen born to 22- to 24-year-olds was born at low birthweight (CDF 1989a: 25). Whatever a community's attitude toward contraceptive services for teenagers, it is shortsighted, given the high cost of intensive care for low-birthweight infants, not to provide readily accessible prenatal care to every teenager who becomes pregnant.

Adolescent health clinics can be funded in a number of ways. One of the most likely is through the Maternal and Child Health Block Grant under title V of the Social Security Act, which provides federal funds to state health agencies for women's and children's health services. In 1986, 18 states had comprehensive school-based adolescent health clinics, most of which were funded in part by title V funds. In Jackson, Mississippi, a network of model school-based clinics was developed through a community health center, and Wisconsin and West Virginia also have enlisted community health centers to help serve teenagers. Schools themselves generally provide some health services for their students, although school health programs vary a great deal. A demonstration program sponsored by the Robert Wood Johnson Foundation found that expanded school health programs could be successfully managed in most school districts with minimal increased costs (CDF 1986a: 18).

The teenagers of today will be the workers—or the welfare recipients—of the future. The greater the number of teenagers who receive the help they need in adolescence, the greater the number of productive young adults this nation can count on to be the scientists, teachers, and business leaders our nation so urgently needs.

Child Care: An Investment with a Double Return

Child Care for America's Work Force

As an investment in human capital, good child care yields a double return. First, the availability of child care gives the mothers of young children the option of joining the work force in order to support or help support their families. Second, good-quality child care helps prepare children for success in school and thus increases their chances for productive lives of their own.

But decent child care at affordable prices is hard to find. In 1987, more than 10 million children younger than six and nearly 25 million aged six and older needed some type of child care while their parents worked. However, existing spaces in licensed child care centers and regulated family day care homes can accommodate only an estimated 2.9

children. This means that millions of children are at risk of receiving substandard child care, and an unconscionably large number receive none at all. Between 2 million and 7 million children, including an estimated 1.5 million children younger than five, take care of themselves or are watched by other children for all or part of each day (Rosewater 1989: 11).

The lack of reliable and affordable child care not only prevents some parents from joining the labor force; it also reduces the effectiveness and productivity of those who do have jobs. In 1985, for example, one working mother in twenty reported lost time from work the previous month as a result of failed child care arrangements (U.S. Bureau of the Census 1987: 14). Among parents surveyed by the American Federation of State, County, and Municipal Employees, 28 percent of those with children aged 12 or younger said they had given up a job or promotion because of child care problems (CDF 1987c: 4). Among mothers not in the labor force, 36 percent of those with annual family incomes of less than $15,000 and 45 percent of single mothers said they would look for work if affordable child care were available (U.S. Congress 1989: 18).

The cost of good-quality child care averages more than $3,000 a year in urban areas, which is far more than low-income families—especially those with more than one preschool child—can afford (CDF 1987c: 4). American families in general spend an average of 1 percent of their total family income on child care for their preschool children, but poor families spend an average of 20 to 26 percent (Rosewater 1989: 8).

Congress recognized the long-term cost-effectiveness of providing child care assistance when it linked government-subsidized child care to mandatory job training and employment programs for AFDC parents under the Family Support Act of 1988. The benefits of increased worker productivity and family self-sufficiency also accrue to our economy when other low-income families receive help in paying for decent child care. For example, the Colorado Department of Social Services reports that providing child care assistance to low-income working families so they can remain self-supporting costs only 38 percent of what it costs to provide AFDC and Medicaid benefits to those families (CDF 1987c: 6).

Most states devote part of the federal funds they receive through the title XX Social Services Block Grant of the Social Security Act to help subsidize child care for low-income families, but the proportion of title XX funds used for child care varies widely from state to state and averages only about 18 percent of title XX funds nationally. Moreover, that 18 percent is cut from a shrinking title XX pie. Although the number of families that need child care has grown steadily, the federal title XX appropriation for fiscal year 1988 in inflation-adjusted money was less than one-half of what it was in fiscal year 1977 (CDF 1988b: 1–5).

Because good child care is expensive and scarce, our nation is moving

toward a two-tier child care system that threatens to reinforce the dep-
rivations already associated with poverty. In 1985 less than 33 percent
of four-year-olds whose families had incomes below $10,000 a year were
enrolled in preschool programs, while 67 percent of four-year-olds
whose families had incomes of $35,000 or more a year attended pre-
school (CDF 1987c: 7).

By failing to make sure that all children have access to good-quality
child care and early childhood education programs, the nation will for-
feit a ready-made opportunity to help prepare disadvantaged children for
school success and thus save billions later in remedial education. A policy
of neglect will drive up the future costs of educating these children because youngsters from stressed homes are more vulnerable than others
to the negative effects of overcrowded, inconsistent, and nonnurturing
child care.

Research tells us that in order to develop intellectually and socially,
all young children, but especially disadvantaged children, need to be in
small groups with low ratios of children to caregivers. Despite this
knowledge, however, there are no minimum standards for group size in
child care programs receiving federal funds. In some states, child care
standards are so poor that they not only fail to ensure an environment
for learning, they actually threaten the well-being of many children. For
example, in 1988, 30 states did not regulate group size for preschoolers
in child care. Twelve states had infant-to-staff ratios higher than 7:1 for
18-month-old babies. And 11 states permitted five or more infants to be
cared for in family day care homes by one provider without an assistant.

Although the training, attitude, and skillfulness of child care staff are
crucial to the quality of child care, seven states allowed totally untrained
persons to staff day care centers. Seventeen states required no ongoing
training for teachers in child care centers, and 42 required none for home
care providers (CDF 1988b: 45).

In 1990 Congress passed the nation's first comprehensive child care
legislation, designed both to help improve the quality of child care services and to help low-income families pay for care. The Child Care and
Development Block Grant authorizes $2.5 billion for the states over
three years and "necessary" amounts thereafter. The grant requires no
state match; each state receives funds according to a formula. Families
that earn up to 75 percent of the state's median income are eligible for
child care assistance. Congress appropriated $731.9 million for fiscal
year 1991. The 1992 appropriation should rise to $825 million.

In addition, $300 million a year for five years will be available for
child care under the Aid to Families with Dependent Children (AFDC)
program. These funds will subsidize child care for working families that
cannot afford to pay for child care and are thus at risk of going on wel-

fare. Since these are entitlement funds, no congressional appropriation is necessary.

The new federal child care dollars will help the states meet the child care needs of working families, but they are not intended to supplant state investments in child care. Moreover, the states remain primarily responsible for ensuring the quality of child care services. Therefore it is critical that the states implement the new federal programs carefully while continuing to invest state resources in child care.

Child Care for Teenage Parents

For teenage parents, child care can spell the difference between earning a high school diploma and thereby a chance to become self-sufficient, and dropping out of school and facing long term economic dependency. Yet teenage mothers who wish to stay in school or participate in vocational training have very few child care options. The vast majority of schools do not offer child care; child care provided by family members is unreliable, and other child care is expensive. Unable to solve their child care problems, teenage mothers typically drop out of school, remain isolated at home with their babies, and often get pregnant again before they are out of their teens. One-third of all teenage mothers have second pregnancies during their teenage years.

Fortunately, school systems and social service agencies are beginning to recognize the importance of offering child care at or near schools so that teenage mothers may have the opportunity to become independent and productive adults. In addition to allowing teenage mothers to stay in school, special child care programs for young parents can serve as a focus for organizing comprehensive support services that may include health care, tutoring, family counseling, job counseling, and parenting education. Because these programs help relieve the stress and the sense of isolation that beset teenage parents, they also reduce the potential for child abuse and neglect and thus decrease the demands on child protective services.

An example of a successful prenatal and child care program is the Family Learning Center in Leslie, Michigan, which combines the services available from the state departments of Education, Public Health, Mental Health, and Social Services in one facility. Begun in 1975, the center draws pregnant teenagers and teenage parents from seven rural high school districts. The program accommodates 26 babies and their mothers and stresses high school graduation, vocational preparation, and the development of parenting skills. Between 1985 and 1990, 92 percent of its senior students graduated, and 94 percent of its seventh- to eleventh-graders stayed in school. Only 2.4 percent of the participating students had repeat pregnancies (Eakins 1990). The infants in the program have lower-than-average rates of medical complications: in 60 births, only one child was born prematurely and four were born at low birthweight (CDF 1987b: 10–11).

Head Start

In Head Start, the nation has a preschool program of comprehensive services for disadvantaged three- to five-year-olds that ideally should serve as a model preschool program for all young children who are poor. Head Start not only prepares children for school; it also strengthens the families that participate and energizes the communities in which Head Start programs are located. The Head Start presence encourages communities to pay greater attention to the needs of poor students and leads to greater involvement of parents in local schools.

The key to Head Start's broad success is its commitment to the dual principles of comprehensive services and family involvement. Since malnourished, hungry children cannot learn efficiently, Head Start provides hot meals. As a result, Head Start children have higher intakes of protein, calories, and other essential nutrients than do peers who do not attend Head Start. Since untreated vision, hearing, and other medical and dental problems impede physical and intellectual development, Head Start screens for and treats these conditions and immunizes participating children against childhood diseases. In 1986–87, more than 97 percent of Head Start enrollees received necessary medical care, and more than 96 percent were brought up to date in their immunizations (CDF 1988a: 192).

Head Start strengthens the families of enrollees by providing such preventive services as family counseling and problem solving, assistance to family members in coping with substance abuse, and referral to other assistance programs such as the federal food stamp program. Based on the precept that children, parents, and the program itself all benefit from the active involvement of parents, Head Start enlists parents as partners in the children's learning. Four in five parents of Head Start children get valuable experience both in working and in parenting by providing volunteer services to the program. In addition, one-third of Head Start's paid staff are parents of former or current Head Start students (CDF 1988a: 192).

Research consistently shows that children who attend Head Start score higher on IQ and achievement tests and are more likely to meet the basic requirements for elementary school than are children in control groups. A number of studies also suggest that once Head Start students have started school, they are less likely than are students in control groups to be placed in special education classes or held back in school (CDF 1988a: 192).

As Ernest Boyer also points out in Chapter 6 of this volume, research on preschool programs similar to Head Start confirms that later-life benefits can be significant. He notes the Perry Preschool Project in Ypsilanti, Michigan. Another long-term study, which examined a comprehensive preschool program in Harlem in New York City, found that at age 21 graduates of the program had an employment rate double that of a control group; one-third more of the program participants had a high school or high-school equivalency diploma, and about 30 percent more had gone on to some form of postsecondary education (Schorr 1988: 194–95). And according to the House Select Committee on Children, Youth, and Families, $1 invested in good preschool education returns $6 in savings in special education and welfare costs, and in higher worker productivity (U.S. Congress 1988a: 7).

Despite Head Start's effectiveness in preparing children for school, this nation is still a long way from providing Head Start education for all of its disadvantaged children. As a result of inflation since 1981 and the increase in the number of poor three- to five-year-olds, the Head Start appropriation was actually less per eligible child in 1986 than it was in 1981 (CDF 1988a: 194). Although 2.5 million disadvantaged youngsters are potentially eligible for Head Start, the program's fiscal year 1989 budget was so inadequate that only 18 percent of eligible children— about one in six—was enrolled (CDF 1989b: 27).

In 1990 Congress acknowledged Head Start's unique effectiveness by authorizing for the first time a series of funding increases which, if appropriated, will allow all eligible three- and four-year-olds and 30 percent of eligible five-year-olds to participate by 1994. The Head Start appropriation for fiscal year 1991 is $1.95 billion. Congress should appropriate $4.3 billion for 1992 as the next step toward full funding.

Nonschool Programs

Many children who grow up poor lack adult supervision and structured opportunities for recreation and learning outside of school. Yet teenage pregnancy rates, gang culture, and the lure of drugs in many poor neighborhoods make it vital that all children have constructive ways to fill their free time before and after school and during the summers. This nation is losing far too many of its youth to hopelessness, violence, and drug abuse. Forty-nine cities across the nation have reported street gangs dealing in narcotics. The number of juveniles arrested for *violent* crimes increased 9 percent between 1984 and 1986, even though there was an overall decrease in juvenile crime. Homicide is a leading cause of death among 15- to 24-year-olds (U.S. Congress 1989: 47).

Because low academic achievement and low self-esteem generally go together, disadvantaged youths who have trouble in school need a variety of nonacademic experiences that allow them to gain the life skills and the feelings of self-worth that will help them do better in school and avoid premature parenthood, drug abuse, and violence. Just as good child care and preschool education are cost-effective investments in the educational development of young children, well-planned, well-supervised after-school and summer programs for preteens and older adolescents are cost-effective alternatives to the neglect that breeds isolation, alienation, and antisocial behavior. The supervisor of diagnostic studies for juveniles on probation from the Washington, D.C., Superior Court says that one of the striking characteristics common among youths who commit crimes is their lack of bonding to the mainstream culture through neighborhood activities such as Boy Scouts, church activities, or sports leagues (Kurtz 1989: A30).

Effective community-based programs for preteens and teenagers should offer:

- A variety of recreational activities including individual and team sports
- Educational enrichment that may include tutoring but also include opportunities to apply basic skills in new activities—creating a product, for example, or performing a service
- Interaction with adults who like adolescents, understand their needs, and can serve as positive role models
- Opportunities to practice leadership, to make decisions, and to interact in a variety of activities with peers
- Opportunities for community service. For adolescents of all ages— and all incomes—service to others can be the grounding experience that forges ties to the community, bolsters self-esteem, and encourages understanding of the importance of learning.

Funding for summer and after-school activities is meager and unreliable in this country. When money is tight, free public programs run by libraries, public parks, neighborhood recreation centers, and schools are the first to be cut out or changed to fee-based programs. But even minimal fees generally prevent low-income children from participating. Privately funded programs can and do offer many opportunities to moderate- and low-income students. At a time when violence, drug and alcohol abuse, and teenage pregnancy claim so many poor youth, however, the need to guide adolescents into constructive activities is far too important to leave this function entirely to the private sector, particularly when the nonprofit private sector has been battered by growing demands and diminishing federal contributions. Moreover, many of the public and private programs that do exist are generally targeted either to young children or to older adolescents already in trouble. Youngsters between the ages of 10 and 14 are likely to be forgotten, although their experiences during these highly formative years often determine the choices they make in later adolescence.

Consistent state and federal funding for after-school and summer programs for preteens and adolescents would be a wise investment in human capital formation. It costs an average of $31,000 to keep a juvenile in detention for a year, and that does not include other costs of the juvenile justice system. At more than $31,000 per detainee per year, the savings realized from even a modest drop in detentions would be substantial, making a significant public investment in preventive activities for preteens and teenagers a cost-effective use of tax dollars. Either as a formal or informal aspect of this nation's war on drugs, Congress should appropriate money for preventive summer and after-school programs that offer all preteens and teenagers constructive activities to help them develop the skills, self-concept, and attitudes that will link them to the economic and social mainstream (see CDF 1987d).

Strengthening Families: The Key to Saving Money and Developing Human Capital

Poverty places a family under tremendous strains and increases a child's risk of being placed in a foster home, a group home, a treatment center, or some other type of child care institution. Half of Iowa's foster care children, for example, come from AFDC families, even though these families account for less than 8 percent of all Iowa families (CDF 1989c: 48).

In 1985, 276,000 children in this country lived apart from their families in foster care. On a one-day count in June 1986, an estimated 375,000 children were in foster care (U.S. Congress 1989: 45). If the erosion of American families continues at recent rates, the child welfare system alone could account for a half million children and adolescents in out-of-home care by the year 2000.

The economic cost of failed families is sobering. According to a recent study of out-of-home placement in Missouri, the total annual cost for one year of out-of-home placement ranges from $11,424 for family foster care to $93,075 for in-patient care in a mental health facility. In fiscal year 1988, Missouri spent more than $82 million to place children outside their homes. If current growth rates in out-of-home placement continue, costs are expected to increase by 56 percent by fiscal year 1993 (Citizens for Missouri's Children 1989: viii–ix).

Out-of-home care is a worthwhile investment when it is absolutely necessary and when it reclaims troubled children for productive lives in the future. It is a poor investment when it is used unnecessarily and when it does not have a positive result. Unfortunately, in many states, the child welfare, mental health, and juvenile justice agencies are so overburdened that the quality of the average out-of-home placement is shockingly poor. Nonetheless, a Missouri study found that child welfare workers used out-of-home care as a first rather than a last resort because there were few home- or community-based alternatives and because the child welfare workers were pressured by their unreasonably high case loads. The study also concluded that state foster care systems have a fiscal incentive to place children outside their homes because federal law entitles each child to foster care if needed and gives the states federal funds for foster care maintenance (Citizens for Missouri's Children 1989:ix).

Bureaucratic barriers that prevent children and families from receiving integrated services are one reason child-serving agencies typically produce so few success stories. Depending on how children first come to the state's attention, they are routed into child protective services, mental health services, or the juvenile justice system, which are all separately funded, functionally distinct, and often rigidly restricted in the kinds of help they can provide.

Children's problems, however, are not so neatly compartmentalized. Most at-risk children come from similar family backgrounds and have overlapping, multiple problems. An increasing number of children in the child welfare and juvenile justice systems, for example, have serious emotional and behavioral problems as well as severe educational and health deficits. In Ohio in 1987, two-fifths of the children in state care had problems that overlapped departmental boundaries (CDF 1989c: 51). If these children and their families are to be helped, they need a wide range of complementary services.

Under the present system, however, neither the children nor their families consistently get the kind of comprehensive help that could lead to family reunification and improved functioning. One New Jersey study, for example, reported that one-third of the children leaving foster care during an 18-month period had returned to care within one year (CDF 1989c: 52). In Missouri, one-quarter of the children entering placement in 1988 had been placed outside their homes at least once before, a 66-percent increase over fiscal year 1985 (Citizens for Missouri's Children 1989: vii). Children who endure such stressful and fragmented childhoods are not likely to develop the emotional or educational foundation for future achievement.

Fortunately an alternative to rigidly circumscribed treatment and unsuccessful and unnecessary out-of-home placement is developing in this country. Family preservation services, as this new approach is called, deliver a specially tailored set of comprehensive services through intensive intervention in the family. The child at risk of placement is left in the home if the family agrees to participate. A trained case manager with a small case load—two or three families—is available to the family on virtually a 24-hour-a-day basis for several months. The case manager spends time with the family in the home, concentrates on active aid in solving the family's practical problems, whatever form they take, gives immediate instruction in and help with parenting, and provides an ongoing link with various family support systems. The goal is to enable the family to reach a level of functioning that eliminates the need for removing the child (see Nelson 1988).

Does family preservation work? The evidence is encouraging. Familystrength in New Hampshire is a family preservation program serving families of abused, neglected, or delinquent children. In 1986–87, the average length of treatment for the 180 families served was 4.4 months, at an average cost of $4,800 per family of five. Seventy-six percent of the client families were still intact at the end of treatment. The per-family cost represented less than half of the average cost of foster care placement for one child for one year (CDF 1989c: 50).

Maryland's Intensive Family Services program delivers comprehensive services to families through public agency teams made up of a social worker and a paraprofessional parent aide. Each team serves about six families at a time for a period of three months. At the end of that time, approximately two-thirds of the cases are closed with no further service needed; other families are linked to auxiliary supports. An evaluation of 100 client families revealed that after one year these families were less than one-fourth as likely to have a child in out-of-home care as families receiving traditional child protective services. The families also had a lower recidivism rate after two years. The state estimates that serving 600 families each year in the program can save about $2.5 million a year in averted costs of out-of-home care (CDF 1989c: 50).

The federal government can encourage cost-effective family preservation by eliminating the imbalance between the federal funds available for out-of-home care and the money available for services that reduce the need for placements. This would mean modifying the federal foster care program, the Child Welfare Services program, Medicaid, the Juvenile Justice and Delinquency Prevention Act, and the Alcohol, Drug Abuse, and Mental Health Block Grant to give states financial incentives to develop alternatives to out-of-home placement.

The federal government should also provide new money for state expansion of in-home services and community-based alternatives to institutional placements. In addition, states that reduce the number of children entering out-of-home care should be able to retain the equivalent of the saved federal foster care dollars for use in developing alternative services.

Finally, in order to encourage unified children's services, Congress should amend existing child welfare, juvenile justice, and mental health programs to provide incentives to state child-serving agencies to jointly fund and staff services for youths at risk of placement and for those already in care. States that document interagency collaboration should receive federal money for developing and implementing family preservation services.

While family preservation programs are proving cost-effective in successfully treating families and children in crisis, they are providing another valuable service by leading the way toward even broader changes in the delivery of all social services. Our current antipoverty and family assistance efforts are so fragmented that in one typical county of half a million population, a low-income family would have to apply to 18 separate organizations to receive all the various types of assistance for which its members might be eligible (Levitan, Mangum, and Pines 1989: 3). Many of these programs have their own eligibility rules, their own offices, and their own service delivery systems. Since most of these agencies target their help to individuals, no single organization is responsible for making sure the family as a unit receives the particular combination of services it needs to remain intact and solve its day-to-day problems. Recently, however, a few states and counties have begun using the idea of family preservation as a model for reorganizing their broader social service programs into a more integrated, more responsive whole that focuses on strengthening families, not merely on treating individuals in isolation.

Central to this approach are community-based family centers that are the only intake points for families needing public assistance of any kind. Trained case managers with small case loads determine family eligibility for assistance, analyze family needs, and become family resource brokers, responsible for committing the services to be provided by various agencies and following up on the family's progress. The keys to a successful program, of course, are interagency staff training, collaborative planning, and coordinated funding.

Under current laws, states already have some latitude to set up family centers and rationalize service delivery. For example, states could establish family centers as a means of implementing the Family Support Act of 1988. In addition, however, the federal government can provide important incentives for change by endorsing the concept of family-centered comprehensive services, by giving states planning grants, and by funding pilot projects in a variety of community settings around the country (see Levitan, Mangum, and Pines 1989).

Common sense and experience tell us that integration and coordination are cheaper and more efficient than duplication. With a rationalized delivery system, we should be able to provide more social services for the same amount of money. Even more important, however, integrated family-centered help increases the likelihood that low-income families can achieve economic self-sufficiency and better all-round functioning. The result will be a nation of healthier, better educated, more productive citizens and workers.

Now Is the Time to Act

This nation's ability to grow economically and compete in the international market is being threatened by our inadequate investment in our most important resource: people. Investing in machinery and technology will only take us so far, as IBM Corporation discovered after installing millions of dollars worth of computers in its Vermont factories. Before employees could use the computers properly, IBM had to teach the employees high-school algebra. Employers all around the country are telling a similar story. As Marion Pines and Anthony Carnevale note in their chapter, American industry is currently pouring $30 billion per year into training programs for workers who don't have the skills our economy needs to maintain its competitive status in world trade.

The obvious answer to our human capital deficits is better education. But the complete answer—the answer that makes "better education" more than a slogan—is vastly more far-reaching. In order to learn well, children must get a healthy start in life. They must live in families that have the physical and emotional resources to house, feed, and nurture them and to prepare them for school. They need to be safe and well cared for while their parents work, and as they grow older they must be given opportunities that allow them to develop confidence in themselves as valuable contributors to our society and our economy.

Thus, to invest wisely in human capital, we must invest in families and support their efforts to nurture and educate their children. And our investments must be preventive. To get the most benefit for our money, we must provide assistance *before* a crisis disables a family, *before* a child suffers irreparable harm from unattended health problems, *before* a family is evicted from its home, *before* a child is abused by parents under stress, *before* a child drops out of school or becomes a teenaged parent.

As skilled workers become scarce and our economy threatens to stagnate, we can no longer afford the wastefulness of our current Band-Aid approach to social services. It is not good fiscal policy to allow 70,000 units of public housing to be boarded up and abandoned every year (CDF 1988a: 116), then to spend $3,000 per month per family to provide inadequate temporary shelter (CDF 1989c: 34). It is not good fiscal policy to spend $20 billion per year on prisons while allowing funding for delinquency prevention to be reduced by one-third, as it was between 1980 and 1988 (U.S. Congress 1989: 48). It is not good fiscal policy for a state to spend $6 putting children in out-of-home placements for every $1 it spends on services to prevent child abuse and neglect (Citizens for Missouri's Children 1989: x). And it is not good fiscal policy to deny a pregnant woman comprehensive prenatal care costing $1,200 when it costs an average of $19,000 to save a low-birthweight newborn through intensive neonatal care (U.S. Congress 1988b: 35).

In a $5-trillion economy with a $1-trillion federal budget, the nation *can* find room for spending that reflects more rational priorities. The longer we wait to act, the more human capital we sacrifice and the more precarious our national future becomes. As *Business Week* recently pointed out, "It is time to put our money where our future is" (Nussbaum et al. 1988: 140).

References

Children's Defense Fund (CDF) (1986a). *Building Health Programs for Teenagers*. Washington, D.C.: Children's Defense Fund, May.

—— (1986b). *Model Programs: Preventing Adolescent Pregnancy and Building Youth Self-Sufficiency*. Washington, D.C.: Children's Defense Fund, July.

—— (1987a). *Adolescent Pregnancy: An Anatomy of a Social Problem in Search of Comprehensive Solutions.* Washington, D.C.: Children's Defense Fund, January.

—— (1987b). *Child Care: An Essential Service for Teen Parents*. Washington, D.C.: Children's Defense Fund, March.

—— (1987c). *Child Care: The Time Is Now*. Washington, D.C.: Children's Defense Fund.

—— (1987d). *Opportunities for Prevention: Building After School and Summer Programs for Young Adolescents*. Washington, D.C.: Children's Defense Fund, July.

—— (1988a). *A Children's Defense Budget (FY 1989)*. Washington, D.C.: Children's Defense Fund.

—— (1988b). *State Child Care Fact Book, 1988*. Washington, D.C.: Children's Defense Fund.

—— (1988c). *Teenage Pregnancy: An Advocate's Guide to the Numbers*. Washington, D.C.: Children's Defense Fund, January/March.

Children's Defense Fund (CDF) and Center for Labor Market Studies, Northeastern University (1988d). *Vanishing Dreams: The Growing Economic Plight of America's Young Families*. Washington, D.C.: Children's Defense Fund.

Children's Defense Fund (CDF) (1989a). *The Health of America's Children: Maternal and Child Health Data Book*. Washington, D.C.: Children's Defense Fund.

—— (1989b). *The Nation's Investment in Children: An Analysis of the President's FY 1990 Budget Proposals*. Washington, D.C.: Children's Defense Fund.

—— (1989c). *A Vision for America's Future: An Agenda for the 1990s: A Children's Defense Budget*. Washington, D.C.: Children's Defense Fund.

Citizens for Missouri's Children (1989). "Where's My Home? A Study of Missouri's Children in Out-of-Home Placement." An unpublished report by Citizens for Missouri's Children in cooperation with the Missouri Department of Mental Health and the Department of Social Services, January.

Eakins, Jean (1990). Personal interview, January 10.

Edelman, Marian Wright (1987). *Families in Peril: An Agenda for Social Change.* Cambridge: Harvard University Press.

Johnston, William B., and Arnold H. Packer (1987). *Workforce 2000: Work and Workers for the Twenty-first Century.* Indianapolis, Ind.: Hudson Institute.

Kurtz, Howard (1989). "At the Roots of the Violence." *Washington Post,* April 2.

Levitan, Sar A., Garth L. Mangum, and Marion W. Pines (1989). *A Proper Inheritance: Investing in the Self-Sufficiency of Poor Families.* Washington, D.C.: George Washington University, Center for Social Policy Studies.

Nelson, Douglas (1988). *Recognizing and Realizing the Potential of "Family Preservation."* Working Paper Series, EP-2. Washington, D.C.: Center for the Study of Social Policy, December.

Nussbaum, Bruce, et al. (1988). "Human Capital: The Decline of America's Work Force, A Special Report." *Business Week* September 19, p. 140.

Rosewater, Ann (1989). "Child and Family Trends: Beyond the Numbers." In Frank Macchiarola and Alan Gartner, eds., *Caring for America's Children.* Proceedings of the Academy of Political Science, vol. 37, no. 2. New York: Academy of Political Science.

Schorr, Lisbeth B. (1988). *Within Our Reach: Breaking the Cycle of Disadvantage.* New York; Anchor Press/Doubleday.

U.S. Bureau of the Census (1987). *Who's Minding the Kids? Child Care Arrangements: Winter 1984–85.* Current Population Reports, Series P-70, No. 9. Washington, D.C.: U.S. Government Printing Office.

U.S. Congress. House Select Committee on Children, Youth, and Families (1988a). *Opportunities for Success: Cost Effective Programs for Children Update, 1988.* Washington, D.C.: U.S. Government Printing Office.

——— (1988b). *Young Children in Crisis: Today's Problems and Tomorrow's Promises.* Hearing before the Select Committee held in Los Angeles, California, April 15, 1988. Washington, D.C.: U.S. Government Printing Office.

——— (1989). *Children and Families: Key Trends in the 1980s.* Washington, D.C.: U.S. Government Printing Office.

PART THREE

Roles, Responsibilities, and Resources

11

Human Capital Investment and Federalism

R. Scott Fosler

As the previous chapters of this book have demonstrated, an effective approach to human capital investment involves more than improving the capacity of the work force. Also relevant are policies and practices that affect the size and composition of the work force and the productivity with which it is employed. What is more, work force capacity is itself a complex phenomenon, involving health and supportive services as well as formal education and training. These realities pose an important question: how can such a broad approach be implemented? Where should responsibility for human capital investment be vested? This chapter addresses one portion of the answer to these questions. It focuses on the role of government in setting and implementing human capital policies, and more specifically on the relative roles of federal, state, and local governments and of the federal system more generally.

Historically, the federal system has been viewed as an obstacle to coherent national policy in key policy fields in the United States. The diversity of state political systems and the consequent inequities in coverage and resources that result from extensive decentralization of control have led many to argue that states and localities should play a derivative role in policy arenas that are crucial to national health and prosperity. The argument here, however, is different. While acknowledging a need for active federal leadership, this chapter argues that effective state and local government action is equally essential for progress in the human capital field. Far from seeing America's federal system as an unfortunate burden, I argue that it is a unique asset for developing an effective human capital approach. To achieve this potential, however, both the federal and the state and local governments will have to develop new approaches and styles.

To support this argument, the chapter examines the recent history of human capital and economic policy in the United States, reviews the key components of an effective human capital policy, identifies the inherent disadvantages of the federal government and the inherent advantages of state and local governments that make state and local involvement important, reviews the recent state-local experience in the field, identifies the inherent disadvantages of state and local governments that make federal involvement crucial, and clarifies the role that the federal government should consequently play.

The Evolution of Intergovernmental Roles: Recent History

One of the central rationales for the American federal system has been the opportunity it provides for experimentation. Rather than adopting new policies wholesale for the entire country, the federal system provides an opportunity to "test" them first in particular states and regions. More than that, because it is often difficult to develop a broad national consensus for new policy initiatives, the federal system gives advocates of various initiatives an opportunity to try them out locally in the hope of building broader national support.

For advocates of more effective government involvement in the promotion of American economic competitiveness, the federal system has operated in precisely this way over the past two decades. In the process, two facets of government policy that had long been split—economic policy and human capital policy—were finally united in ways that have great promise for the future. To understand this point, it is useful to review briefly the evolution of intergovernmental roles in human capital and economic policy.

Earlier in U.S. history, the education of the work force was promoted as a means to economic vitality. Horace Mann, as secretary of the Massachusetts State Board of Education in 1848, characterized schools as "the grand agent for the development or augmentation of national resources, more powerful in the production and gainful employment of the total wealth of a country than the other things mentioned in the books of the political economists." But that early connection between human capital investment and economic development soon faded. Education became generally accepted as a routine governmental function and remained a state and local responsibility, while economic policy became the nearly exclusive responsibility of the federal government.

Federal economic policy, meanwhile, became increasingly preoccupied with macroeconomic issues such as fiscal, monetary, and trade policy, and dealt only incidentally with such microeconomic issues as work force development. To be sure, some federal human resource policies have addressed the issue of work force development. For example, the Morrill Act of 1862 established land-grant universities to "promote the liberal and practical education of the industrial classes in the several pursuits and professions of life."[1] And the first federal vocational educational programs date from 1917. But during the Great Depression of the 1930s, the federal government became involved in human resource issues principally as part of its more central concern with economic security.[2] Following World War II, additional federal initiatives addressed the economic needs of specific groups, such as veterans, the elderly, the poor, minorities, and the disabled.[3] The launching of Sputnik in 1957 generated a wave of support for improving public education.

Over time, as each specific need was addressed with specific federal legislation, a potpourri of human service programs accumulated—many of which were administered through state and local governments—with little coordination among them, and no coherent connection with economic policy.[4] It has fallen largely to the states to attempt both to integrate the wide array of human service programs and to reestablish the connection between human resources and economic policy.

The states began to take a stronger interest in economic issues in the early 1970s in response to the pressure of global economic restructuring. They were further motivated by the recessions of the early 1980s, by fiscal pressures from taxpayer rebellions, and by cutbacks in federal financial support.[5] Seeking more effective strategies than the conventional reliance on industrial recruitment ("smokestack chasing"), the states expanded their approach to economic development to include the indigenous development of internal economic assets such as technology, financial capital, physical infrastructure, and the work force (Fosler 1988a).

Pressure for educational reform and skills upgrading quickly became a central focus of policy in many states. This pressure came principally from governors, legislators, and business leaders concerned about deficiencies in the work force, not from professional educators and boards of education. The same economic concern that drove the interest in educational reform has also compelled the states to rethink a wide range of human resource programs—such as job training, vocational education, higher education, welfare, and health care—from the perspective of their impact on the work force.[6]

The election of Ronald Reagan reinforced the state activism. While President Reagan was generally opposed to government initiative in domestic affairs, he also supported the premise that state and local governments should be encouraged to decide for themselves what their citizens wanted.[7] Consequently, a "de facto new Federalism" took shape during the 1980s, characterized by the continuing reduction in federal grants to

state and local government, the virtual cessation of significant new federal initiatives for domestic policy, and the simultaneous resurgence of
activism on the part of state and local government.

Left to their own devices, many states developed imaginative approaches to human capital investment, involving major reforms of public
education, the formation of work force training programs, and the establishment of preschool education initiatives. More importantly, they
linked these efforts explicitly to broader economic development strategies seeking to make the states more competitive economically. In the
process, the sharp divide between economic policy and human resource
policy that developed earlier in this century was, if not eliminated, at
least significantly bridged.

At the same time, there remains a considerable degree of incoherence
in the structure of the nation's human resource policies. Public education
remains a predominantly state-local responsibility, although there is a
clear national interest in educational reform to improve work force competitiveness. Meanwhile, many human resource programs are heavily financed by the federal government, which also shapes their administration, even though many are implemented by state and local government
and are closely related to education. The consequence is a set of highly
fragmented human capital investment policies and programs that can
hardly be characterized as a system.

The Key Components of a Human Capital Strategy

To overcome this fragmentation, it will be necessary to develop a human capital investment strategy and then to sort out the roles of the
different levels of government in implementing it. The first step in this
direction is to review what such a strategy should contain.

Based on recent analysis and the experience of state and local policy
to date, it seems clear that the productive performance and competitiveness of the work force depends on three principal elements. The first is
the *size and composition* of the work force: who is available for work?
The second is worker *capacity*: what do workers know and what can
they do? And the third is *productivity*: are the capacities of workers
channeled into the jobs with the highest possible value added, those
which make the best use of workers' capacities and help develop them
further? Each of these elements is affected by various policies of federal,
state, and local governments, as previous chapters in this volume have
demonstrated, and as Tables 11.1, 11.2, and 11.3 make clear. Thus, as
Edelman stressed, education will have little impact in the absence of good
health and secure child care. Similarly, Danziger underlined the importance of other poverty-reducing measures beyond education; Marshall

Table 11.1   Policies Affecting Principal Determinants of Work Force Size and Composition

Determinant	Policy
Population size	
Birthrate	Policies affecting birthrates
Mortality rate	Health care policies
Migration	
Domestic	Regional policies
Foreign	Immigration policy
Demographic characteristics, (age, sex, race, cultural background, etc.)	Civil rights and antidiscrimination policy, and planning for work force development
Labor force participation rate	Tax and benefit incentives; policies affecting accessibility to jobs (such as child care)
Participation in informal markets	Opportunities for volunteer service; summer youth programs; policies affecting family and social structure; and the underground economy

stressed immigration policy that is crafted to serve human capital goals and then is enforced; Boyer insisted on the importance of early years; and Barrett called for policies that free women for high-productivity jobs. The tables also make clear the point emphasized by Hornbeck: that structural systemic alteration is essential.

Work Force Size and Composition

More specifically, Table 11.1 shows the principal factors that affect work force size and composition (what labor economists would refer to as labor supply) and various governmental policies that influence those factors.

A wide variety of policies affect the size and geographical distribution of the population and the ability of would-be workers to actively enter the work force, get to the workplace, and satisfy minimal personal requirements that would permit them to remain in their jobs.

Factors that could improve this facet of human capital include:

- Elimination of barriers to work force participation, especially for disadvantaged workers;
- Provision of support for workers with special needs, such as child care for working parents

Table 11.2   Policies Affecting Principal Determinants of Workers' Capacity

Determinant	Policy
Early childhood development	Policies affecting prenatal care, infant and child health, child nurturing and development, family integrity
Basic knowledge and ability	Policies affecting preschool education, primary and secondary education, remedial programs, influence of other social institutions
Advanced knowledge and ability	Policies affecting college, university, continuing adult education
Employment-oriented knowledge and ability	Policies affecting employment-oriented elements of the foregoing, high school and for-profit vocational education, government job-training programs, military training, professional schools, employer-based education, work experience

- Establishment of immigration policy that accounts for work force needs
- Adjustment of tax and benefit policies to minimize disincentives to labor force participation
- Encouragement of nonmarket work and volunteer service to meet community needs and thereby help to reduce the costs of business and government.

Capacity of the Work Force

Table 11.2 summarizes the principal factors that affect workers' capacity and the policies that influence those factors.

These begin with good health in infancy, followed by the development of character traits that affect attitudes toward learning, habits of work, and ability to get along with others. Such traits are influenced from the start of life by parents and by a variety of social institutions—family, neighborhoods, health care and religious institutions, television, and day care centers—that in turn are affected by policies at all levels of government. Capacity is further affected by basic education, and for those students who do not go to college, by various training programs that prepare them for entry-level employment. And in the future, work force competitiveness will necessitate lifelong learning.

Policies that could affect the *capacity* of the work force include:

- Health policies that prevent debilitating illness which undermines the ability to learn and perform—beginning with prenatal care
- Target programs for the educationally disadvantaged, beginning with infancy and early childhood and continuing through primary, secondary, and higher education, as well as work force training and supportive services
- Restructuring of primary and secondary education to strengthen incentives for performance
- Educational improvements in priority areas such as reading, writing, computing, science, and problem solving
- Strengthening of higher education, especially below the level of the top universities, and assuring access to qualified students
- Restructuring of employment, training, welfare, and lifetime education programs to form an integrated approach to work force development.

Work Force Productivity

The third major element of human capital investment is work force productivity, which is affected by a wide range of governmental policies, as indicated in Table 11.3. It is here in particular that human capital investment and economic strategy need to be closely related, since the key to work force productivity lies in assuring that workers' capacities are effectively put to use in market-driven industries and firms that are globally competitive.

An economy that fails to provide good job opportunities, to match workers' skills to those jobs, or to assure that those skills are effectively put to use in the workplace is squandering human capacity. What's more, it is limiting the opportunities for further developing worker capacity, since the skills demanded and learned on the job ultimately determine the standards for what people need to know in order to remain competitive in global markets. Maintaining a vital economy at the leading edge of technology and world markets is therefore critical to assuring that workers will develop the knowledge and skills that will keep them competitive in the future.[8]

Federal macroeconomic policy bears the principal responsibility for promoting general economic vitality.[9] But microeconomic policies—at both the federal and state-local levels—play an increasingly important role in assuring the competitiveness of the U.S. economy. The states' ini-

Table 11.3 Policies Affecting Determinants of Work Force Productivity

Determinant	Policies
Economic vitality and employment opportunities	Policies affecting macroeconomic conditions, economic development in specific industries, technologies, and places; enterprise culture and self-employment; temporary and part-time employment opportunities
Placement matching capacity to the job	Policies affecting career and job counseling, job placement and organized access to jobs, labor force information
Mobility (among jobs, vocations, industries, regions)	Policies affecting dislocation assistance, benefit portability, welfare-to-work programs, Unemployment Insurance, workers' compensation
Motivation	Policies affecting compensation, hours of work, and other motivating factors
Workplace	Policies affecting management and conditions of employment (occupational safety and health, labor relations, work rules, worker rights, etc.)

tiatives in technology, financial capital, physical infrastructure, natural resources, and other areas have made important contributions. Pennsylvania's Ben Franklin Partnership, for example, provides financial incentives for businesses and universities to work together to commercialize technology (Osborne 1988). States are also working more directly with businesses in an effort to assist them in improving their productivity. The Michigan Modernization Service, for example, provides technical assistance to upgrade firms in traditional industries.

Factors that could improve the productivity of the work force include:

- Effective economic policies that promote economic growth, stability, productivity, and international competitiveness for the U.S. economy in general
- Regional policies that account for variations in economic conditions throughout the country
- Regional policies that account for variations in economic development programs
- Integration of work force development and economic development programs

- Increased flexibility of the work force through better labor force information, effective job placement, portability of worker benefits, and development of an integrated system for worker transition to new jobs, vocations, firms, industries, and locations
- Increased flexibility and better management *within* the workplace, including attention to policies that protect, motivate, and assist workers in their employment.

The Case for State/Local Involvement

Given the importance of improved human capital investment to the economic health of the nation, a strong case can be made for active federal involvement in the design, funding, and execution of human capital policies. Only the federal government, after all, has the authority to set national priorities and energize national commitment. What is more, the federal government has a far more flexible fiscal structure and is therefore in a better position to generate resources in support of broad national priorities. Finally, the federal government can ensure at least a basic level of activity throughout the country and thus ensure a degree of equity in the pursuit of major national priorities.

Given the breadth of policy measures that must be coordinated to pursue an effective human capital investment strategy, however, central design and administration from the national level is impractical even if it were desirable. For a variety of reasons, however, it is not even desirable. To the contrary, a strong case can be made that the ideal structure of a human capital investment strategy for the United States is one that builds on, and rationalizes, the prevailing mode of American federalism, which involves a thoroughgoing blending of federal, state, and local responsibilities in the design and conduct of public policy. Five factors argue strongly for active state and local involvement in this field, albeit within the context of a strong federal role.

Existing State/Local Investments

The first, and most obvious, reason for involving state and local governments actively in any future national human capital investment strategy is that these governments are already deeply involved in these fields and are likely to be the principal actors for the foreseeable future.

State governments in particular have been assuming greater responsibility for such elements of the human-investment system as education, job training, employment service, unemployment insurance, and workers' compensation. In 1988, the total bill for nondefense purchases of goods and services by all government in the United States was $661 billion. State and local governments accounted for 88 percent of that total, nearly 40 percent of which went for education. And over 90 percent of those education expenditures were covered by states and localities through revenues they raised themselves. There has also been a shift in responsibility for education from the local to the state level, a trend that had already begun in the 1960s due to pressures to desegregate schools and equalize funding among local school districts.[10] State-local funding patterns, however, vary widely. At the extremes, the state may fund as much as 90 percent of school costs (in Hawaii) or as little as only 11 percent (in New Hampshire).

In addition to shouldering most of the responsibility for public education, state and local governments also play a major role in other elements of capacity building:

- *Community colleges.* In 1986, state and local governments spent $12 billion.
- *Vocational education.* In fiscal year 1985, state and local government spent $9 billion, or 13 times the $700 million spent by the federal government.
- *Adult education.* In fiscal year 1986, the state and local expenditures of $320 million were three times as great as federal expenditures of $112 million.
- *Retraining.* According to a 1986 report by the National Governors' Association, states funded 17 types of retraining programs totaling approximately $137 million. Federal funding of programs for dislocated workers in 1986 totaled $188 million.
- *Welfare to work.* According to the General Accounting Office, state and local spending in 1985 was $68 million, compared to federal expenditures of $196 million. Since that year, state expenditures have increased rapidly. California's GAIN program included $214 million in state general revenues for fiscal year 1989. (NAB 1988: 9).

One of the more promising developments in efforts to improve the capacity of the work force is the integration of related programs in education, training, and social services. Some states are experimenting with comprehensive programs to coordinate services to young children and teenagers at risk, programs to prevent school drop outs, early childhood education programs, and skills assessment programs to identify and help at-risk students. Schools are also being used as an institutional focus for coordinating a variety of social services supportive of overall educational improvement. For example, New York's Schools as Community Sites program has earmarked 14 schools for the coordination of educational, social, health-related, recreational, and instructional support services. New Jersey's School Based Youth Services coordinates related services of the state's departments of human services, education, labor, and health at the school level.

Allowing for Regional Diversity

The U.S. economy is composed of diverse regional economies and the labor markets that serve them, and the states and their local governments are in a prime position to provide the kind of tailored policy attention that these diverse conditions require.

The core economic regions are metropolitan areas, which are defined principally by where people live and by the range of their commutation from home to work. A series of metropolitan areas and their associated hinterlands, in turn, typically interact to form broader economic regions, such as the Northeast, or the Midwest.

Regions vary enormously in size, composition, and direction of growth. In 1988 parts of the Northeast were facing severe labor shortages, while some areas of the Midwest still had high concentrations of unemployment. Minneapolis graduates over 90 percent of its high school students, compared to 50 percent in Louisiana. As conditions change, moreover, policies need to be adjusted accordingly. Oklahoma confronted labor shortages during the oil boom years but suffered high unemployment in 1988. Such tailored responses are best fashioned at the state and local levels, not the national level.[11] The question of how to facilitate the mobility of labor among regions in response to varying economic conditions and job opportunities, however, requires national attention.

Integrating Economic Functions

State and local governments play an important role in integrating the institutions and programs that educate and train the regional labor market with other aspects of economic development and civic enterprise.

The states' training programs are increasingly tied to their economic development programs. The Bay State Skills Corporation in Massachusetts, for example, functions as a broker to match businesses that have specific training needs with training institutions that can meet those needs. "Customized training," which for many years was provided as part of a recruitment package of incentives to attract businesses to the state, today is geared increasingly toward helping businesses already in the state to upgrade their work forces.

States are also linking economic development programs with efforts to bring low-income and disadvantaged workers into the work force. For example, Illinois's Project Chance "markets" employable welfare recipients to business. Some states attempt to create new job opportunities in distressed areas through community-based development (Roberts 1988).

While the debate over national economic strategy bogged down in ideological confrontations over the relative merits of "industrial policy" versus "market" approaches,[12] the states evolved a pragmatic synthesis. Virtually every governor—Democratic and Republican—and key business leaders in nearly every state began to fashion a pragmatic strategy to address the economic pressures their states were facing.

Several states have explicitly linked economic development and human capital investment strategies. For example, Michigan, under the leadership of Democratic Governor James Blanchard, made Human Investment Strategy a key element in its program to modernize Michigan's economy. Maine, under the leadership of Republican John McKernan, established a Human Resource Development Plan encompassing 15 state agencies that operate 26 programs spending a total of about $1 billion per year, "an investment in . . . workers to ensure that they possess the education and skill levels necessary to compete for jobs in a changing economy" (McKernan 1988). The Maine Plan intended to ensure that "human resource and economic development activities are coordinated and supportive of each other in order to achieve the state's economic mission" (McKernan 1988).

Some communities are discovering that their ability to develop effective economic and human capital development programs depends in large measure on the status of their civic infrastructure.[13] Moreover, the very importance of the civic dimension, and the fact that effective civic infrastructure depends upon educated and involved citizens, underscores the importance of factoring in civic education and preparation for citizenship as part of the human-capital investment equation.

Experimenting

State and local involvement offers the opportunity for experimentation to test different approaches to human capital investment. As they respond to their own needs and pressures, states and localities gain knowledge and experience that is applicable elsewhere. The Bay State Skills corporation model is now being applied in at least six states. The Minnesota public school "choice" program has been adopted with variations by several states, and is being watched closely by others to see if it will provide the incentive needed to cause widespread improvement in the performance of individual schools, including schools in low-income neighborhoods.

Experimentation at the state and local levels requires a degree of ingenuity tempered by practical constraints that is not commonly seen in national experiments. The Minnesota choice program is a pragmatic hybrid of various voucher, "public choice," and public administration theories that have been debated nationally on theoretical and ideological grounds for many years. It may or may not succeed, but here again there is value in federalism: if a localized experiment fails, the damage will be less than if the experiment had been carried out on a nationwide basis.

The state experimentation has already produced some valuable lessons in childhood education, educational technology, drop out prevention for pregnant teenagers, placing welfare mothers in jobs, and retraining workers for new jobs. There are also important lessons to be learned about the process of government: how to create partnerships among government, business, labor, and nonprofit groups; how to restructure markets to increase competition; how to develop strategy for economic and human capital investment policy; how to strengthen the capacity of communities to deal with their own needs; and how to integrate service delivery.

For example, the state and local experience has demonstrated the importance of government's distinguishing between its roles as a policymaker and a program implementor. Government may decide that a given public goal is worth pursuing, but recognize that the private sector, or a mixed public-private delivery system would be more efficient in pursuing it. In their economic and human development initiatives, the states have learned to set goals but, rather than setting up full-blown government programs to meet the goals, they structure markets so that individuals and institutions have the incentive and resources to achieve those goals. For example, the Michigan Strategic Fund sees itself as a "wholesaler." It identifies gaps in capital markets, and then adjusts laws and provides marginal funds to leverage private financial institutions to fill those gaps. In one instance it detected a gap in seed capital for small firm start-ups and induced banks to establish a loan loss reserve, using modest grants from the Strategic Fund in order to expand loans to start up firms.

State and local governments are learning to be catalysts to get others to act, brokers to bring together actors with mutual interests, leveragers to make the most of scarce resources in several sectors, and partners to work with others on a collaborative basis to determine what works and what does not. They are becoming more sophisticated in tailoring approaches to meet different needs: adjusting the scale of operation, the actors to be involved, the mix of cooperation and competition that is called for, and the marginal use of government resources to stimulate action and get results.

Competing

Competition among states and localities, if properly structured, is a source of energy and creative initiative. Much of the publicity given to state economic development programs has focused on the negative aspects of competitive "smokestack chasing," in which states try to outbid one another with tax incentives and other inducements to attract firms. Even this type of competition has its value and tends to be self-limiting; states that pay too high a price to attract firms suffer the consequences. But the more important feature of state competition is the motivation it produces for each state to make the best use of its own internal resources, including its people. As each state improves its work force relative to others, it also sharpens that state's competitive edge in the global economy, and thus enhances all U.S. competitiveness.

Initiatives fashioned locally are also more likely to motivate and win commitment than are programs that are federally imposed. Local "ownership" builds commitment, and the realization that the gain or failure from the initiative will be reaped locally instills an added incentive to make it work.

In today's global economy, the competition is not just among individuals, firms, and nations, but among regions and social systems. Given this reality, the U.S. federal system can function much as a domestic market economy does: by acting as a crucible to test the capability of the competing units—be they firms, states, or communities—at home, to prepare them for the far tougher competition they will confront on a world scale.

The Imperative of Federal Leadership

Although state and local governments are vital to the design and implementation of the kind of broad human capital investment strategy outlined in this book, they cannot pursue such a strategy on their own. Rather, strong federal leadership is imperative. This is so for a variety of reasons.

In the first place, only the federal government has the perspective and the authority to view the national need in all its dimensions. The economic challenge facing American communities at the present time is in important respects an international challenge arising from the increased penetration of international economic competition into the American market. By virtue of its position as the authoritative voice of U.S. policy in the international economy, the national government has a special responsibility to assist local communities to respond.

In the second place, the kind of effort that will be required to overcome the human capital deficits outlined in this book will quickly exceed local resources. Indeed, as Juffras and Sawhill show in Chapter 13, states and local governments may already be reaching their limits in responding to these challenges on their own. Without some degree of federal assistance, the nation's ability to remain competitive could be severely jeopardized.

In the third place, while many state and local governments have moved actively into the human capital field, some have not. The result is a growing degree of inequality in the capacity of people in different parts of the country to take part in the economic changes taking place around them. The inner city poor in almost all of our states have been particularly disadvantaged as a consequence, in part because of the unavailability of resources and in part because of political priorities that direct resources to other purposes. Only the federal government has the ability to ensure a degree of equity in the way the nation faces up to its human capital challenges.

Finally, the resolution of the nation's economic competitiveness problems will ultimately require much better integration of macro- and micro-economic policies. Yet the macroeconomic policies are the domain of the national government, and are likely to remain so. Establishing a clear national priority for human capital policies within a broader approach to economic competitiveness thus becomes an essential step toward ensuring policy coherence.

While federal involvement in the human capital field is necessary, however, such involvement must differ in content and style from the way the federal government has approached this and related fields in the recent past. In particular, rather than relying on command and control mechanisms, the federal government could usefully borrow from the approach that has seemed to work well at the state and local level. That approach has acknowledged the close link between human capital investment and economic development and recognized the need to mobilize and enlist a wide assortment of actors—from different levels of government and from both the public and private sectors. In other words, federal leadership must be adapted to the reality of extensive involvement of state and local governments and the private sector and structured accordingly. More specifically, federal involvement could take seven principal forms.

Articulating a National Strategy

First, the federal government is needed for the articulation of a national strategy for human capital investment of the kind described above.

Each of the priorities listed under each of the three elements that determine the productive performance and competitiveness of the work force will require detailed consideration of numerous policy choices. It is the task of national leadership—the federal government working in tandem with business, labor, state and local leaders, and other civic groups—to determine how and by whom each of these important issues can best be addressed, the relative priority among them, and how they fit together. Attempting to deal with each issue on a piecemeal basis, without a strategy or framework for comparing the relative importance and relationship of priorities to one another, is likely to produce both waste and missed opportunities.

Educational reform clearly should be one of the key parts of that strategy. But it is only one of a number of issues that require attention. And if educational reform is to be successful, it must be undertaken in the context of reforms in related areas. The establishment of goals for education, moreover, is likely to be a more challenging task than is generally recognized.[14]

Recasting Federal Human Resource Policy

The federal government should reexamine the array of existing federal human resource policies to determine their impact on human capital investment. Most federal policies were adopted with little attention to their economic impact and their impact on the ability of the American worker to compete in the global economy. They need now to be reexamined from that perspective.

In 1988, the federal government accounted for nearly 80 percent of the $557.6 billion in government transfer payments to individuals, for such programs as Social Security, Medicare and Medicaid, and welfare (*Economic Report of the President* 1989).[15] These programs are not generally associated with human capital investment, but they represent a large part of the national budget that goes for human services, and in many instances they are or could be important contributors to improving human capital. Many of these programs are administered by state and local governments, which also play an increasingly important role in financing some of them.

Special attention should be given to assuring that the $557 billion in federal expenditures for individuals helps to maximize, and at least does not impede, work force effectiveness, so that "safety nets" are turned into "ladders" of upward mobility (Friedman 1988). The example of welfare is a case in point. Progress has been made at the state and local levels in revising conventional welfare programs to help recipients find and keep employment. For example, California's innovative welfare program Greater Avenues for Independence (GAIN) requires welfare recipients to participate in training, in remedial education, or in other efforts that will lead to employment. Massachusetts's Education and Training (E. T.) Choices program follows a similar formula, although participation in it is not mandatory for welfare recipients as in the GAIN program in California. Both programs provide other supports, such as child care, to participants who are attempting to enter or reenter the work force.

The Family Support Act of 1988 was intended to incorporate and extend the state experience with welfare-to-work programs. But the preliminary regulations proposed by the U.S. Department of Health and Human Services to administer the act threatened to place even more severe restrictions on the state administration of federal welfare programs. Rather than facilitating further successful integration of welfare and employment and training programs, they could have undermined the progress to date. Reaction from state and local offices persuaded federal officials to amend the proposed regulations.

Promoting Educational Reform

The federal government should take the lead in encouraging the restructuring and improvement of education in the United States. The educational reform movement of the past 10 years has engendered a great deal of activity, much of it imaginative. But the results have been minimal. The current system of education encompasses a vast array of institutions ranging from preschool through continuing adult education. While this diversity can be a strength, it can also be a weakness—as recent evidence suggests—in the absence of a common vision, national goals, and some semblance of order and assurance of accountability.

The president took an important first step in calling the Education Summit with the governors and agreeing to set national goals, increase federal flexibility in legislation and regulation in exchange for greater accountability, and restructure the school system. But unless the general areas of agreement at the summit are followed with specific and meaningful actions, not only will there be little result, but the educational reform effort could be dealt a setback by the perception that the federal government is not serious in its commitment.

Federal leadership is also needed to broaden the concept of education so that it encompasses preschool and continuing adult education, as well as the conventional primary, secondary, and postsecondary institutions. Here again, the summit made progress, expanding the boundaries of education to include early childhood and work force literacy. But the enumeration of concerns must now be followed up with a reconceptualization of the nation's educational system and a specification of the actions required to restructure and improve the performance in each element, and to link related elements where that is required. There is an urgent need to provide all children with an education that will build competence in mathematics, science, and technology.[16]

Over the next six years, nearly one-half of the nation's 2.2 million public school teachers are expected to retire. To replace these teachers would require that over 20 percent of all college graduates become public school teachers. The states have a major role to play here, since most public school teachers are educated in state-run colleges and universities. However, federal support could play a major role in assuring that the next generation of teachers in the nation's schools are adequately prepared and more representative of the diversity of students.

Supporting the Disadvantaged

The federal government should expand its historical role of supporting the disadvantaged in their efforts to prepare for and secure productive employment. For children at risk, this requires an expansion of early childhood programs. The Committee for Economic Development (1985, 1987a) places early childhood education for the disadvantaged at the top of the national agenda and estimates that it would cost about $11 billion per year to assure that most at-risk students began their formal schooling with adequate preparation (Phypers 1988).

The American Agenda, a private project co-chaired by former presidents Ford and Carter, recommended increased federal funding at the rate of $2 billion per year for eight years to cover eligible children under prenatal care, Head Start, the Special Supplemental Food Program for Women, Infants, and Children (WIC), and compensatory education programs. Many of these programs currently service only a fraction—less than 20 percent in some instances—of eligible children. All depend heavily on state and local funding and administration, but without federal support they will not begin to meet their goals.

There is also a need to clarify existing national policy, such as the Chapter 1 definition of "educationally deprived students," as well as to fund additional grants for schools with the highest concentrations of poverty, so that those children in greatest jeopardy can be better targeted (U.S. Congress 1987b).

Developing Knowledge about Human Capital

There is a need for a strong federal role in the development, collection, and dissemination of knowledge regarding human capital. This includes the promotion and structuring of research, experimentation, development, demonstration, assessment, evaluation, and dissemination of knowledge related to education, training, and productivity enhancement. For example, the educational technology and learning systems in use in most public schools today—including hardware, software, and methods—are outdated. But resistance to change and the lack of resources for the development and application of new approaches inhibit the use of techniques that are spreading rapidly in the private sector, others that have been developed in the armed services, and still others that have been applied successfully in a few public schools but have not been widely replicated. Each state also needs more reliable information on the successes and failures of programs in other states. A major federal effort of program evaluation and information dissemination would cost little in national investment terms but could have enormous payoff by permitting states and localities to rapidly adopt the best practices of their peers.[17]

The federal government should promote more disciplined experimentation at the state, local, and regional levels. The public education system has a tendency to alternate between rigidly holding fast to outmoded practices, on the one hand, and adopting wholesale untested new theories of educational reform on the other. There is a need for structured innovation—at the school, district, and state levels—to test new approaches, build on those that are promising, and reject those that prove wanting. A similar approach to experimentation is needed in other areas of human resources, and in community wide efforts to integrate various facets of the human capital system such as health care, education, training, and social services.

The federal government should also expand its labor market information services to provide the kind of detailed and market-segmented information that would be useful to human capital investment planners and policymakers in regional markets. One study found that unemployed steelworkers in Youngstown, Ohio, who participated in public training programs actually fared worse in finding new jobs than those who did not participate, because the programs were using outdated information (Dyer 1987: 307). The reauthorization of the Carl T. Perkins Act, which intended to establish an occupational information system geared toward the needs of work force training programs, presents an opportunity to reassess labor market information needs.

Improving the Federal Policymaking Process

The federal government should revamp its current policymaking machinery, which is ill equipped for the task described above. Ideally, a new institutional structure for human capital investment strategy should be developed within the context of a new institutional structure for national economic strategy that accounts for the interdependence of policies regarding global issues, national security, science and technology, human resources, industry-specific issues, and traditional macroeconomic questions.[18] But even in the absence of a more integrative national economic policymaking process, a more comprehensive policymaking process for human capital investment strategy should still be created. There are several options.

Policy integration should begin at the top, with the articulation of national goals and investment strategy by the president. At a minimum, the White House Domestic Policy Council should play a prominent and ongoing role in this task.

Another option would be to establish a council on human investment to develop a national strategy, advise the president on human resource issues, and coordinate the implementation of strategy. The council might be composed of the Secretaries of Education, Labor, Health and Human Services, Housing and Urban Development, and Commerce, as well as representatives from business, labor, private education, and state and local governments.

A third option would be to structure such a council along the lines of the Council of Economic Advisers or the Council on Environmental Quality. It would then consist of experts on human capital investment, including people with state and local government, as well as private-sector, experience.[19]

A policy-integrating mechanism, such as a joint committee on human investment strategy, or a bipartisan caucus or task force, should also be established in the Congress.

Providing Intergovernmental Leadership

Finally, the federal government should take principal responsibility for assuring that the intergovernmental system is working optimally to facilitate effective human capital investment. That task should begin with a recognition of the impressive strides that have been made by states and localities in recent years, and of the major role that state and local governments can play in the future.

Toward "Economic Federalism"

The basic thrust of the argument developed here is thus that American federalism provides an important asset for the operation of a more effective human capital investment strategy. At the same time, to live up to its potential, the federal system will have to be altered in crucial ways to acknowledge both the importance of federal leadership and the necessity of active state and local involvement. In a sense, the argument of this chapter has been that two important changes are needed in the American federal system to take on the challenge posed by the intersection of human capital and economic policies—one conceptual and the other organizational. In this section I summarize and illustrate these two kinds of changes.

The Conceptual Challenge

In the past, such terms as "marble cake federalism," "picket fence federalism" and "dual federalism," have characterized the distribution of functions among levels of government. Various iterations of "new federalism" have connoted the desire by a succession of presidents to shift power from the federal to the state and local levels. John Shannon, a former executive director of the Advisory Commission on Intergovernmental Relations, has characterized the recent struggles of state and local government in adjusting to federal cutbacks as "fend-for-yourself federalism."

The need today is for "economic" or "investment federalism" which would mobilize the federal system in the interest of developing the nation's capacities, both to deal with an array of domestic needs and to ensure that the United States remains competitive in the new global economy. Mobilizing the federal system for investment will require action along two parallel and mutually reinforcing tracks: *cooperation* to bring the interrelated features of the system into harmony; and *competition* to stimulate each governmental jurisdiction and region to develop its own potential.

The cooperation track might be characterized as "partnership federalism" or "team federalism." Its purpose would be to coordinate and harmonize mutually supportive activities such as education, training, welfare, health care, and related social services. The competition track might be characterized as "challenge federalism" (National Civic League 1988). Greater cooperation to achieve mutual goals does not preclude competition among jurisdictions to bring out the best in each. Appropriately structured, competition among states and localities can tap positive sources of energy to correct deficiencies, develop potential, and sharpen their competitive edge.

The cooperative and competitive features of federalism should go hand in hand. The former would work to establish a base of support for the poorer jurisdictions, protect the disadvantaged, and coordinate mutually dependent programs. The latter would encourage jurisdictions to compete by developing their own potential. Cooperative and competitive approaches could be blended through such mechanisms as the "base-plus formula" provided in welfare reform legislation, which establishes a base line funding for each state but makes additional federal funds available on a sliding sale for those states that expand their education and training activities for welfare recipients. The "challenge grant" is similar in concept, except that it might limit federal awards to states that won a competition for new or improved programs to strengthen human resources (National Civic League 1988).

As the national partner in the intergovernmental system, the federal government should look to the states to learn ways in which it can act as a system arranger, a catalyst, a broker, a partner, and a wholesaler to assure that public investments at the margin are effective in encouraging or helping those other institutions (e.g., state and local government and businesses) to increase their own investment, or to improve the return on the investments they are already making. This does not mean simply "scaling up" successful state government programs to the national level on the assumption that what worked at the state level can be applied nationally. Many of the state programs have been successful precisely because they were carried out at the state level, where they could be tailored to specific regional and local needs. Successful efforts in one state may not be as effective in other states, nor will they necessarily work on a national level. The key will be to extract the principles on which successful state programs are based, and to apply them judiciously at the national level. Federal attention should also focus on the critical points of intersection in the administration of human resource programs. For example, despite some significant efforts at the federal level to coordinate job training, welfare, economic development, health care, and education programs, there remain serious gaps and overlaps among the federal Departments of Labor, Education, and Health and Human Services in the administration of interrelated programs such as those dealing with preschool education, child care, and work force literacy.[20]

Integrating Delivery Systems

A second step to improving the federal system is to focus on the practical task of integrating delivery systems that involve actors at different levels of government. This is important in its own right, since the most skillful formulation and coordination of policies will mean little if programs are not delivered to the people who need them. However, a focus on delivery systems can also be a practical way of forcing attention to the broader problems of policy in a political and governmental system that is rarely inclined to take a broad and holistic view of public policy. Delivery systems for employment and training offer a case in point.

The experience to date—both in the United States and abroad—suggests that effective human investment systems have several important features. They are broadly conceived to include education, training, placement, mobility, productivity, and support services. They are locally or regionally based, with local coordinating councils responsible for tying together related programs—within a single local government jurisdiction, between the public and private sectors, among neighboring jurisdictions in the same region, and among the different levels of government—so that those programs are tailored to local needs and capacities. Regional policy is developed through a broadly conceived human investment council. And government works with business, labor, and education to establish goals and education standards and to encourage state, local, and private participants to develop flexible programs tailored to the needs of their region.[21]

Some states are attempting to develop the Private Industry Councils (PICs) into more broadly based human investment councils. The principal federal job training program, the Job Training Partnership Act (JTPA) of 1982, targets the disadvantaged and thus addresses only a very small fraction of the total human capital investment need in the United States. Moreover, present funding permits the JTPA system to serve only about 5 percent of the eligible population. However, in the years since its inception, the JTPA delivery system has become a focus in some communities for integrating several elements into a progressively broader "work force investment" system.

The JTPA legislation redirected federal jobs programs for the chronically unemployed away from public employment—which had been the principal target of its forerunner, the Comprehensive Employment and Training Act (CETA)—and toward private-sector jobs. It also gave principal responsibility and wide latitude for program administration to state and local governments. To reflect the emphasis on private-sector jobs and local responsibility, JTPA placed the principal administrative authority in local Private Industry Councils (PICs).[22] The PICs typically include representatives from an array of both public and private entities that are involved in work force development: business, organized labor, education, economic development agencies, the employment service, welfare agencies, and community organizations. They are thus in a position both to develop consensus on goals, and to act as a bridge to coordinate diverse but related work force development programs.

The PICs operate within a Service Delivery Area which encompasses one or more local jurisdictions (usually counties) with a combined population of at least 200,000. Thus, there may be more than one PIC and one Service Delivery Area in a given metropolitan area, a source of fragmentation in several labor markets. In each Service Delivery Area, the PIC designates a service provider, such as a nonprofit organization or community college.

While the PICs are closely associated with the JTPA programs, they are not precluded from administering other programs. Maryland, for example, sees the PIC system as the base for a broader "work force investment system"; the state's welfare-to-work program (Project Independence) and drop out prevention program (Maryland's Tomorrow) are both administered through the PICs, together with the JTPA program. Massachusetts has given its PICs an even broader role, redesignating them "Regional Employment Boards" and giving them oversight responsibility for aspects of vocational education, community colleges, adult basic education, entry-level training (provided by the Bay State Skills Corporation), target assistance for refugees, and training and educational services provided by public housing authorities.

The JTPA legislation also created state job training coordinating councils (SJTCs) to oversee the program at the state level. In some states, the SJTCs have widened their purview to include a broader range of training programs, including vocational education, welfare-to-work programs, rehabilitation services, and postsecondary institutions. For example, Maryland's SJTC, called the Governor's Employment and Training Council, was responsible for initiating the "work force investment" concept that gives the local PICs responsibility for welfare-to-work and drop out prevention programs. New Jersey is reconstituting its SJTC as a State Employment and Training Commission charged with general responsibility for work force training in the state. Other states, however, have maintained a narrow focus for the SJTCs or have otherwise treated them as perfunctory federal requirements, and hence they have been of little value.

No state to date has integrated education fully into work force development, in part because the public education system appears to be too big and too powerful to be treated in the same way as other parties involved in work force investment (although Maryland in its drop out prevention program, Maryland's Tomorrow, has made the education systems and the employment and training systems full partners, with joint responsibility for implementation and outcome). It is critical to get educators and trainers to see themselves as a team attempting to assist the same constituency (some 40 percent of JTPA funds are currently allocated to "youth" under title IIIA). It would be a major improvement if educators would accept their responsibility and not see JTPA as a dumping ground for "bad kids," and if JTPA officials would stop viewing educators as having failed in their chance with students.

State job training coordinating councils could be developed into far more effective tools for integrating work force development programs, especially if they were integrated with the educational system. Recent federal legislation has moved in the right direction by giving the councils greater responsibility for welfare-to-work and dislocated worker programs, but greater flexibility is still needed (NAB 1988: 12).

The PIC system is far from perfect. In fact, it has flaws built into its design. It has been implemented with varying degrees of effectiveness by different states and localities. And it is still relatively new and maturing, even in those places where it has been effectively handled. But for all its deficiencies, the system has demonstrated some important strengths. It permits both comprehensiveness and flexibility, and it is adaptable. It is grounded locally and—to the extent practicable—organized on the basis of regional labor and economic markets. It integrates related public and private programs. It recognizes the key role played by the state in linking programs on a geographical basis. And it uses the fiscal and administrative powers of the federal government in an attempt to leverage other resources and to get key actors with related interests to work together in a fashion tailored to the particular needs of their regions. As a base on which to build more effective work force development programs, either for the disadvantaged or for the work force more generally, it also offers the advantage of being on the ground and functioning, with an increasing number of people familiar with it and committed to making it work.[23]

There are also potentially serious drawbacks to using PICs or other program-specific councils as a base for developing a more comprehensive approach to human investment. Merely adding programs to such an agency's responsibilities without restructuring and integrating them can be administratively burdensome, especially if each new program maintains its individual mission, financing stream, reporting requirements, and oversight structure. For example, Maryland's attempt to consolidate three programs in the PICs—welfare-to-work, drop out prevention, and job training—has added substantially to the overhead needed to meet the administrative reporting requirements of each program. Existing boards, moreover, are likely to retain the identification of their original missions; some PICs, for example, may find it very difficult not only to expand their interest and capacity beyond training, but also to encompass more numerous classes of employees (let alone the work force as a whole) when their original mission was to assist only disadvantaged workers.

While the efforts of some states and the experience with some federal legislation suggest potential, it will be a challenge for the federal system to overcome the accumulation of fragmented programs, the culture of narrowly conceived responsibilities, and old-fashioned turf battles to reshape and integrate delivery systems to fit local needs.

Conclusion

The intergovernmental dimension of human capital investment involves more than simply determining an appropriate distribution of responsibilities among the federal, state, and local levels. It poses a major challenge of problem conceptualization, political bargaining, system design, and practical administration.

Over the past decade, state and local governments have been actively experimenting with more productive ways of developing their human resource potential, and have laid both the conceptual and practical bases for a major national leap forward. Today, they continue their efforts and constitute a base for a major national effort. But further accomplishment now depends heavily on national action—not to supplant the initiatives of states and localities, but to supplement and support them. With effective federal leadership, the apparent complications could be minimized, and the federal system could be turned to maximum advantage as a unique American asset for developing a globally competitive work force.

Notes

1. Agricultural experiment stations were established in the Hatch Act of 1887, and the agriculture extension service was formally created by the Smith-Lever Act of 1914.

2. During this period such programs as the Job Service, Aid to Dependent Children (later Aid to Families with Dependent Children or AFDC), Social Security, Unemployment Insurance, and the National Labor Relations Act were created to enhance economic security.

3. These federal initiatives included the GI Bill of Rights of 1944, the National Defense Education Act of 1958, the Manpower Development and Training Act of 1962, the Civil Rights Act and the Economic Opportunity Act of 1964, the Higher Education Act of 1965, and Medicare and Medicaid.

4. Levitan, Mangum, and Pines (1989) provide a useful inventory of most of these programs.

5. Federal grants to state and local governments peaked in 1978 both in real terms and as a proportion of total state-local revenue, and have been declining ever since. The federal contribution to state-local revenues declined from 18.7 percent in 1978 to 13.6 percent in 1987. While federal aid increased in nominal terms during that period from $70 billion to $115 billion (equivalent to a rate of 5.7 percent per year), state and local revenues grew at the more rapid rate of 8.5 percent per year.

6. At the winter meeting of the National Governors' Association in 1989 the governors adopted policy changes that dealt with child care, health care for the uninsured, vocational and technical education, early childhood development, new technologies for the classroom, mental health services, and federally subsidized supplemental food programs for women, infants, and children (WIC).

7. In 1981, as part of his "New Federalism" package, President Reagan proposed a "swap" of government services with the states, in which the federal government was to assume responsibility for health programs while the states assumed responsibility for welfare programs and many other programs in such areas as economic development and transportation. The proposal faltered when the states concluded that the cost would be unfavorable to them.

8. It is worth recalling that when the concept of human capital, as it was developed in modern times by Schultz (1959, 1961, 1963) and Becker (1960), was first applied in the developing countries in the 1960s, it produced mixed results. Investment was shifted from physical capital toward human capital, and to education in particular. This had the positive result of increasing general educational levels and the pool of more highly educated people. However, excessive faith in "manpower planning" that failed to adequately account for the demand side of the labor market also produced serious shortages in some occupations

and surpluses in others. Moreover, many students who received education that did not prepare them for any occupation became the source of discontent. As one analyst noted at the time, "There is a tendency to talk of the 'needs' for development as if they were quite independent of the actual structure of job opportunities in the economy. . . . Cumulative errors in the projections of a whole range of manpower needs can ultimately add up to an alarming misallocation of scarce resources" (Foster 1966 1: 411).

9. State and local governments also have significant potential influence on private sector investment through the management of state and local pension funds, which are currently valued at $600 billion. Private pension funds are valued at $1.2 trillion. The state of California alone manages $130 billion in public pension money, the state of New York $39 billion, and New York City $33 billion. These institutional investors have enormous potential influence on the investment strategies, management, and governance of corporations. The public fund managers by and large have been more inclined than private pension funds to invest for the long term, and a recent ruling by the Department of Labor permits them even wider latitude to do so under the "prudent investor" provisions of the Employment Retirement Income Security Act (ERISA). Some states are setting aside pools of their pension funds for higher risk investments geared toward economic development in these states; for example, Michigan's 5-percent set-aside for venture-capital investment created a pool of some $400 million.

10. Local government has no explicit standing in the U.S. Constitution, which gives to states the exclusive right to establish political "subdivisions." The principal responsibility for education traditionally has been delegated by the states to their local governments.

11. Successful private-sector initiatives also have been tailored to the particular conditions of regional labor markets. For example, efforts by TRW and General Electric to work with small businesses to train machinists and tool and die makers were centered in the Cincinnati area. In the "employer 5 percent solution," employers agreed to hire one disadvantaged young person for every 20 workers; the Urban Affairs Partnership sponsored such a program in Philadelphia and was able to place 1,000 disadvantaged youth in 18 months.

12. Some analysts, such as Robert Reich (1984), argue that the federal government is already deeply involved in microeconomic management in such areas as science and technology and defense, but simply does not acknowledge it. Even such a generally conservative economist as Herbert Stein maintains that federal economic and budget policy should take a broader view of the allocation of all national resources, not for the purpose of detailed direction of economic activity, but to more intelligently identify the true impacts on and needs of that part of the economy that is or inevitably will be influenced by government (Stein 1988). For example, the debate over Social Security focuses on how payroll tax and benefit levels will affect the availability of funds for retirees in 20 years. A far more important question is whether today's children are being properly educated to become productive employees in an economy capable of supporting future retirees.

13. The National Civic League has developed a "civic index" that defines the elements of "civic infrastructure." They are citizen participation, community leadership, government performance, volunteerism and philanthropy, intergroup

relations, civic education, community information sharing, capacity for cooperation and consensus building, community vision and pride, and intercommunity cooperation.

14. For example, there is general agreement on the need to strengthen science education, but substantial disagreement on how it should be improved and by whom. In a position paper published in *Science* magazine in October 1988, during the presidential campaign, then Vice-President Bush argued that the federal government should "consider helping states set up schools that would give our most gifted and talented students the chance to learn as much science and math as their abilities will allow," and that such "schools of excellence" be used to improve the skills of science and math teachers. (The Reagan administration eliminated National Science Foundation funding for science education in 1984.) However, the National Science Teachers Association disagreed, arguing instead that if the United States is to compete internationally, it must "broaden the pool" rather than "skim the cream" of science and math capacity among the population.

15. The federal government has been mandating increased state responsibility for entitlements. For example, states now pay half the cost of Medicaid, and this amount has grown from $2.7 billion, or 3 percent of state expenditures in 1969, to a projected $36 billion, or 11 percent of state expenditures in 1990 (Peirce 1989).

16. The National Center on Education and the Economy (1989) has outlined a federal leadership strategy in *To Secure Our Future: The Federal Role in Education.*

17. The Omnibus Trade and Competitiveness Act of 1988 provided for the creation, in the Department of Commerce, of a clearinghouse on state and local initiatives on productivity, technology, and innovation. It is not clear at this point whether or to what extent the clearinghouse will cover human capital investment issues.

18. The Omnibus Trade and Competitiveness Act of 1988 provides for a Competitiveness Policy Council consisting of 12 members from business, labor, government, and academia appointed in equal numbers by the president, the Senate, and the House of Representatives. The council is to act as an advisory body to identify economic problems affecting U.S. competitiveness and recommend coordinated, long-term strategies for dealing with those problems. It remains to be seen what effect such a council may have.

19. Any of the above options could build on the work of the National Commission for Employment Policy in its efforts to strengthen federal work force development policies.

20. The Council of Chief State School Officers (1987) has proposed a Model State Statute to Provide Educational Entitlements for At-Risk Students, which among other measures, calls for preschool child development programs to be made available to three and four year-old children who are at risk for educational failure, and would establish an entitlement to enable young people who have dropped out of school and are beyond the age of compulsory attendance (generally those 16 through 20) to re-enroll in school.

21. This emerging pattern bears similarity to the systems used in Germany and Sweden. In both countries, government, business, and labor cooperate at all

levels: national, regional, and local. Both countries integrate training and income support for the unemployed, a strong job service with mandatory job listings, and sufficient funding for one employment and training professional for every 500 workers (Spring 1987: 162). In Sweden, a regional board comprised of government, business, and labor representatives coordinates an array of programs—training, wage subsidies, retirement, welfare, job creation, relocation assistance—according to local needs and changing conditions (Nilsson 1988). During periods of labor shortage, the emphasis is on training to match worker skills with business labor needs. During economic downturns, the focus shifts to job retention, creation, and attraction, and adjustment assistance for workers in shifting to new vocations or locations.

22. It is important to distinguish between the JTPA program and the PIC delivery system through which it is administered. Proposals to "tighten" the JTPA program in order to prevent the "creaming" of the most job-ready candidates for employment and focus on the genuinely hard-to-employ should not be equated with restricting the role of the PIC delivery system. The PIC system could still serve as the base for a broadened "work force investment" system, even if the JTPA program were narrowed.

23. A 1987 survey by the National Alliance of Business (1988) gave JTPA generally high marks while highlighting some of the barriers to further improvement, including turf battles, an encumbered bureaucracy in the employment service, inflexibility and lack of performance orientation in vocational educational training, and lack of encouragement by welfare agencies for their clients to move into the work force.

References
American Society for Training and Development (1988a). *Measurement of Training Fact Sheet*. Alexandria, Va.: American Society for Training and Development.
——— (1988b). *The Organization and Strategic Role of Training Fact Sheet*. Alexandria, Va.: American Society for Training and Development.
Becker, Gary S. (1960). *Human Capital*. Princeton, N.J.: Princeton University Press.
Carnevale, Anthony P., Leila J. Gainer, and Ann S. Meltzer (1988). *Workplace Basics: The Skills Employers Want*. Washington, D.C.: American Society for Training and Development and U.S. Department of Labor.
Center for Education Statistics (1987). *Digest of Education Statistics*. Washington, D.C.: U.S. Government Printing Office.
Committee for Economic Development, Research and Policy Committee (1985). *Investing in Our Children: Business and the Public Schools*. New York: Committee for Economic Development.
——— (1986). *Leadership for Dynamic State Economies*. New York: Committee for Economic Development.
——— (1987a). *Children in Need: Investment Strategies for the Educationally Disadvantaged*. New York: Committee for Economic Development.
——— (1987b). *Work and Change: Labor Market Adjustment Policies in a Competitive World*. New York: Committee for Economic Development.
Council of Chief State School Officers (1987). *Elements of a Model State Statute*

to Provide Educational Entitlements for At-Risk Students. Washington, D.C. Published in-house by Council of Chief State School Officers.

Domenici, Pete V. (1988). "The Poor in the Reagan Years: . . . And a Great Misconception." *Washington Post,* November 11, p. C7.

Dyer, Barbara (1987). *Federal and State Roles in Economic Development.* Washington, D.C.: Council of State Planning and Policy Agencies.

Economic Report of the President (1989). Washington, D.C.: U.S. Government Printing Office.

Executive Office of the President (1989). *Historical Tables, Budget of the United States Government, 1990.* Washington, D.C.: U.S. Government Printing Office.

Fosler, R. Scott, ed. (1988a). *The New Economic Role of American States.* New York: Oxford University Press.

———. (1988b). *The Political and Institutional Implications of Demographic Change.* Washington, D.C.: Committee for Economic Development.

——— (1988c). *State Economic Development and the Disadvantaged.* Cleveland: Council of State Community Affairs Agencies (COSCAA), June 22.

——— (1989). *Demography and Jobs in Southern California.* Washington, D.C.: Committee for Economic Development.

Foster, P. J. (1966). "The Vocational School Fallacy in Development Planning." In Blaug, ed., *Economics of Education.* Oxford: Pergamon Press.

Friedman, Robert (1988). *The Safety Net as Ladder.* Washington, D.C.: Council of State Policy and Planning Agencies.

Gray, William H. (1988). "The Poor In the Reagan Years: A Great Divide . . ." *Washington Post,* November 11, p. C7.

Grinker, Nathan J. (1988). *The Limits of Social Policy.* Cambridge, Mass.: Harvard University Press.

Johnston, William B., and Arnold H. Packer (1987). *Workforce 2000: Work and Workers for the Twenty-first Century.* Indianapolis, Ind.: Hudson Institute.

Levitan, Sar A., Garth L. Mangum, and Marion W. Pines (1989). *A Proper Inheritance: Investing in the Self-sufficiency of Poor Families.* Washington, D.C.: Center for Social Policy Studies, George Washington University.

McKernan, John R. (1988). "An Educated and Skilled Workforce." Augusta, Me: Government of Maine.

National Alliance of Business (1985). *Shaping Tomorrow's Workforce.* Washington, D.C.: National Alliance of Business.

National Center on Education and the Economy (1989). *To Secure Our Future: The Federal Role in Education.* Rochester: National Center on Education and the Economy.

National Civic League (1988). *Sustaining Civic Momentum: Prospects for a Challenge Federalism in the 1990s.* Denver: National Civic League.

National Commission for Full Employment (1989). *Report from the Leadership Roundtable.* Washington, D.C.: National Commission for Full Employment.

National Governors' Association (1986). *A Time for Results.* Washington, D.C.: National Governors' Association.

Nilsson, Jan-Evert (1988). *Managing the Spatial Impacts of Industrial Change: The Swedish Case.* Stockholm: Swedish Export Group on Regional Studies, Ministry of Industry.

Osborne, David (1988). *Laboratories of Democracy*. Boston: Harvard Business School Press.

Peirce, Neal (1989). "Many States Are Playing Budget Roulette." *Arizona Republic* (Phoenix), March 6.

Phypers, Dean (1988). "Federal Budgetary Views." Presentation to the National Economic Commission. Washington, D.C.: Committee for Economic Development.

Regional Institute of Southern California, Southern California Association of Governments, and the Roosevelt Center for American Policy Studies (1989). "Recommendations for ETP Policy in the SCAG Region." Prepared for the California Employment Training Panel, Los Angeles.

Reich, Robert B. (1984). *The Next American Frontier*. New York: Penguin Books.

Roberts, Brandon (1988). *States and Economic Development: Expanding Opportunities for Employment and Self-Sufficiency*. Washington, D.C.: Council of State Community Affairs Agencies (COSCAA).

Schultz, T. W. (1961). "Capital Formation by Education." *Journal of Political Economy*, 61, no. 4.

———— (1963). *The Economic Value of Education*. New York: Columbia University Press.

Spring, William (1987). Prepared statement before the U.S. House of Representatives, Committee on Education and Labor, Washington, D.C.

Stein, Herbert (1988). *Governing the $5 Trillion Economy*. New York: Oxford University Press.

Swedish Institute (1986). *Swedish Regional Policy*. Stockholm: Swedish Institute.

U.S. Congress. House. Committee on Education and Labor (1987a). *Education and Training for American Competitiveness*. Hearings held in Washington, D.C., on February 10, 11, 19, 25, and March 4, 11, and 12, 1987.

———— (1987b) Statement of John Brademas as President, New York University, February 10.

———— (1987c) Statement of David W. Hornbeck as president of the Council of Chief State School Officers and Superintendent of Schools, State of Maryland, February 10.

U.S. Departments of Labor, Education, and Commerce (1988). *Building a Quality Workforce*. Washington, D.C.: U.S. Government Printing Office.

12

Financing Human Capital Investment

Jason Juffras and Isabel V. Sawhill

As previous chapters in this book have shown, the resources embodied in people will be crucial to the nation's ability to meet the challenges of the future. We need workers with the knowledge and adaptability to drive the growth of an economy increasingly dependent on information and problem solving rather than land and capital. We also need citizens who have the basic skills and judgment to act competently as parents, as members of communities, and as participants in the political process. In short, investments in human capital—defined here as spending on education, training, health care, and other activities that enhance individuals' skills and capacities—are vital to public welfare.[1]

The public in recent years has increasingly recognized the importance of human resource investments. The most prominent example of this concern is the educational reform movement that gathered momentum during the 1980s, leading state legislatures to increase teachers' salaries, raise graduation standards, and mandate basic skills testing. Other human resource issues, such as training for welfare recipients and child health care, have commanded public attention as well, resulting in new policies. Yet if we are to continue transforming a growing national consensus for more human capital investment into policy, the nation will need to commit sufficient money to the task.

Recent federal policy debates illustrate how fiscal constraints limit the development of effective human resource policies. For example, the 1988 Family Support Act was widely hailed as landmark legislation that would restructure the public assistance system to educate and train welfare recipients. But the funding was insufficient to enroll more than a small percentage of those eligible for such programs, even though the programs have generally been found to be cost-effective (Gueron 1986:

19). Many policymakers also agree that prenatal, infant, and child health care represent sound investments, but the federal government has broadened Medicaid coverage for pregnant women and children only incrementally in recent years because of the high costs involved. Finally, evidence that preschool education greatly benefits poor children has convinced many observers that the federal Head Start program, which serves only one of every five eligible children, should be expanded. However, as Congress reviewed legislation late in the 1980s to increase Head Start funding, lawmakers from both political parties agreed that the federal budget deficit permitted only a modest addition.

These examples suggest that the nation is currently unable to fund human capital investments at a level that reflects their importance to the economic and social health of the nation. To confront this problem, we must examine the government's role in financing human capital investments. Accordingly, this chapter first examines why *private* investments in education, training, and other forms of human capital are likely to fall short of socially desirable levels. It then reviews past trends in *public* support for human resource investments. Finally, and most importantly, it discusses current fiscal constraints that inhibit new public spending on human capital programs—especially at the federal level—and considers some innovative financing strategies that could ease these budgetary limits.

Government Intervention in Human Capital Markets: Rationale, Trends, and Implications

The Rationale for Government Intervention

Economic theory postulates that under certain conditions the independent actions of consumers and producers seeking to maximize their welfare will yield socially desirable outcomes. But in human capital markets these conditions are not met. Rather, there are a number of well-known arguments for public intervention to improve the functioning of the market.

First, society as a whole gains from having an educated citizenry, for reasons more far-reaching than the private benefits that education brings. Educated people make better consumers, better parents, better voters, and better members of their communities. Second, a number of impediments tend to interfere with the functioning of human capital markets unless public intervention occurs. For instance, the mobility of labor leads to underinvestment in training. Firms may underinvest in training because they fear that employees will leave, preventing the firm from reaping the full benefit of any investment. At the same time, individuals will be reluctant to pay fully for training that might not be useful in another job. Thus both the employer and the worker will tend to devote insufficient sums to training because the payoff is uncertain.

Another impediment to the functioning of human capital markets is the relative unavailability of credit. Credit markets for human capital investment are not well developed, partly because the loans are not used to purchase tangible assets that can serve as collateral.[2] Even if credit or another source of money is available, education and training involve a considerable amount of risk that discourages such investments. For example, it is difficult for an individual to predict the value of education, since its benefits will accrue over a long period while the economy and society change.

Finally, there is the problem of imperfect information. People may not know which skills to invest in, or who provides the best education and other instruction (Bendick and Egan 1982: 38–41).

These impediments, or *inefficiencies,* in the functioning of free markets for human capital create a rationale for government intervention to ensure that society realizes the full benefits of investments in people. Besides this economic justification for government's promotion of human resource investments, a concern for equity has long motivated government policy in this area. In a society committed to equal opportunity, public investments in human capital are viewed as a way of compensating for the fact that children from different socioeconomic backgrounds do not start out with equal chances in life.

These efficiency and equity arguments for public investment in human resources may be even more powerful as the United States enters the 1990s, as noted earlier in this volume. As the growth of the nation's labor force slows to 1 percent annually during the 1990s and the skill requirements of jobs continue to rise (Johnston and Packer 1987: xix, 97–101), economic growth will depend more critically on workers' abilities and productivity. The globalization of markets for goods and the increased mobility of capital only reinforce the importance of the resources embodied in people. While investments in human capital will be important to the economy on a broad scale, they will also be important to ensure that disadvantaged groups, such as the nation's 13 million poor children or the growing numbers of people living in troubled inner-city neighborhoods, can contribute to society and share in its opportunities.

Trends in Public Investment in Human Capital

Government in the United States has long accepted the responsibility of helping to develop the capacities of people. This commitment is expressed most powerfully in the case of education. During the 1985/86 school year, federal, state, and local governments poured $197 billion into education, a sum which amounted to 73 percent of total educational expenditures during that period.[3] The public sector also makes a much smaller—but still important—investment in job training, mostly through the federal Job Training Partnership Act (JTPA). Outlays for JTPA, which are projected to be $3.8 billion during fiscal year 1989, supplement private training expenditures of a far greater magnitude. The American Society for Training and Development has estimated that training provided by businesses through formal programs costs $30 billion annually, while the informal training provided on the job represents an investment of $90 to $180 billion yearly (see Chapter 9).

While the public commitment to human capital investment is substantial, we need to assess—as background for our discussion of financing strategies later in this chapter—whether it is growing or declining. We use public investment in education and training at all levels of government as our measure of human capital investment because these are the categories of government spending with the most direct impact on productivity. While other public programs do affect people's skills and knowledge, the investment component of these programs is difficult to isolate.[4]

The Federal Role: A Commitment to Investment in the Disadvantaged Wanes during the 1980s

The federal government has a long history of commitments to human capital investments for broad segments of the population. Some of the most prominent threads in this pattern are the Morrill Acts of 1862 and 1890 encouraging the creation of agricultural and mechanical colleges; the GI Bill of 1944 providing educational vouchers to World War II veterans; and the National Defense Education Act of 1958 promoting the study of science and engineering.

With the advent of President Johnson's War on Poverty in 1964, the federal government assumed responsibility for a new national commitment to invest in the skills of the disadvantaged. Using data provided by Burtless (1986: 35), we estimate that three-quarters of total federal human capital spending between 1963 and 1985 was targeted to poor people. From an intergovernmental perspective, it can be argued that this targeting of federal human capital programs to the disadvantaged is logical; because states and localities must compete to attract or retain businesses and middle-class families, they have an incentive to keep taxes low and may neglect certain needs, including those of the disadvantaged.

Human capital programs such as Head Start, the Job Corps, and Pell grants for college students became the centerpiece of Johnson's War on Poverty because they reflected the popular view that programs for the poor should help poor people to become self-sufficient. During this period, human capital expenditures grew rapidly from a very small base,

Figure 12.1 Federal investment in human capital, 1962–89.

(Data are from Office of Management and Budget 1989a: 63–67; Office of Management and Budget, *Budget of the United States Government: Appendix*, various years; Congressional Budget Office 1982: 5; General Accounting Office 1982: 10; U.S. Department of Labor 1975: 43.

more than tripling in real terms between 1965 and 1968. During the early 1970s, the expansion of human capital programs slowed due to stagflation and disillusionment with some of the programs, but strong growth resumed again during the mid to late 1970s (Office of Management and Budget 1989a: 63–67) (Fig. 12.1).

During the 1980s, the almost continuous growth of federal human capital spending was reversed, as President Reagan secured a 21 percent real cut in outlays for human resource programs in the Omnibus Budget Reconciliation Act of 1981. As a result, such spending declined from $25.4 billion in fiscal year 1981 to $20.1 billion in fiscal year 1982. Job training programs for the disadvantaged suffered the sharpest cuts; funding declined from $7.4 billion in 1981 to $4.3 billion in 1989 (1982 dollars) or by 42 percent, as the Comprehensive Employment and Training Act was replaced by the smaller JTPA.[5] After the initial cuts in 1981, however, Congress protected most education and training programs from further reductions, leaving estimated expenditures on human capital programs for 1989 equal in real terms to those of 1982. Large federal budget deficits perpetuated this stalemate in spending throughout the 1980s.

While federal spending on education and training dipped by 21 percent in real dollars between 1981 and 1989, federal human capital in-

Figure 12.2 Human capital investment as a percentage of federal social-welfare and investment spending, 1962–89.

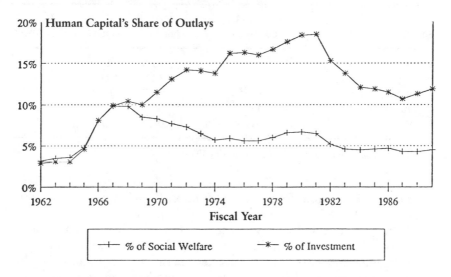

vestments declined even more steeply as a percentage of the gross national product (GNP); this ratio decreased by almost two-fifths between 1981 and 1988.[6] Human capital also represents a declining share of federal expenditures, down from 3.6 percent of total outlays in 1981 to 2.3 percent in 1989. Finally, as shown in Figure 12.2, human capital outlays have been shrinking substantially in recent years as portions of the nation's social welfare spending, which includes health care, income maintenance, education, employment services, training, social services, veterans' benefits and services, and total investment spending (the sum of the nation's investment in physical capital, including national defense, research and development, and education and training).[7]

The State and Local Role: Steady Growth in Investment in Education

As the federal government reduced its human capital investments during the 1980s, state and local governments assumed a more visible role, as Scott Fosler showed more fully in the previous chapter. The federal government was partly responsible for this shift, as its large budget deficits and cutbacks in aid to state and local government encouraged the lower levels of government to rely more on their own resources. Motivated as well by concerns about economic growth and international competitiveness, state and local governments channeled much of their energy and initiative into human capital programs, raising teachers' salaries, tightening graduation standards, and beginning drop out prevention programs. Promising initiatives were also numerous in prenatal care, par-

Table 12.1 Education Expenditures by Source of Funds and Level of Education, 1985–1986 (in billions of dollars)

Source	Elementary and Secondary Education	Higher Education	Total	% of Overall Total
Federal government	9.9	13.6	23.5	8.7
State government	73.2	32.2	105.4	39.1
Local government	65.0	2.7	67.8	25.2
Private sources	13.6	59.1	72.8	27.0
Total	161.8	107.7	269.5	100.0

Source: National Center for Education Statistics 1988: 31.

enting education, and drug abuse prevention (Committee for Economic Development 1987; National Governors' Association 1987).

While the state and local governments have clearly served as sources of ideas and innovations in domestic policy during the 1980s, their roles in financing human capital are characterized more by continuity than by change. State and local governments have long borne primary responsibility for administering and financing education. As shown in Table 12.1, state and local governments provided 64 percent of education funding during 1985/86, reflecting a contribution of $105 billion by state governments and $68 billion by local governments (National Center for Education Statistics 1988: 31). These sums represent almost all of state and local governments' investment in human capital. State and local governments continue to provide the bulk of support (85 percent in 1985/86) for elementary and secondary education, while a majority of the funding for higher education (55 percent in 1985/86) comes from private sources (National Center for Education Statistics 1988: 31).

Overall, state and local governments increased their investment in education by 40 percent in real dollar terms between 1970 and 1986.[8] But these aggregates hide as much as they tell, since financing trends differed between state and local governments and between elementary and secondary education and higher education. Furthermore, the raw figures on education spending between 1970 and 1986 are deceptive because school enrollments were changing markedly, as described below.

Total spending for education by the states grew by a healthy 72 percent in real dollar terms between 1970 and 1986. The increase in state funding was largest at the elementary and secondary level, where real expenditures rose while the school population shrank by 12 percent (National Center for Educational Statistics 1988: 10). The result was a 90-percent increase in state spending per elementary and secondary school

Figure 12.3 State per capita spending, elementary and secondary education, 1970–86.

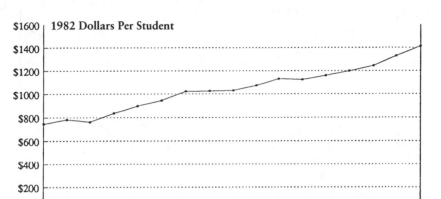

(Data calculated using information from the National Center for Education Statistics, various years.)

student during the 1970–86 period (Fig. 12.3). Meanwhile, state dollars for higher education also increased sharply, but the university population grew rapidly as well (by 32 percent), so that state funding per student between 1970 and 1986 grew by only 31 percent (Fig. 12.4).[9]

Between 1970 and 1986, total education spending by local governments grew by 8 percent in real dollar terms, a 9-percent increase, far smaller than the increases in spending by state governments. Yet on a per-student basis, the local contribution, which goes almost entirely (96 percent) to elementary and secondary education, increased by a more solid 23 percent during this period because of the enrollment decline mentioned above (Fig. 12.5). While state spending for elementary and secondary education grew much more quickly than local spending between 1970 and 1986, some of this differential can be explained by education reform plans that shift fiscal authority to state governments so that money for education is distributed more evenly among local districts.

Overall, these patterns reflect a healthy growth in real spending for education between 1970 and 1986, particularly at the elementary and secondary level. Combined state and local investment per student increased by 51 percent in elementary and secondary education during that time period and by 13 percent for higher education after adjusting for inflation. However, the trends are positive only in absolute, not in rela-

Figure 12.4   State per capita spending, 1970–86, on higher education.

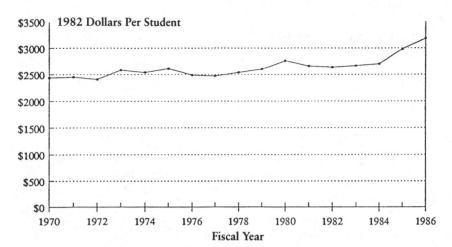

(Data calculated using information from the National Center for Education Statistics, various years.)

tive terms. Between 1970 and 1986, state and local education spending dropped slightly from 4.4 percent of the GNP to 4.1 percent.[10] Gold (1990: 18–19) has likewise found that state spending for education was slightly lower (3.2 percent) as a percentage of personal income in 1987 than in 1976 (3.33 percent). Education also declined from 40 percent of state and local general expenditures in 1970 to 35 percent in 1986.[11] Similarly, education has declined as a share of state and local social welfare outlays, from 66 percent in 1970 to 55 percent in 1986.[12]

State and local governments have also become more involved in other forms of human capital development besides elementary, secondary, and higher education: job training for disadvantaged or dislocated workers, education and training programs for welfare recipients (hereafter called "welfare-to-work" initiatives), and preschool education being among the most notable examples. However, the limited data available suggests that most of these new efforts are small, showcase programs. Innovative programs are numerous, but most state and local governments do not have the interest or the resources to mount intensive human resource programs in these areas.

In job training, for example, federal activity dwarfs that of the state and local governments. While these lower levels of government spent $5.2 billion on labor training and services in 1986 (Peters 1988: 23–25), the bulk of the money came in the form of grants from the federal government (Office of Management and Budget 1989a: 284). While at least 44 states have job training programs—many of which were initiated dur-

Figure 12.5   Local per capita spending, elementary and secondary education, 1970–86.

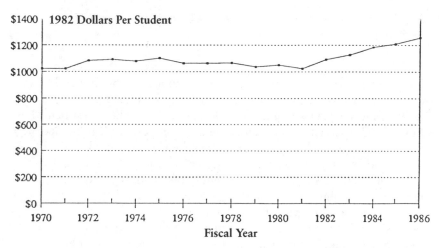

(Data calculated using information from the National Center for Education Statistics, various years.)

ing the 1980s—these are mostly pilot programs with funding ranging between $45,000 and $12 million (Ganzglass and Heidkamp 1987: iii).

State welfare-to-work and preschool education programs show a similar pattern. Welfare-to-work initiatives proliferated even before the Family Support Act of 1988 required each state to develop such a program; by 1986, 25 states operated programs providing a full array of education, training, and supportive services (Nightingale and Burbridge 1987: 74). However, the programs have been quite small; in 1986, only 4 states offered comprehensive services to a large portion of the welfare population (Nightingale and Burbridge 1987: 93). The states provided only $67 million for welfare-to-work initiatives in 1985 (General Accounting Office 1987: 40), compared to a $195 million contribution from the federal government. Similarly, the number of states offering preschool education programs increased from 8 in 1980 to 26 in 1987, but a recent survey showed that the programs served only 140,000 students in 1988, at a cost to the states approaching $200 million (Marx and Seligson 1988: 18–21). The federal Head Start preschool program is much larger, serving about 450,000 children at a cost of $1.2 billion in 1989.[13]

On the whole, although state and local governments have increased their investments in education, they appear to be facing too many other pressing responsibilities to expand their human capital investments much into other areas. The job training, welfare-to-work, and preschool education programs run by state governments are promising prototypes, but the widespread replication of these ventures remains uncertain.

Implications of Current Government Efforts to Promote Investment in People

This chapter and others in this book have argued that human capital investments are particularly critical to the modern economy and to society. Nevertheless, public investments in people have not risen substantially to meet this growing need. Federal human capital investments have fallen by 21 percent in real terms since fiscal year 1981; this decline is even sharper when human capital investment is measured against GNP. The trend in human resource investment at the state and local level is much brighter, as state and local spending for education rose in real dollars by a combined 40 percent between 1970 and 1986. Nevertheless, these sectors of government now spend less on education as a percentage of GNP than they did in 1975, when that ratio began falling from its most recent high. If it were decided—under the premise that human capital investments in the 1990s should be at a high point given their increasing importance—that total government spending for human capital investment should make up the same percentage of GNP as during the peak years, government would have to increase its investments in human capital by some $33 billion annually. This increase would augment total government investment in human capital, which stood at $202 billion in 1986 (the last year for which complete figures are available), by more than 15 percent.

Would increased federal, state, and local investments in human capital of this magnitude really benefit society? There is considerable evidence that human capital investments are worthwhile to individuals—the economic return from education has widely been found to range from 5 to 15 percent, for example, without even taking account of the social benefits of education. But the aggregate impact of the investment is less clear. Although there are strong reasons to believe that human capital investments are important, particularly as we shift toward an economy based upon information and communication, documenting the impact is not easy. The individual may reap economic gains from education because he or she has a credential that leads employers to expect better performance on the job, even if the skills gained are of limited value and contribute little to the output of the economy. Likewise, while many public programs to build human capital—the Job Corps, preschool education, and welfare-to-work initiatives, for example—have been found to be cost-effective,[14] others have either not been evaluated or have been found to be ineffective.

It is beyond the scope of this chapter to assess the quality and effectiveness of the variety of different forms of human capital investments undertaken by government. The authors are under no illusion that increased spending on schools, training programs, or other forms of human capital will always translate into higher productivity or improvements in social welfare. Nevertheless, we assume that additional investment in people's skills and capacities could significantly benefit society *if the money is devoted to the most effective programs.* Keeping this important caveat in mind, we focus now on alternative ways of financing new spending in this area.

Financing Strategies for Human Capital Investments

In the first part of this chapter we argued that private markets underinvest in human capital and that public spending has not kept pace with the need to equip people with the education and skills needed to meet the economic and social challenges of the future. Many researchers have stressed these ideas and outlined their implications (see for example Litan, Lawrence, and Schulze 1988; Thurow 1985; Committee for Economic Development 1987; or Secretary of Labor's Commission on Workforce Quality and Labor Market Efficiency 1989). But these arguments may have no more than academic significance should current fiscal constraints continue to limit new spending initiatives. This section addresses the financing problem.

We begin with a discussion of why funding new human capital initiatives through conventional budgetary procedures—the most desirable approach in principle—is unlikely to yield significant new resources for such investments in practice. We then consider alternative financing mechanisms, including: (1) earmarked taxes; (2) mandated private-sector spending; and (3) greater state and local financing. These options deserve scrutiny because current federal budgetary pressures are likely to compel legislators and program advocates to consider them. While each of these alternatives may be of some use in supporting human capital investments, each poses significant problems as well. The challenge for policymakers wishing to increase national investments in people is to identify the situations in which each financing tool can best be employed, and to determine how the combined use of the available financing tools can contribute to an effective national human resources policy. Finally, we examine another alternative financing mechanism—tapping some of the growing Social Security surpluses—and explain how this option could help solve the funding dilemma hindering human capital programs.

The Conventional Budget Process: Human Resource Programs Are Vulnerable While the Federal Budget Crisis Persists

The nation could choose to pay for more human capital investments simply by committing additional federal, state, and local money to education, training, and similar activities during yearly budget reviews. Such additions to human capital spending could be in the form of direct outlays or tax subsidies. This conventional method of budgeting, in which legislators distribute general revenues (or tax preferences) across a wide range of programs, is arguably the most economically efficient and equitable financing mechanism because it is relatively flexible and comprehensive. As priorities change, lawmakers can redirect money to meet the new needs. Of course, political stalemates and the lobbying of special-interest groups can paralyze the conventional budget process, as they did at the federal level throughout the 1980s. But such disputes can stall any budgetary system. Overall, the conventional budget process is still preferable to other financing mechanisms—such as raising revenue on a program-by-program basis—because it encourages lawmakers to consider the whole range of public needs and decide which ones represent the best uses of tax dollars.

Despite the merits of funding programs through the unified budget process, over the next five years this financing mechanism is likely to yield money for human capital investments only at the state and local levels. As is well known, the federal government persistently ran large budget deficits throughout most of the 1980s, with the deficit as a percentage of GNP reaching a postwar high in 1983 before declining to less alarming levels later in the decade. Because federal budgeting involves only one government, instead of the 50 states and some 80,000 local governments, we shall focus in this section on conventional budgeting at the national level and return to the role of state and local governments in financing human capital investments later in the chapter.

Many economists have persuasively outlined the dangers of federal deficits (see, for example, Gramlich 1984; or Minarik and Penner 1988), so there is little need for us to repeat those analyses or describe the constraints the deficit has imposed on spending in numerous areas. The critical point is that deficits will probably remain stubbornly high, limiting any new initiatives in the human capital area. The Congressional Budget Office predicted in 1989 that the annual deficit would exceed $125 billion at least until 1994 under current policies (Congressional Budget Office 1989: xi). The shortfalls exceed $250 billion annually during the same period if the Social Security and other trust fund surpluses are excluded from the totals (Congressional Budget Office 1989: 51). While the president and Congress may cut these deficits to comply with the

Gramm-Rudman-Hollings deficit targets requiring a balanced budget by 1993, many lawmakers appear unwilling to accept the tax increases or the cuts in entitlement programs needed to reduce the deficit significantly.

Because many items in the federal government are difficult to cut for political or statutory reasons, domestic discretionary programs—including human capital programs—have borne a disproportionate share of budget cuts in the 1980s, dipping from 27 percent of total outlays in 1981 to 16 percent in 1988.[15] These programs remain vulnerable in the 1990s. Federal entitlement programs such as Social Security, in which benefits are guaranteed to all people meeting certain criteria, do not require yearly appropriations. Outlays for entitlements have grown rapidly since the mid-1960s, leaving less room in the budget for other needs. Other budgetary commitments, such as those for military weaponry that is already in the pipeline, or interest payments on the national debt, are similarly difficult to cut. Such factors increased the share of expenditures classified by the Office of Management and Budget as "relatively uncontrollable" to 76 percent in 1989. With the federal budget carved into so many slices reserved for different purposes and constituencies, there will be little left over for such human resource investments as education, training, and preventive health care.

Because advocates of greater spending on human capital programs are unlikely to secure additional federal outlays, some may seek to accomplish the same objective through new tax subsidies. Although legislators stripped away many tax preferences in the Tax Reform Act of 1986, reducing estimated tax expenditures by more than $225 billion in fiscal year 1991 (Congressional Budget Office 1988a: ix-x), these forgone revenues are still projected to amount to $333 billion during that same year—some 28 percent of projected outlays (U.S. Congress. Joint Committee on Taxation 1989: 19). President Bush has proposed new or extended tax subsidies for child care, enterprise zones, capital gains, and private savings, emphasizing that tax subsidies preserve private market incentives and avoid the creation of new government bureaucracies. Nevertheless, the deficit constrains tax subsidies as well as direct outlays, for both compound the nation's budgetary problems. In addition, many members of Congress who invested so much energy in achieving the compromises of the Tax Reform Act of 1986 have said that they do not want to allow tax preferences to proliferate again, narrowing the tax base.

Until the federal government reduces its budget deficit significantly, the only feasible way to increase human capital investments through the regular budget process may be through small increases in education, training, and preventive health care programs that are part of larger deficit reduction packages. Policymakers might be able to justify small increments to human capital spending—no greater than several billion dollars—by arguing that such investments are as important to increased productivity and economic growth over the next 10 years as shrinking the deficit.

Alternatives to Normal Budgeting: Creative Funding Schemes Proliferate

As federal deficits mounted during the 1980s and popular opposition to increased taxation remained high, policymakers have searched for other ways to fund programs.

Option 1: Earmarked Taxes

One alternative lawmakers have increasingly employed is earmarking revenues—that is, requiring by law that all or part of the revenues from a particular tax serve a given purpose or program. Earmarked revenues have been useful because they allow legislators to expand programs that taxpayers are willing to support without requiring an increase in deficits or in across-the-board taxes. Furthermore, earmarked taxes may provide something like a market test for new or expanded programs because beneficiaries are asked to pay the costs. Earmarked or dedicated taxes were used to fund the federal Medicare Catastrophic Care Act of 1988 (financed, until its repeal, through an addition to the monthly Medicare premium as well as a supplemental premium tied to income); education reforms in South Carolina, Mississippi, Indiana, Arkansas, and Tennessee; and economic development, housing, and infrastructure programs in many cities and towns.

Earmarked taxes come in many varieties. They differ in purpose and in scope. At the state level, for example, taxes on motor fuels, motor vehicle registration, sales, tobacco, and alcoholic beverages are frequently earmarked (Gold, Erickson, and Kissell 1987: vii). Earmarked tax burdens may be widely shared (like the payroll taxes used to finance Social Security) or imposed on one group (as when companies that dump pollutants are taxed to finance environmental protection). Because earmarked funding plans can differ so widely, we will examine their merits in financing human capital investments using three examples: (1) a plan to dedicate part of the Unemployment Insurance (UI) payroll tax to create individual training accounts, (2) an idea to restructure the higher education financing system by making repayment of student loans contingent upon income, and (3) a proposal to create a "Children's Trust Fund" by increasing the payroll tax and reserving the proceeds for children's programs. The analysis of these three schemes will illustrate some of the most important ways in which one can design an earmarked tax.

Earmarking unemployment insurance funds for training. This plan would require workers and businesses to set aside a portion of Unemployment Insurance (UI) payroll taxes to create individual training accounts (ITAs) for workers. Although the parameters may vary, most of the ITA proposals follow the same basic structure (see, for example, Congressional Budget Office 1985: 65–68; or Choate 1982: 42–45). Under one prototype, employers and employees would each pay eight-tenths of 1 percent of a worker's wage up to a combined total of $500 annually. Collections would continue until an employee had an ITA of $4,000 through these contributions and the accumulation of tax-free interest. The money could be withdrawn for training purposes deemed allowable by law or regulation.

The training financed by ITAs could reduce unemployment as well as contribute to skill development throughout the economy and throughout a worker's career, enabling people to assume new responsibilities or prepare for new jobs. ITAs would greatly increase job training funds and provide a stable revenue base for skill development in the future. The Congressional Budget Office has estimated that a typical ITA proposal would generate at least $25 to $30 billion annually in job training funds (Congressional Budget Office 1985: 66), far greater than current federal training expenditures, which approach $4 billion annually.

Nevertheless, the ITA concept has its flaws. Like many earmarked financing plans, the ITA would be a somewhat blunt, inflexible tool. If priorities changed, it would be difficult for lawmakers to reallocate the money earmarked for ITAs. Ironically, the earmarking of UI payroll taxes to develop ITAs might encourage saving more than training because individuals might decide not to use the funds. Furthermore, by placing training decisions solely in the hands of workers, ITAs might fail to spur training in the fields most essential to industry or the economy.

This training tax also raises distributional and efficiency concerns. Like most payroll taxes, this increase in the UI tax would be regressive, since it would be capped at a certain level of income ($31,250 under one plan). The ITA plan would also fail to promote training among people who are unemployed, not in the labor force, or not working in covered employment, and would provide fewer immediate benefits for low-wage than for high-wage workers. Finally, this increase in the UI tax would fuel inflationary pressures if employers tried to shift costs to consumers and would reduce employee compensation if it were shifted to workers.

California and Delaware have both implemented less ambitious and more flexible versions of these training tax plans that correct some of the deficiencies described above. California dedicates 0.1 percent of its UI funds and Delaware imposes a 0.1 percent UI tax on employers to provide a range of training services, including customized training for businesses, retraining for dislocated workers, and skills instruction for the disadvantaged. These plans seem better designed to promote training where it is most needed because the money can be allocated to different types of training; however, the funding is modest (about $55 million in California and $2 million in Delaware) and may have little impact on the level of training if legislators provide less for job training from the states' general funds (Ganzglass and Heidkamp 1987: 17).

Another way to generate more resources for job training would be to increase the wage base used to calculate the federal UI tax as average wages increase, and use the proceeds for training. Increasing the wage base above its current $7,000 level to reflect the growth of average wages in the economy each year could generate more than $4 billion during the first four years after the plan was implemented (Congressional Budget Office 1985: 54–55). In addition, gradually raising the UI wage base would be desirable on equity grounds alone since the current tax is highly regressive.

Income-contingent loans for higher education. This earmarked tax proposal would restructure the nation's system for financing higher education. The federal government would guarantee loans to all student borrowers. But instead of repaying the loans over a given period at a fixed interest rate, students would pay back a fixed portion of their income throughout their careers in the form of an increment to their payroll taxes. Under a version of this plan developed by economist Robert Reischauer, students would pay back 0.24 percent of their income for every $1,000 they had borrowed (Reischauer 1987: 19). Therefore, a student with $10,000 in student loan debt and an annual income of $20,000 would have to pay 2.4 percent of his or her income, or $480, per year. This plan would deliver a subsidy from people with higher incomes to those with lower incomes. An adult with an annual income of $30,000, for example, would repay more of his or her loan than would someone with an annual income of $20,000 and the same amount of student loan debt. As a whole, the student loan program would become self-financing because the tax rate would be set to equalize loans and repayments over time.

This financing strategy would have several advantages. All students could use these loans to help them meet the mounting costs of college education, which have risen far faster than inflation over the past two decades (Congressional Budget Office 1988b: 2). Furthermore, the burden imposed by the additional payroll tax would be progressive, unlike that imposed by the ITA plan discussed above. This feature would also relieve pressures upon students to take high-paying jobs instead of less lucrative employment that may be more socially valuable. At the same time, the income-contingent loan system would also reduce budget costs because it would be self-financing. Taxpayers would no longer have to pay the subsidies embodied in Guaranteed Student Loans or pay default costs.

The merits of this financing plan hinge on a number of philosophical and practical questions. One issue is who should bear what share of the tax burden necessary to support higher education. Some might argue that this loan program should incorporate a general subsidy because higher education benefits society, but eventually such a subsidy would imply a redistribution of income from those who do not go to college to those who do. Another issue is the fairness and the feasibility of requiring high-wage earners to subsidize the education of people who earn less or nothing at all (people who have dropped out of the labor market to raise children, for example). The structure of the income-contingent loan program creates incentives that might undermine its financial integrity. On the one hand, the program's flexibility allows people to substitute loans for personal and family contributions, implicitly lowering the price of higher education. Thus, the income-contingent loan program might encourage marginal students—those not likely to do well in school and earn higher incomes later—to pursue more education. At the same time, the program gives students expecting to earn high incomes a reason to forgo participation, since they may have to subsidize others. This result could undermine the financial basis for the loan program.

Children's Trust Fund. This proposal would gradually increase the payroll tax by three-tenths of 1 percent over five years and dedicate the money to children's needs. The tax would yield $20 billion in new revenues in the fifth year after enactment, according to estimates by Jule Sugarman, who introduced the idea (Sugarman 1988: 2). The motivation for the plan is as political as it is substantive. Federal assistance to children declined by 4 percent in real terms between 1978 and 1987 (U.S. Congress. House Committee on Ways and Means 1989: 1231–33), even as the poverty rate for children increased by 25 percent. Sugarman's plan, in effect, would earmark revenues for children in order to push their needs toward the front of the budgetary queue (Sugarman 1988: 5–7).[16]

The Children's Trust Fund would increase public investment in children by 80 percent, providing that spending on children from general revenues was maintained. The proposal would also help equalize resources and opportunities for children, who are now the poorest age group in society. Nevertheless, proposals like the Children's Trust might simply intensify the conflict among interest groups for separate financing sources, particularly since this plan loosens the connection between payment of the tax and entitlement to benefits. The paradoxical result could be less money for discretionary programs, such as those meeting the needs of children, as more revenues are linked with particular programs. It is not unreasonable to expect that other claims—particularly those of the elderly for long-term care—will receive priority for additional payroll tax revenues because there is a clear connection between taxes paid throughout one's working life and an entitlement to benefits when one is elderly.

Concluding observations on earmarked taxes. Obviously, the merits of earmarked taxes for human capital investments must be evaluated on a case-by-case basis. The basic mechanics of each plan are critical, as shown in the income-contingent student loan example. Each tax also has different distributional and economic impacts. But some common themes emerge from the discussion above. Earmarked taxes may be a useful element in a financing strategy for human resource programs because these programs should increase productivity and earnings, allowing people to repay society for the assistance they receive. This principle is most clearly embedded in the Reischauer student loan plan. However, in the same vein, one could argue that everyone benefits from education as a child and should have a responsibility to "pay back" the societal investments in their future through an earnings-related payroll tax dedicated to children. Alternatively, people can be asked to accumulate money for such investments in advance. This approach, which is illustrated by the individual training accounts, can only work for adult training programs. Despite some obvious benefits, earmarked taxes must be judged with great care because they limit lawmakers' flexibility and protect programs from tough budgetary decisions.

With those caveats in mind, we believe that earmarked financing will be most effective when the following conditions are met. (1) There should be a clear connection between the revenue source and the services provided, to prevent people from shifting the costs of favored programs to others and to maintain discipline in the use of earmarked taxes. (2) The class of people who bear the tax should be relatively able to pay; otherwise, the progressive tax system will be undermined. (3) The earmarked tax should be designed in a manner that ensures that overall spending on the program being funded will increase (Gold, Erickson, and Kissell 1987: 27–28). (4) The revenue source should grow at a consistent and steady pace with the rest of the economy, preventing spending from fluctuating unpredictably.

Option 2: Mandated Private-Sector Spending

One way to accomplish public purposes with little or no budgetary impact is to mandate that private employers provide their workers with certain benefits. Such regulatory approaches—like the minimum wage increase enacted in 1989 and the parental leave bill passed by Congress in 1990—became increasingly attractive as budget deficits precluded direct action to accomplish public objectives.

Although mandated-benefit plans have not been used to finance human capital investments, these policies could easily be applied to this area. The most likely extension of mandated benefits would be in the case of training, since employers already bear much of the responsibility for occupational skill development. A French program illustrates the use of employer mandates to increase training. French firms with more than 10 employees must devote 1.1 percent of their wage bill to allowable types of training, in addition to setting aside an additional 0.5 percent of payroll for apprenticeships. Those employers who do not provide training must pay a tax earmarked for government-sponsored training. This money can be used to train people who are unemployed or out of the labor market, and balances public and private control over the kinds of training provided. By mandating that workers' groups participate in the formulation of training plans, the French government also ensures that employees' needs are considered. One study has found that the French system has doubled the amount of money employers spend on training (Bendick and Egan 1987: 17–18).

From a societal perspective, one can justify a mandated training program on the ground that firms tend to underinvest in their employees because they cannot be sure that workers will stay with the firm. The government mandate can benefit all because businesses will be able to choose from a pool of more productive workers, while employees will have greater skills and command higher wages. Furthermore, employers can usually make better judgments than individuals or governments about what kinds of training are needed. They also have the facilities and skilled personnel to provide many kinds of training more efficiently than other institutions.

Nevertheless, mandated benefits have their share of disadvantages. First, to the extent that additional training (or education or health care) is provided, it will not be costless. Although the added costs may at first reduce profits or be shifted to consumers in the form of higher prices, such expenses are likely to reduce workers' compensation or decrease employment opportunities in the long run. While other financing mechanisms are also costly, in the case of mandated benefits the costs are so hidden that it is more difficult for lawmakers to decide if the benefits of the policy outweigh the costs. For example, estimates of the impact of minimum wage increases on employment and inflation vary widely (see for example Minimum Wage Study Commission 1981); recent job loss projections associated with raising the minimum by between $1.00 and $1.30 per hour have ranged from less than 100,000 to almost 2 million.

Mandated benefit policies also bring with them a host of implementation difficulties that may be particularly pronounced in the case of human resource investments. There are so many different types of training that it will be difficult to set and enforce training guidelines for firms. These practical problems may create both inequities and inefficiencies. Firms that provide a lot of on-the-job, informal training may be penalized because those contributions to human resource development are difficult to measure. It will also be difficult to know whether firms have actually increased the amount of training they provide in response to a government mandate, since firms may simply direct their managers to repackage and relabel existing activity as training, impeding efficiency while producing little in the way of new training.

One other inefficiency in the use of mandated benefits to finance human capital investments deserves mention. Because there are so many different skills that make people productive workers and responsible citizens, legislators are likely to impose mandates that focus on inputs (dollars spent on training) rather than on outputs (a certain number of workers trained in a particular skill), as in the French system described above. This design removes the incentives for firms to find the least expensive ways of fulfilling the mandate because they must devote a certain amount of their resources to training regardless.

Option 3: State and Local Financing

Increased funding for human capital investment might come from state and local governments. As noted earlier in this chapter, these levels of government increased their support for education by 40 percent in real terms between 1970 and 1986 and became leaders in policy innovations during the 1980s. While the federal government accumulated deficits, state and local governments balanced their books during the 1980s (49 states have constitutional amendments requiring them to balance their budgets). Finally, state and local governments have often found that raising taxes to finance human capital investment—particularly better education—makes a region attractive to businesses seeking to relocate and encourages local businesses to remain.

However, the state and local fiscal situation is more complicated than this discussion would suggest. First, while the states and localities do appear able to increase their human resource investments, this capacity is limited. Over the last 20 years, state and local governments have assumed more responsibility in a variety of areas, such as economic development, health care, and corrections, reducing the proportion of state and local budgets allotted to education. While their role has been expanding, state and local governments have seen some of their fiscal base erode due to federal policies. Federal aid as a percentage of state and local outlays has declined from 27 percent in 1978 to 18 percent in 1988 (Advisory Commission on Intergovernmental Relations 1988: 35), while a larger share of the remaining federal aid (52 percent in 1988) flows to individuals through programs such as Medicaid and Aid to Families with Dependent Children instead of to governments. Furthermore, the Tax Reform Act of 1986 eliminated the federal deduction for state and local sales taxes. The ending of this subsidy particularly hurt state governments, which relied on sales taxes for 33 percent of their revenue in 1986, according to the Advisory Commission on Intergovernmental Relations (1988: 60–61).

As state and local governments entered the 1990s, their solid fiscal footing became much more shaky, underscoring the difficulty of founding a human capital financing strategy on state and local efforts alone. A regional slowdown in New England during 1989 spread to half or more of the states in 1990, reflecting a wider downturn in economic growth. After at least 20 states slashed their fiscal year 1990 budgets and another 30 states raised taxes, the prospects for fiscal year 1991 remained dim. Projected year-end balances for fiscal year 1991 stood at 2.7 percent (Miller 1990: 9), well below the 5 percent benchmark many experts consider necessary to protect states against recession. Parallel problems occurred in many cities, including New York City and Washington, D.C.

States also differ widely in their ability and willingness to support government programs. According to the Advisory Commission on Intergovernmental Relations (1988: 44), in 1986 state and local expenditures per capita, expressed as a percentage of the U.S. average, ranged from 73 in Arkansas to 178 in Wyoming. A comparable index of state and local governments' tax effort (which relates the level of taxation to an index of fiscal capacity) ranged from 64 in Nevada to 156 in New York (Advisory Commission on Intergovernmental Relations 1988: 92). While state and local governments have a vital role to play in developing and implementing human capital programs, leaving the nation's human capital strategy chiefly to the fiscal and political vagaries of thousands of state and local governments may not ensure a coherent or adequate national policy.

Investing the Social Security Surplus in Human Resources: An Earmarked Financing Plan That Would Serve Broad Public Goals

Another way to fund human capital investments would be to use the growing surpluses in the Social Security Trust Fund for this purpose. The basic argument in favor of this proposal is that the retirement of the baby boom generation beginning about 2015 will impose an enormous fiscal burden on the working-age population. However, if the nation can enlarge its economic base by improving productivity, this task will be less onerous. Earmarking part of the Social Security surplus for investments in people would be one way to increase productivity and ready the nation for the demographic challenges of the next century. This proposal might be the best alternative method of funding human capital investments during a time of tight budgets because the money would serve a broad national goal, could be used flexibly, and would distribute benefits widely. In these respects, the idea of dedicating Social Security surplus funds to human resource investments retains some of the benefits of the standard budget process described earlier.

The demographic challenge facing the nation when the baby boom generation retires during the next century is reasonably clear. By 2020, there are expected to be 50 percent more people over the age of 65 for every person between the ages of 20 and 64 than there were in 1980 (U.S. Congress. House. Committee on Ways and Means 1989: 89). The fiscal implications of this development are harder to project, but one estimate is that maintaining current policies for Social Security and Medicare will absorb 11 percent of GNP by 2030, compared to 6.8 percent in 1990 (Palmer 1988: 183).

Between now and 2015 when these fiscal burdens materialize, the Social Security Trust Fund will build rapidly. The Social Security Amendments of 1983 instituted a series of payroll tax increases that are being phased in until the year 2000, generating excess revenues for the Trust Fund. Furthermore, the baby boomers are entering their prime working years in the 1990s and will themselves have a relatively small cohort of retirees to support. As a result, annual Social Security surpluses are projected to rise from $40 billion in 1988 to a peak of $172 billion in 2010 (in 1988 dollars). While some believe this money can later be used to relieve the fiscal strains associated with the retirement of the baby boom generation, this belief rests on a fundamental misunderstanding of how the system operates. By law, the Social Security Trust Fund must invest its reserves in Treasury securities. The Treasury spends the money it receives from the Trust Fund, leaving it with paper IOUs. These securities will be redeemed on a large scale beginning in about 2030, when the annual Social Security surpluses turn into deficits. At that time, the government will have to repay large sums to the Trust Fund. To do so, it must either raise taxes, reduce other spending, or increase its borrowing. One way or the other, the public will pay. That public is today's children and those who will be born during the next decade or two.

Currently, the government is doing little to prepare the nation for the challenge of supporting the retirement of the baby boom generation. The Social Security surpluses are presently being used to offset part of the deficit accumulating in the rest of the budget and are thus largely underwriting the government's regular operating expenses. Many economists (for example, Aaron, Bosworth, and Burtless 1989) and legislators have argued that the government should not rely on these surpluses to finance its current expenses. A better use for the money would be to finance more public and private investment, thereby raising productivity and standards of living. (More public investment occurs when outlays for research, infrastructure, and human resource programs are increased.

Table 12.2   Social Security Surpluses and the Budget Deficit under the
Gramm-Rudman-Hollings Timetable

1. 1990–92	Throughout this period, the Social Security surpluses will offset part of the deficit in the non-Social Security part of the budget. The Social Security surplus increases yearly, masking the shortfall in the rest of the budget.
2. 1993	The unified budget must be balanced, which means that the Social Security surplus—projected at $103 billion that year (Congressional Budget Office 1989: 46)—equals the deficit in the rest of the budget.
3. After 1993	The Social Security surplus exceeds its 1993 level, growing annually to a high of $172 billion in 2010. Although much of the Social Security surplus is still financing the deficit in the government's other accounts, the annual growth in the surplus relative to its 1993 level creates a surplus in the unified budget—money which could be reserved for investment. One option is to use half of these new funds for human resource investment and the other half for private investment.

More private investment is accomplished by using budget surpluses to retire outstanding debt, thereby lowering interest rates and encouraging new investment in industrial capacity.)

Before the nation can make these investments, however, lawmakers must first make significant progress in reducing the federal budget deficit. As of this writing, the Gramm-Rudman-Hollings legislation specified that the budget should be balanced by fiscal year 1993. If this target is met, the nation could then begin devoting some of the mounting annual Social Security surpluses to investment in both the public and private sectors. Even if the unified budget is balanced, the growth of entitlements will continue to squeeze out discretionary human resource programs, making some new funding source for these activities desirable. Table 12.2 illustrates this complex relationship between the Social Security surplus and the budget deficit and how that dynamic will change according to the deficit reduction timetable.

Reasonable people may disagree about whether increases in public or in private investment will best serve to further the goal of increasing future productivity. But it is likely that one way to raise living standards in the future is to ensure that the next generation is healthier, better educated, and better able to generate and apply new knowledge to the production process. This provides justification for using some of the Social Security surplus to achieve these objectives. Education, training, drug abuse prevention, preventive health care, and nutrition programs would be obvious candidates for expansion. To complement these human resource investments, some of the surplus might also be used to retire federal debt, easing upward pressure on interest rates and encouraging more private investment in new industrial capacity.

One possibility would be to earmark equal shares of the Social Security surplus for additional public and private investment once the budget deficit is eliminated in 1993. Specifically, half of any annual increases in the Social Security surplus above its 1993 level (Table 12.2) would be used to fund an *increase* in spending on *qualified* human resource programs; the other half of those annual increases would be used to retire government debt and make more room for private investment. Although some of the Social Security surplus would still be used to finance the deficit in the government's other program accounts, this contribution could be thought of as supporting the investment component of those other programs. According to the Office of Management and Budget, federal investment outlays for nondefense purposes totaled $73 billion in 1988 (Office of Management and Budget 1989d: D-3). If these investment outlays grow with inflation, they will be roughly comparable to the Social Security Trust Fund's contribution to regular government outlays, which should be slightly over $100 billion in 1994. As a practical matter, this proposal translates into establishing a new set of targets after 1992 for (1) the size of the surplus in the unified budget deficit, and (2) the proportion of total federal outlays devoted to human resource programs.

Substantial sums would be available for investment if the Social Security surplus were allocated in this way beginning in 1994. The money earmarked for new human capital investments between 1994 and 2005 would total $264 billion (1989 dollars). This is an average of $22 billion per year—assuming that current projections of the size of the surplus prove realistic and that the rest of the budget remains balanced after 1993.[17] This money would almost double the federal government's 1988 education and training spending of $26 billion. Comparable amounts would be available for private investment as the government accumulates an overall budget surplus during this period. The risk is not that there would be insufficient resources but that they would be spent unwisely. For this reason, Congress would need to specify what kinds of spending would qualify as a human capital investment and would have to resist political pressures to use a very broad definition. One option would be to require that the productivity-enhancing capacities of any new or existing program be independently and carefully evaluated before it could qualify for funding the Social Security Trust Fund surplus. However, if money from the increasing Social Security surpluses is allocated wisely, it will generate large sums of money that can be used flexibly to fill a range of public investment needs. In its focus on a broad national goal—increasing productivity to raise living standards for the challenges of the next generation—this earmarked financing plan avoids the disadvantages of other dedicated taxes, which often serve narrow goals or target their benefits to a particular group.

Conclusion

The United States faces an impasse in human resources policy as it enters the 1990s. While Americans are increasingly recognizing the growing importance of human capital to the economy and the larger society, particularly as more and more jobs require brains instead of brawn, policies are not keeping pace with these trends. Part of the problem is clearly financial: large federal budget deficits have held federal expenditures for education and training essentially constant since 1982, despite considerable concern during the 1980s that our commitments were inadequate. State and local governments have steadily increased their investment in education, but—burdened with other responsibilities as well—they devoted a smaller share of their spending to education in 1986 than in 1970.

Clearly, increased expenditures cannot substitute for well-designed policies. Nor will every dollar devoted to human capital investment yield benefits. But if lawmakers draw upon decades of experience and evaluation research in designing programs to provide education, training, preventive health care, and other human capital investments, the money may yield immense benefits. During the 1980s, public expenditures shifted away from human assets toward public consumption and physical assets. The pressing problems facing the nation as it enters the 1990s—the changing nature of work and the changing composition of the work force, the rise of international economic competition, the increasing poverty of children, and the growth of an underclass in the nation's inner cities—suggest that some reorienting of spending priorities is in order. Using recent peaks in federal, state, and local human capital spending as an indication of what the nation should spend today, one can conclude that the nation should devote as much as $33 billion more annually to investments in people.

In the next several years, it will be difficult for the government to raise anything like $33 billion annually for human capital investment. The persistent federal deficits—and the Gramm-Rudman-Hollings deficit reduction target of a balanced budget by 1993—constrain the growth of all federal programs, but this pressure may be greatest on domestic discretionary programs, including human resource programs. Although, in principle, financing any program through a comprehensive, regular budget review—what we refer to as the "conventional" budget process—is the optimal method, in practice, efforts to boost spending on human cap-

ital are likely to involve alternate financing mechanisms, such as earmarking taxes, mandating that employers invest in the skills of their
workers, and relying on state and local governments to assume more of
the burden of human capital investments. The advantages and disadvantages of these mechanisms are discussed above.

While these alternative financing mechanisms may be of some use in
financing human capital investment during a time of tight federal budgets, they also have a number of disadvantages. Earmarked tax proposals, for example, can create a sense of entitlement and prevent money
from being allocated to more productive uses as circumstances change.
Mandated benefit plans shift fiscal pressures to the private sector, but the
resulting higher business costs would be passed on to consumers in the
form of higher prices or to employees in the form of lower wages.

Increased state and local financing of human resource investments
does not necessarily involve the economic and budgetary distortions of
earmarked taxes or mandated benefits. But problems with coordination
and control limit the utility of this approach, and the nation's thousands
of state and local governments vary widely in their willingness and capacity to support human resource investments.

While in the short run lawmakers may have to use these three alternative financing mechanisms to provide money for human capital investment, we suggest a fourth, more radical, proposal—using some of the
growing Social Security surpluses to provide significant new resources
for human capital investment after 1993. While the Social Security surpluses accumulating between now and 2030 are designed to prepare the
nation for the retirement of the very large baby boom generation beginning about 2015, these surpluses represent nothing but IOUs to the Social Security Trust Fund. The Trust Fund invests its surpluses in Treasury
securities and will call in these notes during the next century when the
baby boomers retire. Thus, the fiscal pressures associated with the retirement of the baby boom cohort have merely been deferred. To pay back
its obligations to the Social Security Trust Fund after about 2030, when
the annual Social Security surpluses vanish, the government will be
forced to adopt painful measures—raising taxes, cutting spending, or
both.

One way the nation can ready itself for this demographic and fiscal
challenge is to enlarge its economic base by increasing productivity. If the
unified budget deficit is balanced in 1993 according to the Gramm-
Rudman-Hollings targets, some portion of the growth in the Social Security surplus after 1993 could be used for human capital investment
that would raise living standards and make the nation more able to support rising Social Security outlays in the twenty-first century.

Notes

The authors thank Steven Gold and Barry White for their helpful comments on an earlier draft.

1. As is the case throughout this book, the definition of human capital used in this chapter differs from other commonly used formulations. While many scholars use the term to include migration and the search for information, we do not treat those activities in our discussion here because migration and search involve changes in someone's *external* environment, not personal capacities. However, we include noneconomic capacities such as the nurturance of children and contribution to one's community, whereas most researchers focus primarily on the economic implications of investment in human resources.

2. Student loans may be the best example of this market imperfection. Because loans for higher education do not involve a form of collateral, private credit markets in this area were underdeveloped, leading the government to create loan programs for students when it passed the Higher Education Act of 1965.

3. These data are provided by the National Center for Education Statistics (1988: 31). However, these figures may slightly underestimate the public contribution to education because federal aid to students for higher education is classified under private tuition payments. Furthermore, the federal contribution to education through tax expenditures is not included in the data.

4. Many analysts have grappled with the particularly tough question of whether public health care spending is a form of human capital investment. Kendrick (1976) and Eisner (1988) deal with this issue by classifying one-half of public health care dollars as human investment. However, we believe that most public health expenditures do not have the developmental effects embodied in the idea of human capital investment. For example, most federal public health dollars go toward acute care in hospitals or long-term care in nursing homes and institutions for the developmentally disabled.

5. The public service employment that was a major part of CETA is not included in these calculations. If public service employment were included under the category of job training, the drop in real funding would have been 57 percent between 1981 and 1989.

6. Federal investment in human capital has always been minuscule compared to GNP. In 1981, federal investment in education and training was 0.00000776 percent of GNP; by 1987, it had fallen to 0.00000476 percent.

7. The data cited here were derived from the following: Office of Management and Budget (1989a: 63–67); Office of Management and Budget, *Budget of the United States Government:* Appendix (various years); Congressional Budget Office (1982: 5); General Accounting Office (1982: 10); U.S. Department of Labor, *Manpower Report of the President, 1975* (1975: 43).

8. These are the authors' calculations using data from the National Center for Education statistics reprinted in editions of *The Statistical Abstract of the United States.*

9. Our calculation of enrollment in higher education uses data from the National Center for Education Statistics (1988: 142) but treats three part-time students as the equivalent of one full-time student.

10. These are the authors' calculations using data from the National Center

for Charitable Statistics reprinted in editions of *The Statistical Abstract of the United States*.

11. This calculation is based on data presented in U.S. Bureau of the Census *Statistical Abstract of the United States* (1972: 415) and (1989: 272). There is some double-counting in these figures because a small share of state and local education expenditures comes from federal grants.

12. This calculation uses data presented by Bixby (1989: 34–35).

13. It is important to note that the federal government is providing additional funds (over $300 million in fiscal year 1989) for the preschool education of handicapped children. State and local governments must supplement this federal contribution, furthering the growth of preschool education programs at the state and local levels.

14. Even in these cases, one cannot assume that the programs are cost-effective in the aggregate. For example, people who benefit from programs building their skills and aptitudes may find it easier to obtain employment, but they may at the same time close off jobs to others. The issue, as in the case of general education, is whether the programs increase productivity and the general welfare or simply redistribute benefits among people without a net gain to society.

15. Calculations are based on data provided in Congressional Budget Office 1989: 66.

16. Interestingly enough, there are already Children's Trust Funds in most of the states. In 1984, 29 states dedicated money to the prevention of child abuse and neglect (Gold, Erickson, and Kissell 1987: 24). However, the funds, which are often underwritten by marriage license fees or voluntary income tax check-offs, are quite small; almost all took in less than $1 million in 1984.

17. Authors' calculations using "Alternative II-B" (Board of Trustees 1989).

References

Aaron, Henry J., Barry P. Bosworth, and Gary Burtless (1989). *Can America Afford to Grow Old? Paying for Social Security*. Washington, D.C.: Brookings Institution.

Advisory Commission on Intergovernmental Relations (1988). *Significant Features of Fiscal Federalism, 1988 Edition*. Vol. 2. Washington, D.C.: Advisory Commission on Intergovernmental Relations.

Bendick, Marc, and Mary Lou Egan (1982). *Recycling America's Workers: Public and Private Approaches to Midcareer Retraining*. Washington, D.C.: Urban Institute. Research paper.

———— (1987). "Promoting Employer-Provided Workers Reskilling." Copy of testimony presented to the Joint Economic Committee, United States Congress, 100th Congress, 1st session, September 29, 1987.

Bixby, Ann Kallman (1989). "Public Social Welfare Expenditures, Fiscal Year 1986." *Social Security Bulletin* 52 (2): 29–39.

Board of Trustees, Federal Old-Age and Survivors Insurance and Disability Insurance Trust Funds (1989). *1989 Annual Report of the Board of Trustees of the Federal Old-Age and Survivors Insurance and Disability Insurance Trust Funds*. Washington, D.C.: Social Security Administration.

Burtless, Gary (1986). "Public Spending for the Poor: Trends, Prospects, and Economic Limits." In Sheldon H. Danziger and Daniel H. Weinberg, eds.,

Fighting Poverty: What Works and What Doesn't. Cambridge: Harvard University Press.

Choate, Pat (1982). *Retooling the American Work Force: Toward a National Training Strategy*. Washington, D.C.: Northeast-Midwest Institute.

Committee for Economic Development (1987). *Children in Need: Investment Strategies for the Educationally Disadvantaged*. New York: Committee for Economic Development.

Congressional Budget Office (1982). *CETA Training Programs—Do They Work for Adults?* Washington, D.C.: U.S. Government Printing Office.

———— (1985). *Promoting Employment and Maintaining Incomes with Unemployment Insurance*. Washington, D.C.: U. S. Government Printing Office.

———— (1988a). *The Effects of Tax Reform on Tax Expenditures*. Washington, D.C.: U.S. Government Printing Office.

———— (1988b). "Trends in College Tuition and Student Aid Since 1970." Staff working paper.

———— (1989) *The Economic and Budget Outlook: An Update*. Washington, D.C.: U.S. Government Printing Office.

Eisner, Robert (1988). "Extended Accounts for National Income and Product." *Journal of Economic Literature* 26 (December): 1611–84.

Ganzglass, Evelyn, and Maria Heidkamp (1987). *State Strategies to Train a Competitive Workforce*. Washington, D.C.: National Governors' Association.

General Accounting Office (1982). *CETA Programs for Disadvantaged Adults: What Do We Know About Their Enrollees, Services, Effectiveness?* Washington, D.C.: U.S. Government Printing Office.

———— (1987). *Work and Welfare: Current AFDC Work Programs and Implications for Federal Policy*. Washington, D.C.: U.S. Government Printing Office.

Gold, Steven D. (1990). "State Finances in the New Era of Fiscal Federalism." In Thomas Swartz, ed., *The Changing Face of Fiscal Federalism*. Armonk, NY: M. E. Sharpe.

Gold, Steven D., Brenda Erickson, and Michelle Kissell (1987). *Earmarking State Taxes*. Denver: National Conference of State Legislatures.

Gramlich, Edward M. (1984). "How Bad Are the Large Deficits?" In Gregory B. Mills and John L. Palmer, eds., *Federal Budget Policy in the 1980s*. Washington, D.C.: Urban Institute Press.

Gueron, Judith M. (1986). *Work Initiatives for Welfare Recipients*. New York: Manpower Demonstration Research Corporation.

Johnston, William B., and Arnold H. Packer (1987). *Workforce 2000: Work and Workers for the 21st Century*. Indianapolis, Ind.: Hudson Institute.

Kendrick, John (1976). *The Formation and Stocks of Total Capital*. New York: Columbia University Press.

Litan, Robert E., Robert Z. Lawrence, and Charles L. Schulze, eds. (1988). *American Living Standards: Threats and Challenges*. Washington, D.C.: Brookings Institution.

Marx, Fern, and Michelle Seligson (1988). *The Public School Early Childhood Study: The State Survey*. New York: Bank Street College of Education.

Miller, Gerald (1990). "Goodbye to Good Economic Times." *State Government News* 33(7): 9–11.

Minarik, Joseph J., and Rudolph G. Penner (1988). "Fiscal Choices." In Isabel

V. Sawhill, ed., *Challenge to Leadership*. Washington, D.C.: Urban Institute Press.

Minimum Wage Study Commission (1981). *Final Report*. Vols. 1 and 6. Washington, D.C.: U.S. Government Printing Office.

National Center for Education Statistics (1988). *Digest of Education Statistics, 1988*. Washington, D.C.: U.S. Government Printing Office.

National Governors' Association and Council of State Governments (1987). *Focus on the First Sixty Months: The Next Steps*. Washington, D.C.: National Governors' Association.

National Governors' Association and National Association of State Budget Officers (1989). *Fiscal Survey of the States, March 1989*. Washington, D.C.: The National Governors' Association and the National Association of State Budget Officers.

Nightingale, Demetra Smith, and Lynn C. Burbridge (1987). *The Status of State Work-Welfare Programs in 1986: Implications for Welfare Reform*. Washington, D.C.: The Urban Institute. Research paper.

Office of Management and Budget (1989a). *Historical Tables: Budget of the United States Government, Fiscal Year 1990*. Washington, D.C.: U.S. Government Printing Office.

—— (1989b). *Budget of the United States Government, Fiscal Year 1990*. Washington, D.C.: U.S. Government Printing Office.

—— (1989c). *Budget of the United States Government, Fiscal Year 1990: Appendix*. Washington, D.C.: U.S. Government Printing Office.

—— (1989d). *Special Analyses: Budget of the United States Government, Fiscal Year 1990*. Washington, D.C.: U.S. Government Printing Office.

Palmer, John L. (1988). "Financing Health Care and Retirement for the Aged." In Isabel V. Sawhill, ed., *Challenge to Leadership*. Washington, D.C.: Urban Institute Press.

Peters, Donald L. (1988). "Receipts and Expenditures of State Governments and of Local Governments: Revised and Updated Estimates, 1984–87." *Survey of Current Business* (Department of Commerce) 68(9): 23–25.

Reischauer, Robert D. (1987). "HELP: A Student Loan Program for the Twenty-first Century." Unpublished discussion paper.

Sugarman, Jule (1988). "Financing Children's Services: A Proposal to Create the Children's Trust." Unpublished paper.

Thurow, Lester (1985). *The Zero-Sum Solution*. New York: Simon & Schuster.

U.S. Bureau of the Census (1972). *Statistical Abstract of the United States, 1972*. Washington, D.C.: U.S. Government Printing Office.

—— (1989). *Statistical Abstract of the United States, 1989*. Washington, D.C.: U.S. Government Printing Office.

U.S. Congress. House. Committee on Ways and Means (1989). *Background Material and Data on Programs within the Jurisdiction of the Committee on Ways and Means*. Washington, D.C.: U.S. Government Printing Office.

U.S. Congress. House. Select Committee on Children, Youth, and Families (1988). *Opportunities for Success: Cost-Effective Programs for Children, Update 1988*. Washington, D.C.: U.S. Government Printing Office.

U.S. Congress. Joint Committee on Taxation (1989). *Estimates of Federal Tax*

Expenditures for Fiscal Years 1990–1994. Washington, D.C.: U.S. Government Printing Office.

U.S. Department of Labor (1975). *Manpower Report of the President, 1975.* Washington, D.C.: U.S. Government Printing Office.

13

New Paradigms for Action

David W. Hornbeck

When Lester Salamon and I embarked on this project, we both had a strong suspicion that the United States faced some serious human capital problems that were jeopardizing its economic future. We were significantly less clear, however, about how much consensus we would find among a collection of distinguished social scientists and policy analysts as to the scope and character of the problems or what should be done about them. Yet, despite substantial differences, the chapters in this book appear to share a number of common themes.

There is, first of all, a common work force needs analysis. Every author makes it clear that few manual laborers will be required in the future. Rather, there will be greater need for people who can think, who can formulate a moderately complex thought and express it coherently both verbally and in writing, for people who can solve problems and relate well to a team of others. Moreover, given the expectation that workers will increasingly change not only jobs, but occupations as well, it will be necessary for the new worker to learn to learn for a lifetime.

There is, secondly, a common optimism that we know what to do programmatically to cope with our human capital problems and even how to do it. Education in both its precollegiate form and through college; social support services, including health care and child care; family strengthening; and initiatives to alleviate poverty generally are among the program ingredients proposed.

There is, third, the common view that coordination is necessary: not only is the all too frequent phenomenon of disjointed, redundant, and even contradictory action expensive, but also the extra power resulting from collaborative effort is necessary to pierce the difficulties bred by generations of poverty, poor education, and economically unproductive lives.

Fourth, there is a common theme that continued failure to invest in people will be more costly than doing the job correctly. Prevention, investment in the early years, and helping families help their children are emphasized repeatedly in different ways. This emphasis, and the evidence of the success of such efforts, contrasts with the costs of prison, public assistance, higher special education placement rates, a lifetime of poor health, and most importantly, new cycles of generational poverty which result in an increasingly large base of poverty.

In the fifth place there is substantial agreement that these endeavors call for concerted efforts from all levels of government and from both the public and the private sectors. Indeed, it is essential that the different levels and sectors become involved both powerfully and aggressively if we are to meet the emerging needs of the work force. Without making the distinctions too sharp, there is a sense that vision, leadership, and a strong contribution to financial equity are called for at the federal government level; that additional financial equity efforts, strong incentives to collaborate, and the tailoring of initiatives to more regional or local circumstances must be emphasized at the state government level; that delivery of services in a collaborative fashion is important at the local government level; and that business can help to provide certain essential ingredients, such as the identification of necessary work force characteristics and the insistence that the "system" produce people that exhibit them, as well as the provision of political power to initiatives that will yield sufficient resources and/or the redistribution of resources required to produce the necessary results.

Sixth, it is clear to all that greater resources must be provided. While all levels of government and the private sector must help, there is agreement that the federal and state governments must bear the primary responsibility for resources. Only at those levels can the equitable distribution of funds be achieved.

Seventh, there is in these chapters an often stated concern that we are not at the moment doing even what our present laws require. For example, Ray Marshall makes it clear that there is no justification for *illegal* immigration. The availability of a properly trained work force is served by immigration laws tailored to deal with whatever training of unskilled people is needed and then by the enforcement of these laws. Nancy Barrett emphasizes the enforcement of equal employment opportunity laws, the absence of which "results in a self-perpetuating cycle of underinvestment in female human capital and is a serious 'market failure' in our economy."

The eighth and one of the strongest themes of several chapters is that education is absolutely essential, but that the facts, most forcefully presented by Danziger and Edelman, clearly demonstrate that education alone is not sufficient. Other poverty alleviating and socially supportive policies and services, such as income transfers and health care, are also needed. While such noneducational attacks on poverty may not equip the present adult generation to meet our work force needs, they set the stage for reducing the incidence of poorly equipped workers in the next generation.

Ninth, there is here a common view that we are increasingly a nation divided; that the gap between the haves and the have-nots is growing. Concern is expressed that our democratic institutions are threatened. Implicit is the assumption that the economic prosperity of the nation is heavily dependent upon the stability of this sometimes fragile experiment we call democracy.

Finally, there is a common perception that there is *not* a sense of urgency within this country about the problems we face in meeting our work force needs. This last point is perhaps the most important and is the take-off point for this chapter. Owen Butler, the former chief executive officer of Procter and Gamble and presently the chairman of the Committee for Economic Development, stated it well in a speech to a meeting on middle level education called by the Carnegie Corporation in June 1989. He observed that on December 7, 1941, 3,581 Americans were maimed or killed at Pearl Harbor. The next day, President Roosevelt called for and the Congress issued a Declaration of War on Japan. *Weekly* in the United States today, significantly more students drop out of our elementary and secondary education schools. Those drop-outs are as effectively maimed or dead as the Americans at Pearl Harbor. Yet nothing even approaching the reaction to Pearl Harbor has occurred. Unless or until this changes, we will not solve the human capital problem.

Systemic and Structural Change

The cumulative message of the preceding chapters is that incremental change is insufficient. Systems must be radically altered to produce what the nation's economy demands in a work force. With one-quarter of all students and one-half of all disadvantaged students dropping out (Doyle 1989: E14), and with the actual performance even among those who stay and graduate being rather low (Applebee, Langer, and Mullis 1989: 6), we know that the product of America's public school systems is significantly inadequate. A few more social studies courses or three credits of mathematics rather than two, or lengthening the school year so that we do for 220 days what we have previously done for 180 is not going to produce the magnitude of change that is needed.

Health, social services, and other institutions trying to cope with the nonacademic needs of youth are also falling significantly short. For example, exhortations to say no to sexual activity or to drugs are inadequate to change the fact that 25 percent of all sexually active teenagers contract a sexually transmitted disease (Carnegie Council on Adolescent Development 1989: 25) or the fact that America holds the dubious distinction of having a very high rate of teenage drug and alcohol use (Greenbaum 1989: 46).

Adult education programs in schools and community colleges have tried hard, but the fact remains that tens of millions of Americans remain functionally illiterate (Kozol 1988: 17; French 1987: 24–25). Private-sector groups have also made extraordinary public contributions, such as ABC-TV's pro-literacy effort in Project Plus, but fundamental structural changes are necessary in the way literacy services are delivered in America if we are to attack the literacy problem effectively. Employment and training programs do an increasingly good job, but they serve only 5 percent of the population, and many argue that this 5 percent represents just the "cream of the crop" (Job Training Partnership Act Advisory Committee 1989: 7). Higher education serves well at least the highest achieving 25 percent of those going to college, but fails miserably in even retaining nearly 50 percent of those who begin college (Tinto 1987: 1). Unprecedented and profound change is necessary.

In calling for such significant change, it should be noted that I do not long for the "good old days." I frequently hear the nostalgic observation, for example, that if the schools were as good as they used to be we would not have the serious problems to which this book is devoted. That is highly questionable. Schools are not worse than they used to be. Indeed, it may be said that they are too much like they used to be despite the significantly different world in which they exist. Consider this:

- If our economy were still dominated by agriculture and manufacturing, the product of our schools would be fine.
- If ours were a nation that still officially sanctioned segregation in schools and public accommodations, the disproportionately high drop-out rates among blacks and Hispanics would not be of great concern.
- If the fastest growing segment of the work force were white males, whom we have historically served relatively well, and not women, blacks, and Hispanics, whom we have historically served poorly, the product of our schools might be considered barely adequate.
- If ours remained a nation in which citizenship did not even confer the right to vote without paying a poll tax, it would not matter that our schools and other human capital related institutions contribute to the growing gap between the rich and the poor.

• If our world were still one in which the United States had palpable economic and defense superiority and nations such as Japan and Germany remained defeated enemies instead of allies and economic competitors, the product of our schools and other contributors to our human capital reservoir would remain adequate.

Similar observations can be made with regard to other human capital related institutions. Some may argue, for example, that child care was handled well in by-gone days, forgetting the fact that over 70 percent of mothers of school-age children and 52 percent of married women with children below the age of one now work (U.S. Bureau of the Census: 386). The fact is that returning to what we may perceive to be the "good old days" in any of our institutions is, of course, impossible. The United States and the world in which it exists have changed in fundamental ways. The human capital development infrastructure, however, is simply not producing what is required in the face of this worldwide change. The alteration of our human capital development institutions must be as fundamental as the changes in our economic institutions and other parts of our social fabric. This will require structural change. Our paradigms of thought must change. In many instances, doing more of or a better job of what we are presently doing will be insufficient. In each of the preceding chapters, the author makes clear that our human capital institutions are not simply in need of refinement. They are in need of a fundamental retooling. Greenberg, for example, does not argue that the Defense Department, which he notes is our principal source of research, should merely refocus its resources internally. Rather, he makes the case for expanding the research capacity outside Defense and, by implication, reducing it inside Defense, and he adds that the research must be targeted in an integrated way on human capital investment issues. Boyer makes clear that a simple series of add-ons will not do the job in the schools. He supplies the statistics that demonstrate how imperative it is to improve the school success of young people with whom we have failed historically *and* substantially raise the performance of *all* students *simultaneously*. Marshall makes clear the national indecision about appropriate immigration policy and its consequent incoherence and lack of enforcement. Edelman notes such serious deficiencies in the scope and depth of social services that the problem is one of kind, not just degree. She underlines her point by noting the fractured character of a system that can require a single family to go to dozens of separate agencies to secure needed services. My intention is not simply to restate each author's perspective; rather, it is to make clear that timid initiatives, or ones that are too narrowly or categorically targeted, or ones that have a short life expectancy or that are modest in scope will not meet the crises we face.

What must we do to set in motion the catalytic, synergistic forces that will lead organizations and human beings to do what needs to be done? How do we provoke a kind of self-actualizing momentum that does not rely on constant governmental prescriptions for what to do next? Are there mechanisms which can be created that will lead ordinarily unrelated institutions and people to work together, to connect to one another? I wish to emphasize the tools that are available to make change and the categories of analysis which may help us refine our thinking about the program initiatives we need to take.

Generic Policy Tools Used to Provoke Change

What are the basic tools we have available to initiate and sustain real change? I believe there are six:

Demonstration projects. This is a time honored approach. Due in part to such efforts, we are able to declare that we know what works and what doesn't. In theory, we believe that if a particular approach to a problem works, it will be picked up by others and become normative on a widespread basis. Regretfully, there is little or no guarantee that demonstration projects actually lead to widespread systemic change. Most often, demonstration projects cease altogether or assume some different form when the extra funding or priority status associated with them ceases.

Charismatic leaders. Certainly unusual leadership can effectively generate and sustain change—so long as the leadership remains. More than a decade ago, the Ford Foundation issued a report (*A Foundation Goes to School*) examining the results of its expenditure of many millions of dollars over a ten-year period on education. One of the key findings was that frequently when the leaders of a program left, the impact of the program was significantly reduced (Ford Foundation 1972).

Money. If sufficient money is offered, behavior can almost always be altered. The other authors have made clear that additional resources will be necessary, and Sawhill has written powerfully about strategies to produce such additional resources. While it is clear that human capital problems are not limited to the poor, every author has made clear that the poor face these problems disproportionately. That means that not only are additional resources needed, but that both present and additional resources must also be distributed differently.

Nonetheless, for at least three reasons spending more money cannot be the primary strategy for overhauling nearly every large human capital system in the country. First, there is—or there appears to be—not enough of it. Second, there is enough evidence that money alone does not produce the necessary results to cause a critical mass of elected officials and other power brokers to argue that the connection between more money and intended results is unclear at best (Mullin and Summers 1983; Hanushek 1981). Third, as a practical matter, the concentration of poor people in the cities and the flight of the middle class will likely diminish the political power of cities as a result of the reapportionment following the 1990 census. Thus, a frontal assault on state elected officials for more funds as the primary instrument of change, at least on behalf of poor people, is unlikely to succeed.

Lawsuits. A successful lawsuit clearly has the capacity to define and sustain systemic change in institutions. Court opinions can even help alter cultural mindsets. In the field of education, for example, over the past three and a half decades there have been several rounds of precedent-setting lawsuits that have provoked fundamental change. *Brown v. Board of Education* (Brown 1954) declared the concept of separate but equal schools to be unconstitutional. While we have neither fully achieved desegregation of schools nor moved very far toward genuine integration, *Brown* has led to extraordinary and continuing change, not only in schools but in every facet of American life. Another group of school-changing suits is associated with school finance. These include Texas's *Rodriquez* (San Antonio 1973), California's *Serrano* (Serrano 1971), and New Jersey's *Robinson* (Robinson 1973) cases. Some did better than others in producing more money for poor schools, but each was a centerpiece for educational reform. In the early 1970's, the *PARC* (PARC 1972) suit in Pennsylvania and the *Mills* (Mills 1972) case in the District of Columbia established that disabled students were to be accorded a free and appropriate education, a conclusion embraced and expanded upon in 1975 with the passage of P.L. 94–142, the Education for All Handicapped Children Act. These lawsuits affecting disabled students have launched a revolution that has radically changed the lives of individual children, taking them from under the proverbial staircase and providing many with an independent existence, and they are changing how the nation thinks about disabled people as well. In the 1980's, lawsuits in a number of cities including Kansas City (Kalima Jenkins 1986), St. Louis (Liddell 1981), and Milwaukee (Board of School District 1987), resulted in millions of new state dollars flowing to those cities to further the physical desegregation of children, as well as in the establishment of program initiatives to overcome the educational vestiges of segregation. Finally, at this writing the most recent court decision having a major system-changing impact on education is the Kentucky suit, *Council for Better Education v. Rose,* (Council 1989). That case, filed as a school finance case, concluded with the court's declaring the *entire* elementary and secondary education system of Kentucky unconstitutional, including its school board, its curriculum, its methods of training teachers, and its assessment programs. It ordered the Kentucky General Assembly to create a whole new system in which all children are likely to succeed. In

April, 1990, they enacted a sweeping comprehensive law which will result in school structures and practices that are very different from most that exist across the United States.

Other legal theories in this field are being developed, including one that asserts that if education is critical to the fundamental well-being (economic, social, and civic) of each individual, and if we know how to achieve success with virtually all students, then there is a legal duty to do so (Ratner 1985). Whether that theory will be sustained by a court, one cannot say. The point, however, is that the lawsuit continues to be an effective way to provoke broad-based systemic change.

Labor contracts. To continue with examples from the field of education, in several cities, among them Miami and Rochester, labor contracts have evolved as the vehicle that is helping to define and stabilize significant new educational structures. In each, the driving factor is a site-based, shared-power feature. While this feature is crucial to educational change, it is the use of the labor contract to achieve it which is of interest here. Since both teachers and administrators must buy into a changed structure to make it work, a labor contract is a viable way to give expression to such a partnership. Any contract in nearly any institutional setting can be an effective vehicle to define roles. It can set forth appropriate incentives and disincentives related to the parties' performance and thus provoke and sustain structural change.

Legislation. There are, of course, many examples of using legislation to provoke and sustain systemic change. As noted above, the 1975 Education for All Handicapped Children Act is one good example. Others over the years include the Social Security Act, Medicare, Medicaid, the 1964 Civil Rights Act, and the Vocational Rehabilitation Act. Each of these resulted in paradigmatic change. Not accidentally, each is an entitlement, enforceable in court. Each unleashed large systemic, structural change in practice and thinking.

As these comments suggest, demonstration projects and charismatic leaders can be useful, but there is little evidence that alone they can sustain the type of change that is required. Additional money spread around differently will be critically important, but it too cannot do the job alone from a substantive point of view, and for political reasons it will not be abundantly available to do the job. Court orders and/or legislation (I subsume contracts under legislation since they define required outcomes and activities), must be our primary vehicles to provoke and sustain the magnitude and kind of change that is necessary.

I should note that the relative roles of court orders and legislation (and contracts) are often quite different. Court orders can be exceptionally good vehicles for creating a sufficient sense of crisis and an imperative to act so that supporting legislation can be enacted. It is difficult to overstate the importance of such a vehicle, since the magnitude of change to which this volume is directed is so great that such change can only be created out of a sense of having no other option. Wars, natural disasters, and large-scale public movements such as the civil rights movement are also capable of producing sweeping change; a court order can constitute a controlled societal counterpart to these forces. When sweeping, *sustained* change occurs, however, it generally happens through legislation. I know of no examples of such change not associated with legislation that reflects the nature and definition of the relevant crisis.

The issue then is the nature of the legislation that is necessary in the human capital context to provoke sufficient sustained and penetrating change. This change must lead the most diverse nation in the world to concentrate its imagination, will, and resources to produce a work force over the next generation that will permit the United States to maintain (or regain) its economic and democratic leadership position internationally.

The other authors have provided ample program suggestions. I come at the issue a bit differently. With the program suggestions as a backdrop, I offer an analytic schematic as a practical way for policymakers, corporate and civic leaders, and elected officials to think about legislative initiatives that are comprehensive and powerful enough to do the job.

Characteristics Essential to Provoking Significant Change

The legislation (or contract) must include seven bedrock characteristics if it is to have a truly catalytic impact. Such legislation must create a new commitment to solve the deep-seated problems impeding human capital development described so well by Arnold Packer in Chapter 2; it must create new institutional arrangements and connections that are sufficient to achieve the desired ends; it must create a new realization among elected officials that more money will likely yield greater results; and it must initiate a self-actualizing and self-perpetuating momentum that will develop a life of its own, resulting in the long-term commitments necessary to basic change. In setting forth these characteristics, it is important to emphasize that the catalytic and synergistic impact expected of the type of change provoking legislation contemplated here commonly requires all seven characteristics. If one of the seven is left out, the effort is likely to fail.

Clear and Realistic Initial Assumptions

In designing the legislation, one must first examine the assumptions that will underlie the effort. For example, in Chapter 6 Boyer affirms two assumptions that would be central in sustaining broad-based educational change. He notes that we must believe that all students can learn and that we know how to teach all students successfully.

Another illustration of this point about assumptions is made clear by Barrett's, Edelman's, and Packer's contributions that note the radically different nature of family structure today as reflected in working mothers. Are we to assume that this fundamental change will reverse itself? Or shall we assume the contrary, setting the stage for legislation that helps find new ways to meet the nurturing needs of children and ways of providing support to families that facilitate family preservation?

Another way of looking at facts and assumptions is to note that the demographic and economic facts set out by Packer make clear that the United States does not have sufficiently competent workers today, nor will we have in the future, based on the performance of students presently in schools. Historically, our moral assumption has been that if the opportunity exists for a student to learn (or for an adult to become literate), it is his tough luck, and his alone, if he does not seize that opportunity. We have constructed social policies on that assumption. To assume the contrary, that a student's failure to perform or an adult's failure to be literate strikes at the heart of the nation's survival, not just the individual's well-being, is to change radically the character of the legislation.

My point is simply that in designing legislation of the type envisioned, one must begin by being clearheaded about one's assumptions, about why one is crafting the legislation in the first place.

Clearly Defined Outcomes

Common sense tells us that success in achieving an objective is directly connected to how clear the objective is. The only exceptions are a consequence of serendipity. Nevertheless, most of our human capital development systems are framed primarily around inputs, not outcomes. The Family Support Act of 1988 gives much more emphasis, for example, to whether welfare recipients *participate* in education programs than to whether the system actually *results* in greater numbers of recipients with a high school (or college) diploma. The Education for All Handicapped Children Act (1975) focuses exclusively on whether school systems follow certain procedures, not whether more disabled students can read, write, and calculate sufficiently well to live independently. In contrast, the Job Training Partnership Act (1982), of which Pines and Carnevale and Fosler write, is one of the few pieces of legislation to focus on outcomes such as actual job placements.

It is not possible to achieve the kind of outcomes we envision without being specific as to what those outcomes are. Moreover, it is necessary to define the quality and scope of the desired outcomes. Using the Job

Training Partnership Act as an example again, and as Pines and Carnevale note, one of the frequent criticisms of its outcome definition is that it encourages "creaming." If, however, the outcome sought and rewarded was not just job placement, but job placement for the most difficult to serve and job placements of a certain quality in terms of pay and future prospects, one would quickly eliminate that charge.[1]

Crafting outcomes can be a very tricky process. Boyer clearly affirms the importance of higher graduation rates, but asserts that equally important is the outcome of higher achievement levels. Thus he makes clear the imperative that to achieve the high graduation rates reflecting higher achievement levels will require success with the same young people with whom we have failed even with lower standards. Only by being so clear about the objectives will we be able to understand the magnitude of the challenge and be in a position to achieve it.

Similarly, Edelman strongly affirms a family preservation strategy for achieving the measurable outcome of increasing the number of families that stay together. Clearly, she also affirms the importance of a nurturing, safe environment for children, reflected perhaps in a measurable outcome of fewer child abuse situations. These twin objectives could be treated as contradictory, but if we define them carefully—together—a system can treat them as complementary.

It is difficult to overstate the importance of crafting intended outcomes with precision in measurable ways if the new restructured systems are to achieve them. Such carefully crafted outcomes that reflect the dimensions of intended quality and quantity will not assure attainment, but the absence of such outcome definition will almost surely result in intended outcomes not being achieved.

Assessment Strategies

It is, of course, not enough that we should define the outcomes we hope to achieve. We must also design a system that permits us to know whether and/or when we have achieved them. Such an assessment system will also permit us to understand better what contributed to our attaining or failing to attain the intended outcome. Finally, it is impossible to hold any institution accountable absent a good assessment system.

Again, precision is important. Stewart, in his chapter on higher education, notes that more than 50 percent of high school graduates begin college. In many ways, however, the more important fact is that a substantial and increasing number do not finish, particularly among minorities. Yet these facts tell us little about the quality of the education inside the college or university. It is vital that we be able to assess the product of our institutions of higher education. How shall that be done?

In public schools, the issue of assessment is equally crucial. Boyer and others call for much stronger accountability in the schools. Presently, as he notes, we rely on standardized, nationally normed tests. Such tests have at least one fatal flaw: they simply define how one is doing when measured against others. Thus, if the norming sample of students performs badly, it is relatively easy for a student, class, or school to be "above the norm." That is the reason a criterion-referenced test is desirable. If the criterion is, for example, the ability to do a certain level of algebra, one either can or cannot meet it. The desirability of having available a national assessment instrument (such as the National Assessment of Educational Progress) derives at least in part from the fact that if everyone (or an appropriate sample in each school, district, and state) took the same criterion-referenced test, we would know how students performed against a given standard. *In addition,* with the test being administered nationally, we could compare individual performances with the national performance as well as against other states, districts, and schools.

Whether one is determining the impact of child care initiatives (Edelman); colleges (Stewart); jobs programs (Pines and Carnevale); enforcement of equal protection laws (Barrett); immigration policy (Marshall); financial equity (Sawhill); the integrated results of vertical governmental policy (Fosler); antipoverty versus education improvement efforts (Danziger); research and development thinking (Greenberg); or any of the other programs and policies recommended by this volume's authors, one of the central ingredients will be assessment strategies.

Rewards and Sanctions

While I would reiterate the assertion that each of these characteristics is essential and that absent any one of them the system is insufficient, the factors most often absent are serious rewards for institutional success and serious sanctions for institutional failure. At the moment, if a child care center is particularly nurturing, or a social services unit is able to maintain a high number of intact families, or the students in a school graduate at high rates with exceptional skills, or an unusual number of public assistance recipients receive their Graduate Equivalency Diploma (GED), little happens to the institution or to the employees. Sometimes there are certificates or invitations to meet the department head, mayor, governor, or president. Sometimes, if an institution succeeds, money is actually taken away from the institution on the theory that it is not needed since the problem is not as severe.

In contrast, if an institution fails badly, most often nothing of significance occurs. Students cannot read. Children are taken from their families or left in their families and then abused. Poor performance can continue year after year with no consequence. If an abused child dies, there is sometimes a criminal prosecution of an individual social worker. In three or four states, if a school system is absolutely at the bottom academically *and* is a failure from a management perspective, the law permits a takeover. (Fewer than ten of the nation's 16,000 school districts at this writing have been the object of such initiatives to date.) The law permits the withholding of funds if a government entity fails to do something the law requires. That rarely happens, and if it did, it would likely impact the client population far more than the serving institution or its staff. Indeed, when sanctions do exist, they are most often designed to hurt the clients. When students fail, they cannot get their driver's license, or cannot play football. Nothing happens to their superintendents, principals, or teachers. Public assistance recipients lose their grants if they don't do certain things. Nothing happens to their social workers. Present sanctions punish failing clients; rarely do the sanctions also relate to the institutions or the employees who have the responsibility for helping clients succeed. It is essential that we have the incentives and disincentives (rewards and sanctions) sufficiently powerful and interrelated to motivate institutions and the people who staff them to be successful.

Staff Development

Pines and Carnevale, as well as others, note the enormous investment by the private sector in the education and training of staff. Estimates of those expenditures range as high as $200 billion (Doyle 1989: E68), an amount that exceeds the annual expenditure in all of public elementary and secondary education. Too large a proportion of those funds is spent because America's schools and colleges do not do their jobs well enough. But the majority of the money is spent to upgrade skills, introduce employees to new products or skill requirements, and generally keep them current in a productive manner.

If we are to restructure institutions by changing our assumptions and the level of our outcome expectations, assessing performance differently, and placing greater responsibility for institutional performance on local levels or work units, it is essential that we equip staffs to do these very different jobs differently. Corporate America has recognized this need; government and schools have not devoted nearly so much attention to it. America's public sector acts as though its employees should know or be able to do whatever is needed when they take a job; whenever that is not so, the practice generally is for the employee to engage in the additional training at his own expense and on his own time.

The legislation we are addressing must account for the staff needs of the institution(s) undergoing restructuring. Continuing education and training are a critical part of that, but pre-service training, general compensation, and working conditions are vital considerations as well. The whole thrust of this volume relates to the initiatives necessary to produce a quality work force. My point here is that we cannot neglect the issues of a quality work force in the institutions which are themselves seeking to produce a quality work force in the wider marketplace.

Site-based Shared Decision Making

Who among us will accept happily the responsibility implied in the foregoing sections if it is unaccompanied by a significant measure of authority to make the decisions necessary to result in the required outcomes? At the same time, who among us can legitimately deny accountability when we have the authority and flexibility to make the decisions affecting outcomes for which we have professional responsibility?

There are two key components associated with placing significant authority at the level closest to the object (most often clients) of the institutional effort. One is the authority itself. If it is given, it cannot be subject to being overturned arbitrarily or capriciously. Second, authority cannot be given and then effectively usurped by the promulgation of a host of regulations at some other level of authority.

Interagency or Institutional Connectedness

It is increasingly clear that single service institutions alone cannot produce the quality and quantity of human capital the nation needs. It will be essential for legislation to create mechanisms that, in effect, force the interagency connections necessary to achieve the outcomes that generate the rewards referred to above or merit the sanctions that flow if an institution is unsuccessful. There are many mechanisms available. The legislation can assign authority to one institution over another. Or, appropriations can be made contingent upon two or more agencies agreeing on a particular course of action. Or, when more than two agencies are involved, decisions can be made on the basis of majority rule. What is clear is that a measure of compulsion is required to have the necessary degree of sustained interaction between otherwise independent agencies.

Illustrations of Change-provoking Characteristics

The essential characteristics of agents of change and the impact among and between them can be better understood if illustrated, and I will provide two such models. The first is in the context of proposing a strategic approach to restructuring public education. The second will focus on the nonacademic well-being of children and families.

Basic Educational Change

I choose education as one of the two primary areas to illustrate the application of the seven characteristics because it is clearly the perspective of every author in this book that if the public education system were producing what our economy and democratic institutions required, the rest of what needs to happen with respect to human capital development would be much easier.[2]

Assumptions

Two of the three assumptions which must underlie a sufficient restructuring of schools are those mentioned by Boyer: "All students can learn at high levels" and "We know how to teach all students successfully." Fortunately, examples of success are plentiful. Broad public visibility was given in the movie *Stand and Deliver* to students from Los Angeles's Garfield High School who passed the Advanced Placement calculus test. Other examples include the work of people such as Yale's James Comer (emphasizing a school-based management model involving parents and all others with a vested interest in the school) (Comer 1984; 1980), Georgia State's Asa Hilliard (emphasizing the critical role of persistent high expectations) (Hilliard 1988: 195ff), Stanford's Henry Levin (emphasizing that acceleration of a student's work must replace remediation as the method to deal with students who are not performing up to standards) (Levin 1987), and Johns Hopkins's Robert Slavin (emphasizing cooperative learning, early intervention, and assuring from the beginning that a student does not fall behind) (Slavin 1989; Madden, Slavin, Karweit, and Liverman 1989; Slavin 1983). From the work of these individuals and many more, we know strategies that work with youngsters who are poor, who come to school with language deficits, whose home support is minimal, who exhibit characteristics generally associated with youngsters whom we put at risk and who ultimately fail in the public schools of America. The work of the late Ron Edmonds, the father of the so-called Effective Schools Movement, underlines the same point. He emphasized that the schools were usually successful if they exhibited five characteristics: (1) the principal's leadership and attention to the quality of instruction; (2) a pervasive and broadly understood instructional focus; (3) an orderly, safe climate conducive to teaching and learning; (4) teacher behaviors that convey the expectation that all students will obtain at least minimum mastery; and (5) the use of measures of pupil achievement as the basis for program evaluation (Edmonds 1982: 4).

The third assumption is that *what* we teach should be basically the same for all students in the sense that it is commonly challenging. But the strategies that schools and teachers should use in working with students should change based on what is successful in an individual school or classroom. Thus, *how* we teach, *when* school is in session, *where* teaching and learning occurs, and *who* teaches should be the variables. And the criterion for answering those four questions with respect to a given student or class should be "whatever works"!

If all students can learn at high levels and the knowledge exists to be successful at teaching them, it follows in the context of the third assumption that where one fails with a student, one must examine one's answers to the *how, where, when,* and *who* questions instead of simply blaming the student alone for the failure. The "system" must exhibit the attitude that *it* has not yet succeeded. The "system" must adopt a new mixture of *how, where, when,* and *who* until the student succeeds.

It is easy enough to state the assumptions. It is another matter to translate them into reality. To act on these premises for all children requires a different school system, a different school culture, and a significant change in the rules of the game.

Outcomes

It is not enough to embrace a set of assumptions. In pursuit of systemic change in the context of a comprehensive legislative strategy, we must identify our objectives, the outcomes we wish to achieve.[3] While there are a variety of appropriate indicators, consideration should be given to at least four basic areas: academic achievement (reading, math, writing, science, history, geography); good citizenship (behavioral characteristics reflected in lack of expulsions, suspensions, and other modes of discipline, demonstration of the ability to participate effectively in community service, participation in in-school governance, clubs and other citizenship-related activities); physical and mental fitness (decrease in drug and alcohol use and pregnancy, reduction of diseases subject to immunizations, reduction of students with preventable or treatable physical or mental conditions that interfere with school performance); and post-high school success (job success, college/postsecondary education entrance and completion, good military record.

Clearly, different outcome categories and indicators than these are possible. What is essential is that one systematically consider what economic, social, civic, and health goals are important in a given state or community and what measurable indicators will reveal whether the goals have been achieved by schools and school systems.

It is also in the context of crafting the outcomes and indicators that one will determine the quality as well as the quantity of the results. Outcome definition will reflect, for example, whether depth or breadth of curriculum is to be emphasized. It will reveal whether higher-order thinking skills or simply decoding words and learning rudimentary math are the priority. Various outcomes will have to be considered in relationship to one another. For example, if one focused exclusively on improving average test performance in a school, one could achieve that objective by "pushing out" the students who are difficult—which would obviously result in unintended consequences.

Assessment

If the new comprehensive system is to be outcome-based, careful attention must be paid to assessment strategies. The selection of outcome indicators will be informed by the availability of sound assessment instruments. Some may argue that sufficiently good instruments do not exist for use in policy and consequences-related considerations. This is not accurate. Among instruments from the National Assessment of Education Progress (NAEP) battery and the tests available from private test developers are ones sufficient to make a solid beginning. In addition, there are state-required tests and school-district-designed assessment strategies that could also be considered part of the initial effort.[4]

Whether NAEP testing is made universally available or not, however, we should also begin developing even richer assessment strategies. Areas of appropriate exploration include portfolio assessment, structured expressions of teacher judgment arising from classroom observations, student participation in class discussion, and evaluation of student exhibits, demonstrations, and performances. Substantial work on these assessment strategies is well under way in Vermont, Connecticut, New York, and California. In addition, the Educational Testing Service is investing time and funds in developing new approaches. Progress is not limited to this country. Indeed, in the context of performance-based testing, the Applied Performance Units developed in England for national use represent cutting-edge practice (Wiggins 1989; Archibald and Newmann 1988).

All of these assessment observations are related to academic objectives. Similar sensitivity is required in carefully defining appropriate assessment tools in the other areas as well. In citizenship, a method should be developed for expressing qualitative aspects of participation activities. For example, a different value could be placed on community service sustained over a period of time versus a one-time good deed. With respect to physical and mental fitness, new problems arise as we confront legal and even constitutional issues (self-incrimination, search and seizure). Nevertheless, indicators of good health are available. Perhaps a school system should plan to have all students undergo a physical exam in the fourth, eighth, and twelfth grades as a health counterpart to the academic testing program. Again, the emphasis must be on carefully determining assessment strategies that measure the outcomes to be achieved. In some areas, such as measuring post-high school success, it is relatively easy to define adequate indicators (wage level, retention in a non-dead-end job, completion of college, satisfactory military record). What is difficult is accessing the information. Special effort is necessary to track the high school graduate.

The point is that having a strong and appropriate assessment program is as important as having good outcome definitions. Being able to assess student and school success will permit informed policy judgments to be made at the state and system levels; at the classroom and school level, assessment can lead to a school's succeeding with nearly all students in the context of high expectations. Good assessment will inform the answers to the strategy questions shaping instructional options outlined above: *how* teaching is done, *who* does the teaching, *when* it is accomplished, and *where* it occurs.

Finally, it will be necessary to define "the successful school." That definition will flow from a calculus of weighted outcomes that will permit the identification of the "successful student." This can be done in ways that do not require all students to be the same. For example, the standard could require some achievement of minimum success in all areas and outstanding success in one or two; or, alternatively, greater success across the board could define the successful student, as could any number of other combinations. On that basis, "the successful school" would then be one in which the proportion of successful students had increased by a certain percentage since the last assessment period. Such an approach has the advantage of emphasizing constant improvement within the framework of measuring one's performance against one's own past performance. Thus, schools will compete on an essentially level playing field.

Rewards and Sanctions

If outcomes are to have real meaning, consequences must be attached. The assessment process focuses on *school* success, not individual teacher success. This emphasizes the importance of the school staff's working as a team, of teachers helping one another, of the staff's being concerned and communicating with one another about the same children. There should be a spectrum of consequences considered, with the school as the unit of measurement. I offer the following to illustrate one possible spectrum. They are arranged from positive to negative:

- Prominent visibility and various forms of public recognition should be accorded successful schools.
- Substantial school-wide financial awards for school staff, including teachers, cafeteria workers, custodial staff, etc., would be crucial.

- Special discretionary funds could be made available for a staff to develop instructional program initiatives in which they are particularly interested.
- Special opportunities could be provided for staff to participate in professional development opportunities they select or create.
- Remunerative opportunities for teachers in successful schools to provide technical assistance to staff in less successful schools should be available.
- Timely performance feedback to unsuccessful schools must occur.
- Parents and other members of the public should be informed of a school's poor performance.
- Additional resources, staff development, and technical assistance should be targeted to help the staff of an unsuccessful school design and implement successful changes in practice.
- Continued lack of success would result in required plans of action and reduced local decision-making flexibility.
- Students in an unsuccessful school should be given the right to choose to transfer to a successful school.
- Loss of rank, longevity, or cost-of-living pay increases for all staff in an unsuccessful school should be considered.
- Dismissal of school management and other school staff should result if a school is persistently unsuccessful.
- Dismissal of district administrators should result where multiple schools or substantial proportions of a district's students are persistently unsuccessful.

The challenge of developing a sound set of consequences is to have alternatives and to use them sensitively, making certain that all parties understand the repertoire of rewards and sanctions and the circumstances which give rise to each or to various configurations of different ones. One important and difficult issue is to avoid the "rich get richer" syndrome. Measuring school success by emphasizing improvements is one way to do this. In addition, the successful should be rewarded, but the unsuccessful must be more helped than punished.

Site-based Shared Decision Making
If our comprehensive system places significantly greater responsibility on school-based staff as reflected in a rewards and sanctions system that includes large financial bonuses and the threat of dismissal, it is essential that staff have significant decision-making authority. That authority must go beyond the right simply to be consulted on important matters. It should include certain powers related to the choice of personnel; to budget decisions within the framework of an allocation of operating funds from the central office; to staff control of curriculum and instruc-

tional practice, including issues related to discipline; and to all scheduling decisions within the context of fixed, system-wide school-year and bus schedules.

Related to the transfer of authority to the school level, the legislation must provide for the elimination of regulations at the local or state level which would inhibit the ability of school staff to make the decisions they deem necessary to school success.

Staff Development

This book is devoted to the issue of the development of human capital. Clearly, the issue is central to the schools' ability to produce successful students. Boyer noted in Chapter 6 that the quality of the teacher force is crucial. In the new structure, comprehensive legislation must address the pre-service training of teachers, the continuing education of present teachers, and the certification requirements that set the conditions for entry into the profession.

With regard to all three areas, it is necessary to begin to link training and certification to the new system—the assumptions, an outcome system, new assessment strategies, a different incentive plan, and greater responsibility for making substantive instructional decisions. Pre-service considerations should include greater expertise in subject areas, sensitivity to the developmental and cultural characteristics of the students, and in-depth contact of teacher candidates with schools and students in the form of on-the-job training.

Continuing education should be market driven. With greater responsibility for achieving high expectation outcomes, schools and school districts will need to tailor carefully their in-service training funds to strategies likely to have the greatest productivity. Most states and districts will have to add non-classroom time so that teachers can engage in productive continuing education.

With regard to certification, in addition to the suggestions listed above under pre-service training, it is important to consider alternative certification patterns such as the one that exists in New Jersey that facilitates certification of career changers and liberal arts college graduates.

Interagency or Institutional Connectedness

What goes on in school will be crucial to a student's educational success; for many students, however, support beyond the schoolhouse is necessary. Among other elements in the community, social services and health support services will also be essential to school success. Thus, another important task that must be reflected in the legislation is the identification of the range of health and social services that is required, of existing gaps in service capacity, and of alternative sources of essential service that may exist or need to be developed.

Genuine cooperation with and delivery of service from noneducational, human service agencies will not occur automatically. Specific mechanisms must be designed to accomplish these objectives. There are many areas that could be explored. Rewards and sanctions could be designed for other agencies based on the health or well-being of students enrolled in schools in their service areas. Certain funding sources (and, thus, continued staff employment) could be made contingent on the joint development and successful implementation of strategies directed toward certain health and social service outcomes. A school district could be granted actual power over certain health and social service agencies or over certain functions within those agencies. School systems could be required to meet certain objectives, such as seeing that no child forgoes breakfast. That would likely lead, for example, to greater cooperation with the United States Department of Agriculture, which can pay for the breakfast program.

Only through specific legislative action that creates an appropriate array of incentives and disincentives related to the health and social barriers to learning faced by many students will those barriers be eliminated.

Systemic Change Based on the Affirmative Responsibility for the Well-Being of Children and Youth

In this section, I will illustrate the way in which the same essential characteristics could productively be embodied in another piece of legislation related to the nonschool needs of children and youth. Just as every author in this book makes clear the central role of schools and academic prowess in the development of human capital, nearly every author asserts that the nonacademic well-being of children and youth is necessary as well. Pregnancy, sexually transmitted disease, infant mortality, poor health care, physical and sexual abuse, drug and alcohol use and abuse, lack of supervision, suicide, increasing poverty, and families stressed to the point of disintegration are all facts of life for many children in this society; and the children and youth who are reflected in these statistics will be a significant part of the pool from which our work force will be drawn in the future. Our nation's support strategies for our youngsters are not working. I would again argue that this problem has become so large and broad and the stakes so great that a systemic solution is as necessary here as it is in the world of schools.

At the state level, we should promulgate legislation that would create a new affirmative duty for government to assure the health and nonacademic well-being of each child until age 18 or graduation from high school, whichever comes first. That duty would begin during a mother's pregnancy with appropriate prenatal care, extend through the early years of life in the form of support of both mother and child, and as a child becomes school age, the duty would apply before and after school, on weekends, and in the summer.

At the present time, government attempts to fill the gaps for children and youth. It adopts an attitude of "we'll do the best we can, and if we don't reach all the children adequately, we regret it," with the result being the existence and proliferation of the problems outlined above. During a time when we did not "need" all our children, this was an economically viable way to approach their care. If we lost one, or one hundred, or one thousand it did not matter economically. We know from Arnold Packer's demographic analysis that this laissez-faire attitude is no longer tolerable.

Clearly, a major objection to the assumption of such a sweeping affirmative duty to assure the health and nonacademic well-being of every child would be the charge of "big brotherism." What comes to mind are the circumstances from 1852 to 1918 related to compulsory school attendance. During those years, the economic and civic needs of the nation were such that state after state adopted compulsory attendance laws (Cremin 1988: 297–98). A social policy decision was made and translated into the statutes that universal schooling was necessary to maintain our democratic institutions and undergird economic growth. Prior to compulsory school attendance, children and parents were as free to do as they wished with regard to schooling as they are today with regard to the time before and after school. Compulsory school attendance laws limited their freedom because we made a decision as a society that our economic and civic well-being depended on it. We face a similar situation today. It is clear that we are not going to return to being a predominantly rural nation, with families in which one parent works and the other cares for the two children. Neither are we going to resume being a nation in which the poor, people of color, and those whose first language is not English are invisible. They constitute more than one-third of our population today. Their children are disproportionately at risk. We cannot economically afford the loss.

I recommend that the affirmative duty to assure the well-being of children and youth be vested in a Board of Children and Families. I envision this board to be patterned after school boards (at both the state and local levels). It would be elected, perhaps on the same jurisdictional basis as school boards (thus encouraging what will need to be a high level of cooperation). At the local level, the Board of Children and Families would have the authority to raise taxes, as most school boards do. (They should also have the authority to charge, on a sliding-fee basis, for certain services.) At the state level, as with schools, it would be necessary to address issues of financial equalization among and between local jurisdictions. I recommend that the enabling legislation vest "ownership" of school facilities with the Board of Children and Families before and after school, on weekends, school holidays, and during the summer. Similarly, where school buses are "owned" by the school system, the enabling legislation should provide for joint "ownership" and use. In fact, of course, the taxpayers "own" facilities and buses. The issue is who uses them and controls them and on behalf of whom? Our present system of buildings and buses that too often stand idle during nonschool hours would give way to maximum use on behalf of a jurisdiction's children and families as they relate to academic and nonacademic needs.

I pause to comment on the relationship between the local Board of Children and Families and the local school board (as well as their appropriate counterparts at the state level). As I will explain below, the new board's responsibility will be designed in an outcome-based, consequences-driven format. If the school board's responsibilities are similarly drawn (as described in the previous section of this chapter), each will have a powerful incentive to collaborate with each other. Each may ask the other to help with certain functions. For example, certain health-related functions may be wholly assumed by one of the entities; bus operation, by the other; facility maintenance by one, not both; actual supervision of certain activities, such as immunizations or school breakfasts or afternoon homework sessions, may, by agreement, be vested with one entity and not the other. The point is that the enabling legislation should make clear what outcomes are expected of each. The context created should reflect minimum regulatory impediment and maximum flexibility so that these two powerful vehicles functioning on behalf of children can work together.

I turn now to describe briefly the manner in which the legislation creating the State Board for Children and Families and its local counterparts could reflect the seven essential characteristics outlined previously. While the creation of an affirmative duty and a new structure to meet it would constitute systemic change, it would not in and of itself assure the well-being of America's children any more than the existence of school systems with an affirmative duty for the academic success of students has resulted in that objective.

Assumptions

Several assumptions would be important to the effectiveness of this legislation. For example, it should be assumed that the effort would be supportive of the family unit, being careful not to detract from the family. There may be some areas of child need in which the family will play the dominant role—before school care and breakfast, for example. In others, such as after school support, the Board of Children and Families may play the central role. The board would have the responsibility to work with the family to sort out the balance of roles. A second assumption is that a child's existence is not one of independent segments, unrelated to each other. The support from the board should reflect a certain degree of seamlessness among and between the nurturing services required.

I suggest, for example, that the board's staff *not* be organized along categorical, programmatic lines. Rather, I would urge that the primary organizational pattern be one of collaborative units responsible for the outcome or program areas organized around communities of people to be served. Thus, one could have a team composed of people who can respond to health, child care, family support, counseling, and employment needs located in and responsible for a community served by a particular elementary school or by a certain school feeder pattern.

Outcomes

The types of outcomes that could be used to define the responsibilities of the Board of Children and Families include: (for preschoolers) the number of low-weight babies born, the rate of infant mortality, the incidence of certain physical or mental handicaps, the readiness of children to begin school, and the proportion of children with appropriate child care; (for elementary schoolers) the proportion of children contracting diseases totally preventable by immunization, the proportion of children with uncorrected vision or hearing impairment, the number of child abuse cases, the number of children taken away from their families and placed in other settings, the proportion of children with appropriate before- and after-school child care, and the proportion of children suffering from any health problem which is reasonably preventable or treatable; (for secondary schoolers) the proportion of girls who are pregnant, the rate of drug use, the rate of alcohol use, the incidence of smoking, the proportion of young people suffering from any health problem which is reasonable preventable or treatable, and the proportion of unemployed (or unoccupied) youth.

Assessment

The assessment strategies will, of course, be dependent on the nature of the outcomes. In some instances, good data systems already exist. (Infant mortality rates are an example.) In other instances, such as child abuse, the data are dependent on the numbers of cases being detected or reported, both of which are frequently unreliable measures. In such areas, it will be necessary to consider new information-gathering strategies. In still other areas, such as readiness to begin school, the standards are very ill-defined and will require significant additional thought. As with physical and mental fitness, ascertaining the facts in areas such as drug use may pose legal issues and require innovative and perhaps indirect methods of assessment.

In addition to the actual assessment indicators, a system will be required to define a successful unit of the Board of Children and Families (the counterpart to a "successful school"), and here careful thought is necessary. For example, as noted earlier, if too much weight is given to preserving an intact family, it is possible that one could encourage child abuse; the opposite, of course, is also true, for if one is too quick to remove a child, the family can be destroyed. The point is once again that the assessment strategies must be sensitive in measuring how well outcomes are achieved, but not so rigid as to provoke unintended consequences.

Rewards and Sanctions

The legislation must contain rewards for those units that are successful in achieving desirable outcomes. If GED's among public assistance recipients increase during a certain time period, the contributing staff should be rewarded; if the proportion of intact families goes up while the number of foster children and incidents of child abuse go down, responsible staff should be rewarded; exemplary child care programs should also be rewarded. There should be a range of reward levels including the same generic categories as those suggested for successful school staff—recognition, financial bonuses, special training opportunities, etc.

When there is a failure, there should be sanctions. Again, the sanctions should focus on the responsible units and should include notoriety, loss of pay, loss of decision-making authority, and the possibility of dismissal.

Site-based Shared Decision Making

The staff serving a particular geographic area—perhaps, a school attendance area—must have broad powers of discretion. Youth organizations, religious institutions, potential job sites, possible community-service placement opportunities, health care, and all of the community support resources which will play an important role in a local staff's meeting its responsibility will differ from one community to the next. Families, their mores, and their cultural heritage will vary. A local unit's staff must have the flexibility to use its budget and its abilities in a way that is responsive to the outcomes that have been set and the priorities established among them.

Staff Development

Staff must be well trained to respond to the interrelated health and social problems that the Board of Children and Families must address successfully. In many areas, this will require consideration of higher pay to attract better people. In others, training in how to work in teams will be necessary. Child care staff must understand the developmental needs of children; youth employment workers may require training in job development and job placement; health-related personnel may require both initial training and continuing education.

Interagency or Institutional Connectedness

By definition, the Board of Children and Families must embody connectedness. The relationship to schools is a clear beginning point, where the board in fact is co-operator of what we now call school buildings. Social services, nutrition programs, and health initiatives will all fall under the jurisdiction of the board.

There are many ways the work of the board could be organized. One approach could be through family service centers at the elementary level and youth service centers at the middle and high school levels. The family service centers could be patterned on similar centers in Connecticut or Kentucky. They could include program components such as: full-time preschool child care; before-and after-school care which would become full-time during the summer and when school is not in session; an integrated approach to home visiting, group meetings, and monitoring child development for new and expectant parents; literacy training for parents of preschool children; support and training for family day care home providers since these provide day care for many children; health services and/or referral to health services. The youth service centers could be patterned on the successful model in New Jersey. They could include program components such as: primary and preventive health services; referrals to health and social services; employment counseling, training, and placement; summer and part-time job placement; drug and alcohol abuse counseling; family crisis counseling; pregnancy prevention services.

In whatever organizational form the work of the board is done, another key aspect of its interagency character is reflected in the fact that it would assume responsibility for a variety of functions presently vested in other agencies. For example, responsibility for assuring appropriate prenatal care for all pregnant women would be vested in the new board. Similarly, the new board would administer such federal programs as Maternal and Child Health (MCH), Women, Infants, and Children (WIC), and Early and Periodic Screening, Diagnosis, and Treatment (EPSDT) programs. This pattern of bringing together what are in most states almost exclusively federal programs and having them support a broad affirmative duty to succeed with children and families is a pattern that would be programmatically and fiscally important in the new board's meeting its responsibilities.

Let me also underline the fact that the affirmative duty of which I speak is not limited to the poor. Increasingly, the problems of pregnancy, drug and alcohol abuse, and other societal pathologies are penetrating the suburbs and the lives of the middle class and well-to-do. The nature of the response may be different, but the affirmative duty should be no less real. The board in Scarsdale, New York, may meet its health responsibility by knowing that the children are covered by Blue Cross-Blue Shield and are cared for by private physicians. In Baltimore, Maryland, a school-based health clinic may be the vehicle for carrying out this duty. The point is that we are not operating on the "well-being by exception" basis which has been the source of increasing numbers of youngsters falling between the cracks. Instead, all children and youth are covered.

Conclusion

Our present practice of incrementalism or ad hoc treatment and uncoordinated effort is wholly inadequate to raising the next generation of human capital either in school or outside of school. The previous two segments of this chapter are proposals for the dramatic change in thinking and practice that is required. "Trying hard" or "doing the best we can with what we've got" are no longer meaningful standards. More is required if we wish to have the quantity of quality workers required to compete successfully in the international marketplace. The other authors have made equally clear that a similar paradigmatic change in the way we think about other contributing institutions or segments of our society is necessary.

There is widespread agreement about the components of the various systems that define the quantity and quality of our human capital. Moreover, our problem is not the lack of knowledge about what works to produce thinking, skillful, productive citizens regardless of background. The problem, rather, is twofold. First, it is a systems problem. We are not clear about our objectives. The incentives and disincentives within and between systems do not enhance the coordinated productive outcomes of the systems. Assessment tools are inadequately developed and coordinated. Decision-making authority is misplaced. Continuing education and other staff development strategies are undervalued. Substantive coordination within and between agencies is almost nonexistent. Second, we have a will and imagination problem which, not surprisingly, is partly a result of the first problem. We have not recognized the seriousness of the issues we face.

Solutions lie at hand. They will require carefully calibrated, comprehensive, and integrated approaches. They will require being clearheaded about a small number of strategically sensitive objectives, the attainment of which will result in a strong ripple of other positive consequences. Success must not be left to chance. Responsibility must be fixed. All of this must be done legislatively.

Will such far-reaching legislation, which includes the poor and minorities, be passed? History teaches us that the answer is "probably not." The fact, however, that the lifestyles of even the rich, middle-class, and powerful will deteriorate absent aggressive action of the kind described throughout this volume gives me pause—and even more—a measure of hope.

Notes

I wish to acknowledge my gratitude to the Carnegie Corporation of New York. Their generous support permitted the time to develop the thoughts in this chapter. The views, however, are those of the author.

1. This recommendation was also made by a Department of Labor task force chaired by Marion Pines in a report issued in 1989, which called for a substantial targeting of the JTPA on the most difficult to serve.

2. The strategy presented here grows out of work and thinking which took shape during 1986–87, when I served as president of the Council of Chief State School Officers. The council produced two documents to which I refer the reader. The first is a policy statement entitled "Assuring School Success for Students At-Risk." The second is "Elements of a Model State Statute to Provide Educational Entitlements for At-Risk Students." The latter entitles children and youth at-risk for school failure to those educational and related services that are reasonably calculated to lead to high school graduation. The model statute is basically a civil rights statute. It embodies an enforceable entitlement. I remain enthusiastic about that approach and suggest that any jurisdiction with the courage to pursue it should do so. It is clear, however, that a majority of elected officials is not inclined today toward the enactment of entitlements no matter how morally correct they may be or how wise from an economic perspective. Thus, the strategy outlined in these pages is an effort to initiate the movement necessary to achieve the same ends through a different configuration of incentives and disincentives.

In April 1990 the Kentucky General Assembly passed and Governor Wallace Wilkinson signed into law a far-reaching piece of education legislation that embraced all of the essential characteristics described here. That legislation was based in part on recommendations I had the privilege to make to the legislature as one of its consultants. Thus, the similarity is not a coincidence.

3. In the educational arena, a focus on outcomes was given significant impetus in January and February, 1989, when President Bush and then the National Governors' Association identified a set of national goals for education for the year 2000. The goals are:

- All children in America will start school ready to learn.
- The high school graduation rate will increase to at least 90 percent.
- American students will leave grades four, eight, and twelve having demonstrated competency in challenging subject matter including English, mathematics, science, history, and geography, and every school in America will ensure that all students learn to use their minds well, so they will be prepared for responsible citizenship, further learning, and productive employment in our modern economy.

- U.S. students will be first in the world in mathematics and science achievement.
- Every adult American will be literate and will possess the knowledge and skills necessary to compete in a global economy and exercise the rights and responsibilities of citizenship.
- Every school in America will be free of drugs and violence and will offer a disciplined environment conducive to learning. (National Education Goals, adopted by the members of the National Governors' Association on February 25, 1990)

4. With respect to NAEP, its governing law should be amended to permit its unimpeded use at the school and school district level. Presently there is a limitation which prohibits any use that might result in school or school system comparisons.

References

Applebee, Arthur N., Judith A. Langer, and Ina V. S. Mullis (1989). *Crossroads in American Education*. Princeton, N.J.: Educational Testing Service.

Archibald, Doug A., and Fred M. Newmann (1988). *Beyond Standardized Testing: Assessing Authentic Academic Achievement in the Secondary School*. Reston, Va.: National Association of Secondary School Principals.

Brown v. Board of Education, 348 U.S. 886 (1954).

Board of School Directors of City of Milwaukee v. Thompson, 84-C-877 (filed in Eastern District of Wisconsin 1987).

Carnegie Council on Adolescent Development (1989). *Turning Points: Preparing American Youth for the Twenty-first Century*. Report of the Task Force on Education of Young Adolescents. New York: Carnegie Corporation.

Comer, James P. (1980). *School Power*. New York: Free Press.

——— (1984). "Home-school Relationships as They Affect the Academic Success of Children." *Education and Urban Society* 16 (3): 323–37.

Council for Better Education v. Rose, Docket #88-SC-804-TG (June 8, 1989).

Cremin, Lawrence A. (1988). *American Education: The Metropolitan Experience 1876–1980*. New York: Harper & Row.

Doyle, Denis P. (1989). *Endangered Species: Children of Promise*. Reprinted from *Business Week*, October 15, 1989.

Edmonds, Ronald R. (1982). "Programs of School Improvement: An overview." *Educational Leadership* 40 (3): 4–11.

Ford Foundation (1972). *A Foundation Goes to School: The Ford Foundation Comprehensive School Improvement Program, 1960–1970*. New York: Ford Foundation.

French, Joyce N. (1987). *Adult Literacy: A Source Book and Guide*. New York: Garland Publishing.

Greenbaum, Stuart (1989). "Youth and Drug Abuse: Breaking the Chain." *USA Today* 118 (2534): 45–47.

Hanushek, Eric A. (1981). "Throwing Money at Schools." *Journal of Policy Analysis and Management* 1: 19–41.

Hilliard, Asa G. (1988). "Public Support for Successful Instructional Practices for At-risk Students." In Council of Chief State School Officers, *School Success for Students at Risk*. Orlando: Harcourt Brace Jovanovich, p. 195–208.

Job Training Partnership Act Advisory Committee (1989). *Working Capital: JTPA Investments for the 90's*. Washington, D.C.: U.S. Department of Labor.

Kalima Jenkins v. Missouri, 807 F.2d 657 (8th Circuit 1986).

Kozol, Jonathan (1988). "There Is Little to Celebrate." In Gary E. McCuen, ed. *Illiteracy in America*. Hudson, Wis.: Gary E. McCuen Publications, pp. 16–19.

Levin, Henry M. (1987). "New Schools for the disadvantaged." *Teacher Education Quarterly* 14 (4): 60–83.

Liddell v. Board of Education, 667 F.2d 643 (8th Circuit 1981).

Madden, Nancy A., Robert E. Slavin, Nancy L. Karweit, and Barbara J. Liverman (1989). "Restructuring the Urban Elementary School." *Educational Leadership* 46 (5): 14–18.

Mills v. Board of Education, 348 F. Supp. 866 (1972).

Mullin, Stephen P., and Anita A. Summers (1983). "Is More Better? The Effectiveness of Spending on Compensatory Education." *Phi Delta Kappan* 64 (5): 339–47.

PARC v. Commonwealth, 343 F. Supp. 279, 281–303 (E.D. Pa. 1972).

Ratner, Gershon M. (1985). "A New Legal Duty for Urban Public Schools: Effective Education in Basic Skills." In 63 *Texas Law Review* 777.

Robinson v. Cahill, 303 A.2d 273 (N.J. 1973).

San Antonio Independent School District v. Rodriquez, 411 U.S. 1 (1973).

Serrano v. Priest, 96 California Reports 601; 487 P.2d, 1241 (1971).

Slavin, Robert E. (1983). *Cooperative Learning*. New York: Longman.

——— (1989). "Cooperative Learning and Student Achievement." In Robert E. Slavin, ed., *School and Classroom Organization*. Hillsdale, N.J.: Lawrence Erlbaum Associates, p. 129–56.

Tinto, Vincent (1987). *Leaving College: Rethinking the Causes and Cures of Student Attrition*. Chicago: University of Chicago Press.

U.S. Bureau of the Census (1989). *Statistical Abstract of the United States: 1989*. 109th edition. Washington, D.C.: U.S. Government Printing Office.

Wiggins, Grant (1989). "Teaching to the (Authentic) Test." *Educational Leadership* 46 (7): 41–47.

Index

Aaron, Henry, 142
Adolescent Resources Corporation, 279
Adult education, 306, 363
Advisory Commission on Intergovernmental Relations, 349
Aerospace technology, 231
Agriculture, 17, 45, 363; immigrant labor, 98, 99, 100; productivity, 7, 70, 75, 232
Aid to Families with Dependent Children (AFDC), 87, 88, 250, 253, 261, 271–72, 282, 287, 348
Alba, Francisco, 129
Alcohol, Drug Abuse, and Mental Health Block Grant, 289
Alcohol abuse, 278, 279, 286, 385–86
American Agenda project, 314
American Association for the Advancement of Science, 181
American College Test (ACT), 172, 173, 188
American Economic Association, 3
American Federation of State, County, and Municipal Employees, 281
American Institute of Physics, 225
American Society for Training and Development, 331
American Telephone and Telegraph Company, 58
Antidiscrimination laws, 9, 30, 89, 361
Apollo space program, 227, 229
Apprenticeship, 254, 261, 347
Arkansas, 349

Asian Americans, 46–47, 206; immigrants, 96, 97, 101, 102, 103, 109, 112–13, 114, 132
Association of American Universities, 232
Atkinson, Richard C., 227–28, 235
Atlanta, Ga., 181
Automobile industry, 12, 14

Baby boom, 46, 206; in labor force, 15–16, 44, 45, 49–50, 65, 115, 134; retirement, 16, 36, 44, 51, 54, 349, 350, 354
Baltimore, Md., 279, 386
Banks, 243
Barrett, Nancy S., 17, 203, 301, 361, 369
Basic School (proposed), 184
Bay State Skills Corporation, 307, 308, 320
Bell, Jerry A., 226
Bell, Terrel H., 198
Bennett, William J., Jr., 198
Berg, Ivar, 2, 7, 21
"Big science," 223–24, 234, 237
Biotechnology, 224
"Birth dearth," 15, 16, 44, 51, 115
Birth rates, 16, 44, 50–51, 54, 70, 95, 240, 271
Blacks: education, 23, 24, 61, 133, 173, 194, 203, 206, 207, 363; education, relation to income, 20, 21, 146–50, 151, 152–53, 159, 209; immigrants and, 19, 122, 123, 131, 136 n. 7; infant mortality, 275; in labor force, 46–47, 54, 240,